2

WITHDRAWN FROM THE LIBRARY

UNIVERSITY OF WINCHESTER

KA 0245261 8

Composing the Music of Africa

Composing the Music of Africa

Composition, Interpretation and Realisation

Edited by

MALCOLM FLOYD

Ashgate

Aldershot • Brookfield USA • Singapore • Sydney

© Malcolm Floyd and the contributors, 1999

All rights reserved. No part of this publication may be reproduced, stored in a retrieval system, or transmitted in any form or by any means, electronic, mechanical, phoptocopying, recording or other wise without the prior permission of the publisher.

The authors have asserted their moral right under the Copyright, Designs and Patents Act, 1988, to be identified as the authors of this work.

Published by

Ashgate Publishing Limited
Gower House
Croft Road
Aldershot
Hants GU11 3HR
England

Ashgate Publishing Company
Old Post Road
Brookfield
Vermont 05036-9704
USA

Ashgate website: http://www.ashgate.com

British Library Cataloguing in Publication Data

Composing the Music of Africa: Composition, Interpretation
and Realisation.
(Ashgate Studies in Ethnomusicology)
1. Music--Africa. 2. Folk Music--Africa.
I. Floyd, Malcolm, 1958-
780.9'6

Library of Congress Cataloging-in-Publication Data

Composing the music of Africa: composition, interpretation and
realisation/edited by Malcolm Floyd.
(Ashgate Studies in Ethnomusicology)
Includes bibliographical references and index.
ISBN 1-85928-143-5 (hardcover)
1. Music--Africa--History and criticism. 2. Folk Music--Africa--
History and criticism. 3. Composition (Music). I. Floyd, Malcolm.
II. Series.
ML350.1C66   1998
780'.96--dc21

97-45088
CIP
MN

ISBN 1 85928 143 5

This book is printed on acid free paper

Printed and bound in Great Britain by MPG Books Ltd, Bodmin, Cornwall

KING ALFRED'S COLLEGE
WINCHESTER

780.96
/FLO

KA 8245261S

Contents

Part II: The Changing Faces of Music

Ashgate Studies in Ethnomusicology

General Editor's Preface

The aim of this new series is to encourage ethnomusicological study (with 'ethnomusicology' defined very widely), which has significance for all those involved in it. The series is interested in work which emphasises the relationships between people and music in cultural context, as individuals within communities and which acknowledges a varied range of contributions and looks to beneficial outcomes for those 'being researched' as well as for the 'researcher'. To this end it supports what might be regarded as a dialogic praxis, of collaborative discursive action and reflection, in which the researcher might become part of the facilitation of a particular focus, in time and place. It is also an intention to enable the investigation and problematising of ethnomusicological practices, and to discuss ways of clarifying such issues and addressing them.

There is a place in the series for the 'traditional' studies of particular musical practices, where these are related to cultural and functional significance, and where they give an insight into modes of representation and transmission. This is particularly true where the research process gives those sharing the information a new and useful view of their own activities. Innovative and experimental work that is appropriate to the principal aims of the series is also encouraged.

Malcolm Floyd

King Alfred's, University College Winchester

List of Figures

Contributors

Lara Allen conducted her research into *kwela* music at the University of Natal where she received her MMus (cum laude) in 1993. She has presented papers at international conferences in southern Africa, Europe and America. The recipient of several scholarships, she is presently completing a PhD at Queens' College, Cambridge.

James Flolu has worked in all sectors of Ghanaian education, and in 1995 completed a DPhil on Ghanaian music education at the University of York. After a period as Visiting Lecturer at King Alfred's, University College Winchester, he has returned to Ghana as a Lecturer in the Department of Music Education at University College of Education, Winneba.

Malcolm Floyd studied at London, Exeter and Oxford Universities, and then taught in Kenya for seven years. In 1984 he won the Kenya Music Festival prize for performance on a traditional instrument (a Luo one-stringed fiddle). He has had work published in Kenya and Britain, and was the editor of *World Musics in Education*. Currently he is Senior Lecturer and Head of Music at King Alfred's, University College Winchester, and General Editor of 'Ashgate Studies in Ethnomusicology'.

Kenneth Gourlay studied English at Oxford, and gained his PhD in Karimojong' music from the University of East Africa in 1971. He worked as a teacher and lecturer in England, Uganda, Papua New Guinea and Nigeria, finishing as Senior Lecturer at the School of Oriental and African Studies, London University, and published a wide range of articles internationally. The editor and publishers are grateful to Mrs Gourlay for permission to reprint this article by her late husband.

Christopher James was born in Zimbabwe, and learnt the piano, clarinet and organ. After studying accountancy for two years he emigrated to South Africa and became a music student at the University of Pretoria. During 1983-85 he continued his studies at the University of Cincinnati, and during this period some of his compositions were performed. He is currently teaching music at the University of South Africa. He has a keen interest in the fusion of African and European musics, and is working on a symphony entitled 'Paradise Regained' which is to be dedicated to the President of South Africa, Dr Nelson Mandela.

Adel Kamel graduated from the Faculty of Musical Training and then the Conservatoire in Cairo. In 1977 and 1978 he studied at the Kodaly Institute in Kecskemet, Hungary, and in 1992 completed his doctorate in Coptic music at the Institute of Coptic Studies in Cairo. He combines his post as university professor with journalism and composition.

Gerhard Kubik gained his PhD in ethnology from the University of Vienna in 1971. His major interests are African and African-American cultures, African systems of ideographic writing, the psychology of culture-contact and so on. Since 1959 he has undertaken fieldwork in 16 countries of sub-Saharan Africa, and also Brazil. He has written over 200 articles, and a number of monographs and books. in 1980 he was appointed Professor, attached to the Institute of Ethnology at the University of Vienna.

Geoffrey Poole is Senior Lecturer in Music at Manchester University. His 40 compositions engage both with European tradition and a broader world view, with African music growing in importance after a two-year residency at Kenyatta University (Nairobi) from 1985 to 1987. He is currently Visiting Fellow at Princeton University, while fulfilling a novel commission for the Halle Orchestra with Javanese Gamelan.

Hans Roosenschoon was born in The Netherlands, emigrating to South Africa a year later. In 1976 he won a composition scholarship from the Southern African Music Rights Organisation to study at the Royal Academy of Music in London under Paul Patterson. Since returning to South Africa his work has been performed regularly, both there and internationally, and he has received many commissions. In 1987 he won the Standard Bank's 'Young Artist of the Year Award', and in 1991 was awarded a DMus by the University of Cape Town. He is currently a Lecturer at the University of Orange Free State in Bloemfontein.

Janet Topp Fargion was born in South Africa, and did her first degree in ethnomusicology at the University of Natal, including research into gumboot dance. She then studied at the School of Oriental and African Studies, University of London, completing her PhD on *taarab* music of Zanzibar in 1992. She is currently curator of the International Music Collection at the British Library National Sound Archive in London.

Trevor Wiggins is Director of Music at Dartington College of Arts, University of Plymouth. His current research is the recreational music of the Dagara people of northern Ghana. He has undertaken large periods of field research, and his publications relate both to this research and his interest in teaching world musics.

1 Introduction: Composing the Music of Africa

Malcolm Floyd

It will be apparent from the complete title of this book that the authors are looking at composition in a range of guises. The adjusting of a phrase to fit new words, the appearance of a new phrase, a new individual contribution to a known song, a new song, a new symphony, all come within our meanings of composition. In some cases there is intensive preparation, in others the performative act of utterance simultaneously embodies the act of composition. In 1903 Albert Lavignac discussed the nature of composers and composition in his book *Musical Education*. For him:

> No study ... can result in producing a composer worthy of the name out of any individual who is not natively endowed with that entirely special instinct that leads one to create and invent combinations of sounds, and which in various degrees is called having ideas, having the creative faculty, and lastly, having the sacred fire, or having genius. (1903: 241)

As to how this 'special instinct' is to be recognised, he comments:

> ... many young composers reveal their vocation from infancy, by the propensity for putting their ideas down on paper, when as yet they know none of the theoretic elements except what they have been able to divine. (Ibid.: 242)

So for Lavignac composition has theoretical constructs, and is to be perceived as existing when written down. A composer has a special instinct, which is innate. In considering the optimal environment for composition, 'to favour its growth and blossoming', Lavignac sets it against the worst conditions, which include:

> ... living in some forlorn region far from every intellectual centre, isolation, or association exclusively with common people who are totally destitute of instruction, the absence of all affection, employment in manual labour of a kind that demands no intellectual effort, ignorance of all manifestation of any art whatsoever, in a word, all that constitutes the most brutish existence. (Ibid.: 243)

It might be seen as unfair to Lavignac to expect his cultural conditioning to stand up to examination nearly one hundred years after his book was published, for situations of which he could have little awareness or understanding. However, it does perhaps make clear a particular attitude to composition and composers that is questioned and generally found to be incomplete by the authors of this book.

This is not to say that there are not 'special' people doing 'special' musical things in Africa, or that notation is always irrelevant, or that environment and training are not important. Rather that music is composed, interpreted and realised in a range of ways that have significance and value within their contexts, and have the potential to inform practice and comprehension beyond their original contexts, in a musical world that has always been a meeting ground, with resulting 'convergences and collisions' (Kartomi and Blum, 1994).

Africa has written about its music itself. Not only in academic musicological ways, but through investigating cultural function and change in novels, where music is included both as part of the organic whole, and for its roles as mode of expression of a culture, and as a mode of mutual interpretation between culture and individual. Conflict between cultures, or between the micro-culture of the individual and identifiable meta-culture, which attempts to hold all the individuals in relationship, is often played out in this latter mode.

Camara Laye in *The African Child*, (an autobiography of a 'son of Malinke' in what was then French Guinea, now Guinea) describes a performance by a praise singer designed to persuade his father to work quickly and effectively at producing an item of gold jewellery:

> The praise-singer would install himself in the workshop, tune up his cora ... and would begin to sing my father's praises ... The harp played an accompaniment to this vast utterance of names, expanding it and punctuating it with notes that were now soft, now shrill ... I could tell that my father's vanity was being inflamed. (1955: 23)

Later, when Laye's father had been persuaded to undertake the work, there is a relationship apparent between the creative processes of goldsmith and praise singer:

> While my father was slowly turning the trinket round in his fingers, smoothing it into perfect shape, [the praise-singer] during the whole process of transformation, had kept on singing his praises, accelerating his rhythm, increasing his flatteries as the trinket took shape, and praising my father's talents to the skies.

Indeed, the praise-singer participated in a curious - I was going to say direct, effective way in the work. He too was intoxicated with the joy of creation; he declaimed his rapture, and plucked his harp like a man inspired; he warmed to the task as if he had been the craftsman himself ... He was no longer a paid thurifer; he was no longer just the man whose services each and anyone could hire: he had become a man who creates his song under the influence of some very personal, interior necessity. (Ibid.: 29-30)

There is much here to which Lavignac would relate. There is a person perceived as having a particular gift, which has been nurtured, and is valued. The importance of keeping a record, which for Lavignac requires notation, is achieved by the praise singer through the use of a strongly developed and frequently exercised memory, and the use of traditional patterns and formulae as an aid to that memory. Laye also considers that the praise singer moves beyond the acknowledged, and paid for, function of the composition; there is an internal drive, which may remind us of Lavignac's 'sacred fire'.

On the other side of the continent the Kenyan writer, Ngugi wa Thiong'o, also gives music particular significance in dealing with the central issues he writes about. *Petals of Blood* (1977) deals with the new capitalism, colonial oppression, and the struggle against 'a more severe and deadly exploitation by an alliance of foreigners and the class of newly-propertied Africans' (back cover). There are references to music, often as cultural signifier, throughout the book, and in one case Ngugi laments the disappearance of a traditional drink that was closely linked to occasions of composition:

Theng'eta is the plant that only the old will talk about. Why? It is simple. It is only they who will have heard of it or know about it ... Nyakinyua says that they used to brew it before the Europeans came. And they would drink it only when work was finished, and especially after the ceremony of circumcision or marriage or itwika, and after a harvest. It was when they were drinking Theng'eta that poets and singers composed their words for a season of Gichandi, and the seer voiced his prophecy. (Ngugi, 1977: 204)

The *Gichandi* is a seed filled gourd and is used in competition as described by Senoga-Zake:

Commonly two players, especially old men, used to challenge each other in a market place. They shook their instruments and

> chanted poems or told stories, or even had a question and
> answer style warbling. Whoever lasted longer than the other ...
> won and took possession of the other's gicandi. (Senoga-Zake,
> 1986: 165)

Later in the book, Ngugi describes a wedding celebration, in which some of
the central characters of the novel are involved in singing, which, although
based on what is known, is also highly adapted to these particular
circumstances:

> Under the emotion of the hour, Munira suddenly tried a verse he
> thought he knew. Njuguna and Nyakinyua were making it
> sound so easy and effortless. But in the middle he got confused.
> Njuguna and Nyakinyua now teamed up against him:
>
> > You now break harmony of voices
> > You now break harmony of voices
> > It's the way you'll surely break our harmony
> > When the time of initiation comes.
>
> But Abdulla came to the rescue:
>
> > I was not breaking soft voices
> > I was not breaking soft voices
> > I only paused to straighten up
> > The singers' and dancers' robes.
>
> Nyakinyua's voice now drifted in, conciliatory, but signalling the
> end of this particular dance. She asked in song: if a thread was
> broken, to whom were the pieces thrown to mend them into a
> new thread? Njuguna replied, turning to Karega: it was thrown
> to Karega for he was a big warrior, Njamba Nene. (Ibid.: 209)

There is in this still something of the notion of gradations of skill in
singing/composing, but it is a skill that all have access to, and all need to
maintain for full involvement in demonstrations of cultural identity, to
understand what is happening and to affect it.

In *Devil on the Cross*, Ngugi considers the 'composer' as Lavignac would
have understood the term. Gatuiria is a young Gikuyu man, who has
studied music at an American university, and is now researching traditional
music at university in Kenya. He is also a composer:

> My ambition and dream is to compose a piece of music for
> many human voices accompanied by an orchestra made up of

all kinds of national instruments ... I often hear with the ears of my heart flutes and trumpets blown by a choir of herdsmen in the plains, the drums of the whole land call on the youth of our country to go to war ... I seize pen and paper write down the message of the voices before they are carried away by the wind. (Ngugi, 1982: 59-60)

What we see here is somebody who is fully absorbed in plans to integrate the many communities of his country through music, and is planning to achieve it through ways that do not perhaps originate in his own culture, but which are appropriate for assimilation, because of the fact that 'composition' itself is well known and practised. Later on, Gatuiria's plans are much further developed, and he plans to finish his piece in honour of his fiancée:

> ... Gatuiria had decided that his score would be Wariinga's engagement ring ... during tomorrow's ceremony Gatuiria intended to offer her the two hundred sheets of music, the fruits of two years of the labour of his heart. (Ibid.: 226)

So Gatuiria would appear to meet Lavignac's criteria: having special instincts, a 'sacred fire', the ability to infer or apply theoretical constructs, and being nurtured in an appropriate environment. There is also the idea that the score is the music. And in a sense, anyone wishing to combine all the cultures of Kenya musically would have to work outside the traditional practices of any one of them, precisely because of their cultural loads.

What these novels, and many others, perhaps show about the nature of composition in Africa is its groundedness in a people's life. It is communal expression and signification, and a vehicle for individual interpretation of that. Through the relationship between this individuality and communalism it embodies cultural dynamism. Composition in Africa is seen as a medium for change and integration inter-culturally and internationally, as well as intra-culturally. It may be that this book will reveal some of the dynamic processes and products of this medium.

The book

This book looks at music from several parts of Africa; from Egypt to South Africa, from Ghana to Kenya. It investigates a range of styles and types; traditional, popular, contemporary and syncretic. It is written by a variety of scholars, some African, and all of whom have spent considerable time in Africa in connection with their researches. We have included transcriptions wherever possible, to give a flavour of the music, although we are all well aware of the significant limitations of these. There are also references to recordings, and some of those are held centrally, in places such as the British Library National Sound Archive, thus making access easy for those in Britain at least. Recordings are also held in the National Archives of most countries in which our research has been based.

I would like to record my thanks to King Alfred's, University College Winchester for supporting this work through the granting of sabbatical time, and for financial support; to Maureen Blaydon for most of the music setting, and particularly to Emma, my wife, who has put up with my absences and supported both me and my work.

Bibliography

Kartomi, Margaret J. and Blum, Stephen (1994), *Music - Cultures in Contact. Convergences and Collisions,* Basel: Gordon & Breach.

Lavignac, Albert (1903), *Musical Education*, New York: D. Appleton & Co.

Laye, Camara (1955), *The African Child*, London: Fontana. [Extracts reprinted by permission of Harper Collins Publishers Ltd.]

Ngugi wa Thiong'o (1977), *Petals of Blood*, London: Heinemann.

Ngugi wa Thiong'o (1982), *Devil on the Cross*, Oxford: Heinemann. [Extracts from the two books above are reprinted by permission of Heinemann Educational Publishers, a division of Reed Educational and Professional Publishing Ltd.]

Senoga-Zake, George (1986), *Folk Music of Kenya*, Nairobi: Uzima.

2 Melodic and Rhythmic Aspects of African Music

Christopher James

African music has long-standing traditions and has produced a vast variety of beautiful and impressive music. Apart from a few specialists, Europeans have only relatively recently begun to appreciate and understand the rich tapestry of African musical styles.

Music making is such an important part of African social and cultural life that it is performed regularly in a wide diversity of social settings. When communities come together, music usually forms an integral part of the activities. Music is played for purely recreational purposes, or it may enhance ceremonies or rites (Nketia, 1975: 21).

Africans assume that all normal people have some musical ability and are therefore capable of taking part in a musical performance (Blacking, 1973: 34). Thus when music is performed by a group or tribe it becomes a shared creative experience which enriches community life (Nketia, 1974: 22). Musical performance cannot therefore be separated from social activities. Even in urban communities it is an essential component of cultural life (Coplan, 1985: 4).

Music is generally performed by groups of musicians who lead the others in dance and song; however, it is sometimes performed by individuals (for example, a herd boy playing his flute). At important ceremonies and celebrations music is fundamental to the proceedings. But it may also be used to aid tasks, such as grass cutting or threshing. Music is performed at many events, but not necessarily on every social occasion or for every collective activity (Nketia, 1975: 29). In fact there are times in the year when certain African societies deliberately refrain from making music.

When a 'Westerner' enjoys music, he or she usually sits passively and listens. But the African will become so absorbed that s/he becomes a participant. Chernoff, in discussing African aesthetics, states that there can be no meaning without participation. He claims that for a Westerner to understand and appreciate an African musical event, he must 'slow down his aesthetic response, and glide past his initial judgement' (Chernoff, 1979: 33). In discussing the music of the Venda, Blacking mentions that music expresses emotions and attitudes that have already been experienced and thereby enhances the social meaning of the gatherings which it serves (Blacking, 1967: 23). Thus, to understand African music fully, it ought not to be divorced from its social and cultural context.

In spite of the great diversity of African musical styles and idioms there are a number of common features and characteristics. I shall illustrate some of these during the course of this chapter.

Part one of the chapter deals with melodic features. Part two is devoted to the complexities of rhythmic organisation.[1]

Melodic features

A Westerner's initial response to African music may be 'it is so repetitive'. Repetition is an important formal characteristic contributing to the design and structure of African music. However, the type of repetitious patterns used by Africans can be extremely complex. Most music (except where composers deliberately avoid it) contains some repetition. What is important is how the African musician achieves variety and maintains interest within a cyclical framework, not the mere fact that the music is repetitive.

Many African melodies are based on scales of a few tones, for example, four, five, six or seven. The concept of modulation within a piece of music is foreign to African thinking. In listening to African music we ought therefore always to be aware of the very stable tonic note or chord, one to which all the other pitches relate.

In hexatonic or heptatonic melodies the size of the intervals does not always correspond to those in the major or minor scales used by European composers. Often the octave is divided into equidistant steps, so the concept of tone and semitone as found in Western scales is absent from African scale patterns. Jones concludes that wherever the equiheptatonic scale is used it consists essentially of two factors: first the notes divide the octave into seven equal intervals; and second, these notes are always tuned to a standard set of absolute pitches (1980: 69).

Our first example of African melody is a short love song composed by a young man from the Tutsi people of the Congo. The piece is entitled 'Lama', meaning 'lament', and a translation of the text reads as follows:

> Why do I love you when you do not respond,
> I have written you letters and you do not answer,
> I have sent you messengers and you turn them away,
> Why do I love you when you do not even notice me.

The structure of this lament is very simple. A soloist starts it and the chorus sings repetitive motifs in drone-like fashion at appropriate moments. Phrases overlap between the soloist and chorus. Figure 2.1 shows a transcription of the first section of this song. Note that the melodic structure is hexatonic. Also, the piece has only one rhythmic motif which is employed throughout the song. This is in sharp contrast to some of the other examples we shall be examining.

Figure 2.1 'Lama': lament, Tutsi, Congo

The second example (Figure 2.2) was sung by a Bobwa man from Northern Congo. This humorous song is accompanied by an *mbira* (a type of finger piano) playing a cyclic pattern in a hexatonic scale. The text deals with the timeless theme of the mother-in-law, a translation of it being 'every time he goes out, his mother-in-law comes to borrow a bunch of bananas'.

The melodic style is akin to speech (which of course makes transcription of the vocal part difficult). It could be called 'parlando style' (Rycroft, 1985: 14), which is a combination of speech and song. Sometimes the soloist sings distinct pitches; at other times the quasi-speech patterning determines the rhythmic structure of the vocal part. Ekwueme claims that because speech and music are closely allied a tune may easily switch from music to spoken words of indefinite pitch. In so doing, it may be decorated by glissandi and other forms of note bending which may obscure the intonation (1974: 52).

Mbira pieces often have fixed musical structures, and do not generally have a specific beginning or end. *Mbira* compositions contain characteristic cyclical patterns that provide a framework for elaboration and variation supporting the creative expression of the performer (Berliner, 1978: 52). This pattern repeats fairly consistently even though the phrase structures of the vocal part and the accompaniment are seldom synchronous. The scale used has six tones. Interest is maintained in the vocal part by varying the length of the phrases.

**Figure 2.2   'Amana': humorous song with *mbira* accompaniment,
              Bobwe, Northern Congo**

The third example demonstrates rhythmic variation applied to a melody. This song is a lament entitled 'Chidilo cha Mindonga' and is sung by a soloist; later in the piece a small chorus joins in. Notice how the descending melodic line is carefully varied according to the text. Although the rhythmic variations are subtle, the general contour of this descending melodic pattern is always perceivable. Melodies which start on a fairly high pitch and descend to a low pitch are a common feature of African music (Ekwueme, 1974: 48).

The melody is heptatonic and is suggestive of modal music. Many African melodies resemble some of the medieval modes employed by European composers. The melodic structure of this particular example corresponds to the mixolydian mode which is frequently encountered in medieval church music.

Figure 2.3 shows the opening few bars which contain the essential structural material.

Figure 2.3   'Chidilo Cha Mindongo': Chopi, Mozambique

In the following example the song is built on a six-note scale. It is a humorous one entitled 'Kayuni' and comes from the Tumbuka people in Malawi.

It begins with an introductory motif sung by the soloist, which is answered by the chorus. This statement and answer (or call and response) principle is a noteworthy characteristic of much African music. The introductory section is repeated, after which the remainder of the verse follows. Overlapping of phrases between the soloist and chorus is apparent. Observe the melodic contour; again it starts on a high pitch, then descends to a lower one. The whole of the first verse is shown in Figure 2.4. After the verse has been repeated, the soloist improvises in a very humorous fashion against the basic motif which the chorus sings. Syncopation and complex rhythmic patterns (largely determined by the text) are attractive features of the soloist's part.

There is ostinato (particularly in the chorus section), and the final result is aesthetically pleasing on account of the tremendous interest maintained by the soloist.

The transcription shows that the song is based on four melodic and rhythmic motifs (one of which is derived from another). These motifs determine the structure and help provide unity.

Figure 2.4 'Kayuni': Tambuka, Malawi

The next piece, 'Mkazi wa Mulomo' [to be found on the disc referred to in note 1], is played on the *mogogodo*, a loose note xylophone, by two Malawi boys of approximately 12 years in age from Chikwaka district. Children are taught to play instruments and sing at a very tender age, particularly those born of musical parents.

The ten-note xylophone that these boys play is tuned to a pentatonic scale. The rather quick tempo and interesting rhythm aptly portrays the character of this work, the title of which is 'Mkazi wa Mulomo' meaning 'the talkative woman'. The lower part emphasises the pulse by employing a repetitive cyclic pattern. The upper part improvises melodic phrases above this ostinato pattern. Although the upper part is improvised, the lower part ensures that a definite cyclic structure is maintained, thereby providing a clear formal design for the piece as a whole.

A fine sense of rhythm is required to play this work, particularly by the boy playing the improvisatory upper part. Notice how the melodic patterns of the upper part generally enter on a weak beat or weak portion of a beat. What is important about the rhythm is that the lower part cuts and defines the pulse, thereby leaving room for the other rhythm to be heard clearly. As Chernoff states, the African instrumentalist 'concerns himself as much with the notes he does not play as with the accents he delivers' (1979: 60).

Rhythmic characteristics

Most African music contains recurring cyclical patterns, and rhythmic complexity is a hallmark or African music. The scholar A. M. Jones has stated:

> Rhythm is to the African what harmony is to the Europeans, and
> it is in the complex interweaving of contrasting rhythmic patterns
> that he finds his greatest aesthetic satisfaction.[2]

The rhythmic component of most Western music is divisive in concept. Whether the metre has two, three or four beats the stress on the first beat determines the rhythmic structure of the music. In African music, especially drumming, the first beat of the bar often receives no stress. Instead it is felt by the musicians (or supplied by the dancers). The African approach to rhythm is that at least two separate and independent rhythms should occur simultaneously, thereby producing in combination rhythmic complexities not found in most Western music. In Western music rhythmic patterns reinforce and emphasise the essential metric pattern, whereas in African music separate rhythmic patterns conflict with one another to produce polyrhythmic combinations and multi-metric patterns. Our first example of African rhythm, although fairly simple, clearly demonstrates this principle.

This short composition is a duet played by two Chopi girls from the Zavala district of Mozambique. It is played on two four-note ocarinas (small gourd wind instruments). Figure 2.5 shows the opening few bars of this duet. Notice that the upper melody accentuates the first and third beats of the metre, whilst the lower one emphasises the second and fourth beats. The effect is similar to hocket, a characteristic of many medieval and renaissance compositions.

Figure 2.5   Duet played by two Chopi girls (opening few bars only)

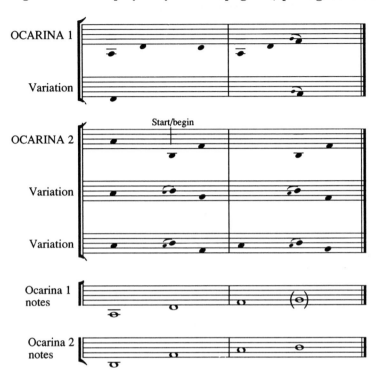

Figure 2.6 is performed by Soga men from Uganda. The performers include one playing a flute, two drummers (playing a drum each) and handclappers. The colourful title 'Bwomera envu' means 'When your hair turns grey, you are getting old'. The flute player plays a descending melodic phrase which undergoes subtle rhythmic and melodic variation during the course of the piece. The drummers each play fairly simple contrasting patterns which when superimposed provide much momentum and vitality. In Figure 2.7 notice that the first drummer stresses the first, third and fifth beats of the metre whilst the second drummer accentuates the second, fourth and sixth. The resultant pattern would not be counted, but felt by the performers (Koetting, 1986: 60). Handclapping occurs on every beat, and thus contributes to the rhythmic complexity. Nevertheless, four independent rhythmic patterns are observable in this rather beautiful example of African music.

Figure 2.6 'Bwomera envu': Soga, Uganda (opening four bars)

Figure 2.7 demonstrates a group of six African musicians complementing one another to form a complex rhythmic pattern. Each player plays only one pitch on his instrument. The rhythmic interlocking effect can only be produced by each player's knowing exactly when to play his note. The playing of these individual notes is always accompanied by some bodily movement (Ekwueme, 1974: 61).

The unusual metre is a fine example of additive rhythm. Instead of a regularly recurring pattern of three or four beats, groups of four, five, six and seven notes may be used in duple and triple patterns (Nketia, 1975: 129-31). In this example duple and triple metres are combined.

By listening to the music and examining the transcription we notice that the metric structure is established by the two treble horn players who play a regular rhythmic pattern. This pattern acts as a time line and guides the other players (Ekwueme, 1974: 61). The lower four horn players often play in between the pulses, thus causing a syncopated effect. Since the players do not generally play on the first beat of the bar, the effect of this silent beat helps to create the forward or dynamic motion in the music (Agawu, 1986: 79). Note that there is some rhythmic activity on almost every quaver in this piece. Each player plays his own specific rhythmic pattern and the final effect is created by each playing his own pattern at the appropriate moment. The composite result is an engaging composition which successfully shows some of the complexities of African rhythm.

Figure 2.7 'Rwakanembe': Nyoro horn players, Uganda

Many African compositions reveal different structural levels as a component of their design. In the previous example we saw how the two upper horn parts provided the time line and thus the essential framework of the composition.

The concept of structural levels in music was first developed by Heinrich Schenker, who postulated that Western music consisted of three different structural levels. Ekwueme has applied Schenker's principles to rhythm and form in African music. He concludes that African rhythm is based on a skeleton - a background structure which he calls the 'form' of the music and which is often reducible to a 'call and response' pattern. The middleground and foreground levels of African music are determined by the presence of both constant and variable rhythmic and melodic patterns and by assessing whether the variable patterns are essential or unessential to the architectural structure of the composition (Ekwueme, 1976: 28).

By applying Ekwueme's concept of rhythm and form to our next example, you will notice that the background level is supplied by a bass drum which defines the time line and pulse of the composition. The other drums contribute to the middleground level and the horns, which appear about halfway through the piece, are foreground material. However, what is fascinating about this example is that the middleground drums start off the composition and only after this rhythmic pattern has been established is the bass drum introduced.

The dance song entitled 'Mavumbala' (also to be found on the record) is played by Mayogo men from the Congo. The instruments are: seven *mbar* wooden horns, a *kekese* basket rattle, *Mbili* metal wrist bell, two pod drums, two conical laced drums, two small slit drums and a double metal bell.

Our next example is played by five Lozi men from Zambia. They accompany their singing with a nine-note *silimba* xylophone. The *silimba* xylophone is built on a rough frame standing about three feet above the ground. Each of the keys has a separate calabash resonator. The instrument is tuned to a hexatonic scale. The piece is called 'Mulala karimukwa panga' ('Mulala stole money').

Even without a transcription the five-part structure of the piece (shown in Figure 2.8) can be recognised. The cyclical accompaniment provides continuity and unity, while at the same time creating a degree of variation by subtle alteration of repeated phrases. The vocal parts demonstrate the call and response pattern mentioned earlier.

Figure 2.8   'Mulala karimukwa panga': Lozi, Zambia

macrostructure	A	B	A	B	A
vocal parts		c and r		c and r	
accompaniment	recurring cyclical patterns, slightly modified.				

The final work is by Chopi musicians from Mozambique. Hugh Tracey regards their artistic integrity and musical achievements as perhaps unexcelled in Africa. This composition entitled 'Lawanani michanga sika timbila tamakono' ('Come together and make music for the new year') is played by six musicians on *timbila* xylophones. Chopi musicians often play music with large ensembles, with as many as fifteen instrumentalists participating.

The macro-structural design of the work is shown in Figure 2.9. In the introduction one player establishes the full cyclical pattern and tempo of the piece, after which the full instrumental ensemble plays variations on the basic material. The ensemble is then augmented by the addition of a chorus consisting of dancers. A short coda the same length as the introduction concludes the piece. Note that the instrumentalists play through the entire work, thereby fulfilling a primary role. The chorus is of secondary importance. Observe also the descending vocal lines in the chorus sections.

Figure 2.9 'Lawanani michanga sika timbila tamakono' Chopi, Mozambique. Composed by Mzeno of Gomukoma

	Macrostructural design		timing
A	Introduction		17"
B	Full instrumental ensemble		1'23"
C	Chorus	50"	
D	Instrumental interlude	10"	
C'	Chorus	50"	1'50"
A'	Coda		17"
			3'47"

Conclusion

This chapter has tried to illustrate some of the important melodic and rhythmic phenomena of African music, to introduce some stylistic and aesthetic features of African musical thought.

It has been observed that the role of music in African societies is fundamental and pervasive. African melodic formulae are still the subject of much debate amongst scholars, and African rhythmic principles are beginning to exert a profound influence on contemporary Western composers. For me, to live in Africa without taking cognisance of its rich variety of music would be akin to observing the sun without feeling its warmth.

Notes

1. All the music examples quoted have come from Hugh Tracey's two
    collections, 'The Music of Africa' series and the 'Sound of Africa'
    series. Some details relating to performers, instruments and texts have
    been gleaned from the record jackets.
        All the transcriptions in this chapter were completed by Andrew
    Tracey (International Library of African Music), Rhodes University.
    The notations should not imply a certain scale or tuning, nor do they
    correspond to absolute pitch. Some transcriptions are transposed for
    easier reading.
2. Quoted in Chernoff (1979: 40), from Jones (1954: 26-47).

Bibliography

Agawu, V. K. (1986), '"Gi Dunu", "Nyekpadudo", and the Study of West
        African Rhythm', *Ethnomusicology*, **30**, 64-83.
Berliner, P. F. (1978), *The Soul of Mbira*, Berkeley and Los Angeles:
        University of California Press.
Blacking, J. (1967), *Venda Children's Songs*, Johannesburg: Witwatersrand
        University Press.
Chernoff, J. M. (1979), *African Rhythm and African Sensibility*, Chicago:
        University of Chicago Press.
Coplan, D. P. (1985), *In Township Tonight! South Africa's Black City
        Music and Theatre*, Johannesburg: Ravan Press.
Ekwueme, Laz E. N. (1974), 'Concepts of African Musical Theory',
        Journal of Black Studies, **5** (1), 35-64.
Ekwueme, Laz E. N. (1976), 'Structural Levels of Rhythm and Form in
        African Music', *African Music*, **5** (4), 27-35.
Jones, A. M. (1954), 'African Rhythm', *Africa* **24**, 26-47.
Jones, A. M. (1980), 'Panpipes and the Equiheptatonic Pitch', *African
        Music*, **6** (1), 62-9
Koetting, J. (1986), 'What Do We Know about African Rhythm',
        Ethnomusicology **30**, 58-63.
Nketia, J. H. K. (1975), *The Music of Africa*, London: Gollancz.
Rycroft, D. (1985), 'Zulu Melodic and Non-melodic Vocal Styles', paper
        presented at the Fifth Symposium on Ethnomusicology,
        Grahamstown: Rhodes University Printing, pp. 13-28.
Yeston, M. (ed.) (1977), *Readings in Schenker Analysis and Other
        Approaches*, New Haven and London: Yale University Press, pp. 3-
        37.

Part I

The Making of 'Traditional' Musics

3   Egyptian Folk Music

Adel Kamel

Since the time of the pharaohs, Egyptian folk song has gone along with the life of the Egyptian person from his birth until his death, expressing his happiness and grief, sharing in all occasions. From the moment of an Egyptian infant's birth, a song or hymn takes its way to his ears. The song plays with him, puts him to sleep and appears at beautiful celebrations. Then come lullabies, with the singers caressing and playing with the child.

When the infant is one week old, he is put in a cradle full of grains such as wheat and corn, and while he is being rocked steadily the family sing special songs. Another kind of infant song is for circumcision. The child to be circumcised, along with friends, relatives and other groups of people, marches along the streets with musicians and dancers of both sexes. While the operation is being performed they all keep singing. After a few years we find the child himself performing certain songs and even inventing some while playing with his fellows.

Traditional folk singing

Work songs

The song '*Hedaa el Ebel*', ('the merchant who rides the camel') seems to be one of the oldest national folk songs. '*Helalia*' is a song fishermen sing while they are pulling in the nets. It encourages the physical strength of the group through singing '*Hela-Hela*'. In the song they describe their voyages at sea.

Songs for cotton gathering begin with a part praising the *Kholi*, the person who is responsible for bringing the girls to gather the cotton. He is also responsible for conducting their work and paying their wages. In these folk songs the girls perform *zagharitte* in his honor. The *zagharitte* is 'played by women's tongues' (like a trill played on musical instruments).

Marriage songs

Weddings are very social events, occasions when poor people, as well as the rich, celebrate with very specific traditional features. Weddings are not short ceremonies as is often the case in modern societies. What usually takes place is that the bride's family choose the bridegroom for their daughter, thus having the right to interfere. The young couple ready to be married go through several ceremonies, although these differ from one area to the other.

They start at the engagement where a gift is presented (usually gold) the night before the wedding. Then comes the wedding, and I remember seeing - as a child in my little village (Zoeir) - that the wedding day starts with a procession from the bride's house with her mother, father and brothers. She comes out of the house wearing a wedding dress, usually red, then the father or brother carries her on a horse. She is preceded by a group of musicians playing beautiful deep tunes and there is a kind of freedom in this happy music. At the same time it is a farewell to her family and her father's house where she was born and grew up.

When the procession arrives at the bridegroom's house, he steps forward and carries his bride to his room accompanied by his mother or any of his aunts or his sisters. After he performs what is known as 'deflowering the virgin' he shows the handkerchief with her blood stains to his family, her family and the whole village people, through the window. He feels proud because of the virginity of his bride. So the girl's family dance, and sing, being happy that their daughter honoured them.

There are various types of marriage song in Egypt. There are songs for the engagement, others for the night before the wedding (*El Henna*), wedding songs, and songs for the day after the wedding (*sabaheia*) to make sure of the bride's happiness. *Zagharitte* is also performed.

Pilgrim songs

Moslems of the world go on pilgrimage to *Bate - Allah* or *Kaaba*, 'God's House' in Saudi Arabia. This occasion is greatly celebrated, no less than weddings. A religious man (*Sheikh*) comes to recite some of the Koran, with poems and religious praises to the Prophet Mohammed. These songs start as soon as the pilgrims apply to go on the journey, and continue while arranging what is needed to be taken with them. The house is painted with folkloric designs relating to the occasion, such as painting a ship, or an aeroplane or the Holy Koran, then writing sentences to congratulate the person going and wishing him a happy return.

There are two kinds of wording for pilgrim songs. One to be sung before the departure of the person on their pilgrimage. The other is recited after his return. All this takes place in big processions of relatives, friends and lovers, singing religious pieces. The texts are about the occasion, the journey and its purpose, praising the Prophet Mohammed, and giving good wishes for the person's happy journey and a safe return. The singers also ask God to fulfil their dreams that they may also visit the tomb of the Prophet Mohammed.

Epic songs

Egyptian history is full of these epics of love and heroism, like those about the hero Abou Zeid el Helali, and Hassan and Naima, the Egyptian Romeo and Juliet. These are not simple stories related by the old to the young, but they are complete dramatic stories and complete musical stories, that are sung by poets on the *rabab* from their beginnings to their ends. Egyptian civilisation is full of other epics like those that speak about revenge in the epic known as 'Adham el Sharkawai'. Other epics give us examples of patience and endurance like 'Ayoub' which is sometimes also called 'Nasa and Ayoub'.

The Zar

This is a kind of old folkloric dancing which still remains. It seems to be a remnant of old religious dancing, according to the Egyptian author Ahmed Roushdy Saleh:

> The first ritual beliefs about primitive folkloric art are the sites of *El-Zar*. There are just barbaric dances which remind us of what we read about primitive group dancing, that is performed for richness, or sending away a fierce animal or frightful darkness.

This is disputable. The *Zar* has its own tradition with a fixed dramatic shape, and is accompanied by rhythmic music that adds to the depth of this drama. These rhythms reach a state of violence, after starting quietly. This gradual proceeding to a climax shows, without doubt, a dramatic shape.

Death songs: eulogies

These hymns are very similar musically to work, pilgrims', and some wedding songs. They are similar in their musical construction and their way of being sung. What differs is the wording only. This kind of song is about to be forgotten, especially after the disappearance of the job of the *Naddaba*, the person specialising in saying these words. This is happening because of the modernisation of Egypt, and also because religion forbids this kind of mourning. It involves reciting some words, folk poems and lamentations in a free way, saying good things about the deceased as well as asking for faith, acknowledging that everybody will die, and that only God will remain.

The instruments of Egyptian folk music

Aerophone

Suffara: or *Sallameia*, is a tubular reed flute open at both ends, with six holes.

Instruments with single reed:

Arghul: It is a double clarinet. The tube on which the melody is played, has six holes, the other tube is longer. There are two kinds of *Arghul*, one 60-85cm, the other 180-250cm. Other kinds of *Arghul* are called *Tommary, Orma, Zummara.*

Instruments with double reed:

Muzmar: It is a simple oboe made of wood whose tube ends in a conical bell. It has eight holes. There are three kinds of *Muzmar*, they are different only in size, *Sibs, El-Muzmarel Soieedy, Tiet.* The smallest plays the melody, the others play a 'basso sostenuto'.

Chordophone

With plucked strings:

Qithar: or *Tanbur*. It has five metal strings strung over a sounding box. It is found in South Egypt (Aswan).

Semsemeia: It is similar to *Qithar*, and mostly found in the Canal zone.

With bowed strings:

Rababa: It is the oldest violin type in Egypt, with a sounding box made of coconut with the top removed and over which a skin of leather is stretched. It has only two horsehair strings, and is held vertically, the lower part resting on the player's knee.

Membranophone

Tabla: or *Darabukka* or *Doholla*. It is made from pottery with a wide neck, its mouth is covered with a thin goat or fish skin, and it is played with the fingers. It is the principal percussion instrument of the folk orchestra.

Rikk: or *Tambourin* or *Duff*, it has discs of metal which create a
                   special effect.

Idiophone

Sagat: Pairs of small copper cymbals, put on the fingers. Small ones
                   are called *Torra*, big ones (15 cm) are called *Kass*. The Coptic
                   Church uses an identical cymbal pair called *Naqqous* together
                   with a triangle called *Teryanto*.

We have to remember that some instruments have different names in
different parts of the country. Moreover, various fortuitous objects are
sometimes used to accompany songs: spoons, or bottles, or glasses struck
with a key or knife!

Folk music in Nubia

The Nubians inhabit the area from the Sudanese border up to Aswan in the
North. They lived originally in scattered communitites; yet the majority
now live in Aswan in what is called the new Nubia beween Luxor and
Aswan, because their native area was drowned by Nasser's lake, after the
building of the High Dam. They differ from the rest of the people of Egypt,
having their own customs, traditions and language, in addition to Egyptian
- Arabic. Due to their geographical position they have come more into
contact with, and have been more influenced by, African art and folklore.
This is clear in their use of the pentatonic mode.

Example 3.1

The main musical instruments are the *tar* (drum) with its different sizes,
and a string instrument called the *tannboura* which resembles the
semsemeia of Port Said, the pharaonic guitar or *kenara*. It has five strings,
like the pharaonic instrument, and is adjusted to the same mode or tonality
(pentatonic), and is played the same way. It is the only instrument that is
used in this part of Egypt, either alone or to accompany dancing and
singing. Nubians use the *tannboura* very cleverly, and can link lines in

parallel. Every group has a different rhythm, but they join together without the slightest defeat, rather in wonderful harmony.

Inhabitants of this area tend to use several voices polyphonically, and solo and group singing and dancing depend mainly on composed polyrhythmic accompaniments. They also have a special style in clapping the hands which is not mere keeping the rhythm, as in other parts of Egypt. This clapping has a role and a separate line that could be considered a tune in itself, or a melody of rhythms.

The Nubians have special dances with very slow movement, while we find the music and the rhythm strong and lively. Men dance together in groups and it is very rare for women to participate, for their role is secondary; one dancer, or two at the most, may join in performing some special dances. Group performance prevails, where all the people present, without exception, participate either by dancing, or playing the *tannboura* or *tambouus*, clapping or singing in the form of a dialogue.

Music in Nubian rituals - birth

The mother gives birth to her child and the midwife carries him on a white piece of cloth taken from a kind man's robe. After a week the child is taken to the River Nile because in Nubia every child is the son of the River Nile. When the day is fixed for the child to appear, people of the village, relatives and neighbours gather together and walk in a procession towards the Nile. They carry the child, who is still wrapped in the white cloth for blessing, in such a way that he is facing the Nile. Some ladies in the procession carry bread, and they are all led by a young boy holding two daggers in his hands, dancing while the others sing. When the procession reaches the Nile, they wipe the face of the child with the water.

Music in Nubian rituals - marriage

Customs and traditions of Nubian marriage resemble those of other parts of Egypt, except for the wedding procession of the bride and bridegroom. The people walk in a big procession after dinner, heading for the house of the bride. Relations of the bridegroom carry with them his bedding which consists of a pillow, blanket and a cover. Then the women stand together in several rows. In front of them stand men of the village, keeping a space of at least three metres between them. They clap their hands in a rhythm called *Al Ketshad.*

Example 3.2

Then they sing the wedding song. With the singing they dance the *Aragio*, a well known Nubian dance.

The Dance starts accompanied by a rhythm of ♩s then it is performed as is shown in Figure 3.3,

Example 3.3

Music in Nubian rituals - death

When a death occurs, female relatives of the deceased start screaming so that the people of the village know about the tragic event that has taken place. Women go to pay their condolences, and so do men after they close their shops, or leave their work in the fields. After the burial is over the women go to the house of the deceased, speaking about the tragedy. When they come close to the house they start to weep slowly, then suddenly it becomes higher and higher when they meet with any of the deceased's relatives. Then screaming starts and they start beating their cheeks in this rhythm:

Example 3.4

Conclusion

These are just a few examples of the rich inheritance which fills the history of folklore in Egypt. We will not be the first people who have tried to search their old history in order to use their inheritance in artistic development.

And in spite of the very humble steps we have taken in this field, we still have much in front of us. We still have to classify what is still with us now. By doing this we may discover the size of our dreams and how we might realise them.

Bibliography

Braddock, J. (1960), *The Bridal Bed*, London: Robert Hale.

Breasted, J. H. (1906), *Ancient Records of Egypt*, Chicago: University of Chicago Press.

Coon, C. S. (1965), *A Reader in General Anthropology*, London: Jonathan Cape.

Gorer, Geoffrey (1945, repr. 1983), *Africa Dances*, London: Penguin.

Krappe, A. H. (1898, repr. 1962), *The Science of Folklore*, London: Methuen.

Lane, E. W. (1898), *An Account of the Manners and Customs of the Modern Egyptians, Written in 1833-1835*, London: Gardener.

Murray, M. (1972), *The Splendour that was Egypt*, London: Sidgwick & Jackson.

Nazeer, William (1959), *Egyptian Customs in Past and Present*, Cairo.

Stromback, Dag (1970), *Folklore*, Uppsala: Institute for Philology, ARV.

Tiberiu, Alexandru (1967), *Folk Music in Egypt* (research made in collaboration with Emile Azer Wahba), Cairo.

4 The Roots of Ghanaian Composers

James Flolu

Despite all the developments in child psychology, a lot remains to be discovered about children's natural talents and potential, some of which adults underrate, do not notice or unconsciously suppress. The arts, particularly music, are victims of this attitude; and music education in Ghana is one of the most obvious sufferers. This chapter surveys the underlying musical experience of Ghanaian children and the extent to which they are involved in music creatively.

Generally, children's attempts at music composition, although valuable, have been overshadowed by the achievements of professional creative musicians (Ainsworth, 1970: 43). It is often argued that children cannot be true practitioners until they have acquired knowledge and skill (Walker, 1983: 96). Although those who support this argument do not always indicate precisely when such knowledge and skill should be acquired, the argument implies doubt about children's capacity to compose acceptable music. Plummeridge, (1980: 39) suggests that we consider seriously the question of standards, so as not to 'trivialize, or make meaningless' the notion of creativity. But what is the standard, and who sets the standard? As he has pointed out, these are notoriously difficult questions with which art has been confronted. Nevertheless, the tendency markedly to distinguish a child's composition from that of the established composer (Plummeridge, 1980: 38) - with a criterion set by the adult - has often blinded us to the significance of children's compositions.

Consider, for example, the case of language acquisition which begins at birth. We do not say that the young child with limited vocabulary, sometimes coining words to express himself, is not speaking a language because his range of vocabulary is not as extensive as that of the adult. Before the child attains school age, he has already learnt to speak the language of his home.

There is an abundant literature on how children acquire and master the knowledge and skill of spoken language (see e.g. Skinner, 1957; Chomsky, 1959/1969; Piaget, 1970; Gleitman and Wanner, 1982; Bruner, 1983). Despite the divergencies and controversies in the theories of language acquisition, there is some agreement that, apart from adult intervention and the general environmental influences, there is a natural process by which normal children learn to speak. Children hear people speak, and they have access to a 'corpus or sample of language in the utterances they hear' (Harris, 1990: 76). Even so it has been noted that; 'children's utterances are frequently characterised by novel combinations of morphemes and words which are not found in normal adult speech' (ibid.: 74). They imitate and improve language until they establish a medium of communication (Coates, 1993: 251). Even in cases where adult speech becomes ambiguous children bootstrap

> their way into the linguistic system, making use of whatever information they can extract from the surrounding environment (linguistic and non-linguistic) and their own predispositions (innate or acquired) for processing linguistic information. (Plunket, 1993: 43-4)

To a considerable extent, there is close agreement between the pattern of language acquisition and that of musical knowledge and skill in that, from the time of birth, children have lived with and through, some form of music provided by the same sources and facilities which provide for the learning of language. Undoubtedly, through the interaction with their environment, children often acquire some skill with which they manipulate the sound materials according to their own interests, capabilities and rules 'generated spontaneously' (Harris, 1990: 74). It has been suggested that children begin to utter their first words around the age of 12 months, and around the age of 18 months they begin to combine words (De Villiers and De Villiers, 1974: 13). Therefore, both speech and music can be viewed as developing skills, during the acquisition of which, children become increasingly capable of organising sound, rhythm and linguistic structures at several levels concurrently (Clark, 1974: 1).

According to Moog, (1976: 52-4), at between four to six months, children become actively attracted to music: they listen to music attentively, and often will turn towards the sound stimulus with an 'unmistakable expression of astonishment'. Some 6-month-old children even stop feeding to turn towards the music. Moog also discovered that children of the same age, at the same time that they begin to produce speech babbling, are also capable of making musical babbling: 'speech babbling is produced in the 6 or 7 months old infant by talking to him; musical babbling only occurs if music is sung or played to him' (1976: 60). This supports Kodály's conviction that music education should begin at birth.

Pond (1981) has observed that even young children have some hidden skills and talents which emerge when the opportunity to express themselves is provided. Three major conclusions were arrived at by Pond. First, young children have an 'innate apprehension of the function of formal procedures when sounds are being structured'. Secondly, improvisation with voice or other instrument is central to the promotion of innate musicality of the children. And thirdly, the children's constructional predilections are photo-polyphonic; that is, 'the free use of polyphony is the end that is most consonant with their musical instincts' (Pond, 1981: 11). Shelley (1981) has pointed out that young children, given the natural classroom setting with instruments, time and privacy, demonstrate a rich variety of musical behaviours which tend to surprise adults. The child's music, she writes, 'is unique and strange to the adult due to its unpredictable duration, rhythmic complexity and elusive totalities' (Shelley, 1981: 26). In recent years interest in children's musical expression has been growing steadily. Among the many British studies of children as composers, Swanwick and Tillman (1986) have traced the sequence of musical creative development through four stages, each of which is further divided into two, resulting in a spiral of eight cumulative and cyclical developmental modes:

- **mastery** - sensory response to sound materials - evolving into manipulative control (0-5 years)
1   *Sensory* (0-3 years): There is a strong desire to explore the nature and sources of sounds; the child is fascinated by and attracted to different characteristics of timbre, intensity, and duration of sounds.
2   *Manipulative* (4-about 5 years): The child begins to gain control over the techniques of handling instruments and sound sources.

- **Imitation** - personal expression moving towards the vernacular (4-9 years)
3   *Personal experiences* (4-7 years): Direct and spontaneous personal expression of musical feelings begin to emerge.
4   *Vernacular* (7-9): Shorter melodic and rhythmic patterns start to appear with repetitions; structure of phrases is more precise and coherent than before.

- **Imaginative play** - the speculative merging into the idiomatic (9-14)
5   *Speculative* (10-13): Improvisation and extemporisation become evident.
6   *Idiomatic* (12-14): Structural surprises become more firmly integrated; there is interest in adult musical communities.

- **Meta-cognition** - from symbolic value to systematic development (from 15 years)
7   *Symbolic* (from 15 years): The child gradually becomes aware of his own musical experiences and growth; musical discrimination begins to take place based normally on the nature and intensity of experience.
8   *Systematic* (from 15 or 16 years): Knowledge of generally accepted principles of creative construction is reflected in the child's musical compositions.

Swanwick and Tillman's model was replicated in further research in Cyprus with parallel results (Swanwick, 1991). This framework enables Swanwick and Tillman to see the mastery of compositional skills as a developmental process, beginning with an embryonic and primitive stage and moving progressively to an advanced stage where the child's composition manifests an understanding of musical concepts. However, all the stages seem to be characterised by technical complexities; what distinguishes a late childhood composer from an early childhood composer appears to lie in the former's ability to handle abstract musical phenomena, as well as the fluency in verbalising his or her artistic intentions. The model provides a general pattern for understanding the nature of children's compositions and has some important implications for curriculum development, and in particular for the assessment of students' compositions.

A recent research project presents a slightly different but no less significant view. A study of selected songs from the work of three 5- to 7-year-old children

> (a) [demonstrates] that the invented songs of 5- to 7-year-olds may present a complex picture of the integration of 'materials' and 'expressiveness' in structurally organised wholes (perhaps more so than their instrumental pieces would do); the songs suggest that features which Swanwick and Tillman would put later may, in fact, occur quite early. They also show (b) each child constructing an agenda to meet her personal needs; and (c) suggest that a child may be working in various modes of the development sequence suggested by Swanwick and Tillman all at the same period. (Davies, 1992: 24)

Coral Davies reaches the conclusion that children of 7 or 8 years are capable of taking part in the artistic process and 'need not pass through any qualitative organisations' (Davies, 1992: 47). She also finds that the children demonstrate a grasp of the 'meaning, significance and structure of time' (ibid.: 47), and she is convinced that:

> the organisation and relationships of musical events in time are fundamental to music's meaning and that we should expect structural considerations to be important as soon as a child begins to be musically articulate. (Ibid.: 19)

The only known study on Ghanaian children's musical behaviour was conducted in 1967, presumably in response to Nketia's (1966) call for a psychological investigation into the musical background of African children. The study was designed to test the singing, listening and creative experiences of Ghanaian primary school children. Children were asked to listen to recordings as well as to their own performances of various categories of songs. Later they were asked to complete a questionnaire designed to test their musical awareness and preferences. It was discovered that songs in the children's indigenous languages were recalled better than those in the foreign languages; the music the children liked best *to be taught* was religious music (hymns), although the music they liked best, and would like to compose, was contemporary Ghanaian (pop and highlife) music; Ghanaian traditional music was among the least preferred. From the pattern of children's answers, Ampom Darkwa concluded that 'the children made their choices out of the development of increased understanding of pattern and mood in music' (Darkwa, 1967: 18). The study did not, however, go on to explore the children's creative experiences in music.

Improvisation in cradle songs

In Ghana music is a living and practical activity. Improvisation and composition occur as a matter of course. In dance music, for example, without the dance the music is incomplete. The dancer's contribution thus becomes that of a co-composer. The dance arena serves as a platform for an interplay of musical creativity; each performer endeavours to add a new variation to the dance, drum rhythm or song.

The transfer of musical knowledge to children begins right from birth. The baby's first cries are considered as vocalises in preparation for singing; and the traditional midwife will often say: 'Brilliant, you are potential singer, you have brought life'. Music thus symbolises life. The child begins to receive music lessons straightaway. Nursery rhymes and lullabies are sung to the baby by the mother or by other close relatives of both the household and the neighbourhood. A mother going about her domestic chores may often be heard singing. This is to assure the baby of her presence and that it is not deserted, as a complete silence may soon lead the baby to cry. Mothers are expected to entertain their children with music; and an incapable mother may be teased:

> Beautiful baby, charming baby,
> Your mother admires you,
> But cannot make music for you;
> It's a pity.

Often, a father, grandparent, or relative may rock the baby to music as the mother busies herself in the kitchen, and he or she will be surrounded and supported by all the children in the household. The baby often responds to these musical gestures with movement and musical babbling. This indicates the baby's interest. The babbling sound is treated as musical theme and may form the basis for improvisation, an adult starting, then all the children taking turns. Here is the beginning of musical invention for both the new born and older children. Thus, training in spontaneous composition begins even before the child utters the first spoken word. In Ghanaian homes the singing of well-known nursery songs such as 'O Amavi', 'Eyibe ne, ne, ne', 'Tutu Gbovi' (see Egblewogbe, 1974), and others, often found in publications described as 'children's songs', is reserved for less creative spontaneous composers and may be sung merely for pleasure or sometimes as accompaniment to formal games; although, as I shall shortly show, they may be re-created. (I can recall that we sang some of these mostly at school.) Ghanaian children do not sing them for the purpose of lulling their younger ones. On the contrary, what appears to be a true cradle song is that where composition and singing arise by chance - the presence of a crying or an enthusiastic baby. Sometimes older children, and even adults, will deliberately incite a baby to cry to give them the opportunity to test their creative skill from which immense pleasure is derived. In spontaneous composition the musical themes are derived from nonsense words and rhythmic sounds imitative of various sounds around - the bleating of goats, singing of birds, the sound of the corn mill, or of passing vehicles, and indeed any sound (that is immediately perceivable).

Finnegan (1970) and Nketia (1975) have noted that the performance of cradle songs serves as the medium through which the singer exhibits creative skill in a spontaneous expression of feelings, thoughts and emotions as well as the exhibition of creative skill. In fact, both authors were concerned with the poetry of the songs composed by adults, which of course have no direct relevance for children. Children seem to be more interested in sound and rhythm, and the sound of the poetry of such songs is more important to them than the meaning of the words, which they make no attempt to grasp. It seems to be true that in the performance and composition of cradle songs, the source of enjoyment is primarily a musical one. This should not be taken to imply that children do not make up meaningful texts when they invent cradle songs. A child may sing to a younger one, 'Stop, stop, stop. Father is coming, mother is coming', or 'I have an egg, if you cry again, I won't give it to you ... '. Here, the child does what makes sense to him or her.

Well-known songs, whether sung in the context of cradling or in other games, may be re-composed. My own experience, which of course is not peculiar, will illustrate the creative attitude of children in their involvement in this activity. As schoolchildren, we had learnt a cradle song, from whom I cannot remember, but it had been widely sung in the village in which I grew up. Indeed, entertainment is ceaseless even in the face of hunger and the baby is teased, it wants nothing except food:

Solo:	They drummed for him,
Chorus:	With no avail.
S	They cried for him,
C	With no avail.
S	They sang for him,
C	With no avail.
S	Rather, he wants to suck the breast,
C	*tsutsupo, tsutsupo, tsutsupo.*

To and from school, we would sing it to tease those of our friends who had previously been punished or reprimanded for some offence at home or at school. In this context while the chorus remained the same, the soloist invented new words to suit the situation; for instance, 'They spanked him/her', or 'they slapped him', or 'they knocked him', 'father/uncle/mother scolded him', 'It's a shame'. The last two lines would be repeated as many times as we desired, often to the accompaniment of rhythms we provided on our books, with tools, sticks and pencils. An interesting factor was that, to avoid a direct reference, as this could sometimes lead to acrimony, the soloist improvised his part according to rhythm in various ways, nonsense words, humming, making body gestures, hand signs and facial signals. This is a commonplace experience for Ghanaian children.

   Increase in the rate of the composition of lullabies is even faster than that of population. Most of these excellent compositions and their composers are limited to households, neighbourhoods, and villages. No matter how voluminous it may be, no compilation of cradle songs will exhaust the repertoire nor provide a truly representative sample.

Music in games

Participation in music continues as the child begins to join his peers with whom he makes music at play and in games. Songs may be used to accompany games or may be interspersed with play activities, alluding to some undesirable behaviour, or teasing friends. Shame songs may be sung to ridicule the child who has formed the habit of begging for food, as the text of the following Ewe song indicates,

   The beggar approaches,
   Keep it [your food] away!

Similarly, children who have lost their front teeth may be teased:

> I set a trap for voloe [a bird]
> Voloe did not enter
> Alata wide, wide, wide.

Or those who have had their heads shaven because of hair lice may be welcomed to the playground with the following words;

> The shaven head
> Does not eat fried fish
> Fried fish came out
> Of the broken spot.

Frequently, in teasing songs, the purpose is not to offend, but rather to create fun. In fact, those who are offended at being teased may be ostracised from other games; for to children this is one way of testing people's sociability and tolerance. These songs may have very little or no melodic shape, but the accompanying rhythmic, dance and dramatic gestures are what makes them interesting. There are also games which are purely musical in content. Sometimes the games are organised and supervised by adults; but often the games which children enjoy most are those which appear to have been composed by themselves.

Musical games are performed at home or in the streets by children to pass their time pleasantly during the evening hours. The sense of community and group involvement which characterises the social lives of the African is reflected in children's games. In fact it would be very difficult or perhaps impossible to derive any form of enjoyment from these games without such coordination of individual effort. In each game everyone has a role or a set of roles to play. There are rules governing the performance of each game; and there are also appropriate penalties for breaking any of the rules. Without these, the essence of the games will not be achieved.

African parents are excited and delighted to see their children play leadership roles in such games and some psychologists believe that a child's choice of games and the roles s/he plays in them reveal a great deal about her/his personality (Jersild, 1968: 299). In fact, the cultural educational value of Ghanaian children's games has attracted scholars' interest (for example, Egblewogbe, 1974; Turkson, 1989), but the creative resources of musical games have yet to be investigated. It is nevertheless obvious that children give to and derive pure musical meaning from the games, and this can be noticed from the musical materials they create (Walley, 1976).

Musical games are exciting; the number of variations can be overwhelming. The songs which accompany the games are the children's own compositions, often in monophonic singing with varying degrees of rhythmic freedom, contrasts of vocal range and with intense agility. Frequently, the songs are repetitive, sung with precision and articulation, the words covering a limited range and usually related to the intention of a particular game. Outside the context of games the words can be difficult to translate; sometimes what may sound like mere nonsense words have special meaning for the actors which can only be derived from the actions which accompany their singing.

Rhythmically they are organised on a steady recurring beat; one that is easy to locate and which encourages foot tapping, arm swinging and, indeed, the movement of the whole body. As in cradle songs, the games are not merely for playing: they provide opportunities for musical creativity - composition and improvisation - far beyond our immediate notice. Participation and enjoyment are derived from the interweaving relationship of sound, rhythm and body movement in a dramatic medium. Musical games provide a wellspring for creative improvisation for the musically enthusiastic children. Let us see how spontaneous composition arises in the context of a typical Ghanaian game.

Kiti Kangbɛ

The game is played by both sexes usually of the same age group. Children sit, or sometimes squat, in a circle with a stone in each child's hand. The leader announces the start of the game, 'Ekpe, ekpe' ('stone, stone') and all the actors hit their stones on the floor as they respond, 'kpo kpo kpo kpo ... ' roughly, to the rhythm of quaver beats in simple time. Then the leader continues, 'kpo kpo trikpo' with the chorus responding 'kpo':

    Leader: *kpokpo trikpo*
    Chorus: *kpo!*

    Leader: *kpokpo trikpo*
    Chorus: *kpo!*

As soon as the leader sings 'Kiti kan(m)gbɛ', each child passes the stone anti-clockwise to a neighbour as they respond 'kangbɛ h-rr gbɛ'.

    Leader: *Kiti kamgbɛ*
    Chorus: *kamgbɛ h-rr gbɛ*

Leader: *Kiti kamgbɛ*
Chorus: *kamgbɛ h-rr gbɛ*

This may go on for a number of times. Thereafter, the leader introduces a wide range of songs. Apart from the introductory activity, the songs accompanying this game are not peculiar, and they may be selected from other categories - marching songs, hymns, pop and highlife - provided they are rhythmically convenient.

This description provides only the skein of the game; how the threads are woven together is difficult to describe in words, and unless one observes the children directly in the act, it would not be easy to perceive the musical challenges the game offers. In the course of the game, the leader may introduce several musical surprises; he or she may decide to vary the tempo abruptly, or to bring the game to a sudden end, and may even change her/his mind after the signal for rounding off has been introduced. Through an appropriate musical gesture, s/he may suddenly invite any member of the team to take up the leadership. The leader may use body and facial gestures to signal variations as desired; any member can be called upon to introduce a song, and after such a person has had a turn will also call a fellow; this is the time when new songs are spontaneously invented, taught and sung without disrupting the smooth flow of the game. While maintaining the tempo, and according to rhythm, a lead singer may begin by saying, 'it is coming, get ready, my song is coming soon, are you ready? OK, it goes like this ... '. All these are considered as part of the game and are responded to musically. Inability to cope with these surprises leads to automatic elimination, and therefore all children endeavour to sustain their musical sensitivity, smartness and alertness. 'Kangbɛ' is just one example of the opportunities available to Ghanaian children for displaying their talents for spontaneous musical creativity.

Spontaneous creativity in folk tales

The performance of folk tales serves as one of the main means by which both children and adults share musical experiences and activities directly. The enjoyment of folk tales lies in the extent to which the audience interact with the narrator, by way of comment, dialogue and with music and dance. Music, drama and dance are integral parts of the performance. Songs begin, accompany and end every story. Once again this is another opportunity for spontaneous composition, and both children and adults have equal opportunities for expressing their musical and dramatic ideas.

Although many of the songs - the introductory and concluding ones especially - could be melodic, the most interesting ones are the *glite fenohawo* (witness, verification or digression songs) which are purely rhythmical These are usually short and may be based on burden texts, and sonic mnemonics extracted from the narration to illustrate or reinforce an important stage of the story. This must be done in such a way as to excite the imagination of the audience whilst at the same time not disrupting the smooth flow of the narration. Finding an appropriate spot to introduce a musical event calls for attentive listening and creative ability, for when a song is introduced at the wrong stage there may be no response from the audience or the response may be in form of booming to show it is out of step.

Digression songs may be well known to the audience but also new ones could be introduced spontaneously, singer after singer, until the narrator cuts in or the group becomes tired. One singer may say, 'No! that was not how they sang it'; or 'I was there, but I heard it differently; it goes like this ... '. Frequently when a singer believes there is something musical to offer, although it may not be directly related to the story, he or she will manage to create an additional scene. For example, a *glite fenola* (witness singer) may say to the narrator: 'That day, as your characters were doing that, I was also working on my farm on the other side of the river when I heard birds/animals singing ... '. Dance and dramatic movements are also introduced spontaneously by other members of the audience: 'and the monkey was dancing like this ... ; and the elephant that way; and the housefly', and so on. Sometimes too, singers may use the avenue to allude to some recent social event or to tease the opposite sex. If it is a teasing song an appropriate musical response usually follows immediately, or at a later stage of the narration.

When the music sounds completely new, the Ewe for instance, call it, *ahatso ha* (untrue song) and the singer, *ahatso ha dzila/kpala* (singer/composer of untrue songs). It sounds as if it is uncomplimentary, but that is how all spontaneous compositions and their composers are described; contrary to the literal meaning, it emphasises the newness of the music and the novelty of the composer. During story telling sessions, games and other play activities which require this practice, the absence of 'untrue composers' is immediately felt and often regretted.

The songs which, however, become part of the general repertoire of folk tales are those judged by the group to be 'good': they may be sung over and over again at various stages of the same narration, or used in other stories and may be carried to neighbouring villages by visiting relatives.

Creative imitation of adult music

Imitation as an intrinsic tool for the acquisition of knowledge and basic skills has received much attention from educators and psychologists. It is usual to find groups of children, a few hours or days after the celebration of festival, church anniversary and open day, trying to re-create the music which accompanied those celebrations. It is amazing to see how these children cooperatively coordinate their individual memories to 'compose' their personal experiences as an integrated form. Individual members of the group may serve as teachers, conductors, master drummers, singers and soloists according to what they had previously seen. Despite some authors' assertions about cultural exclusivity (for example, Kwami, 1989), there is evidence that all the music associated with cultural events considered to be purely adult affairs is still open to children. Thus, they may be involved, in their own way, in the performance of cult music and dances, execution songs and funeral music. For example, when, during a funeral celebration, the professional *atumpan* drummers take a break, children may be seen imitating on the same drums. This is tolerated and fostered, as it is the actual funeral which provides the only direct opportunity for acquiring the music associated with its celebration.

It is generally assumed that children merely copy adult musical models, but more objective listening and observation reveals that this is not always the case. Children re-compose - re-create - the adult musical models, create new rhythms and compose new songs to suit their peculiar interests and purposes. Novelty is the overriding principle in this kind of imitative activity and children are aware that they are indeed making something new. Children will tell their peers, 'Let us sing/play it this way or that way', or, 'Let us use this ... instead of that' and will be proud when they succeed in teaching their friends something new.

Not long ago, when I asked some Primary 1 and 2 children in the Volta Region to sing the Ghana National Anthem, they were quick in pointing out that they had two versions, 'the school version and our own version'. I realised that in both versions the first lines were the same, but in the children's own version, the rest of the lines were substituted with a collection of proverbs and nonsense words, melodically and rhythmically arranged to enable the performance of body gestures on the last line to express what they meant. After singing they warned me not to teach it to other children since this was their own composition. Even they were protecting their copyright!

Direct instruction

Children also receive direct instruction. Among the Dagomba, for instance, 'drummers take their sisters' and daughters' children to rear and train in their profession' and a 'drummer who is well-known for his ability will have children other than close kin sent to him' (Oppong, 1973: 47-55). Indeed, the only way to become a skilled performer is to start at an early age. Among the Yoruba, 'the son of a master drummer often goes about with his father playing either the *donno* drum or the little drum called *gudungudu*' (Nketia, 1968: 3). Children remember their teachers. They will often say 'Let us sing *Wofa* (uncle) Kwame's song', meaning the song uncle Kwame 'taught us'.

The Ghanaian child's musical environment is not limited to that of indigenous music of Ghana. Their musical environment also includes popular band music, such as highlife and Afro- and Latin-American music, brass band music and Sunday school songs. Through the mass media, radio and television, by the use of cassette recorders and players, through the presence of migrant workers and farmers, children are exposed to the music of other African tribes as well as other parts of the world. The Ghanaian children reorganise their experiences into action by imitating and re-creating whatever they see or hear. Through this children acquire a wide basis for musical ideas and knowledge.

Ghanaian children, as in other African societies, by virtue of their presence in the community, assimilate the musical practices of the environment. On hearing musical sound children may spontaneously run out of their homes, even sometimes leaving their food behind, towards the direction of the music. They are the first to express interest and are the first group of spectators to arrive at any musical scene. Frequently they get so close to the performers that they (the children) are seemingly even prepared to take over from the performers. They do not discriminate between different kinds of music.

This chapter has described the musical backgrounds of Ghanaian children. It has concentrated on the facilities, resources and opportunities which promote music making rather than specific examples of music that can be found. This broad and diverse range of experiences has influenced the rate and direction of the Ghanaian children's musical growth, and enhanced their readiness for the practice and appreciation of music. It points out that their musical environment, the roots of the musical heritage are potentially wider and even more sophisticated than that of the adult.

Bibliography

Ainsworth, J. (1970), 'Research Project in Creativity in Music Education', *Council for Research in Music Education*, (**22**), Fall, Champaign: University of Illinois and Ray Page Superintendent, 43-8.
Bertonoff, D. (1963), *Dance Towards the Earth: on a UNESCO Grant in Ghana*, trans. I. M. Lask, Tel-Aviv: Alityros Books.
Blackemore, C. (1988), *The Mind Machine*, London: BBC Books.
Bruner, J. S. (1983), *Child's Talk: Learning to Use Language*, Oxford: Oxford University Press.

Chomsky, N. (1959/1969), *The Acquisition of Syntax in Children from 5 to 10*, Research Monograph 57, Cambridge, MA: MIT Press.

Clark, R. (1974), 'Performing without Competence', *Journal of Child Language*, **1** (1), May, 1-10.

Coates, J. (1993), 'The Language of Appreciation through Talking and Making', *Educational Review*, **45** (3), 251-62.

Darkwa, A. (1967), 'Music Education for the Primary School Child', unpublished MS IAS University of Ghana Legon, Accra.

Davies, C. (1992), 'Listen to my Song: a Study of Songs Invented by Children Aged 5 to 7 Years', *British Journal of Music Education*, **9** (1), March, 19-48.

De Villers, J. G. and De Villers, P. A. (1974), 'Competence and Performance in Child Language: Are Children really Competent to Judge?', *Journal of Child Language*, **1** (1), May, 11-22.

Egblewogbe, E. Y. (1974), *Games and Songs as Educational Media in Eweland*, Tema: Ghana Publishing Corporation.

Finnegan, R. (1970), *Oral Literature in Africa*, Cambridge: Cambridge University Press.

Fridman, R. (1976), 'Affective Communication through the Baby's Sonorous Expression: Relation to Mental Health and Future Musical Activity', in *Challenges in Music Education ISME Yearbook*, Perth: University of Western Australia Department of Music.

Harris, J. (1990), *Early Language Development: Implications for Clinical and Educational Practice*, London and New York: Routledge.

Gleitmen, L. R. and Wanner, E. (1982), 'Language Acquisition: the State of the Art', in E. Wanner and L. R. Gleitmen (eds), *Language Acquisition: the State of the Art*, Cambridge: Cambridge University Press.

Jersild, A. (1968), *Child Psychology*, Englewood Cliffs, NJ: Prentice Hall.

Kwami, R. (1989), 'African Music, Education and the School Curriculum', PhD dissertation, University of London, Institute of Education.

Loane, B. (1986), 'Thinking about Children's Compositions', *British Journal Music Education*, **1** (3), 27-36.

Medinus, G. R. and Johnson, R. C. (1976), *Child and Adolescent Psychology*, New York, London and Toronto: John Wiley.

Merriam, A. P. (1964), *Anthropology of Music*, Evanston, IL: North Western University Press.

Moog, H. (1976), *The Musical Experiences of the Preschool Child*, trans. C. Clarke, London: Schott.

Nketia, J. H. (1966), 'Music Education in African Schools: a Review of the Position in Ghana', in *International Seminar on Teacher Education in Music*, Ann Arbor, MI: University of Michigan.

Nketia, J. H. (1968), *Our Drums and Drummers*, Tema: Ghana Publishing House.

Nketia, J. H. (1975), *The Music of Africa*, London: Victor Gollancz.

Oppong, C. (1973), *Growing Up in Dagbon*, Tema: Ghana Publishing Corporation.

Piaget, J. (1970), 'Piaget's Theory', in P. H. Mussen (ed.), *Carmichael's Manual of Child Psychology*, 3rd edition, New York: John Wiley.

Plummeridge, C. (1980), 'Creativity in Music Education: the Need for Further Clarification', *Psychology of Music*, **8**.

Plunket, K. (1993), 'Lexical Language Acquisition and Vocabulary Growth in Early Language Acquisition', *Journal of Child Language*, **20** (1), 43-60.

Pond, D. (1981), 'A Composer's Study of Young Children's Innate Musicality', *Bulletin of the Council for Research in Music Education*, **(68)**.

Shelley, S. J. (1981), 'Investigating the Musical Capabilities of Young Children', *Bulletin of the Council for Research in Music Education*, **(68)**, 26-34.

Skinner, B. F. (1957), *Verbal Behaviour*, New York: Appletoncentury Crofts.

Swanwick, K. (1991), 'Further Research on the Musical Development Sequence', *Society for Research in Psychology of Music and Music Education*, **19** (1), 22-32.

Swanwick, K. and Tillman, J. (1986), 'The Sequence of Musical Development: a Study of Children's Composition', *British Journal of Music Education*, **3** (3), 305-39.

Turkson, A. R. (1989), 'Music and Games in Early African Childhood Education', *African Music Education*, University of Cape Coast, Department of Music no. 7.

Walker, R. (1983), 'Innovation in the Music Curriculum: New Ideas from Canada and Great Britain', *Psychology of Music*, **11**, 86-96.

Walley, S. C. (1976), 'Music Models and Children's Plays: a Programme of Teacher Preparation for Early Childhood Education', in *Challenges in Music Education ISME Yearbook*, Perth: University of Western Australia, Department of Music.

5 Drumming in Ghana

Trevor Wiggins

West Africa, especially Ghana, has always been known for its variety of drum ensembles. Although some early white visitors referred to the 'heathen noise' of the music, many others were impressed. Unfortunately, we can have little idea how the music sounded until recordings began to be made in the twentieth century. Drum music is not written down but is an 'aural' music passed down from one generation to another. This process is also one of change. When one person learns from another they cannot perform the music in exactly the same way so each process of transmission results in variation. Equally, people do not want to play music in the same way as their teacher. Music is something which identifies you and says something about you, so you want to make sure you have your own voice, not one you have borrowed. In Ghana there are many different tribal groups. Most of these will have their own language or dialect which may be more or less different from that of their neighbours. There are close links between language and music so there is a similar richness and diversity to the music of Ghana.

Of course, not all Ghanaian music is for drums. There is a wide range of instruments, some traditional, some developed from traditional instruments and some imported from other areas of West Africa. The *gonje* is a one-string fiddle probably originally from Nigeria which is now used in Ghana. The *atenteben* is a flute like a recorder which was developed by the late Dr Ephraim Amu from simpler traditional flutes. Animal horns of different sizes are played as an ensemble. The xylophone with 14-18 keys is common in the north-west of the country, but the most common instrument after the voice is the drum. This is found in a vast range of shapes and sizes ranging from something maybe 30 cm high through to massive instruments often used for ceremonial purposes which are up to 2 m high and 1 m across.

Drums are usually in sets of between two and five drums although some parts may have more than one person playing. The different drums have a clear function within the ensemble; they will usually be tuned to different pitches and one will act as the leader while the other drums have simpler more repetitive parts which sometimes change in response to the lead drum. The parts in drum ensembles integrate in a wide variety of ways and explore the range of rhythmic interaction to an extent unparalleled in Western music. This integration is so complete and at such a speed that it is extremely difficult, if not impossible, for a Western musician to work out what is going on. Some of this problem lies in the Western way of listening. In the West we tend to use staff notation at an early stage of our learning. Staff notation is an extremely useful and powerful tool, but this also means that, in some respects, it is severely limited. In fact, we are so used to staff notation that we tend to hear through it. When faced with a new piece of music our understanding rests on an identification of such features as the time signature, the beat and a unit we can identify as a bar. This is a problem for much West African music. There may be several time signatures operating concurrently and different parts may effectively have their barlines in different places. This will also be a problem with understanding the music examples in this chapter. I have decided to use staff notation because so many people are familiar with it but I will also need to continually point out how it is misleading as a model for the music.

Ghanaian people do not learn their music from notation. It is all around them and they have probably heard it since before they were born. They will not conceive of it in western terms. A Ghanaian drummer would look mystified if asked 'Where is the beat?' However, if you ask, 'Where is the dance step?' your answer might be much more useful and instructive. Dance and singing are part of the music for most Ghanaians. My notations are a transcription of what I have been taught or what I have observed myself. They represent one possible version of this music interpreted through my ears, which may work in a similar manner to yours. To begin I want to look at a piece of music where the pulse is relatively easy to identify. '*Sikye*' (pronounced see-chi) is from the *Akan* area of Ghana around the regional capital, Kumasi, Ghana's second city. It uses an ensemble of four drums together with a bell and a rattle. As with many ensembles, the bell and the rattle act as timekeepers. They have a sound which the other players and the dancers can hear clearly over the rest of the sound. Their parts are usually unchanging throughout the piece and the rattle part in particular often has more than one person playing the part - sometimes as many as ten people. '*Sikye*' has the simplest bell and rattle parts of any piece I know:

Example 5.1

but even this simplicity becomes much more difficult when the rest of the ensemble begins to pull against it. Example 5.2 shows how the rest of the ensemble begins this piece. The *donno* is sometimes called a talking drum. It is about 60 cm long with a wooden body shaped like an hourglass. There are two heads which are connected by leather thonging. Thus, by squeezing the drum under your arm you can raise the pitch by, maybe, a fifth. The notation here shows when the drum should be high and low in pitch.

Example 5.2

The *donno* part immediately establishes a quaver pulse against the crotchet of the bell and is repeated every two crotchets giving a hierarchy of relative pulses. The high drum part adds another level to this introducing a semiquaver pulse. Being played with sticks, its high sound cuts clearly through the sound of the other drums. The low support drum is played with the hands using pitch to designate which hand and which sound to play. The pitches used for this also indicate the relative pitch of the sounds produced by the drum when played, but should not be understood as precise pitches.

Example 5.3

LH	RH	LH	RH	LH	RH	LH	RH	LH	RH
bass	bass	open	open	mute	mute	slap	slap	soft fill	soft fill

These are all the symbols used in the transcriptions for playing a drum with the hands or sticks. A **bass** note is played in the centre of the drum with the hand flat and bounced off the drum head. An **open** note is a bounced stroke played with the hand flat at the rim. The rim of the drum should come under the top of the palm towards the fingers. When an open stroke is played with sticks, the sticks are bounced about one-third of the way across the drum head. A **mute** sound is played in the same position as an open stroke. With the hand you do not bounce it off but continue to press the head quite firmly, giving a shorter note with a pitch about a tone above an open sound. The same technique is used with sticks: the stick is not bounced off but presses the head, not too hard, giving a sonorous click. A **slap** can be a conga-style slap or an open slap with the hands towards the centre of the drum head. The sound should be relatively high in pitch. A **soft fill** is a quiet conga-style slap which is used by good drummers to keep a rhythm moving so that there are no gaps in the sound.

The low support drum reinforces the rhythm of the high drum in the first half of the pattern then interlocks with it in the second half. It also establishes another pattern length lasting one bar in my version, but its real function only begins to emerge when the master drum begins its first main pattern.

Example 5.4

The two parts coincide every two crotchets but the rest of the time they are mainly interlocking producing a composite rhythm like this:

Example 5.5

The effect will sound more interesting than this looks through the effect of the different sounds and pitches of the drums. It is as though the two drums are holding an intricate conversation threading in and out between each other. The master drum then proceeds to lead the ensemble and the dancers through a series of variations and sections. The master drummer has to know both the drum and the dance parts as there are signals in the lead part which both the other drummers and the dancers must respond to. The first variation is a technique found in many drum pieces where the existing rhythm is made into a longer pattern by the substitution of one unit of the basic rhythm with alternative material which is often quite simple. In this case, the basic unit is the half-bar rhythm seen above a) which is substituted by four quavers b) with the sequence **a a b a**. This sequence is also very common.

Example 5.6

The next variation for the master drum is again a substitution for one unit. What is substituted are two slaps which suddenly reinforce the rhythm of the low support drum instead of interlocking with it. This can be used in either the sequence **a b**, or **a a a b** as shown in Example 5.7:

Example 5.7

After these variations the master drum needs to move to the next section. There is a signal for this to warn the dancers and drummers that this change will happen. A version of Example 5.7 is played with only one slap. This rhythm is repeated and leads to the next section. The change signal needs to be a distinctive rhythm which is played only at this point.

Example 5.8

The main rhythm for the next section is this:

Example 5.9

Initially this sounds and looks quite different from the first section, but on closer examination you can see clear links with the previous main rhythm. The sequence of sounds has been changed so that the bass and open sounds now fall at different points against the bell pattern, although still in the same relation to each other. The rhythm has had little changed other than the addition of two semiquavers for a quaver on the 'up' beat. The minimal nature of the rhythmic change can be seen when the resultant pattern of the exchange between the master drum and the low support part is compared to the previous one, but the effect on the ensemble is considerable because of the changed sounds.

Example 5.10

The third section of '*Sikye*' continues to use some of these techniques and adds some new ones. It is introduced with a signal at the end of the rhythm shown in Example 5.6. This new section has a rhythm pattern which is longer than any so far, lasting four bars. It pulls strongly against the bell and rattle pulse so that the low support drum changes its pattern to reinforce the bell part. It is made up of three elements: slaps, open strokes and a link rhythm. The slaps and the open strokes alternate with one getting shorter as the other gets longer (the pattern completely ignores the barlines I have adopted). The sequence could be described as slap-3, open-1, slap-2, open-2, slap-1, open-3, link to repeat.

Example 5.11

The resultant rhythm between the master drum and the low support now looks like Example 5.12. Again a family resemblance with the previous sections can be seen, but the changed sounds, especially the powerful slaps and open sounds on the 'off' beat, give a very different effect.

Example 5.12

To summarise this first piece, the main techniques are the construction using interlocking parts with one part changing in response to another, the substitution of sounds, the extension of rhythmic ideas using a sequence, the composition of a rhythm sequence using additive elements, and the use of a rhythm signal to effect section changes. All the rhythms in this piece fell within a Western rhythmic conception of a basic pulse (semibreve) which is divided into minims, crotchets, quavers and semiquavers (1, 2, 4, 8, 16), but for many pieces of Ghanaian music this is not the case.

To begin to explore other rhythmic ideas I want to begin not with a drum piece but one which uses only clapping. *'Neporu'* is a piece of music from the Sisaala people in the village of Lambussie in north-west Ghana. When it is known that someone has died the women will gather together to perform this music. It has a unison vocal part, which is not shown here, accompanied by clapping. Each woman will have her own rhythm (some are duplicated) which is repeated throughout. The women claim that they always perform it the same way, but there are many small differences on each occasion. It will be led by a different person each time. The leader begins and ends the piece. Since there has just been a death the spirits will be close by and if the leader makes a mistake they may take her as well, so there is a different leader each time, usually one of the oldest women. Notated, the clapping rhythms look like this:

Example 5.13

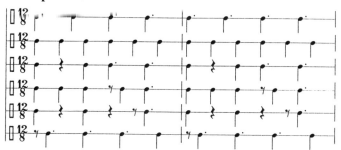

The music is notated in twelve-eight as there is a cycle of 12 pulses before the pattern is repeated, but it is not an indication that there is always a dotted crotchet pulse. The parts and the singing are not absolutely fixed. Each woman may sing her part slightly differently, an effect known as heterophony. The same idea applies to the rhythms, but there is not a word for this idea. The first part I have notated is the dotted crotchet pulse. There are always some women clapping this, but it is not the first part to start - this is usually part four. The second part sets six against the four so there is a constant 3:2 rhythm. Parts two and four move between these pulses using as a basic idea although some notes are often left out. Another idea is found in part six: this is the first part using the dotted crotchet pulse but starting one quaver later (this contrasts with the vocal part which often anticipates the same pulse by a quaver). Part six also coincides with every third quaver of the crotchet pulse. The part which starts, part four, can now be seen as linking parts one, two and six together. Although this piece is comparatively simple (actually, it's not when you try to sing and clap) it contains important ideas which are extended in many other drum pieces, especially the idea of 3:2 and the displacement of a pulse.

Both these ideas can be seen in a piece called 'Asaadua', again from the *Akan* region of central Ghana. This uses two bells: a single peapod shaped bell called *dawuro* and a double bell, with high and low pitches a fifth to an octave apart, usually known as *gankogui*. The interplay of these two, together with the rattle, *trowa*, clearly shows the same ideas. (This piece is notated in six-four as the best compromise, but twelve-eight has an almost equal claim.)

Example 5.14

The *trowa* maintains the dotted crotchet pulse while the *gankogui* has the crotchet, with the additional interest of two different pitches. The *dawuro* moves between these in the sequence ♩. ♩. ♩ ♩ ♩, but adds something else by subdividing the first part of the pattern to establish a quaver pulse. This first half also links between the *gankogui*, coinciding on the second crotchet, and the *trowa* part. The next part to enter is the *tamale* (frame drum). This has a simple dotted crotchet pulse alternating open and slap sounds, but displaced to anticipate the *trowa* part by a quaver. This part enters on the penultimate crotchet of the *dawuro* rhythm and also coincides with the quavers in the same part. The effect is to suddenly make the *dawuro* part sound as though it has become ♪ ♩ ♪ ♩ ♩ ♩ .

Example 5.15

The master drum, when it enters, reinforces the crotchet pulse of the *gankogui* and the barline I have adopted, but this simple part again has a fascinating interplay with the *tamale*.

Example 5.16

When the master drum begins some variations, one of the things it does is to imitate the start of the *dawuro* part, but displaced back by a quaver, thus adding further to the conversation between the parts.

Example 5.17

The idea of parallel pulses within an overall time frame is also found in some complex rhythms played by the Dagomba people of northern Ghana. *'Bamaya'* (together with its related pieces *'Damba' and 'Takai'*) uses just two types of drums, although there may be a number of players. The *Brekete* (also known as *Gon-gon*) is a cylinder up to 60 cm across and deep. It has two heads cross laced to each other so that the drum can be tuned. Each head also has a gut snare to add a buzz to the sound. It is played slung under the left shoulder using a curved stick in the right hand and the left hand playing an open stroke at the top edge of the drum. The drum produces four sounds which are notated like this:

Example 5.18

An **open** sound uses the stick in the centre of the drum to give a powerful sound, considerably louder than any of the other strokes. A **closed** stroke uses the stick with less force and the stick is pressed lightly into the head giving only a sonorous click. A **stick fill** sound is a quiet stroke with the stick, sometimes played towards the top edge of the drum. The other sound is the **left-hand** stroke already mentioned. The muted and hand strokes are used to fill the gaps between the main notes, with the closed stroke being used to stop the sound as a sort of punctuation. Again, it is difficult for the notation to give a sufficient image of the difference between the quality and volume of the sounds and thus, their effect. The other drum used in this music is the *donno* which has already been described.

One of the rhythms in *'Bamaya'* has the *brekete* playing a rhythm which we would clearly identify as twelve-eight time, although some of the variations also suggest a crotchet pulse. The *donno* rhythm against this is very complex. The first half of the bar uses a crotchet pulse with the first crotchet missing - clearly a similar technique to that observed in *'Neporu'*. The second half of the bar uses the dotted crotchet pulse, but makes it a duple, not a triple beat. So, on the third beat of the bar the *brekete* has three soft quavers which the *donno* has to play two against, missing out the first one. The fourth beat has equal duple notes between the *brekete* and *donno*.

Example 5.19

The difficulty here is in holding the rhythmic difference between the *donno* part in the first and second half. This is even more true in one of the variations where the *donno* substitutes two semiquavers for one of the quavers, although this is in response to the straighter pulse that the *brekete* plays in this variation.

Example 5.20

The combined effect of the two parts is that there is a steady pulse at the speed of the half bar in my notation, but this is divided first into three, then four |1 2 3 1 2 3 4 |1 2 3 1 2 3 4 |. Ultimately, this is another extension of the idea of 3:2 parallel pulses, but it makes it plain that each level of pulse can itself be subdivided into either two or three.

Example 5.21

Another rhythm from later in 'Bamaya' shows the level of complexity that this music reaches in using these ideas. It is worth repeating that Dagomba musicians will not analyse or conceptualise the music in the ways I am describing but their sense of rhythm is so advanced that their compositions lead to description in these terms. When heard in isolation the rhythm sounds like this:

Example 5.22

The three loud open strokes at the beginning establish a pulse and these same three notes are soon repeated, but the point at which they are repeated

does not seem to relate to the pulse the first three had established. Each set
of three loud notes is followed by a closing motif using a closed and a hand
stroke and on the second occasion this closing motif is extended. This
extension gives rise to another different pulse for a few beats, which is then
promptly negated by the return of the beginning. A number of musicians
(for example Professor J. H. Kwabena Nketia) have written about the
concept of additive rhythm in African music. This is the idea that many
African rhythms, instead of being built up by the division of notes, are
created by the addition of smaller units, typically two or three notes in
length. This might be a good example of the idea. Counting in quavers, the
time signature shows how the units are built up, giving one bar of 9 and
one of 15. It would not be a satisfactory explanation to view this as a dotted
crotchet pulse with one bar of 3, and one of 5 - the rhythm simply does not
work in this way.

The accompanying *donno* part for this rhythm initially appears to be
unconnected with the *brekete*, but this perception soon changes. The *donno*
enters on the third of the opening loud notes from the *brekete* playing what
we later understand is the pulse (this is also the dance step).

Example 5.23

With the *donno* pulse, the *brekete* rhythm is still asymmetric but we are
more able to perceive the alternation of duple and triple units within the
pulse although these are still disguised by the fact that the first of the
triplets is a quiet hand stroke. It also becomes clearer how 9 + 15 can fit
into four.

To see a more extended version of 3:2 I want to look at the fast section
of a dance called 'Kundum' composed by the Nzema people of the Volta
region in Ghana. There are five parts: bell, rattle, high support drum played
with sticks, and a low support drum and a master drum which are both
played with the left hand and a stick in the right hand. From the beginning
the bell divides the rattle pulse into 3 + 4. This bell part is rhythmically
very close to the standard claves pattern of South America, but that tends to
be syncopated in the first part, whereas this is a very definite triplet. The
high support drum takes the 4-pulse of the rattle and subdivides it in units
of three. The low support drum picks this up and answers it on the last beat
of the bar, creating a combined triplet rhythm ♩♪♪♩ which echoes the first
part of the bell rhythm. The first part of the low support drum goes with the
bell, with the middle note missing. By now, the bell player has to
concentrate to keep the sense of four in the second part of the pattern.

Example 5.24   'Kundum'

As you might by now expect, the master drum moves between these various possibilities. (The note written as a 'B' in this piece is a forceful bounced stroke with the stick while pressing the head with the left hand. (This sound cuts clearly through the ensemble.) At the beginning it keeps the sense of a quaver pulse both by sounding quavers and by anticipating the crotchet pulse by a quaver. The first three variations show standard techniques of substitution of sounds and pattern extension (each section written with repeat signs can be played as often as you like in whatever sequence). The patterns in bars 7-10 combine triple and duple pulses. Bars 11-12 are particularly interesting. There is a sequence of three sounds: two open hands sounds each with a stick 'flam' for emphasis, followed by a bass sound. This sequence is repeated three times but with a slight hesitation before the bass note on the third time. The notation shows quite clearly what is happening. Our ear is drawn to the repeated unit and each start of this seems to set up another almost unrelated pulse. However, the pattern is based on the triplet crotchet and the rhythm unit is slightly displaced each time. These two bars are usually played three times. (A parallel technique called a *tihai* can be found in North Indian music.) The next section is more predictable with continuous triplet crotchets. This moves to quavers in the last three bars which form the stop signal.

Finally, I want to look at a long and complex drum piece from the Ewe people of south-east Ghana. They occupy the coastal region of Ghana and its neighbour, Togo. My comments and analysis will be based on what I was taught by an *Ewe* master drummer, Johnson Kemeh.[1] The minimum set of instruments for this music is an iron bell which acts as a timekeeper, a rattle and three drums. The bell can be either the double bell *gankogui* or the single open peapod-shaped *atoke*. The rattle *axatse* also functions as a timekeeper, usually with a less complex part. The three drums must be accurately tuned relative to each other, although the absolute pitch is not set. *Kagan* is the highest pitched drum and generally has an unvarying part. *Kidi* is tuned a major third lower and usually has a part which responds to the changes played by the master drum, *sogo*, which is tuned a perfect fourth lower than *kidi*. (In a larger ensemble *atsimevu* or *gboba* is the master drum with *sogo* taking a supporting role.) The tuning of the drums is important, not only for the musical sound, but because the Ewe language is tonal and the drums can mimic the language, thereby 'talking' to each other.

'*Ageshe*' (the final e is short as in 'egg') is a fast version of '*Agbadza*' the traditional Ewe war dance. The *gankogui* part is best conceived as being in twelve-eight time.

Example 5.25 ($\quad \downarrow = 120$)

This pattern[2] when first heard by European musicians appears to have three pulses whereas African musicians hear four. The dance step uses the 4-pulse - it is interesting that this make the dance step more a part of the music as it 'fills' some gaps in the pattern more than the 3-pulse. Twelve is also a very useful number in that it can be divided by two, three, four and six - although more of this later. The *axatse* plays either a version of the *gankogui* rhythm or the dance pulse. The *kagan* part also supports the perception of the dance pulse in that it fills in the gaps to maintain a constant quaver beat.

Example 5.26

At this point in the explanation, the time-line could support several interpretations, but the other parts reinforce the dance step.

The *kidi* part changes throughout the piece in response to the rhythms played by the master drum. The master drum part is in clearly delineated sections which each consist of variations around a central idea. The *kidi* part for the introduction uses the 3-pulse and a combination of open and closed strokes.[3]

Example 5.27

This has added another level of possibilities for the listener, but these are still comparatively simple compared to the master drum (*sogo*) part.

At one level the *sogo* part uses the 3-pulse of the *kidi* part. I have beamed the notation to show the repeated unit. If we hear the start of the pattern with the bell it is likely that we will conceive the *kidi* part as beginning with the closed strokes. Another interpretation is to hear the *kidi* part beginning with the two louder open strokes which also coincide with the second dance step. The *sogo* part uses this second interpretation but generally has a softer stroke to coincide with the loud strokes of the *kidi* part so as not to obscure it. Notice the way that this pulse links between the *gankogui* part and the dance step.

Example 5.28

This pulse is then filled in a way which shows a superb understanding of the rhythmic possibilities of the pattern - and all worked out without the aid of notation. If you subdivide the 4-pulse to get an 8-pulse you have a constant three against two (12 against 8). This is quite straightforward, except that it is not directly sounded. Different rhythms are based on either twelve or eight, leaving out some beats and sounding others so that the supporting pulses must be internalised to be understood. But even this level of sophistication is too simple for the master drum. It uses the 8-pulse (dotted quavers) in combination with the 12-pulse (quavers) to achieve three units each lasting for four quavers and thus matching the *kidi* part. However, the order of the elements is not constant in each unit. Whereas the first two units are ♪♪♪, the third unit reverses the order so that the second note of the pattern coincides with the start of the *gankogui* pattern.

Example 5.29

Sogo

There is an additional level of sonic complexity resulting from the sounds used. The second and third notes of each unit are generally louder sounding strokes than the first note. The distance between the two attacks for the second and third notes is also constant. The variation occurs between the first and second note or the third note to the first note of the next unit. This gives the effect of a slightly uneven waltz which at first hearing seems to have little to do with the *gankogui* part. After repeated hearings you realise that there are links and the parts are in a strict relationship to each other, but at the speed that this music is played it is virtually impossible to unravel the elements. As you get used to the sound you may also notice that the first four notes of the bar for *sogo* sound the 8-pulse, although this is somewhat disguised by the different sounds used.[4]

After playing variations around the introductory pattern, the sogo part proceeds through a number of sections. Each section has a basic idea which is then developed both rhythmically and sonically by using different sounds. The first section experiments with the 6-pulse and the 4-pulse. The paradigm might be expressed as:

Example 5.30

Sogo

Both the elements here can be directly repeated to fill a whole bar. The crotchet pattern is then extended:

Example 5.31

Sogo

This of course can, in its turn be extended in the same way as the paradigm, by the repetition of the unit:

Example 5.32

Another variation of this idea changes the rhythm slightly and displaces it, using a similar sequence of sounds which supports the rhythm played by *kidi* at this point:

Example 5.33

The effect of this on the listener (at least, this one) is to cause the whole rhythm to mentally 'flip' to a different starting point, especially if the *atoke* is being used so that there is not a clear start to the timeline.[5]

In the next two sections the *sogo* part continues to explore the possibilities of the 4-, 6- and 8-pulse against the rest of the ensemble. The second section deals mainly with 4-pulse and 6-pulse. Again each element can be extended.

Example 5.34

The third section uses mainly the 4-pulse and 8-pulse in a pattern which starts at the half-bar compared with the timeline.

Example 5.35

This section also has a linguistic joke in the *sogo* part. The main pattern imitates a child at school asking in the *Ewe* language 'Will my mother come, will my mother come for me?' Because of the tonal nature of most West African languages[6] it is easy for a combination of pitch and rhythm to suggest a phrase in the language. This happens frequently in drumming. What is 'said' is often a joke or a comment on a local event but is also used by drummers as a mnemonic as in this example from the latter part of *Ageshe*.

Example 5.36

Al - i me-le ke - se To - yo - ta,   To - yo - ta.

'The girl is wider than a Toyota bus.' There is a close parallel between this and the starting point for the composition of new tunes in the *bɛwaa* xylophone songs of the Dagaare people.

To show some of these complex ideas in operation, here are all the parts for one variation of '*Ageshe*' beginning with the signal to change. This is given by the *sogo,* but *kidi* immediately joins in with the same signal so that dancers and drummers all hear it.

Example 5.37

The change signal is in fours (16-semiquavers) against the threes (12-quavers) of the *gankogui* and *kagan* parts. The bell player has to work really hard not to lose the rhythm at this point. The only part which helps both of them is the rattle. The *sogo* then plays the main rhythm for this section which is broadly in four time. (The notation here gives a fair idea of the sound except that the higher notes will tend to sound louder than the bass notes.) *Kidi* plays its own version of this same rhythm using open strokes (notes F and G) for the louder notes for the *sogo* part, and closed strokes to fill the rest of the rhythm and keep the semiquaver pulse going. You will realise that this means that the *kidi* player must know the music very well. *Kidi* must know all the master drum rhythms and what the *kidi* answer should be. This rhythm suggests the words, '*Television le daa nyesi. Eleasi woa?*' in the Ewe language, meaning, 'My mother has television. Do you have it?' The complexity of the ideas show just how advanced is the rhythmic sense of the unknown composer.

Let me attempt to summarise what I conceive as some of the compositional techniques involved in this music. Some writers have conceived as an essential difference between Western rhythm and African rhythm that it is divisive as opposed to additive. Western rhythm tends to start with the unit of the whole bar and then divide it into smaller fractions, usually by two, but occasionally by three. Much African music on the other hand is made up by the addition of a number of smaller units. Whilst this is a helpful concept in some ways, it does not satisfactorily express the awareness of multiple pulses and their relationships with each other.

In learning this music, the key to understanding for me has always been the dance pulse. This provides a generally stable reference point and often interlocks with the timeline. The timeline is usually the *gankogui* or *atoke* plus *axatse* part or the *kpagru* on the xylophone and uses either a 12-pulse, or an 4/8-pulse. The actual timeline is not a regular beat, but is often a combination of just two note lengths. These are often combined in such a way that if the pattern can be conceived as dividing into two sections, these sections will be of unequal length, thus supporting the concept of additive rhythm. Thus the timeline for '*Ageshe*' could be seen as five plus seven quavers.

There is usually at least one other part, often *kagan*, which supports an unchanging pulse. The *kidi* and *sogo* parts interact with each other in several ways, with *sogo* taking the lead. The lead part has a number of techniques which can be used. There is usually one main idea to each section of the piece. This idea may take a complete cycle of the timeline or it may be repeated two or three times to each cycle. If it takes a complete cycle it will often make reference to more than one of the concurrent pulses. The pulses to which it relates will not usually be in a simple divisive relationship, but may relate by 3:2 or a compound of this (3:4, 6:8, 8:12, 12:16). The same technique may still be employed if the unit is shorter, but it seems to be less common. The start point of the unit may not correspond with the start of the timeline or the perceived start of other parts. Recognisable rhythms may recur with their position changed relative to the other parts.

There are a variety of sounds available from the drum (at least five) which vary in pitch, volume and quality. These can be varied separate from the rhythm and may be used in such a way that they cause the listener's perception of the rhythm to change (for example, moving the position of a strong note). The lead part often interlocks with the supporting part, i.e. the two have a conversation with each other in which it is rare for them both to be speaking at once. The alternative is that the two parts are very similar and, often in this case, moving against the timeline to create a strong alternative pulse or perception. It is not impossible, of course for these two techniques to be mixed. There are many more variations in the lead part than the supporting part which has only one or two possibilities for each section. Each element of the lead part may be taken and repeated, extended or developed in the course of the section. There is a clear delineation between sections (this is often important for the dancers as well) which is indicated by a continuous 'roll' from the lead and supporting drum lasting between one and two repetitions of the timeline.

If a final comment were needed on this wealth of percussion music, one could do no better than to look at the dancers who are performing at the same time. Their engagement with and enjoyment of the music is all any composer or performer could ask.

Notes

1. Johnson K. D. Kemeh was born in Dzodze in the Volta region of Ghana near the border with Togo. He is now based in Accra where he is the senior drumming instructor at the University. He also runs a superb dance/drumming cultural group for young people in Alajo, Accra.

2. When played on *gankogui* the first note of the pattern is sometimes played on the lower bell which helps the perception of the start of the pattern. When played on *atoke* or often on *gankogui* given the speed, it is all played at one pitch thus making more interpretations possible.

3. The sticks are held flexibly in a matched grip. See the previous key for a description of the symbols used.

4. The earlier caveats about transcription, of course, apply here too. I have taken the *gankogui* part as indicating the basic barline structure. The reason for the beaming of the *sogo* part is because I was taught that the *sogo* part starts on the second dance step and because beaming it in units of three shows the structure.

5. For comparison and for a similar effect, listen to Steve Reich, 'Music for Pieces of Wood'.

6. A tonal language is one in which the pitch of the syllables changes the meaning, so the same two syllables spoken low-high, and high-low in pitch will have different meanings.

Bibliography

Arom, Simha (1991), *African Polyphony and Polyrhythm*, trans. Thom, Tuc and Boyd, Cambridge: Cambridge University Press.

Bebey, Francis (1975), *African Music: a People's Art*, trans. Josephine Bennet, New York: Lawrence Hill.

Chernoff, John Miller (1979), *African Rhythm and African Sensibility*, Chicago: University of Chicago Press.

Kinney, Sylvia (1970), 'Drummers in Dagbon: the Role of the Drummer on the Damba Festival', *Ethnomusicology*, **14** (2), 258-65.

Ladzekpo, Kobla (1971), 'The Social Mechanics of Good Music: a Description of Dance Clubs among Anlo-Ewe Speaking Peoples of Ghana', *African Music*, **5** (1), 6-22.

Ladzekpo, Kobla and Panteleoni, Hewitt (1970), 'Takada Drumming', *African Music*, **4**, 6-31.

Ladzekpo, Alfred Kwashie and Ladzekpo, Kobla (1980), 'Anlo Ewe Music in Anyako, Volta Region, Ghana', in E. May (ed.), *Musics of Many Cultures*, Berkeley, CA: University of California Press.

Locke, David (1987), *Drum Gahu*, Indiana: White Cliffs Media Co.

Locke, David (1990), *Drum Damba*, Indiana: White Cliffs Media Co.

Nketia, J. H. Kwabena (1962), *African Music in Ghana*, Evanston, IL: Northwestern University Press.

Nketia, J. H. Kwabena (1962a), 'The Hocket Technique in African Music', *Journal of the International Folk Music Council*, **14**, 44-52.

Nketia, J. H. Kwabena (1962b), 'The Problem of Meaning in African Music', *Ethnomusicology*, **6** (1), 1-7.

Nketia, J. H. Kwabena (1963), *Folk Songs of Ghana*, Legon: University of Ghana.

Nketia, J. H. Kwabena (1964), 'Traditional and Contemporary Idioms of African Music', *Journal of the International Folk Music Council*, **16**, 34-7.

Nketia, J. H. Kwabena (1971), 'History and Organisation of Music in West Africa', in Wachsmann, K. (ed.), *Essays on Music and History in Africa*, Evanston, IL: Northwestern University Press, 3-25.

Nketia, J. H. Kwabena (1975), *The Music of Africa*, London: Gollancz.

Opoku, A. A. (1970), *Festivals of Ghana*, Accra: Ghana Publishing Corporation.

Oppong, Christine (1969), 'A Preliminary Account of the Role and Recruitment of Drummers in Dagbon', *Research Review*, **6** (1), 38-51.

6   The Xylophone Tradition of North-West Ghana

Trevor Wiggins

In this chapter I shall draw particularly on examples from the Dagara people of northern Ghana and Burkina Faso.[1] The Dagara, together with their close neighbours, the Lobi people, occupy a region of north-west Ghana and south-west Burkina Faso straddling the Black Volta river. The other neighbours of the Dagara are the Waale people to the south in Ghana, particularly around the regional capital, Wa, and the Sisaala to the east. The boundaries between these groups of people is far from clear geographically. Individual villages in one area may be either Dagara or Sisaala. The Sisaala men often take Dagara wives but it is very unusual for a Dagara man to have a Sisaala wife. Dagara men think Sisaala women are 'dirty' but their meaning is probably cultural rather than factual. Lobi and Dagaare languages are mutually intelligible, the differences being the equivalent of the dialect change between relatively remote regions of the UK. The Dagaare and Sisaala languages are not similarly related. Few Dagara people speak Sisaala although they may understand some of the language. A fair number of Sisaala people, especially those with Dagara wives in the family, understand and speak some Dagaare, at least sufficient for trading purposes. The countryside in the Dagara region is long grass savannah. The soil is not very fertile and is not deep having many rocky outcrops. There are some *baobab* trees which grow to tremendous girth, but most trees are comparatively small and, near to the villages, are regularly cut back in the search for firewood. There is one main rainy season which lasts roughly from May to October, with little rain outside these months. In the dry season temperatures often exceed 40°C with a hot dry wind called the *harmattan* blowing south from the Sahara. Food for the dry season must be stored and is supplemented by what can be grown in small walled gardens. The gardens must be watered by hand twice a day, so are usually close to a well or a reliable stream. The main town of the Dagara area is Nandom. Nandom has a hospital and a substantial Catholic church but no made roads, mains electricity or telephones. The nearest any of these amenities come is Wa, 120 km south, but they are progressing north and their arrival may have a considerable impact on life in Nandom.

The Nandom area is bounded by the Burkina border about 15 km north and the Black Volta river 10 km west. To the south and east are a number of villages owing allegiance either to Nandom or to other administrative centres such as Lawra (30 km south) or Jirapa (40 km south-east) neither of which are Dagara. Work in Nandom centres mainly around the production of food and drink. The main foods are either rice or a traditional thick millet porridge called TZ (from *Tuo Zafi* which is probably a word from the Hausa language of Nigeria which was the language spoken by official messengers). These staples are eaten with a mainly vegetable stew made from tomatoes and green leaves with processed seeds from the *dawadawa* tree added for flavour and protein. The main local drink is *pito* (local people claim this is an English word but, if it is, it has changed beyond recognition). *Pito* is also made from millet which has been sprouted, boiled and fermented overnight. It is drunk very fresh so the alcohol content increases from a sweet drink with little alcohol in the morning, to a quite potent sour brew with a taste like cider and major headache potential by the evening. Other local occupations include the manufacture of a wide variety of pots and baskets, and the weaving and sewing of traditional cloth. Many of these trades are under threat from imports and mechanisation, with the traditional crafts being seen as old-fashioned. A high proportion of the young men either leave the area completely or travel to the south of Ghana outside the farming season to find paid work and a more comfortable lifestyle.

In Dagara culture, as in many others in Africa, music is central to everyday life, orchestrating and accompanying all significant events from birth to death. The main instrument of the Dagara people is a large 18-bar pentatonic xylophone called a *gyil* which leads and accompanies singing and dancing. A similar instrument is used by many of the neighbouring people. The Sisaala people have instruments which are often bought from Dagara makers who are acknowledged to be experts. The Lobi xylophone makers are also well known but often make smaller instruments with fewer bars and a slightly different tuning. Even the Dagara instrument is not consistent throughout the region. Dagara musicians in Diebougou in Burkina Faso about 50 km north-west from Nandom play a smaller 19-key instrument which is more closely related to the Mandinka *balafon* found in northern Burkina, Mali and across to the Gambia. Throughout the region the xylophone is used for a number of different types of music, particularly funeral music, fetish music for traditional religious ceremonies, and some forms of recreational music.

It is well known that there is no specific word for 'music' in many African languages, as distinct and separate from 'dance' and other aspects of live performance. For example, the Dagara people have a type of recreational performance called *bɛwaa*. The name itself comes from the word *bɛwaare* - they are coming - thus suggesting the coming together of people with a common purpose. There is no audience: everyone participates, as musician, singer or dancer. *Bɛwaa* (sometimes also referred to as *bawaa*) takes place mainly in the harvest season (October-December) on nights when the moon is full. When it is clear that there will be a good harvest people will meet together to sing, dance, play, drink, meet friends, exchange gossip, arrange marriages and so on.

Bɛwaa is also closely related in style and content to *dalaari* which is for children, and *kari* and *nuru* which are performed by women and use only voices and clapping. All of these involve songs. The words of a song are often the first thing to be composed usually by the women. These may then be taken over and used in *bɛwaa*. The words often deal with local events. They may narrate a humorous incident, comment on someone's behaviour, or give advice about how one should behave. Although the references are often quite local the song will often be heard by visitors from the next village who will remember and repeat it, possibly with some alteration and addition, when they return to their own village.

Since most West African languages are tonal[2] the words of a song will begin to suggest a melodic outline which is developed often by repetition or phrase extension. A *gyil* (xylophone) player may become involved here. A good *gyil* player must be able to repeat on his instrument anything which is said, but *gyile* (plural) are pentatonic so he has to make a precise choice of notes, thus establishing the melody more clearly (within Dagara culture *gyile* may only be played by men). The rhythm of the melody also has to fit with the rhythm for the dance step, so this further constrains the possibilities.

The *gyil* player of course, has two beaters. As well as playing the melody (and probably embellishing it) with the right hand, he will add some further accompaniment with the left hand. This additional part may vary according to the skill of the player between a simple 'Alberti' type steady pattern, and a much more complex independent accompaniment with elements of imitation of parts of the melody. Inevitably, this too will be heard by another *gyil* player who will remember the contour of the song and take this back to his village. He will then reproduce the melody, but will make no attempt to copy the accompaniment style of the other player, preferring instead to add his own.

In each place where the song is performed people will dance. The basics of the dance step are fairly universal to fit with the rhythm, but again there will be different versions in different places. The net result is almost like an extended game of 'Chinese whispers', but with words, music, and dance all involved. There is not one single composer or creator, but many, each adding a part to the mosaic. There is not one piece which is subject to different interpretations as with Western music, but an almost continuous variation based around a central paradigm.

If you try to ask someone how the music in one place is different from another you may get a reply which says that the song is the same, but the dance is different. Yet to our ears the music may sound very different. The instruments used may have variations in tuning which make the song sound quite different even though relatively the same bars are played. Each player will perform in their own style which is distinctive and different. Each performance by the same person may involve playing variations in a different order or adding some changes. In the conception of the performer they may play a particular tune the same every time. By this they will mean that they perform the same song, in their own style with some standard variations. Western musicology, in contrast, may point to many areas in which each performance is not the same. There is no correct view here, what is interesting are the different ways that people perceive the music they are playing and hearing.

The instruments used in a typical performance are one or two *gyile*, and a drum, which can be either a *kuor* (calabash drum) or a *gangaar* (short cylindrical wooden drum). In addition, someone will play the *kpagru* (literally 'beating') rhythm on the lowest bar of the *gyil* which is usually reserved for this purpose. When there are two *gyile* the one with the 'sharper' sounding voice will be designated as female and used as the lead instrument. The *gyil* player will also have metal jingles attached to his wrists. The dancers will have similar jingles on their ankles and legs and will also play a regular pulse on a small metal idiophone. The standard *gyil* has 18 keys but is large and heavy. Some players will use a smaller 14-key instrument because it is easier to transport. The 18-key instrument is preferred to the 14-key because when a performer feels inspired the 14-key will restrict his imagination. The 14-key is a Lobi instrument which the Dagara have adopted because you can play some of their music on it and it is lighter when transporting the instrument, but the tuning of the 14-key Lobi instrument and the 14-key Dagaare instrument is different. The 14-key gyil is usually referred to as *lo-gyil*.

The bass part of the xylophone is called *gyil nyaa* - xylophone chest (part of the body) - for funerals you play tunes here late in the afternoon between the time when the sun is hot and its setting. The middle is *gyil sɔg* - xylophone middle, played in the middle of the day. The top bars are *gyil pilɛ* - xylophone low-down (because these bars are closer to the ground) and would be played in the morning. For recreational music where there is singing involved, these ideas are less important than finding a pitch which is comfortable for the singers. The xylophone is played with large heavy beaters traditionally made from raw latex and glue wrapped round the end of a stick about 30 cm long and 2 cm in diameter. The modern alternative replaces the latex with a disc cut from a lorry tyre. The beaters are often called *gyilbie* (lit. xylophone children) but the same term is also used in some places for the bars. Beaters are also called *gyilluɔrɛ* - jumping from place to place, *gyilnɛɛ* - xylophone mouths, or *gyilduɔlɛ* - xylophone stretching. The music of *bɛwaa* is often referred to as *bɛwaa gyile*.

The *gyil* is pentatonic, but instruments vary widely between makers and the interval between adjacent notes can be between 202 and 283 cents. Each maker will normally be quite consistent, tuning each new instrument to an existing one or just to his memory. Thus, when a player is faced with a new instrument he will often play a pattern of alternating notes up and down the instrument, followed by a well-known tune. The purpose of this is to establish 'where its voice lies'. The player may be unhappy starting a tune on one note and begin again one bar higher or lower. The instrument is in tune when the performed tune sounds satisfactory. The tuning is not judged in isolation but is good when it performs the desired function.[3] However, this certainly points towards a conception of the tuning as equipentatonic in many ways.

Given this performance context, what about the actual musical practice? (I am using western techniques and concepts of musical analysis in this discussion.) *Bɛwaa* begins with a song and, in its basic form, this is supported on the *gyil* with a simple accompaniment. The song, '*Bobo Dioulasso tingenbarena*' comes from the Dagaare area of south-west Burkina Faso (Bobo Dioulasso is the main town of the area) and dates from the 1970s. The basic melody and words are:

Example 6.1

This has really only two ideas: the first bar is reworked in the third bar, and the second and fourth bars are identical. Rhythmically the first and third bars have all equal notes, only the order of the notes is slightly different. The rhythm of the second and fourth bars owes quite a lot to the dance rhythm (*kpagru*) which is usually played in the bottom bar of the instrument.

Example 6.2

The left hand of the *gyil* player adds a simple ostinato-like accompaniment,[4] similar in form and function to an 'Alberti' bass, but without the harmonic implications. Apart from the substitution of some notes in the first and third bars, this accompaniment continues without changing style or rhythm throughout the piece.

This simple beginning has many possibilities for small scale variations which explore the detail of the song without ever moving far away from it. At the most simple level, the first note of the right hand is delayed by one quaver adding momentum at the beginning of the bar. The same procedure is also applied to bars 2 and 4, or the pitch of the first quaver of the bar is substituted by a different one.

Example 6.3

The obvious extension of this is to continue the idea, moving the first two notes of bars one and three back one quaver.

Example 6.4

Then all of the notes in bars one and three, introducing the effect of a syncopation across the barline.[5]

Example 6.5

At the level of micro-rhythm there are two main cells resulting from the combination of the two parts: one is ♪♪♩, the other is ♪♪♪♪, and these can be realised in different ways. They are frequently combined in one bar in the stated order:

Example 6.6

And, of course, different notes can be substituted whilst keeping the general phrase shape:

Example 6.7

Although this is all at a simple level, by combining the different variations an interesting and appropriate piece of dance music can be created, at the same time remaining close to the original song.

The further extension of these techniques can be seen in another song, '*Yaya kole zɛlɛ*'. Literally translated the words mean 'Keep on begging, (repeated), If she is happy she will give you love'. Meaning - if you want a woman but she is not interested you should pay her more attention, you may be rewarded with love.

Example 6.8

This is a very well known and liked *bɛwaa* song first heard in 1986. It is performed by most *gyil* players and, therefore, exists in a great many differing versions. As can immediately be seen there are a number of elements even within the nuclear melody which are derived from a single idea. The first three phrases of the melody are nearly identical. They have the characteristic repeated notes at the beginning of the phrase which means that this melody is quickly recognised even in complex variations. The third phrase is extended to balance the first two phrases and this extension draws on elements already heard and also continues the downward curve of the phrase which has been established.

It is also interesting to note that we are in no doubt as to where the metrical stress lies. Without there being the degree of emphasis of the resolution of the repeated notes created in a similar situation by, for example, Beethoven, there is a clear stress on the note following the three repeated notes. From the interaction of the stress and the density referent established by the repeated notes, there is also a clear, unstated accent falling immediately before the start of the second phrase.

As it stands, the main interest in the tune lies in the phrase structure and the interaction between the simple note lengths and the metre. As such, it is an ideal vehicle for further elaboration and variation, having similar features to other themes such as the framework underlying the famous Paganini 'Caprice'.

Of course, no self-respecting *gyil* player would perform the song with just the melody, so differing versions immediately begin to emerge from different performers. A version by Joseph Kobom Taale[6] starts by emphasising the rhythmic impetus of the first three notes then disguising the end of the phrase. The left-hand additions in bar two have three effects: they mirror the opening falling interval of the melody, emphasising it by repetition; they further disguise the 'barline' with a rhythm which hangs across it; and they adumbrate the repetition and pitch fall of the second phrase.

Example 6.9

The same idea is used at the end of the second phrase although the impact here will be slightly different due to its previous audition. The music so far has also alternated between two-part writing and single line, although it could be argued that, by its pitch structure, the single line implies the continuation of two parts. These features are all continued in the extension of the third phrase with the repeated use of the interval of a fourth (however approximate), the dualism of the part writing and the rhythmic idea which drags across the bar line to the return of the first phrase. In the next variation it is the melody which is decorated while the left-hand accompaniment remains unchanged.

Example 6.10

It is generally accepted that a good *gyil* player can be recognised by the speed of his left hand (and *gyil* players take special measures, such as eating food with the left hand instead of the right, to strengthen it). The next variation retains the expanded version of the right-hand part whilst adding more independence and complexity in the left hand.

Example 6.11

The development from the existing left-hand part is clear and one could argue that only four notes have been added or changed, but the effect is more far-reaching than that would suggest. Whereas the left hand was previously primarily an accompaniment (this effect being reinforced by the gaps in its movement), is has now become an independent line with a wider range of notes. It also complements the rhythmic flow of the melody moving it on at significant places. The left-hand part also now has a symmetrical line and contour, connecting the lower register in a broad sweep up to the high note at the beginning of the phrase.

In a performance of *bɛwaa* there will be a number of songs performed without a break, alternating with dance sections. Typically the *gyil* player will begin a song by playing the first phrase which will be recognised by the dancers who will begin singing. The player will then continue to play the tune ornamenting and playing variations around it. At a signal from the lead dancer (usually a whistle) the dance section will begin. The *gyil* player will play a simpler alternating pattern for this section until the return of the tune, or the start of a new tune. During the dance section the dancers will usually be performing a set sequence of steps. As they wear metal idiophones on their legs this will also contribute another rhythm to the overall sound.

An example of a typical song is '*Fra-fra woe kɔ simie yang baa, Fra-fra woe kɔ simie yang baa, Fra-fra woe kɔ simie yang baa. Kɔ simie yang baa, ɛ baa bɛ dunɛ*'. A literal translation of the words is: 'The Fra-fra, joke, farms groundnuts, gives to the dog (repeated three times). Gives to the dog, now the dog doesn't bite.' This is a joke *(woe)* at the expense of the Fra-fra people who, in Dagara opinion are so stupid they farm groundnuts to feed the dog, then they are surprised when the dog doesn't bite. The tempo is around mm 240.

There is an alternating, one-bar pattern to the accompaniment which is also found in the vast majority of *bɛwaa* songs. This starts on adjacent notes and follows a sequence: **1 1 2 1 2 2 1 2** (each number represents one bar). This sequence can also start at different points whilst maintaining the pattern e.g. **1 2 1 2 2 1 2 1**. If there are two *gyile* available then the second player will play variations around the support part as shown below, following the same sequence as the lead part accompaniment. This example starts with bar 1, followed by bar 2 of the sequence.

Example 6.12

Example 6.13   'Fra-Fra woe'

Of course, this again only represents the central idea of the second *gyil* part. A typical elaboration of the part is shown below. Although visually it is quite easy to see the relationship with the paradigm above the aural reality is more complex. The dotted crotchet pulse is maintained throughout, but it occurs in different parts, frequently with the other part anticipating or following the pulse so our sense of rhythm (but not the Dagara sense of rhythm) is confused.

Example 6.14

The tune itself is very simple, utilising only four notes. The word pattern of three lines the same followed by a consequent line is a common model. The melody for each of the first three lines is very similar really only changing to fit the accompaniment sequence. Most songs, like this one, have a 12-pulse (two bars) phrase length, with the *kpagru* being repeated three times against it. (There are also a significant number of songs which use a shorter 8-pulse, like *Bobo*, aligning with the *kpagru*.) The section from bars 10-17 shows a typical elaboration of the melody. There is a small amount of note substitution and a whole phrase (bars 11-12) which is extended. Rhythmically it is quite a simple syncopation across two bars. This is a Western conception, measuring the sound events against where we think the beat should be. For many *gyil* players it is a motor pattern between the two hands, the sequence being left-right, left-right, together, left-right, left-right, together. Melodically it uses a pattern of fourths common in the tune, combining this, in bar 12, with a pattern closely derived from the accompaniment. The dance section (beginning at bar 18) emphasises the accompaniment pattern more, often reinforcing notes from it, for example bars 21, 22, 24, 25. Most of the right-hand part in this section can be seen as just two basic shapes relating to the left-hand sequence. One shape rises. Bearing in mind the pentatonic construction of the instrument the shape could be described as 1-3-5 (bar 21) or 2-4-5 (first half of bar 22.) There is an answering downward shape which can be expressed as 3-3-1 (bar 23) or 2-2-1 (bar 27.) The numbers here are used to show the relationship and not to designate the pitch, thus the note D is referred to as 5 in the upward shape, and 1 in the downward shape. The resultant rhythm from the two parts is ♩ ♪ ♩ ♪, tending to suggest a compound metre against the simple time of the *kpagru*. This again can be seen as a motor pattern: together, together, right-left.

There are some recognised tunes used for the dance sections of songs. They are far fewer in number than the songs themselves and are generally only one phrase long. What seems to have happened is that a particular repeated pattern used in the dance section has suggested a phrase in the language (see endnote 2) and this linguistic phrase has fixed and identified the tune. A common example is *Kpere bandazuziɛ*. The words mean *Shake your head lizard*. The lizard referred to has a red neck and a habit of standing still while performing what look like rapid press-ups with the upper half of its body. The dance at this point involves the male dancers shaking their upper body and shoulders vigorously so the *gyil* player is encouraging to greater exertions. The tune is one phrase long but has two versions to accommodate the accompaniment sequence.

Example 6.15

Kpe - re ban - da- zu - ziɛ   Kpe - re ban - da-zu - ziɛ

The *gyil* 1 accompaniment pattern shown for *Fra-fra woe* is the most common but other rhythms and notes are possible although the sequence is unvarying. Other typical realisations are illustrated below:

Example 6.16

There are also more elements to the variations which cannot be shown here. Each *gyil* has a calabash resonator for each bar which has two or three mirlitons attached. It is not intended that these should buzz equally and evenly for each note. Some may sound more than others; some may sound scarcely at all, and some may have an interesting pulsation to the sound. Makers will tell you that if all the notes buzz evenly and loudly it will obscure the tone of the instrument. The presence of the mirlitons will add another dimension which will vary between each instrument. Some notes will be more prominent than others and the effective length that each note sounds will vary. The notation cannot show this but the effect on the sound is considerable.[7]

The other element which I have not yet mentioned in any detail is the calabash drum, the *kuɔr*. This is made from as calabash up to 60 cm in diameter. A slice is cut off the calabash leaving a circular opening about 30 cm across. The flesh of the calabash is scraped out and the shell dried. A skin is then fitted across the opening (traditionally crocodile skin for the best sound) and glued and nailed in place. The resulting drum when played with the hands is quite loud and very light to transport. It has a clear open sound and a distinctive 'slap' sound but little bass. The head cannot be tuned directly but can be kept at the preferred pitch either by exposing it to heat (the sun or a fire) to raise the pitch, or putting water on the head to lower the pitch. The *kuɔr* part is mainly improvised but there are some typical phrases shown below. Rhythmically the *kuɔr* relates to the accompaniment of *gyil* 1 but also links with the *kpagru* rhythm. The notation here uses the note G for an open sound and D for a slap.

Example 6.17

An alternative version of the *kpagru* part is also shown. The addition of the extra quaver makes the part more open to alternative interpretations and can be heard more as a 2 + 3 + 3 quaver pattern.

When all these elements are put together in an ensemble a complex texture emerges which to Western ears can be quite confusing. The *kpagru* has a very obvious 4-beat repeated pattern but, although there are clearly notes in common with the rest of the ensemble, the precise relationship is not clear. The melody may, according to the song, sound like either twelve-eight or six-four time with either the dotted crotchet or the crotchet as the main pulse. The *gyil* 1 accompaniment often has a clear crotchet pulse and a clear repeated rhythmic unit lasting six crotchets, but the adherence of a player to the rhythm I have shown often varies so that it is precise in its relationship to the other parts at those points I have shown as barlines, but has a much freer feel between those points (some of this can also be seen in the melody of the next song). The *gyil* 2 part tends much more towards a dotted crotchet pulse and twelve-eight barring but this is frequently disguised by the anticipations and delays around the pulse. The *kuɔr* moves between different interpretations of its rhythms. The typical opening bar of the last example can be heard with either a crotchet or a dotted crotchet pulse and many of its other patterns exhibit a similar ambiguity in Western terms.

It is useful to look at another song with all the parts notated to get some idea of the possible interactions. '*Viɛlu daa na Nandomme mi nyu, akuraku*' follows (see Figure 6.1). The words mean 'Very good pito Nandom people drink, wonderful, The rainwater comes, comes, comes and turns to pito then we drink, wonderful'. The song was not written in Nandom but was composed in the early 1960s by people from Tuoper (a village 8 km south-west from Nandom) who always enjoyed the Nandom *pito* when they came to the town. Although *akuraku* does mean 'wonderful' its precise meaning is also 'I'm surprised it's so good!' The melody for this varies rhythmically between the crotchet-quaver feel of bar 1 and the duplet quavers shown in bar 3. Much of the time it occupies a tantalisingly uncertain feel somewhere between the two. The tune also has some bars which use a crotchet beat (bars 6-7) and one bar (bar 8) which uses a typical *kuɔr* rhythm. Structurally the melody follows the common pattern also seen in *Fra-fra woe*. The first two bars are repeated twice more with virtually the only variation being the starting note in the pentatonic scale, with bars 7-8 being the consequence of the words and a melodic contrast. The actual pitch of the melody would be one where men and women could sing in the same register so the first note of the melody might be around middle C or D on the piano. A typical variation of the melody is shown in bars 9-16. The tempo would be around mm 150.

What general principles for musical construction and continuation can be abstracted from these examples of *bɛwaa* music? Many of them can be expressed in ways which find close parallels in music of the European tradition. The presence of the *kpagru* and a dance step which is realised aurally means that there is a clear rhythmic periodicity which elaborations can negate or subvert to a fair extent. The phrase lengths themselves are comparatively short and controlled largely by the song text.

Figure 6.1 'Viɛlu daa na Nandomme mi nyu, akuraka'

These phrase lengths are adhered to in all the examples I have heard. At a micro-rhythmic level there is often a pulse (at the speed of the crotchet in the transcriptions) in the song which can be subdivided by the *gyil* player who can make faster attacks. This is, however, used with some subtlety. There is no point in going quickly to a continuous quaver pattern which has no sense of progression and loses rhythmic differentiation. The beginning of the bar is the preferred point for most of the initial subdivisions. This is often extended and may continue across the bar line to the start of the next phrase or just beyond it.

Pitch variations are limited, but also enabled by the pentatonic tuning. There are fewer notes available but adjacent notes can be easily substituted without sounding like wrong notes and whilst maintaining the contour of the melody. There is some indication that there is a sense of an 'octave' in the substitution and addition of notes from a different register - mainly the low notes of the left hand. The additional notes frequently reinforce part of the pitch content of the melody, either by direct or mirror imitation. There is a clear sense of part writing, almost always two-part because of the physical limitations, but, by implication, there is sometimes a third part present. This raises the question of a sense of harmony. This obviously does not exist in the sense of western syntactical functional harmony. There is a sense, though, in which there is an alternation of two harmonies or harmonic centres.

Although this is usually dance music it is also used as a performance or to accompany songs. There is never a set pattern of variations although the performance generally begins with something close to the original song before becoming more complex. The player will also respond to the level of involvement and excitement communicated by the other performers. The usual form of a performance would be a gradual increase in complexity and density of sound events (although not tempo) taking one or two minutes.

This would reach a sustainable plateau which could continue for 2-5 minutes, during which time the process of variation would be mainly concerned with quite small changes within a complex matrix, At the end of this time the performer might return to a simpler pattern allowing the music to become quieter before just stopping at a suitable point. There is not a sense of climax or of resolution of inherent or generated conflict as in most European classical music.

What I have presented are naturally rather coarse abstractions and an attempt to indicate some general principles. They are not a guarantee that, if you use these ideas you will write African music - there are many more subtleties than I can understand. Because of the process of composition and communication in West Africa we are often not aware of the names or identities of the excellent creative musicians whose output is often labelled 'traditional'. The music they create is appropriate for the occasion and valued by the listeners - a claim which all composers would like to be able to make.

Notes

1. I should make my own views clear. As the product of a European system of music education, I cannot write 'African music'. I can use some of the techniques as part of an extended vocabulary or palette. I can also pastiche African music - as a learning exercise, as a tribute, or as an exploration of the links between one style and another (rather in the manner of Sir Michael Tippett's use of music by Corelli).
2. A tonal language is one in which changing the pitch of syllables changes the meaning. However, the context is also very important. In the context of a song, the meaning would be understood which made sense even if some of the tones in the language were negated by the pitches used in the song.
3. My transcriptions indicate approximate pitch using the nearest equivalent notes from the western pitch system. The following figures relate to instruments I have measured. Since my sample is quite small there may be some instruments which would extend the range. Typical intervals in cents might be:

| Octave 1 | 274 | 224 | 275 | 237 | 242 |
| Octave 2 | 249 | 232 | 225 | 245 | 228 |

4. Most performers play the melody with their right hand and the accompaniment with the left, but there are a significant number who reverse the instrument. One Ghanaian informant suggested that this came from Burkina Faso although no justification was offered. Playing

the instrument in this way is even more dangerous spiritually than normal.

5. Again it is the transcription rather than necessarily the sound which leads to a description in these terms. However, without wishing to suggest the that music itself uses the emphasis of a conceptual barline, I would argue that the mapping of pitch on to rhythm in the construction of the accompaniment leads to an interpretation which supports an understanding in these terms.

6. Joseph Kobom Taale was one of the leading *bɛwaa gyil* performers in Ghana. He was born in Nandom in the Upper West region and began performing nationally at the age of about 16. He taught *gyil* at the University of Ghana for some 20 years and until recently worked as a freelance musician based in Accra. He died in November 1995 after a short illness.

7. For comparison, listen to some of John Cage's pieces for prepared piano and, if possible, experiment with the technique. The mirlitons on the *gyil* are holes cut in the calabash covered with a thin membrane which is loose enough to buzz. Traditionally the material used for this is the egg case of a particular house spider. With the increasing number of concrete block houses being built rather than the traditional mudbrick, these spiders are now quite scarce. The preferred modern alternative is high density plastic carrier bags.

Bibliography

Anderson, Lois (1967), 'The African Xylophone', *African Arts/Arts Afrique*, 46-9, 66-9.

Anderson, Lois (1968), 'A Reassessment of the Distribution, Origin, Tunings and Stylistic Criteria in African Xylophone Traditions', *African Studies Association*, **11**, Los Angeles.

Blench, Roger (1982), 'Evidence for the Indonesian Origins of Certain Elements of African Culture', *Journal of the International Library of African Music*, **6** (2), 81-93.

Chappell, Robert (1978), 'The Amadinda Xylophone: the Instrument, its Music and Procedures for its Construction', *Percussionist*, **15** (2), 60-85.

Cooke, Peter (1970), 'Ganda Xylophone Music: Another Approach', *African Music Society Journal*, **4** (4), 62-80.

Godsey, Larry (1980), 'The Use of the Xylophone in the Funeral Ceremony of the Birifor of Northwest Ghana', unpublished PhD, University of California at Los Angeles.

Herzog, George (1949), 'Canon in West African Xylophone Melodies', *Journal of the American Musicological Society*, **2**, 196-7.

Jessup, Lynne (1983), *The Mandinka Balafon*, La Mesa: Xylo Publications.

Johnson, Thomas F. (1973), 'Muhambi Xylophone Music of the Shangana-Tsonga', *African Music Society Journal*, **5** (3), 86-93.

Jones, A. M. (1960), 'Africa and Indonesia: the Xylophone as Culture Indicator', *African Music Society Journal*, **2** (3), 36-47.

Jones, A. M. (1964, reprinted 1967), *Africa and Indonesia: the Evidence of the Xylophone and Other Musical and Cultural Factors*, Leiden: E. J. Brill.

Kubik, Gerhard (1960), 'The Structure of Kiganda Xylophone Music', *African Music*, **2** (3), 6-30.

Kubik, Gerhard (1962), 'The Endarra Xylophone of Bukonjo', *African Music Society Journal*, **3** (1), 43-8.

Kubik, Gerhard (1963), 'Discovery of a Trough Xylophone in Northern Mozambique', *African Music Society Journal*, **3** (4), 35-51.

Kubik, Gerhard (1964), 'Xylophone Playing in Southern Uganda', *Journal of the Royal Anthropological Institute*, **94** (2), 138-59.

Kubik, Gerhard (1965), 'Transcription of Mangwilo Xylophone Music from Film Strips', *African Music Society Journal*, **3** (4), 35-51.

Kubik, Gerhard (1969), 'Composition Techniques in Kiganda Xylophone Music', *African Music Society Journal*, **4** (3), 22-72.

Mensah, Atta Annan (1967), 'The Polyphony of Gyil-gu, Kudzo and Awutu Sakumo', *Journal of the International Folk Music Council*, **19**, 75-9.

Mensah, Atta Annan (1970), 'Principles Governing the Construction of the Silimba; a Xylophone Type Found Among the Lozi of Zambia', *Review of Ethnology*, **3** (3), 17-24.

Mensah, Atta Annan (1982), 'Gyil; the Dagara-Lobi Xylophone', *Journal of African Studies*, **9** (3), 139 ff.

Saighoe, Francis A. K. (1988), 'The Musical Behaviour of Dagaba Immigrants in Tarkwa, Ghana: a Study of Situational Change', unpublished PhD, Columbia University.

Seavoy, Mary H. (1982), *The Sisaala Xylophone Tradition*, unpublished PhD, University of California at Los Angeles.

Strumpf, Mitchell (1975), 'Ghanaian Xylophone Studies', *Notes on Education and Research in African Music*, (2), Legon: University of Ghana, 32-9.

7 The Making of Karimojong' Cattle Songs[1]

Kenneth Gourlay

> Thinking of the relationship between leader and group leads us
> closer to the character of the performance than thinking in terms
> of the analysis of musical forms. (Wachsmann, 1963)

The object of this article is to demonstrate the processes by which
Karimojong' cattle songs are produced, that is, to trace the stages from the
original impetus to composition to actual performance. As there are some
25,000 males in Karimojong' and thus probably 100,000 individual cattle
songs, this may appear an impossible task. Research has shown (Gourlay
1971), however, that, while no two cattle songs are the same, all are
similar, that is, they embody a musical tradition so rigid that it can almost
be expressed as a formula. I propose, therefore, to examine in detail a
small number of 'type-songs' and to attempt to relate them to their cultural
background.

The Karimojong' and their music

The Karimojong'[2] belong to the large group of East African pastoral
peoples which includes the Nuer and Dinka of the Sudan and the Turkana
and Maasai of Kenya. They inhabit a semi-arid plateau between 3,000 and
4,000 feet in height in north-eastern Uganda. Their mode of livelihood
reveals a means of adaptation for survival in the face of a harsh
environment, climatic uncertainty and social insecurity. Owing to scarcity
and irregularity of rainfall - the dry season from October to March is a
period of almost unrelieved drought - the men practise a transhumant
pastoralism, while the women attempt to grow sorghum in areas of
permanent settlement. Cattle represent not only wealth but are themselves
objects of value and emotional attachment; other cattle-owning peoples are
regarded as:

1. potential sources of supply for the enlargement of Karimojong' herds.
2. enemies (*ng'imoe*) for whom Karimojong' herds are potential sources of
    supply. Open inter-tribal warfare of the past has been replaced by
    clandestine cattle-raiding, but the human characteristics necessary for
    both are preserved and find expression in song. During the 30 years
    before independence, Karamoja as a 'closed district', shut off from the

rest of Uganda. The result of this isolation is that the people have kept their musical culture as a living tradition comparatively free from outside influence.

All Karimojong' music is vocal. Although musical instruments are used in some ceremonies, their purpose is simply to emphasise rhythm. Like most of the other cattle peoples of the Plains-Nilotic language group (Sutton, 1968: 81), the Karimojong' have no drums. Musically they exhibit two different styles: both are Karimojong' in that neither can be mistaken for the music of any other ethnic group, yet each is distinct from the other. The first comprises all traditional communal songs associated with ceremonial occasions such as *akiwudakin*, the cattle gathering at which young herdsmen seek the blessing of the elders before moving off with their herds to dry-season pastures. The second, with which we are concerned here, comprises individually composed songs associated with a particular individual which are performed on social occasions such as beer parties. This 'individual group' dichotomy[3] applies not only to musical style but, as will be seen later, is reflected in performance and is part of the karimojong' way of life itself.

Karimojong' cattle songs

Although the Karimojong' herd is the communal property of a family of full-brothers, every Karimojong' male is directly associated with his own favourite ox (or if fortunate, oxen), to which he shows genuine emotional attachment; he causes its horns to be knocked by a stone into a socially approved shape, cuts its ears to mark the number of human or animal 'enemies' killed, names it according to its colour, hide marking, horn shape or characteristics, styles himself its 'father' (*apa*) and 'immortalises' it in song.

A song in Akarimojong', irrespective of type, is *eete*. Ox-songs are referred to as: a) *eete elope elope* - a man's 'self' song, or one of which he is the 'owner';[4] b) *eete emong'* - literally, 'ox-song'; c) *emong'* - that is, 'ox', a shortened form of the latter. The context usually makes clear whether the song or the animal is intended. All songs are allegedly original compositions, the owner-composer alone having the right to act as cantor in performance,[5] which takes place in conjunction with a group of intimate personal friends.

The genesis of ox-songs

Men compose songs for a number of reasons:

1. Composition is a socially accepted practice, that is, everyone does it.
2. Ownership of a number of songs brings prestige. 'Every man has his song, most men have three or four, the good singer has very many (*ng'ulu alakak*).'
3. Ownership of songs about oxen may compensate for inability to own cattle, especially among young men.
4. Men compose songs because they enjoy doing so.

Composition would appear to be essentially a young man's activity. While older men preferred to sing communal songs, an under-thirty group invariably chose to sing their ox-songs. An older member of this group stated that his songs were composed 'long ago' (*kolong'sek*), that is, when he was a young man.

The basis of almost all songs is an event - not any event, but one which, in Freud's terminology, has a 'traumatic significance' for the singer (1955: 17). Thus one song arises from the experience of nearly being captured by the Pokot (Suk), whilst searching for a runaway animal, another concerns the killing of a lion while herding, several relate how enemy 'spies' are going round and round the temporary cattle camp (*aui*) searching for a way through the thorn-bush fence in order to steal the cattle. Songs thus exhibit two features: a) socially, they stress approved behaviour, for example, they need to show courage in the face of danger while herding; b) on the individual level they have therapeutic value in that, through re-enactment of the event in performance, the singer is able to overcome his fear and even to 'achieve enjoyment through active mastery of a formerly threatening' situation (Freud, 1955: 17).

The event is embodied in a more general topic chosen from the following:

1. Praise of the ox, particularly its size and strength.
2. The begging and giving of oxen - these socially approved practices promote inter-personal loyalty while songs about giving express public acknowledgement of the gift, enable the singer to show pride in his new possession, and perhaps hint that he would welcome a similar gift from others.
3. Characteristics of the ox, for example its fierceness, its habit of wanting to fight with gulls, or the way it breaks through the fence to enter a woman's field.

4. Tying and knocking the horns as described above, including such misfortunes as the need for repeated tying or the fact that the horns were knocked badly.
5. Herding and grazing and their attendant dangers from animals and men.
6. Raiding and warfare in order to obtain cattle.
7. A small group of songs expresses personal emotions or thoughts opposed to the prevailing social ethos but permissible because expressed in song,[6] for example a mission-educated young man sings, 'I wish we were told not to fight', and even a traditional herdsman exclaims: 'It is hard, hard to go and fight.'

The point here is that however different are the original events in the experience of the individual, his choice of subject matter is restricted by tradition to a small number of topics. Even when the thoughts expressed are outside this framework, the mode of expression, that is, song form, follows established practice.

The act of composition

Data on actual composition is difficult to obtain. One singer gave the following account: 'After we sang yesterday (i.e. at the recording session), I went home. I went to *edong'a* (the leaping dance). Someone gave me *ng'agwe* (beer). I got very drunk and started to sing this song. I greeted my girlfriend and she greeting me'.[7] The most prolific composer (I recorded 20 of his compositions) maintained that he 'made songs' while walking. Others mentioned dance expeditions to neighbouring settlements. All occasions involve some form of increased motor activity. Opinions differed as to whether words or music came first.[8] My own conclusion is that much of this process takes place subconsciously at a level where certain acceptable verbal patterns and similar musical patterns co-exist, and that attempted differentiation is a futile exercise.

The majority of songs recorded by a group of selected singers were of recent date - over two-thirds within the last three years and more than half within six months prior to recording. 'Composing a song' does not of course mean that the singer produces a series of different verses, each followed by a constant chorus. What it may mean can only be judged by examining what happens in actual performance. For purposes of exposition it is necessary to consider a) the setting and general manner of performance, b) verbal structure, c) musical sound. Only after this can one attempt a synthesis.

The setting and general features of performance

Ox-songs are performed primarily at beer-parties,[9] that is, in a man's hut or a compound within a settlement. Usually about a dozen people, all close friends, are invited. This is essential both on grounds of space and because every man must know the others' songs. The guests form a rough circle and sit, or recline, on the floor, adopting a relaxed posture, which is the keynote of performance. Almost any position can be used, provided it is possible for the singer to move his arms freely. Each person in turn drinks from a gourd in the centre, starting in a clockwise direction from the door, then proceeding in an anti-clockwise direction. When the urge to sing arises, the senior member present begins and continues until he has 'completed' the song. The probability is, however, that after being given what the others consider a 'fair time', he will be interrupted by a second person who now wishes to sing *his* song. This singer gives an accepted verbal signal, singing of the first song stops, the second begins at once, and the process continues with other singers until there is a pause for further beer or the singers exclaim that they are exhausted. Each song, which lasts from 10 to 15 minutes, may be considered as showing four stages, the length of each of which varies according to the position in the overall sequence. 1) *The start*: The opening words are almost invariably sung softly and at the lowest pitch level. 2) *'Warming up'*: singers place their hands over their ears in a 'resonating posture', volume increases slightly, and there is possibly a slight rise in pitch. 3) *'Identification'*: the soloist, now fully 'warmed up', 'identifies' himself with his ox by moving his arms rapidly into a formalised horn-shape whenever the name is mentioned. 4) *'Ornamentation'*: The soloist indulges in 'octave leaps', that is, one phrase is sung an octave higher than the preceding, then the original pitch is resumed, other singers shout out the names of their oxen (*akiwang'*), women, if present, break into shrill ululations, volume reaches its greatest intensity and the overall pitch level its highest point. In short, each song is a gradual crescendo and a sequence of songs a series of waves of sound.

Song structure

All songs follow an antiphonal leader-chorus pattern with the owner-composer as soloist. Songs thus require a minimum of two people for performance. Conceptually (and practically) a one-man song is an impossibility or, as the Karimojong' express it, 'not interesting'. The singer-composer begins with a four phrase 'opening lead', usually of the pattern A B C D or A B C C, that is, each phrase is different, or the third and fourth may be the same. This is then repeated by the group of 'helpers' and thereafter becomes the chorus. At a point of his own choosing during the singing of this chorus (or a repetition of it), usually in phrases 2 or 3, the composer introduces his first solo; singing of the chorus stops at once, and starts again from its beginning on completion of the solo. Again it is interrupted by a second solo and the process continues in this manner, either new solos or repetitions of those already sung being introduced during the singing of the chorus. If the singer fails to interrupt the group, they complete the chorus and the song ends.[10] This process may be illustrated as follows (S - soloist; C - chorus):

Opening Lead (S): /....A..../....B..../....C..../..C../..D../
                   (This is taken over and used as chorus)

Chorus: (C): /....A..../....B..../....C..../..C../..D../
              /....A..../....B....../....C..../Interrupted by soloist who starts first
                                                solo.

Sequence 1:S1: /..a../..a..//C:/   A / B / C   ) solo entry

Sequence 2:S2: /..b../..b..//C:/   A / B / C   ) solo entry

(Further sequences continue as above until failure of the soloist to enter leads to completion of chorus and end of song).

Final sequence

S: /....x..../....x..../ /C:/   A / B / C / C / D // end of song

Verbal structure

Verbally the chorus (or such phrases of it as are sung) remain constant throughout (except for the introduction, by agreement, of meaningless vocables at the beginning of phrases), and any variety is obtained through the solos alone. This is achieved by means of substitution or permutation. Solos consist of two, three or four phrases, the most common patterns being 'a a b b', or 'a a', that is, one or two phrases, each of which is repeated. The simplest method of obtaining variety in solos is substitution within one variable, as when the solos '_____ , *ianyubo emon anyekonikone a Riono*', 'O (so-and-so), have you seen the ox of your friend, Riono?' are completed by the insertion of the name of one of the singer's friends as the person addressed. Thirty-two different names occur in the course of 38 solos recorded, there being no other verbal change, finally one of the singer's friends found the repetitive element excessive and brought the song to a conclusion!

The same singer, however, demonstrates his manipulative skill in a further song on the subject of tying an ox's horns. The solos follow an 'a a b b' (or b1) pattern, that is, two phrases, each of which is repeated (though the second may be modified slightly). Phrase 1 consists of the following:

1. an opening unit (three alternatives):
    al: *aen* - (he) tied
    a2:   *ekateen* - I made (him) tie
    a3:   *aenen* - (he) has tied several times

2. one of 23 different personal names (p1-p23) which act as subject or object of the verb in 1.

3. a grammatical phrase describing the person in question: either (aa) *ninati ajokan ka eruori* - (the one) who is always pleasant of speech or (bb) *noloti - ka emong'* - the one with the ox (of such and such a colour. 8 different units: bb1 - bb8).

From these the singer produces such different examples as: 'Lokong', who is always pleasant of speech, tied (the ox)'. 'Sagal, who has a black and white ox, has tied (the ox) several times'. 'I made Lokwang, who has a reddish-brown ox, tie (the ox)', etc.

Phrase 2 consists of:

1. an operative verb:
    o1:   I shall catch (the ox) (*ekamunia*)
    o2:   it will be caught (*ikamunia*)
    o3:   it will be tied and tied again (*ilodio*)
    o4:   it will be chased (*iritario*)
    o5:   it will be tied (*eyenia*)

2. an expression of time:
    t1:   tonight (*lolo*)
    t2:   tomorrow (*taparac*)
    t3:   soon (*moi*)
    t4:   when the rain comes (*itimi*)
    t5:   in the far future (*rianu*)

   3.   a concluding phrase (cc):
          ngoloti kaamong' ka atuko - my big ox with a strap.

Further variety is obtained by allowing the expression of time to precede
the verb in some solos and to follow it in others. Hence such possibilities
as:

> Tonight I shall catch my big ox with a strap.
> Tonight it will be caught, will my big ox, with a strap.
> It will be tied and tied again tonight, etc.
> In the far future it will be chased, etc.

In the song as recorded the singer produced 28 solos and only repeated
himself once. This is not entirely surprising as, with such a high degree of
permutability the first phrase allows of 525 different combinations, the
second of 625. The entire solos can however, be reduced to a simple
formula (using the symbols given above) as follows:

$$\mathbf{(aa}$$

$$1 - 3 \quad 1 - 23 \qquad 1 - 8 / (t^{1-5} - o1)$$
$$\mathbf{a} \qquad \mathbf{-p} \qquad \mathbf{...... (bb} \qquad\qquad \mathbf{-cc}$$
$$(o^{2-5} - t1)$$

(The dotted line indicates restricted permutability)

Musical sound

In attempting to analyse the sound of the music, one is faced with what
Seeger (1961:78) calls the 'lingua-centric predicament' that 'one commu-
nicatory medium is relied upon to communicate about another because that
other does not do so'. To the non-specialist, Elizabeth Marshall Thomas'
assertion that songs sung by Dodos young men of northern Karamoja 'begin
and end with cries like bulls or oxen bellowing' (1965: 8) may give a more
accurate impression of the sound than the outline analysis that follows. For
the benefit of the specialist, however, the major characteristics of the sound
of Karimojong' music, as they appear in the selected type-examples
(transcriptions of which appear in the Appendix to this chapter) are as
follows:

Form: The opening lead-chorus consists of four phrases using an ABCC pattern which correlates with the verbal structure. The solo[11] is a single phrase repeated (aa), with the ending modified slightly in the repetition.

Tonal structure: Following Kolinski's classification (1961), the lead-chorus uses a penta 4 structure (aCde) with C as tonal centre, the solo a penta 5 (aCdega), again with C as tonal centre. Choruses tend to use a simpler structure than solos.

Tonal range: While the lead-chorus uses a 7 semitone range (729 cents), the solo covers a complete octave, that is, solos use a wider range.

Melodic movement: Using Kolinski's 1965 method of classification, the lead-chorus begins with a wide up-flexure over the entire tonal range (see diagram), leading up to two pendular movements (2, 3) and concluding with a narrow up-flexure. After the initial movement the whole process pivots on the tonal centre (C) which is strongly emphasised by monotone repetitions in phrases 3 and 4.

In contrast each phrase of the solo begins with a falling one-step movement (in the area of P5), leading to a narrow progressive down pendulum (M2). Taken in succession the two phrases from a wide up-flexure over 7 semitones at their point of juncture, and conclude with a narrow falling one-step movement (m3) leading to the chorus. Movement from the initial tone of Phrase 2 to the initial tone of the chorus forms a step-line-step indirect descent over an octave. Compared with the lead-chorus repetition is less pronounced, being divided evenly between the important tones c, e and a.

Melodic patterns: Certain patterns occur with such frequency as to be considered marks of style. They may almost be considered musical cliches, or at least expectancy patterns, from which songs are made and by which singers learn new songs rapidly. Thus phrase 2 of the lead-chorus (*a ngai-wo-ye*) - rm3-fm3 - is considered common property ('Anyone can use it'.) and five other examples have been transcribed used only in this position. The most common pattern, fm2-fm2 occurs as <u>edc</u> in the solo; both solo and chorus contain examples of fm2-fm3 while the lead-chorus has a falling pentachord (fm3-fm3).

Phrase length: The chorus is a-typical in that all phrases are of equal length (9 eighth notes). More representative patterns would be: 8-10-10-8,6-8-8-9,6-5-7-9, etc. Both solo phrases are the same length.

Tempo: The respective M.M. figures for the lead-chorus and solo are 154 and 180 npm (eighth notes per minute), i.e. neither is particularly fast. Measured in notes per minute, however, the lead-chorus still shows 154 npm but the solo has 279, that is, the rate of singing in solos is faster than that of choruses.

Rhythm: Neither the lead-chorus nor the solo show the prominently marked accentuation found in communal songs[12] and may almost be described as a form of 'free chanting'. The most prominent feature is a series of paired eighth notes (the first is accentuated slightly more than the second), especially in phrases 3 and 4 of the lead-chorus. (In the example the series is broken by a triplet on the opening three syllables of *Lo-si-a-cu-ba* - the verbal speech rhythm here correlating directly with the musical rhythm.) The final tones of phrases 1, 3 and 4 are shown as 'extensions' of the second eighth note of the pair. In practice, although unaccentuated, they may be prolonged and their length may vary in successive choruses. Triplets are more common in solos, especially at the opening (see example). Used in conjunction with an eighth note pair, they produce a 'lateral hemiola' effect.

Synthesis and development

Given the above data, it is possible to 'make' one's own cattle song, and one can only assume that a Karimojong' maker of songs 'knows' what is required of him in order to produce what is socially acceptable. In the course of social learning he has assimilated the approved verbal structures and the formal melodic and rhythmic patterns of the musical sound, and learned how to combine them. In this he resembles Levi-Strauss' 'bricoleur' whose 'universe of instruments' is closed and the rules of the game are to make do with 'whatever is at hand' (1962: 16). No Karimojong' composer, for example, would consider making a song with three phrases only in the opening lead. More important, no Karimojong' would want to! The individual composer's 'freedom' lies in recognising (if only unconsciously) and accepting the limitations imposed by, and operating through, the tradition of the group.

Karimojong' music derives much of its power from this conflict and resolution of inter-penetrating individual and group forces. As Wachsmann remarks in the quotation given at the head of this paper, thinking of this relationship 'leads us closer to the character of the performance than thinking in terms of the analysis of musical form' (Wachsmann, 1963). The relationship is particularly important in the study of Karimojong' music for it not only tells us *how* performances are carried out but suggests the reason why they take the form they do

In the first place, performance of an individual song requires the presence of both leader and group. If the song provides a man with the opportunity to display his skill and gain prestige, he cannot do so without the presence of a group of 'helpers'.

Secondly, although the solo-chorus relationship is at times hierarchical - the group are only allowed to perform their chorus part in its entirety twice and must stop immediately the soloist enters - they have other means of exerting their power: a) if the song itself does not employ acceptable verbal and musical patterns, that is, those known to the group, its performance can be terminated before the soloist wishes and through repeated discouragement, the song may disappear from the repertory; b) if the individual can terminate the group's chorus at will - and, as a song progresses, the soloist's point of entry in the chorus tends to move nearer towards the opening, that is, they have less and less to sing - they may retaliate by encroaching on his solo part, e.g. in the previously mentioned song in which the soloist merely substitutes the name of a different person addressed before asking 'Have you seen the ox?' and so on, the group gradually take over the singing of this phrase until the 'solo' consists solely of the insertion of a new name; c) as noted in outlining the procedure at a beer party, any member of the group can bring the song to an end when he chooses by giving the accepted verbal signal - and the soloist must accept this.

This leads to the third point - the importance of positional fluidity in a sequence of songs. Although every song requires a leader and group, no two successive songs have the same leader or entirely the same group. The individual who is the leader in one song reverts to group status as soon as he has finished. This is inevitable in a society without professional musicians, or (what amounts to the same thing) in which every man is a musician.

Song and society

Finally, the individual-group relationship expressed in the performance of cattle songs may be seen as one aspect of the individual-group relationship found in society as a whole. Two aspects should be noted: a) traditionally the Karimojong' have no chiefs but employ a cyclical age set system of authority which gives members of the senior age group power over members of the junior age group wherever they may be, irrespective of biological age; b) the system of transhumant pastoralism with its attendant dangers necessitates the development in young herdsmen of such qualities as initiative, endurance, courage and self-reliance. Since the herdsmen, as members of the junior age group, are all equal, their mode of existence tends to foster strong individualism and leadership through merit. In time of tension or danger, e.g. when raiding or being attacked, the leader establishes himself through ability and is accepted by the group, when the danger is over, he gives up his leadership and becomes a member of the group indistinguishable from the rest.

The problem is thus how to reconcile the need for strong individualism (which, taken to its conclusion, is the equivalent of anarchy) with social control. The solution is to permit individual initiative when required within the egalitarian junior age group, but to subordinate the entire group to its seniors. Although individual ox-songs are associated especially with young men, they may be seen embodying in performance the conflicting individual-group needs of society as a whole, and so reinforcing socially desirable behaviour and attitudes in a wider sphere. The song-leader is in control and has power to interrupt the chorus as leader of a raid is in control and has authority over his followers - but it is an authority based on consensus and lasts only for as long as the song or the raid itself. Once this role is accomplished, the leader returns to his position as a member of the group from which another member takes on the role of leader for another song or another activity. The positional fluidity of song performance thus appears as embodying social attitudes which permeate the entire culture.

In stressing the need to avoid 'structural studies pursued in isolation', (i.e. simply to analyse musical sound in the esoteric jargon of academies of music), Nketia maintains that African 'music is influenced ... by social, religious, economic or political considerations' and that such problems 'may be reflected in the very structure of the music' (1967: 25-6). Karimojong' cattle songs are an example of this process in action.

If this thesis is correct, it should be applicable to other aspects of Karimojong' music. One would thus expect that in traditional, communal songs, in which the values of the group as a whole are extolled, the individual (that is, the soloist) would be put in his place. This is exactly what happens. In section ceremonial songs the chorus, far from stopping immediately the soloist enters, is continuous, and the soloist is forced to squeeze in his little contribution as rapidly as possible on the chorus' final sustained tone. Instead of leading, he follows. Moreover, while the soloist at a beer party, faced with at most a dozen personal friends who sing softly at the opening so as not to drown him, stands a fair chance of being heard when both he and they are warmed up, the soloist at a communal group song, in competition with two hundred hefty males bawling and stamping, becomes little more that the individual's still, small voice that is all too often lost in the incessant din of society's leg bells.

Appendix: Musical examples

Notes

1. This article was originally written as a seminar paper for the Institute of African Studies of the University of Nairobi, and then published in the Institute's newsletter, *Mila*, vol. 2 no. 1 (1971). It is a summary of part of the author's PhD thesis, and is subject to qualifications which appear in that full version. The editor is grateful to Mrs Gourlay for permission to reprint her late husband's work.

2. For further details of the anthropological background necessaary for an understanding of the Karimojong' and kindred peoples, reference should be made to Dyson-Hudson (1966), Gulliver (1955), Gulliver and Gulliver (1953) and Farina (1965).

3. The terms 'individual' and 'group' are used in preference to 'individual' and 'community' or 'traditional'. While songs of the first type are associated with particular individuals, songs of the second are associated with groups within the community rather than with the community as a whole. Thus there are songs of men's generation groups, (such as the *Ng'imoru* - Mountains, *Ng'igetei* - Gazelles) women's emblem groups (see Gourlay, 1970) and sections of the *Ng'ibokora* (Partridge people), *Ng'itomei* (Elephant people) or *Ng'ipian*

(Spirit people), but not of the entire Karimojong' community. 'Traditional' is rejected because of its associations. While groups songs are of anonymous origin and have been passed from one generation to the next, the concept of a 'living tradition', as exemplified in the ability to trace ancestry back through numerous generations, is alien to Karimojong' ways of thought which rarely go beyond their grandparents and are conditioned by the idea of 'cyclical' progression rather than 'linear' genealogy.

4. The term *elope* can mean 'self', for example *aiong' elope* 'I myself', or it can refer to ownership, for example the head of a settlement is known as *elope*, the 'owner'.

5. On rare occasions a man may allow his closest male friend (or even his wife, if present) to act as cantor. The only examples in my experience, however, were when a) the soloist was incapacitated by a fit of coughing and b) a young and inexperienced singer needed the 'help of an older one to keep the song going'.

6. For the use of song as an artefact which permits 'expression of the inexpressible' that is 'repudiates' the content while the form remains 'non-repudiable', see Devereux (1961).

7. These facts were confirmed by independent witnesses. Previously the singer had maintained that he had only two ox songs, the one he now proceeded to sing was completely new.

8. The question is important as Akarimojong' is a tonal language and it might be argued that the tonal patterns of speech (that is, words) would thus determine melodic movement of the music. Investigation shows that, while there is a tendency towards correlation between the two, this is by no means absolute. Moreover, the existence of correlation does not in itself establish the primacy of either.

9. They may be performed at feasts - which are only glorified beer parties - but those taking part in the singing will be limited to a man's intimate friends.

10. This procedure is not always followed in practice. While a good singer invariably interrupts the chorus, those with less proficiency are often given a further chance, that is, the chorus is repeated a second, or even a third time to give the soloist the opportunity of breaking into it.

11. In order to give a more accurate picture of the sound *as heard* (that is, to avoid concluding the analysis part way through a descending movement) the term 'solo' here includes the opening tone of the chorus which follows.

12. In the Elephant Dance, for example, in which the movements of the elephant are mimed, the tempo is determined by the slow movements of the animal and its ponderous footsteps marked by a series of slow, heavily accentuated beats. Similarly, processional dances at which cattle

are driven take their tempo and rhythm from the slow movement of the beasts.

Bibliography

Devereux, G. (and La Barre, W.) (1961), 'Art and Mythology', in Bo Kaplan (ed.), *Studying Personality Cross-Culturally*, New York, Evanston and London: Harper and Row, pp. 361-403.

Dyson-Hudson, N. (1966), *Karimojong' Politics*, Oxford: Clarendon Press.

Farina, F. (1965), *Nel Paese dei Bevitori di Sangue*, Bologna: Editrice Nigrizi.

Freud, S. (1955), *Beyond the Pleasure Principle*, London: Hogarth Press.

Gourlay, K. A. (1970), 'Trees and Anthills: Songs of Karimojong' Women's Groups', *African Music*, **4** (4), 114-212.

Gourlay, K. A. (1971), 'Studies in Karimojong' Musical Culture', PhD thesis, University of East Africa

Gulliver, P. and Gulliver, P. H. (1953), *The Central Nilo-Hamites*, London: International African Institute.

Gulliver, P. H. (1955), *The Family Herds*, London: Routledge and Kegan Paul.

Kolinski, M. (1961), 'Classification of Tonal Structures', *Studies in Ethnomusicology*, **1**, 38-76.

Kolinski, M.(1965), 'The Structure of Melodic Movement - a New Method of Analysis. Revised Version', *Studies in Ethnomusicology*, **11**, 95-120.

Levi-Strauss, C. (1962) (English trans. 1966), *The Savage Mind*, London: Weidenfeld and Nicholson.

Nketia, J. H. K. (1967), 'Musicology', in D. Brokenshaw and M. Crowder (eds), *Africa in the Wider World*, Oxford and London: Pergamon Press, pp. 12-35.

Seeger, C. (1961), 'Semantic, Logical and Political Considerations Bearing upon Research into Ethnomusicology', *Ethnomusicology*, **5** (2), 77-80.

Sutton, J. E. G. (1968), 'The Settlement of East Africa', in B. A. Ogot and J. A. Kieran (eds), *Zamani: a Survey of East African History*, Nairobi, Kampala and Arusha: East African Publishing House/Longmans, pp. 69-99.

Thomas, E. M. (1965), *Warrior Herdsmen*, London: Secker and Warburg.

Wachsmann, K. P. (1963), 'Musicology in Uganda', *Journal of the Royal Anthropological Institute*, **83**, 50-57.

8 *Embaire* Xylophone Music of Samusiri Babalanda

Gerhard Kubik

My first encounter with musicians of Busoga dates back to November 1959, when I began to record blind *budongo* (lamellophone) performers at the Agricultural Training Centre for the blind, Salama, south of Mukono near Lake Victoria.[1] On 8 December I started to take regular lessons in Kiganda music (*amadinda* xylophone and *baakisimba* drumming) from Evaristo Muyinda, a Kabaka's musician who had also taught some of the blind trainees at Salama. A large *akadinda* xylophone stood in a music pavilion in the residential area of the training centre, and it was regularly played by blind trainees of various ethnic backgrounds, mostly Basoga who had learned Kiganda music from Evaristo Muyinda and the resident Muganda music teacher, Yusufu Bosa. There were also some aliens to the tradition, mostly 'Northerners' (Acooli, Langi etc.) who were trying their hands at the xylophone.

Through my study and practice of *amadinda* and *akadinda* with Evaristo Muyinda and my contact with royal musicians at the *lubirii* (king's enclosure), I was persuaded to assume that southern Uganda - or at least Buganda - was an area where rigid composition techniques and some form of standardisation dominated the scene, providing a relatively narrow margin for stylistic and organisational variation from group to group. While this was perhaps true to a certain extent among disciples of Mr Muyinda, I gradually discovered the relatively wide margin of stylistic variation among performers from the eastern bank of the Nile river: Busoga. I recall a memorable event that took place one afternoon in early February 1960 at the *akadinda* in Salama. In the middle of my usual practice with some of my blind partners, Yusufu Bosa announced that a sighted visitor had come from Busoga who would play a piece. It all occurred very quickly, but fortunately the tape recorder was still running. The visitor and Yusufu took the sticks from us rather abruptly and sat down opposite each other. The visitor began striking part A, with Yusufu interlocking with part B. They played a song from the *embaire* tradition of Busoga: '*Mobuka* ng'komera'.[2] Since Kiganda and Kisoga instrumental tunings are in principle identical - all tuned to a tempered pentatonic framework - there was no problem in using the *akadinda* for this music. What electrified me, however, was the *manner* in which they played this song. I immediately noticed that the combination of the two parts was analogous to that of *amadinda* music: there were two interlocking tone rows (in this song each with 18 strokes). However, the way they played them was remote from the faithful striking of *okunaga* and *okwawula* parts as I had learned under Evaristo Muyinda's tutorship. The two musicians played them as if they were merely abstract lines of orientation, without actually striking all the notes. The accentuation technique was so overwhelming that the original tone rows seemed to dissolve. What resulted was a highly dissective, even interruptive sequence of fast impulses which constituted an overall disjunctive melody, probably representing the vocal theme of '*Mobuka ng'komera*'. My first impression was that they were improvising, but it turned out later through analysis of the tape recording that melodic improvisation was as minimal as it was in Kiganda styles. The constant reshuffling of patterns and reconfiguring of the whole was mainly achieved through accent technique.

Would I ever learn this? Apparently there existed no teaching methods to transmit the art of reconfiguration by accents. My experience that afternoon, however, generated in me an intense desire to do field work in Busoga, a cultural area where so much in the history of the court music of Buganda had apparently originated (Wachsmann, 1971). To organise a field tour immediately thereafter proved difficult, as all my potential companions were blind. This trip only materialised at the end of December 1962. It was the blind *kadongo* (lamellophone) player Waiswa Lubogo who eventually introduced me to Kisoga music in his home village at Bumanya, Saza Bulamoji. As memorable as my first encounter with *embaire* music had been, so was our journey on 1 January 1963, from Salama to Kamuli by road and train and finally on foot, with Waiswa's 35 kg wooden suitcase in my hand on a mile-long walk to the village of his parents.

I was very curious to learn how the third part performed on a fifteen-note *embaire* would be developed. In Salama, our Musoga visitor, together with Yusufu Bosa, had only played the interlocking basic parts. A third player was not found. Would the third player in *embaire* music duplicate an inherent pattern which appeared in the bass, as in *amadinda* music of Buganda?

The first thing I observed in Bumanya with the two groups we recorded in 1963, those led by Venekenti Nakyebale and Yonasani Mutaki, was that the players sitting opposite each other combined the basic tone rows in parallel octaves in the same way as their counterparts in Buganda, but the third player was not restricted to only two notes, as in the *amakoonezi* technique on an *amadinda*. In principle he had five notes at his disposal, which were, however, not always fully used.[3] I noticed further that, although the third player's pattern was basically in an octave relationship with notes distributed across the combining basic tone rows, it could not be determined from which layer of the total image he had picked the tones to form his pattern. Apparently it was *not* an inherent pattern. It seemed that the conscious exploitation of a subjective auditory effect in humans, or what I had described as inherent or subjective patterns in Kiganda music (Kubik, 1960: 12), did not play so prominent a role in Busoga.

Four more years passed before I got back into Busoga for a more intensive survey. This time I travelled in the company of ethnologist Maurice Djenda from the Central African Republic and John Mwase, a Musoga who was by profession a policeman and musician, and who had worked in the national ensemble called Heart Beat of Africa. We had met him at the Busoga District Council near Jinja, and he was willing to accompany us to various villages, beginning with a courtesy visit to Waiswa Lubogo. This survey was carried out during another somewhat shorter stay in Uganda from 6 November 1967, to 31 January 1968. Besides many recordings of other Kisoga traditions, such as *enthongoli* (lyre), *enkwanzi* (panpipes), *amagwala* (horns), the ground-bow *musokolome* and *budongo* groups, we concentrated in this endeavour on *embaire* music. In our overall 1967/68 recorded sample, *embaire* music is in fact represented with no less than 72 items recorded from various performers. In addition, I had also recorded many of these items on 8 mm film, shot for the purpose of later transcription from the silent movie.

Our aim in 1967/68 was to carry out a systematic sampling of many different groups and their repertoire to allow for a comparative analysis of their styles and techniques. In Buganda this had proved increasingly difficult. But in Busoga we were able to record and (in part) film four different *embaire* groups within only a few days in January 1968. The first was a group using an instrument of 15 slats. This group played together with a *enkwanzi* (panpipe) ensemble at village Namisambya I. The other three groups, led by the following musicians, had instruments with a varying number of slats: Sepiriano Kabanda, aged about 20 and from a village near Namisambya, and George Mulabiza, about 18, both had xylophones with 14 slats, while Samusiri Babalanda, about 16, had a large instrument with 18 slats.

In the present context I can only pick one group from this sample: that led by Samusiri Babalanda, which was recorded and filmed near Namisambya I village. My account should be considered preliminary. It focuses only on the xylophone combination technique, not considering the drums, rattle, and so on, which could also be analysed.

I have chosen the group led by Samusiri Babalanda because he was considered the most expert by local residents, and the organisation of his group and what they played deviated from all the others I had recorded before, demonstrating perhaps the breadth of stylistic variety that existed in xylophone music within Busoga at that time. In contrast to the other groups, Samusiri's included four (and not only three) performers on the *embaire*. Evidently each group in Busoga was not merely an exponent of traditional music, but also had a shot of idiosyncratism and personal style.

The presence of four performers made me curious to learn what the players C and D were up to on the smaller slats of the xylophone. What were their tasks? How did they combine their parts? The analysis of Samusiri Babalanda's music from film - an approach I have applied in other African cultures as well - should inform us specifically about the organisation and structure of instrumental performance within this particular group. This approach can then be pursued with a similar evaluation of other *embaire* groups recorded in Busoga, thus demonstrating the advantage of contextual documentation.

Figure 8.1 Basic recording data

Tape No./Track/Item No.	No. 119, track 2, items 1-6
Place of recording	near Namisambya I, Busoga District, Uganda
Date of recording	January 1968
Group leader	Samusiri Babalanda, male, aged *c*.16
Number of performers	9 (4 performers on the xylophone, 3 on different drums, 1 on the flat rattle, 1 hand-clapping)
Performers' first language	Lusoga
Type of ensemble music	*embaire* (log xylophone) music
Musical pieces	1. *Wairugala* (*embaire* performance with drums)
	2. *Baala ndolo* (*embaire* performance with drums)
	3. *Empata egwana mukaire* (*embaire* performance with drums)
	4. *Omukaire amera envu* (*embaire* performance without any accompaniment)
	5. Kisoga rhythm patterns performed with drums and rattle.
	6. Tuning of the *embaire*

Of the six recorded items, only the first four were entire pieces performed on the xylophone. Extracts of these were filmed with 8 mm normal silent movie film in colour at 24 frames per second. After Item 4, I made a few more shots of the xylophone-playing musicians, including close-ups, with the tape recorder no longer running.

The construction of log xylophones in southern Uganda and the materials used for them have been described in detail by several authors.[4] Samusiri's was a large type of xylophone and fell within the margin of variation suggested in those descriptions. It may therefore suffice to reiterate that the instrument's basis is two parallel banana stems and that the keys are separated by thin, and in principle straight, sticks cut from nzo wood (bot. *Teclea nobilis*), which are pierced into the banana stems. One detail, however, that was not noticeable in Samusiri's xylophone was that the slats had been tuned by removing broad chunks of wood from the *upper* middle surface of each slat, especially from those of lower tuning, with apparently only very little taken from the underside.

The accompanying instruments consisted of a flat rattle made of sheet iron and three drums. In addition there was one person clapping hands. Two of the drums were of the type Wachsmann used to call 'Uganda drum', with a cylindro-conical body shape and two skins connected with leather strings. One of them was played with two hands, the other with the left palm and a stick in the right hand. Another was the tall drum, called *mugabe* in many areas of Busoga. It is a relatively small specimen and is held by the musician under the left arm as he sits in a squatting position.

In principle, the four players of the xylophone each had two sticks at their disposal, but musician C only played with one stick, which he held in his right hand. The playing sticks or beaters in this *embaire* group were all about 25-28 cm long and 2.5 cm in diameter. They were held firmly and yet in a flexible way. In conformity with other log xylophone traditions in southern Uganda and elsewhere, the slats were always struck at their extremities, from an angle and at a point in the upper half of the playing stick, as seen in the pictures. An idiosyncratic mannerism of this group (perhaps also fashionable among other *embaire* groups at that time) was to sit with the legs crossed. This was probably by order of the leader, since all four players sat in that manner. The rattle player used a motional technique typical for flat rattles, shaking it sideways and tapping the top of the rattle alternatively with the thumbs while holding it between his two hands.

The tuning of Samusiri Babalanda's xylophone

When their performance ended, I recorded the tuning of the log xylophone,[5] first sounding a pitch pipe (A4 = 440 Hz), then tapping each slat slowly with one of the sticks three times proceeding from the smallest to the biggest slat. In September 1991 I measured the recorded pitches using a Korg Chromatic Tuner WT - 12 (32 Hz ~ 4.2 Hz) from the original tape recording, which was played from a UHER 4000 Report Monitor reel-to-reel tape recorder. For the calculation of cents versus hertz (and vice versa), I used the standard Table of Cents provided by African Music Research (Director: Hugh Tracey) for fieldworkers. The accuracy of the measurements and calculations should be within +/- 5 cents. This figure is acceptable in the comparative study of African tunings, and well within the margin of tolerance of present-day musicians in southern Uganda, as the results of recent experiments carried out with Baganda and Basoga informants by Peter Cooke suggest (Cooke, 1991).

Although the overtone structure of xylophones in southern Uganda is complex (see Schneider and Beurmann, 1990), its discussion would have little relevance in the present context. Musicians in southern Uganda share a musical culture whose tonal ideas are *not* inspired by the natural harmonic series (which is common elsewhere in eastern and southern Africa). Only indirectly do they pay attention to overtone structures as a welcome determinant of the individually of a note on the xylophone or in timbre sequences on rattles, drums, etc. When tuning different instruments together, such as in a group that incorporates a set of *enkwanzi* panpipes and an *embaire* xylophone, attention focuses on pitch or on the 'voice' (*eddoboozi*) of a slat, pipe, etc. - that is, on what makes the sounds identical and *not* what makes them different (the timbre).

Figure 8.2 below gives the tuning in hertz (Hz) and cents of Samusiri's xylophone. Each slat is identified by a cipher, either written plain, underlined, top-lined or double top-lined according to position. These same ciphers are also used for the transcription of the music, thus identifying the slat to be struck. The ciphers ascribed to each slat in Figure 8.2 thereby serve as a key to the transcriptions.

Figure 8.2 Tuning of Samusiri Babalanda's xylophone (recorded January 1968, measured 4 September 1991)

Notational symbol	Hz (hertz, cps)	Cents	Cents intervals
3	1310	1135	
2	1150	910	225
1	996	661	249
5	868	421	240
4	773	221	200
3	667	1165	256
2	587	945	220
1	526	755	190
5	450	486	269
4	392	246	240
3	341	5	241
2	297	963	242
1	260	733	230
5̲	231	526	207
4̲	200	281	245
3̲	179	85	196
2̲	152	1006	279
1̲	130	733	273

The tuning of a new *embaire* can be a laborious undertaking, especially if there is no reference note available for the tuning process, such as from an old xylophone, flute, etc. Prominent overtones, particularly in the lowest keys, distract the ear from the perception of relevant pitches, thus making it difficult to decide upon the desired note. In this cultural area, assessing pitch by ear means to compare first a slat with its neighbour, then jump to the next step in either direction, and eventually to check the octaves. These measures facilitate decisions about relevant pitch. On Samusiri's *embaire*, the three lowest keys 1, 2 and 3 had obtrusive overtones which made it difficult for me as well, even with the aid of the Korg Tuner, to detect what the relevant frequencies were, while it is clear that the musicians must have focused on that part of the spectrum which they could interpret as representing the *lower octave* of 1, 2 and 3. That some of the octaves in *embaire* tunings are typical friction octaves (for example 2 = 2 is minus 43 cents and 3 = 3 is as much as minus 80 cents) makes no difference. Friction octaves are deliberate and serve to make individual melodic lines at different tonal levels more distinctive.

The overall impression of the tuning of this *embaire* (as shown in Figure 8.2) corroborates earlier experiences in Buganda and Busoga (see Wachsmann, 1967). Most intervals fluctuate around values between 230 and 270 cents, while some are a bit smaller, as the step from 4 to 5 with 200 cents, from 1 to 2 with 190, from 5 to 1 with 207 and from 3 to 4 with 196 cents. There is no regularity, however in the distribution of these smaller intervals, and we know that on other specimens of xylophones or lamellophones they can be distributed differently over the range. My conclusion therefore is that it is not intended in this music to establish a whole tone/mirror third dichotomy, but on the contrary to establish an equal temperament within the pentatonic framework. Consequently, there cannot be any concepts of modality either. Instead there are concepts of tonal relationships by which every progression to a neighbouring note, in any direction and from any point of departure, is considered analogous and distances of five notes, struck simultaneously (for example 1 and 1, or 1 and 1), are considered identical. The difference between these octave notes is in their tonal size (one is *oguloboozi*, another *eddoboozi*, another *akaloboozi*), as in the difference between the voices of men, women and children. Equally skipping one step on the xylophone from any starting point, in any direction, is thought to yield intervals that are analogous, in this case relationships somewhat close to a fourth.

Technical terminology from the performers and their tasks in an *embaire* group varies across Busoga; there is no standardised terminology. In this chapter I am identifying the players as A, B, C and D, in order of their entrance. Normally *embaire* music is performed with only three players. The two groups that we had recorded in Busoga in 1963, led by Venekenti Nakyebale and Yonasani Mutaki, used this terminology:

A = *mulangalira*
B = *mugoiti*
C = *mudumi*

Another group, that of the blind *embaire* player Slaiman Waida, aged about 18, whom I recorded repeatedly at Salama in December 1967, used these designations:

A = *omunazi*
B = *omutawuzi*
C = *omukubi ow'obutono*

For comparison, Klaus Wachsmann in Trowell and Wachsmann (1953: 320) summarises different designations (informants not identified) as:

A = *omuleterezi or munsansazi*
B = *omwauzi or omutabuzi*
C = *omuleezi or omukubi w'obuto*

Unfortunately, Samusiri Babalanda, concentrating on performance, showed little inclination to discuss theory with us, and for tactical reasons we abstained from posing penetrating questions about terminology, including his designations for the accompanying drums. Of course, I would have liked to know how he conceptualised the tasks of players C and D in particular, but we observed that he was somewhat evasive and therefore did not want to risk the success of the filming by imposing interruptions.

Playing areas and cinematographic documentation

The lowest slat on the *embaire* of this group was not used by any of the performers. This cuts down the effective range of this eighteen-note xylophone to only seventeen, a number of slats frequently encountered in southern Ugandan log xylophones (see table in Trowell and Wachsmann, 1953: 320). One can speculate about why note 1 was not used. Sometimes log xylophone makers produce surplus keys, but it could also be that Samusiri Babalanda and his performers were not happy with its extreme distortions through overtones. Unfortunately I did not ask the musicians while I was there. But during my evaluation, the moment came to decide how to number the slats (see Figure 8.3). At one point I thought it would be realistic to begin with the No. 1 on the second slat from below; however, lacking crucial comment from the musicians, this would have been difficult to justify, although it would have seemed logical in view of the actual playing areas.

Figure 8.3   Playing areas of the four musicians at the xylophone in Samusiri Babalanda's group as in 'Wairugala' (item 1)

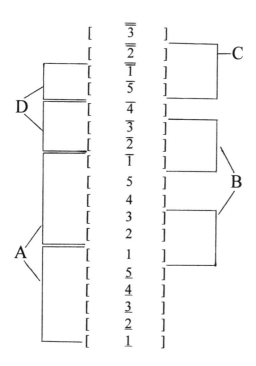

However, this is a minor issue, since the transcriptions can be renumbered at any time, if the need arises. Regarding the playing areas for A, B, C and D, the following observations can be made:

1. The performers adhere to their playing areas in the different pieces, but with small changes.[6]
2. Player A uses the full range of ten slats, with five notes for each hand to play in parallel octaves. He sits with the lower keys at his right hand.
3. Players A and B sit diagonally opposite each other; in fact, the playing area of B is shifted by four slats upward in relation to that of A. This is

remarkable because in several log xylophone styles elsewhere, especially in southeast Africa (Kubik, 1972), the two performers interlocking their parts do not sit directly but rather obliquely opposite each other.

4. The same applies to the range of players C and D, who play in the upper register and whose playing areas are shifted in relation to each other. In addition the different playing areas of the performers are linked in a way which one can schematically represent with square brackets hooked into each other, alternately in the order A-B-D-C.

Figure 8.4   Playing areas and camera position

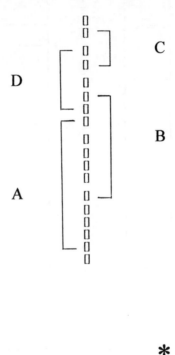

For a comfortable movie documentation of this arrangement, giving maximum visibility to the actions of the four players, I chose an oblique angle for the camera, which was positioned about 1.6 m above the ground and about 1 m from the xylophone at the point marked in Figure 8.4. Due to the constraints imposed by the technical equipment, I was only able in 1967/68 to record the complete pieces on tape, not on film; I could film only short extracts of each piece. Maurice Djenda was responsible for the continuous sound recording, while I filmed approximately 10 to 15 seconds of each piece from a suitable angle, beginning somewhere in the middle of the performance. In view of the enormous speed of this music, this proved sufficient to get several repetitions of the cyclic structures on movie film. Naturally, the variations (especially by player B) were not covered in full by the short shots, but melodic variation is not such a prominent feature of this music that one would have to follow it from the beginning to the end. In retrospect, while evaluating the film material, I found that the short extracts I had intuitively chosen for movie documentation revealed in all cases theme and cycle and, in some, even a few variations.

Elsewhere I have explained the technique of transcribing from film (Kubik, 1972). It is not necessary therefore, to reproduce here the original graph paper containing my frame-by-frame transcriptions of the four pieces obtained from this group. Instead, I will only present the final transference into cipher notation. Cipher or number notation, as some prefer to call it, was first used in Buganda in 1962, in the circle of Evaristo Muyinda. It can be employed with equal benefit for the transcription and notation of music in Busoga. When transcribing xylophone music from film, it is not necessary to consult the sound recordings in order to get an accurate picture of what is played. Frame-by-frame transcription proceeds from the movement alone. Even the speed of the music can be calculated from the movie record, using the simple formula

$$f : p \times 60 = \text{M.M.}$$

These symbols stand for: f = frames per second, and p = the distance between elementary pulses expressed in frames. Here one only has to look at the original transcription on graph paper and note the shortest average distance between two entries (strokes). In the present case, p was two frames for all four items. The speed of the elementary pulsation of this music therefore is: 24:2 x 60 = 720 M.M. This means that the basic tone rows performed by each player were sounded at a speed of 360 M.M.

The only way that such fast music can be played is by thinking of the patterns and tone rows in their own right, as the late A. M. Jones would have said. This excludes any overt or hidden concept of syncopation. The moment player B enters with his tone row (by falling between two notes of the tone row of player A) he thinks of his line as on-beat. And so does player C, who reshuffles the total image from the viewpoint of his own relativistic perception by grouping the beat in terms of three elementary pulses. He also does not syncopate, neither against player A nor B. The only performer whose motional behaviour could be discussed as to where he feels the beat lies is player D, since he plays a pattern which in itself consists of two interlocking lines. However, since no human being can split his or her brain and perceive both left and right hand lines simultaneously as the beat, it must be in one of them. Alternatively it is also inconceivable that the player refers his doubled strokes *only* to the elementary pulsation without any concept of beat because the phrase is structured regularly. The elementary pulsation is an *unstructured* reference line of fast impulses, unconsciously steering a performance in African music.

So where is the beat then? My view is that it lies in player D's right-hand notes, that is, in the first stroke of each pair of strokes. There are comparative and also psychological reasons for this.[7]

Transcription and commentary

Notational symbols:	number	=	stroke
	point	=	non-stroke
	+	=	entrance of part B
	*	=	entrance of parts C or D

The entry points for musicians B, C and D have been marked in the transcription as they occur in the *sound* recordings.

Item 1: 'Wairugala'

Explanation of the title: 'When the Europeans were here (in Uganda), they used to punish us terrible. Why have you punished Africans?'
Filmed extract: 196 frames. Parallel recording: Arch No. B 12615.
Transcription - Elementary pulsation: 720 M.M./cycle: 30 pulses.

```
A    5.1̄.5.5.4.1̄.5.5.5.5.4.2.5.4.4.
     5̲.1.5̲.5̲.4̲.1.5̲.5̲.5̲.5̲.4̲.2.5̲.4̲.4̲.
                           +
B    .2̄.1̄.3̄.2̄.1̄.3̄.2̄.1̄.3̄.2̄.1̄.3̄.2̄.1̄.3̄
     .2.1.3.2.1.3.2.1.3.2.1.3.2.1.3

C    .2̿..5̄..2̿..1̄..2̿..5̄..2̿..2̿..2̿..1̄.

D 1  5̄..1̄..5̄..1̄..5̄..5̄..5̄..1̄..5̄..1̄..
     ..4̿..3̄..4̿..3̄..4̿..3̄..4̿..2̄...4̿..3̄
```

Observations:

Already the first piece on our film is somewhat a surprise. The theme of player A is a tone row of 15 strokes, which results, after combination with the part of player B, in a cycle of 30 elementary pulses. Thus Busoga provides us right from the beginning with evidence that irregular form or cycle numbers (deviating from the usual 12, 16, 23, 32, etc.) are not only common in the esoteric context of Buganda's court music,[8] but also elsewhere in southern Uganda.

Player B at the point marked (+) enters with his part. He divides the 15 strokes by interlocking technique with a repeating group of three notes, beginning this formula with its *lowest* component. As it turned out after examining the other pieces, this three-note group is something like a standard formula for player B in this type of *embaire* music; it is not restricted to just one piece. Structurally, therefore, one cannot consider the tone rows of A and B to be equivalent. Although they combine to form the total image (or 30 pulses in this case), each on its own has a separate identify. Part A, with its tone row of 15 strokes, is an irregular chain, showing no symmetry, in contrast to other pieces, for example Item 2 (see below). Player B inserts what can be described as a formula. Evidently, part A is a *theme* while part B is not.

The cycle number 30 can be divided by three or by five. How do the performers conceptualize this tone row? Do they divide it or do they think of it as an irregular (non-metric) chain? Looking at each part separately, A, B, C and D, we find some configurations suggesting threes, fours, etc. but no constituent notes in any part recur even regularly at a distance of five elementary pulses or five individual strokes. This provides sufficient evidence that there is no structuring by five in this piece, which makes it also unlikely that any of the participant performers would conceptualise of his pattern in a grouping by five, for example as a kind of 5/4 metre.[9]

To the degree that players A and B follow a standard combination technique, so does the upper pair, players C and D. Here, the most surprising observation to be made is that players C and D reshuffle and reconfigure the total image in a way to combine their parts in *triple-division interlocking* (i.e., as on an *akadinda*). Player C strikes a line whose notes are in principle in unison (or in octave relationship) (as on an *amadinda*). After player C reinterprets it all as a 'triple rhythm', player D then interlocks just like an *omwawuzi* on the *akadinda* would, except with one small, but important difference: just before his cycle ends, to be repeated immediately, it has a rhythmic kink. The right hand stroke on slat 2 is anticipated by one pulse, creating the sequence:

$$. \ \bar{1} \ . \ . \ \bar{5} \text{ and so on}$$
$$\bar{4} \ . \ \bar{2} \ . \ . \text{ and so on}$$

which for a moment interrupts or delays the flow of this otherwise regular motion. Certainly it must have some function in the overall combination - but what kind of function does it have? Is it a cue to announce the imminent repetition of musician D's cycle to begin with note 4 (see the transcription of Item 1)? Or is it an aborted vertical hemiola-style (Brandel, 1959: 110)? Alternatively, could it be language based?

Item 2: 'Baala Ndolo'

Explanation: 'The girl is already sleeping. We are late. We are not going to wake her up.' This song refers to the well-known custom of bride kidnapping in Busoga on wedding days.
Filmed extract: 288 frames. Recording: B 12616.
Transcription - Elementary pulsation: 720 M.M>/cycle: 36 pulses.

```
A    4 . 5 . 5 . 3 . 3 . 2 . 2 . 5 . 5 . 4 . 5 . 5 . 3 . 3 . 2 . 2 . 2 . 2 .
     4 . 5 . 5 . 3 . 3 . 2 . 2 . 5 . 5 . 4 . 5 . 5 . 3 . 3 . 2 . 2 . 2 . 2 .
                           +
B    . 1 . 5 . 2 . 1 . 3 . 2 . 1 . 5 . 2 . 1 . 5 . 2 . 1 . 3 . 2 . 1 . 2 . 2
     . 1 . 5 . 2 . 1 . 3 . 2 . 1 . 5 . 2 . 1 . 5 . 2 . 1 . 3 . 2 . 1 . 2 . 2

C    . 1 . . 5 . . 1 . . 2 . . 1 . . 5 . . 1 . . 5 . . 1 . . 2 . . 1 . . 2 .

D 1  4 . . 5 . . 4 . . 5 . . 4 . . 5 . . 4 . . 5 . . 4 . . 5 . . 4 . . 5 . .
  r  . . 3 . . 2 . . 3 . . 2 . . 3 . . 2 . . 3 . . 2 . . 3 . . 2 . . 2 . 2 .
```

Observations:

In contrast to Item 1, the theme introduced here by player A has a bipartite structure, each section having nine notes, totalling 18. There is a clear progression between more than one tonality step, the first centred on 5, the final (at the end of the tone row) on 2. Player B falls in between, with a cycle consisting of groups of threes, incorporating the following variants:

    (a) 3 . 2 . 1 . ;(b) 5 . 2 . 1 . ;   (c)   2 . 2 . 1 . .

These are then strung in a certain order to form a tone row that is more similar to the tone row of player A than was the case with part B in Item 1.

The combination of lines performed by players C and D follows the standard procedure already discussed, and at the end of the cycle of player D there is the expected 'rhythmic kink'.

.5̄..4̄
2̲.2̲..

only melodically somewhat different from the corresponding phrase in item 1.

Item 3: 'Empata Egwana Mukaire'

Explanation: 'It isn't good to lose one's hair while one is still young and become a baldhead.'
Filmed extract: 338 frames. recording B 12617.
Transcription - Elementary pulsation: 720 M.M./cycle: 36 pulses (theme, as played from frames 39 to 110).

```
A    4.5.3.3.2.5.4.3.5.4.4.4.4.2.5.4.3.5.
     4̲.5̲.3̲.3̲.2̲.5̲.4̲.3̲.5̲.4̲.4̲.4̲.4̲.2̲.5̲.4̲.3̲.5̲.
                                        +
B    .1̄.3̄.2̄.1̄.2̄.2̄.1̄.3̄.2̄.1̄.3̄.2̄.1̄.2̄.2̄.1̄.3̄.2̄
     .1.3.2.1.2.2.1.3.2.1.3.2.1.2.2.1.3.2

C    ..3̄..2̄..2̄..2̄..3̄..2̄..3̄..2̄.2̄..2̄.3̄..2̄

D1   .1̿..5̄..1̿..5̄..1̿..5̄..1̿..4̄..1̿..5̄..1̿..4̄.
 r   4̄..3̄..3̄.2̄...4̄..3̄..4̄..3̄..4̄.2̄...4̄..3̄..
     |
```

Variation of part B (between frames 185 and 280):

▼
```
.1̄.3̄.2̄.1̄.2̄.2̄.1̄.3̄.2̄.1̄.4̄.1̄.1̄.2̄.2̄.1̄.3̄.1̄.
.1.3.2.1.2.2.1.3.2.1.4̲.1.1.2.2.1.3.1.

.5.5.2̄.1̄.2̄.2̄.
.5̲.5̲.2.1.2.2.      ... continued with basic pattern
```

Observations:

This is another 36-pulse cycle, but without an explicitly bipartite structure in part A. Part B is the standard three-note phrase 1 3 2 which we have already encountered in Item 1. Here it is altered only in one way, evidently for reasons of tonality and consonance. Player B at his entry point (+) first plays 1 . 2 . 2 ., responding to the 4 . 2 . 5 . 4 melodic passage in part A. This results in the combination 4 1 2 2 5 2 4, establishing a tonal progression that would have been disturbed by the insertion of a 3.

In the reshuffling of the total image by players C and D, a veiled bipartite structure of the piece emerges: Player C's line consists of a grouping of six tonal markers, $\overline{\overline{3}}$ .. $\overline{\overline{2}}$ .. $\overline{\overline{3}}$ .. $\overline{\overline{2}}$ .. $\overline{\overline{2}}$ .. $\overline{\overline{2}}$ .., which is repeated twice identically to fill out the length of the theme of A. Player D then joins with an interlocking pattern that is similar to what he had played in Item 1, but with the rhythmic kink occurring in *two* places.

A variation by player B was captured on the film between frames 185 and 280. It shows a basic technique of melodic variation which is used, however, sparingly: substitution of a few notes. In my transcription above I have written the variation exactly below part B, with the basic line above, so that it becomes evident which notes are varied. The varied notes are marked by horizontal parentheses. In one spot the player substitutes $\underline{4}$. 1 for 3 . 2, in another 1 . $\underline{5}$. $\underline{5}$ for 2 . 1 . 3.

Item 4: 'Omukaire amera envu' *('Old People Have Only White Hair')*

Filmed extract: 308 frames. Archive No. B 12618.
Transcription - Elementary pulsation: 720 M.M./cycle: 18 pulses.

A   5 . 4 . 5 . 4 . 4 . $\overline{1}$. 5 . 3 . 2 .
     $\underline{5}$. $\underline{4}$. $\underline{5}$. $\underline{4}$. $\underline{4}$. 1 . $\underline{5}$. $\underline{3}$. $\underline{2}$.
              +

B   . $\overline{2}$. $\overline{1}$. $\overline{3}$. $\overline{2}$. $\overline{1}$. $\overline{3}$. $\overline{2}$. $\overline{1}$. $\overline{3}$
     . 2 . 1 . 3 . 2 . 1 . 3 . 2 . 1 . 3

C   . $\overline{\overline{2}}$ . . $\overline{5}$ . . $\overline{\overline{2}}$ . . $\overline{\overline{1}}$ . . $\overline{\overline{2}}$ . . $\overline{\overline{2}}$.

D 1 $\overline{5}$ . . $\overline{\overline{1}}$ . . $\overline{4}$ . . $\overline{\overline{1}}$ . . $\overline{5}$ . . $\overline{\overline{1}}$ . .
 r   . . $\overline{4}$ . . $\overline{3}$ . . $\overline{4}$ . . $\overline{3}$ . . $\overline{4}$. $\overline{2}$.

Variation of part B (from frame 1-308) (only one octave transcribed here):

   . 1 . 1 . 3 . 1 . 1 . 3 . 2 . 1 . 2
   . 2 . 1 . 3 . 1 . 1 . 3 . 2 . ⌐1 . 3
   $\underline{. 2 . 1 . 3 . 2 . 1 . 3 . 2 .⌋}$ 1 . 3
   . 2 . 1 . 3 . 2 . 1 . 3 . 2 . 1 . 2
   . 2 . 1 . 3 . 2 . 1 . 3 . 2 . 1 . 3
   . 2 . 1 . 3 . 2 . 1 . 3 . 2 . 1 . 3
   . 2 . 1 . 3 . 2 . 1 . 3 . 2 . 1 . 2
   . 2 . 1 . 3 . 2 . 1 . 3 . 2 . 1 . 3
   . 2 . 1 . 3 . 2 . 4 . 3 . 2   and so on

Observations:

This is the shortest theme we recorded from Samusiri Babalanda; it is only 18 pulses long (or nine strokes in the combined parts A and B). Part A consists of a tone row with (as is usual) irregular melodic accents. Performer B strikes the same three-note interlocking sequence 1 . 3 . 2 . , which he had also played in one or another variation in Items 1 and 3. In fact he varies his formula considerably during the 308 frames of film documentation. A complete transcription of his variations follows my notation of the theme. That part where he returns to the basic 1 . 3 . 2 . phrase during the exposition of the theme is shown with angular horizontal parentheses embracing the respective ciphers. Player C, with his line in triple-division structure, marks what is probably the dancers' beat. It also serves as a marker of tonality. Player D eventually interlocks in triple-division style with the usual $\overline{4}\,\overline{\overline{1}}$. $\overline{3}\,\overline{5}$. basic pattern, always adapted melodically in response to the other constituent parts of the piece. The pattern ends its cycle with the rhythmic kink, with which we are already familiar from the other pieces.

Conclusion and summary

The organisational principles, combination techniques and structural characteristics of the four *embaire* pieces documented from Samusiri Babalanda can now be examined comparatively.

As in Buganda, the titles suggest that there are vocal themes behind these xylophone pieces which are probably sung in other contexts and with the accompaniment of other instruments. In the embaire there was no singing at all, except occasional shouts of a few words that can be heard in the recordings. *Embaire* music is instrumental and, to perform it, the participating musicians must know above all their instrumental parts. It is highly unlikely that the four players on the xylophone and the drummers were all 'humming' the 'song' in their hearts while playing, in order to relate their parts to it. In terms of pure performance economics, this would not make sense. In other words, while there can be no doubt about structural relationships between the total image of these compositions and the 'song' lurking in the background that is never sung, the performance tasks of each participant are at least as important, and here we discover methods in the structuring of movement that would escape our attention if we concentrated on a projective analysis. As in Buganda, one can, of course, try to elicit from the musicians how they *would* sing by mouth the songs behind these instrumental pieces, playing the recordings to them and record the result on a second tape recorder. As interesting as this would be, one has to realise that such a procedure would go beyond the documentation of the tradition as it exists in its own context. As I often experienced in Buganda with my teacher Evaristo Muyinda in the quiet hours at his home in Nabbale, such endeavours inevitably create a laboratory situation. One can adopt either approach at different times and on different occasions. In Busoga the feeling we had was that musicians expected us to remain strictly contextual.

In terms of the building blocks and tasks contributed by each of the four performers on the xylophone, our transcriptions from film demonstrate the emphasis in this culture on individuality. Player A (Samusiri Babalanda) introduces what, in view of its complexity of structure and central importance, deserves to be called a *theme*, or even a 'nuclear theme' as A. M. Jones (1970) would say. It is essentially a tone row, in the documented examples of either 15 elements (or strokes), as in Item 1, 18 strokes (in Items 2 and 3), or merely nine strokes (Item 4). These tone rows consist of irregular accent structures generated by the varying regularity of melodic peaks and nadirs. One piece in the sample, Item 2, had a part A with a bipartite structure.

The interlocking tone row of player B is clearly subordinate in this music, although in its nature as tone row and in its combination technique it is analogous to part A. In all four songs, player B's part proceeds from a three-note group (1 . 3 . 2 .) adapted in one or another form to the melody of part A, or subjected to some melodic variation. This is so even in Item 2, where it was not clear at first. Upon closer examination, one discovers that in this piece part B, as well as parts C and D, are similar to the other songs in melodic context, but this is disguised by the fact that the whole piece is played *transposed* one step downwards in relation to the level of the other songs. Therefore, what appears to be 5.2.1 in part B is in fact the same sequence as in the other songs, namely 1.3.2 (or only one step lower in the equipentatonic tuning). The same applies to part D, in which the sequence

$$\frac{.\overline{4}..\overline{5}.}{\overline{2}..\overline{3}..}$$

is merely a transposition one step downward of what in all the other recorded songs appears as:

$$\frac{.\overline{5}..\overline{\overline{1}}.}{\overline{3}..\overline{4}..}$$

The reader is advised, for comparative analysis of the four pieces, to transpose item 2 one step up in all its parts, hence beginning part A as 5 . 1 . $\bar{1}$. 4 . 4 . 3 . 3 . $\bar{1}$., etc. Then the above analysis will become clearer.

Although my experience with *embaire* music in 1960 made me expect to find the same highly interruptive style in field recordings in Busoga as played at the rehearsal at Salama with the visitor playing '*Mobuka ng'komera*', my expectations were not confirmed. At least the groups that I recorded in 1963 and in 1967/68, including that of Samusiri Babalanda, also played their parts rather faithfully and predominantly in a manner Evaristo Muyinda used to call *okusengejja* (in Luganda). The larger sample therefore shows that the 'truth' is somewhere in between, and the 'freedoms' of improvisation which apparently exists in the performances I heard in the 1960s are in reality minimal, in Busoga as well. It is probably accurate to say that improvisational elements are perhaps a little more prominent in Busoga than they were in the style of Kiganda music that Evaristo Muyinda had taught me, but in Samusiri Babalanda's group, improvisational variation was mostly left to player B. Variation follows a substitution technique by which it is often sufficient to replace one or two notes for obtaining a reshuffling of the pattern or its enlargement to a longer configuration. (Compare player B in Item 2). Sometimes player B adapts one or another note to more closely follow the tonal progressions established by the theme of player A.

In principle, all the simultaneous sounds in this music are in octave relationship. But this principle is occasionally broken, for example in variations developing their own structural force which imposes itself on the whole, and which is also 'broken' or rather neglected when required by the logic pattern formation. For example, deviations from the unison principle in part D are found in the middle of Item 1 ('*Wairugala*') and in several places in Item 2 ('*Baala ndolo*'), because part D has its own melodic and motional logic dictated by its basis structure in al the songs. Such deviations from the octave (or sometimes unison) principle establish a kind of transient heterophony.

The music of Busoga (as that of Buganda) is not built upon concepts of 'harmony', though Ugandan composers at the end of the colonial era, under the influence of value judgements by Western contact persons, fell in love with the term. Joseph Kyagambiddwa used the term 'to harmonise' several times (Kyagambiddwa, 1955). For fear of hurting Baganda friends who were sensitive towards any remarks that seemed to deny 'Africa' any 'higher development' of music, (for which 'harmony' in the Western sense had become a symbol) I used Kyagambiddwa's term in my own early works (Kubik, 1969, etc.), hoping that it would be understood in the wider sense in which I had intended to use it. Today, saying that music in southern Uganda is not based on simultaneous harmonic sound (except some church music, popular guitar music and the work of certain composers aiming at Western contemporary art music) will probably no longer hurt anyone's feelings. Values have changed in the meantime and people have become increasingly aware that music everywhere in the world is always part of complex musical and cultural systems and not an expression of a 'stage' in the development of humankind.

In southern Uganda, although the musical and tonal systems exclude use of 'harmony', there does exist related phenomena which Kyagambiddwa perhaps senses when he talked about 'harmonising' and which many musicians of the region have emphasised when pointing to the 'mellow' quality of the music. These are:

1. principles of consecutive consonance and
2. the tonal steps and progressions between them.

I have analysed these factors in Kiganda music in Kubik (1991). The transcriptions of *embaire* music in part corroborate the existence of these principles in Busoga and in part confirm their absence. While there is no piece that remains only on one tonal level (in contrast, for example, to some xylophone styles of Mozambique where a constant bordun tone plays an important role), progressions between different tonal steps are not always clear-cut.

In Kiganda xylophone music, it was possible to deduce 'rules' about melodic interlocking from the 'behaviour' of the combining tone rows. These rules are quite strict in this case and guarantee the recurrence of various 'consonant clusters' which often define tonal steps and their progressions between them. On the other hand, preliminary analysis of the Kisoga material of 1963 and 1967/68 has shown that, in many places, parts A and B come together in a manner that would be unacceptable in *amadinda* composition. For example, in *embaire* xylophone compositions, interlocking with the same note or even a tone lower or higher is acceptable, as is demonstrated in the combination:

$$\underline{3} \, . \, \underline{2} \, . \, \underline{2} \, . \, \underline{2} \, . \, \underline{2} \, . \qquad \text{(in Item 2)}$$
$$. \, 3 \, . \, 2 \, . \, 1 \, . \, 2 \, . \, 2$$

This gives a sequence of $\underline{3}$ 3 $\underline{2}$ $\underline{2}$ $\underline{2}$ 1 $\underline{2}$ 2 $\underline{2}$ 2 in the total image-something inconceivable on the *amadinda*. In a way, what is acceptable in melodic interlocking and what is not in this form of *embaire* music seems to be closer to the *akadinda* than it is to *amadinda*, because in the former case the stringing (in the resultant total image) of the same note three times, for example 1 1 1, does indeed occur (Kubik, 1969, 1991). The essential difference in the melodic interlocking of the basic parts within the Kiganda and Kisoga xylophone styles seems to lie in relation to fourths or fifths. A prominent feature of *amadinda* interlocking is the preference for the Kiganda-fourth/fifth interval and its predominant use in sections of tonal rest; this in turn creates the consecutive consonance effect. In the *embaire* music that we have examined so far, the use of interlocking fourths or fifths is not such a prominent feature and in some pieces even insignificant; on the contrary, interlocking with unison notes or even in seconds is very common. Probably this is also a basic reason why the rise of inherent auditory patterns in perception plays a less significant role in this music than it does in Kiganda xylophone styles.[10]

The most fascinating discovery in Samusiri Babalanda's type of *embaire* music concerns the tasks of players C and D. In contrast to the *okukoonera* abstraction technique in *amadinda* music of Buganda - here definitely absent - we first note that the four players are organised in pairs, two by two. The pair playing in the lower and middle registers (players A and B) acts as if they were playing an *amadinda*, i.e. in duple-interlocking style, while the two performers in the upper register, C and D, reshuffle the total image as if they were playing it all on an *akadinda* (i.e. in triple-division interlocking style). Typically, player D falls in between, with two notes forming patterns which are essentially what in Buganda would be called 'Katongole':

$$\frac{.\overline{\overline{1}}..\overline{5}.}{\overline{4}..\overline{3}..}$$

however, with the starting point on the higher element of the phrase, namely on note 4 (played with the right-hand stick; see entry points in Items 1, 3 and 4).

Equally fascinating is the small but important difference between a performer D's part in Samusiri Babalanda's *embaire* group and that of an *omwawuzi* on an *akadinda* of Buganda. Player D's cycle inevitably ends with a rhythmic kink, that is with this phrase:

$$\frac{.\overline{\overline{1}}..\overline{5}}{\overline{4}.\overline{2}..}$$

We have already asked what the purpose of this rhythmic break might be. Although I cannot offer an exhaustive explanation, I can make the following observations. First, the 'rhythmic kink' not only occurs with regularity at the end of part D, but it occurs immediately before the recurring entry point of player C. Most significant, however, is that the middle note of the rhythmic kink, namely the 1, also coincides exactly with the entry point for player B (in Items 1, 3 and 4). Isolated from the total image, we thus observe in these pieces an invariable relationship between the three-note formula of part B and the 'rhythmic kink', shown below:

Rhythmic kink	$.\overline{1}..\overline{5}.$
of player D's part	$\overline{4}.\overline{2}...$
Player B's three note	$.1.3.2$
formula (in octave duplication)	

If anything, the 'rhythmic kink' is therefore something like a connection point between the different motional systems (triple-division and duple-division interlocking), here united into one super-system; it is something like the funiculus on which the individual lines hang, the 'window' through which communication between the systems is possible. In this manner, the rhythmic kink is also a *cue* for the participants, showing them where they are.

Lois Anderson has stated with relation to the geographical distribution of the triple-division interlocking as found in *akadinda* music:

> The only style which is comparable to this is that used by the Padhola, although an important difference is the scale structure used. While the Ganda utilize a five-tone scale, the Padhola use a six-tone scale; while six players are required on the akadinda, five play the Padhola xylophone, of fourteen keys ... The Ganda akadinda and the Padhola xylophone styles utilize the same pattern of interlocking ... (Anderson, 1967: 69)

The Padhola is a Nilotic ethnic group settled between Tororo and the south-eastern tip of Lake Kyoga. I had no opportunity to do research among that group, but if the interlocking principle there is indeed the same as in *akadinda* music (the tonal system, whether six notes of not, is a separate issue), one is persuaded to ask from where they obtained it. To the best of my knowledge, log xylophones, if encountered among Nilotes, are there as a result of contact either with speakers of Niger-Congo languages (I.A.5 in Greenberg's classification) or Adamawa-Eastern languages (I.A.6). Triple-division inter-locking techniques with simultaneous perception of a relativistic individual beat is characteristic of several forms of drumming, xylophone music, and so on, of the eastern stream of the Bantu, but it is a trait not normally associated with speakers of Eastern Sudanic languages.

Perhaps our findings with Samusiri Babalanda may throw some light on this question. At least he has provided us with more evidence regarding the distribution of the triple-division interlocking technique in southern Uganda: it is surely found in Busoga. Indirectly, this might reveal something about the history of the *akadinda* in the now defunct royal music of Buganda, considering the intensive presence of Basoga musicians in the king's court during the nineteenth century. Although the *akadinda* in the king's court was considered an esoteric tradition, its interlocking technique is not esoteric at all, but rather one of the basic interlocking principles in wide areas of east and east-central Africa (see Kubik, 1988) and was first described by the late Arthur M. Jones in the *ngwayi* dance of Zambia (Jones, 1934). That it is also found in Busoga is, after all, no surprise. Surprising is the fact that duple and triple interlocking techniques are used simultaneously. Here it might be useful to look at other xylophone ensembles in southern Uganda incorporating four performers. Summarising his field experiences during the 1940s and 1950s in a table on xylophones, Klaus Wachsmann stated that four players, apparently with different roles, shared in the performance of a log xylophone called *endiga* that was found on the southern shore of Lake Kyoga, through Nyoro, Ganda, and Soga (Trowell and Wachsmann, 1953: 320). He gives the terminology for the endiga which presents a variation of what can also be noted among other Basoga musicians:

> A: Omugoisi or Omutabuzi, B: Omuleterezi or Omukubi W'Pbutono, C: Omutabuza or Omwakati. D: Omukubi W'entama.[11]

It is possible that Samusiri Babalanda's music was based on traditions linked with the *endiga*, although I do not recall having ever heard this term in the area of Busoga where we did most of our fieldwork.

The repertoire of *embaire* performances, as documented in Busoga in 1963 and 1967/68, was not restricted to the xylophone alone. Well-known song titles such as, for example, '*Waiswa mugudde*' have been recorded in performances on *budongo* lamellophones, as well as by the *amagwala* ensemble with eight gourd horns.[12] In January 1968 we found on two occasions *embaire* players joining a group of *enkwanzi* (panpipe) performers. Although I cannot ascertain whether this represented an older tradition in Busoga, or whether it was a result of attempts at nationalising music in Uganda (in the manner of the Heart Beat of Africa), it was remarkable in this particular case that *enkwanzi* and *embaire* could play together without difficulty. At least it confirmed the identity of the tonal system across Busoga.

Regarding the flexibility and potential of all these traditions to converge and reconfigure, I would like to conclude this paper with a fictive story. The spirit of a deceased Musoga friend recently told me in a dream:

> Long ago, there was an embaire group like the one of Samusiri Babalanda. In the beginning, the four musicians were good

friends and played beautifully together. But one day they started to quarrel; the performers on the smaller notes accused those of the bigger notes of practicing witchcraft. The arising antagonism and fear between the two pairs intensified to the degree that, one evening, after a violent quarrel, the performers of the smaller notes decided to cut off their section of keys on the banana stems and migrate to another country. Since the two pairs of performers had each played the same songs their own way within their own playing areas, their separation did not destroy the music. In fact players A and B continued to perform how they had always performed on the ten keys which their quarrelsome partners left behind. (There was even one more key at the bottom but it was totally useless, because it didn't sound well.) As time passed, they added two more keys and hired a friend to play with them only on the two top keys added, creating a new configuration of the same music which from then on was performed on an instrument of twelve keys.

The quarrelsome players of the upper register who had cut off seven slats ran away westwards from the Nile river. They also continued to perform this music in the place where they settled, on their fragment of the original instrument to which they referred as a xylophone with 'small' (i.e. high-pitched) notes. They called it with a word beginning with *aka-* ... to express smallness. (The spirit in my dream did not tell me the name exactly.) For some time they played on the seven-key high-pitched xylophone what they had always played. But people in the place to where they had migrated did not like it very much. They were missing the bass. Eventually the players responded to the pressure and recruited from their own offspring young trainees and extended their seven-note instrument by two octaves into the bass. The final product now had seventeen notes and needed five people to be played to everyone's delight. The original players and their clan jealously guarded ownership of what they still referred as their *aka-*... xylophone. This was their new instrument and they were very proud of it. No one outside the clan was trained, only youngsters within their clan. Soon they played so expertly that the king of the country to which they had migrated called them to play in his court. And so it remained as long as the kingdom existed.

Notes

1. See recordings under collection G. Kubik 1959/60, B 4803-5198 in *Katalog der Tonbandaufnahmen* ... , Phonogrammarchiv Vienna, 1966.
2. Rec. B 4931
3. Kubik (1964, 1988: 168-70).
4. See for example Trowell and Wachsmann (1953: 314-20); Kubik (1982: 74-5, 82-3); Kubik (1991).
5. Archive No. 1 B 12618
6. Therefore, illustration 2 refers to one particular piece only.
7. See Kauffman (1980: 395) and Tracey (1981).
8. See my discussion of '*Agenda n'omulungi azaawa*' in Kubik (1991: 79-80).
9. At the moment I can only confirm this statement for the xylophone; the accompanying rattle and drum patterns have not yet been scrutinised with regard to this question.
10. The importance of fourth-interlocking in *amadinda* music is probably also connected to the technique of the *ennanga* (harp), with which *amadinda* music is related, while in Busoga this factor is irrelevant.
11. Here one should note that Klaus Wachsmann's designations A, B, C and D are based on principles different from those I have adopted to describe Samusiri Babalanda's performance organisation. My letters follow the order of entry of each player, while Wachsmann's designations attempt to establish an interethnic comparative scheme whose sketch is given in his table.
12. See Record AMA TR 142, by Hugh Tracey at Bugembe, Bugabula County, near Kamuli in 1950; also Tracey (1973: 321).

Bibliography

Anderson, Lois Ann (1967), 'The African Xylophone', *African Arts/Arts d'Afrique*, **1** (Autumn), 46-9.
Brandel, Rose (1959), 'The African Hemiola Style', *Ethnomusicology*, **3** (3), 106-17.
Cooke, Peter (1991), 'Report on Pitch Perception Experiment Carried Out in Buganda and Busoga (Uganda) August 1990', *ICTM Study Group on Computer Aided Research*, Info. 33, 2-6.
Jones, Arthur M. (1934), 'African Drumming - a Study of the Combination of Rhythms in African Music', *Bantu Studies*, **8** (1), 1-16.
Kauffman, Robert (1980), 'African Rhythm: a Reassessment', *Ethnomusicology*, **24** (3), 393-415.

Kubik, Gerhard (1960), 'The Structure of Kiganda Xylophone Music', *African Music*, **2** (3), 6-30. Corrigenda (1960), in *African Music*, **4** (4), 136-7.

Kubik, Gerhard (1964), 'Xylophone Playing in Southern Uganda', *Journal of the Royal Anthropological Institute*, **94** (2), 138-59.

Kubik, Gerhard (1969), 'Composition Techniques in Kiganda Xylophone Music. With an Introduction into some Kiganda Musical Concepts', *African Music*, **4** (3), 22-72, (1970). Corrigenda in *African Music*, **4** (4), 137. Supplementary notes under 'Letters to the Editor', *African Music*, **5** (1), 114-15 (1972).

Kubik, Gerhard (1972), 'Transcription of African Music from Silent Film: Theory and Methods', *African Music*, **5** (2), 28-39.

Kubik, Gerhard (1982), *Musikgeschichte in Bildern: Ostafrika*. Band I: Musikethnologie, Lieferung 10, Leipzig: Deutscher Verlag für Musik.

Kubik, Gerhard (1988), *Zum Verstehen afrikanischer Musik*, Aufsatze, Leipzig: Reclam.

Kubik, Gerhard (1991), 'Theorie, Auffuhrungspraxis and Kompositionstechniken der Hofmusik von Buganda. Ein Leitfaden zur Komposition in einer ostafrikanischen Musikkultur', *Hamburger Jahrbuch für Musikwissenschaft* ('Für Ligeti. Die Referate des Ligeti-Kongresses Hamburg 1988'), **11**, 23-162.

Kyagambiddwa, Joseph (1955), *African Music from the Source of the Nile*, New York: Praeger.

Schneider, Albrecht and Andreas E. Beurmann (1990), 'Okutuusa Amadinda; Zur Frage aquidistanter Tonsysteme und Stimmungen in Afrika', in Peter Petersen (ed.), *Musikkulturgeschichte: Festschrift für Constantin Floros zum 60. Geburtstag*, Wiesbaden: Breitkopf and Hartel, pp. 493-526 (with Gerhard Kubik and Mpijma Wamala).

Tracey, Andrew (1981), 'White Response to African Music', *Papers Presented at the 6th Symposium on Ethnomusicology*, Music Department, Rhodes University, 10 to 11 October 1980, Grahamstown: International Library of African Music.

Tracey, Hugh (1973), *Catalogue. The Sound of Africa Series*, 210 Long Playing Records ... , vols 1-2, Roodepoort: International Library of African Music.

Trowell, Margaret and Klaus Wachsmann (1953), *Tribal Crafts of Uganda*, London and New York: Geoffrey Cumberlege and Oxford University Press.

Wachsmann, Klaus P. (1967), 'Pen-Equidistance and Accurate Pitch: a Problem from the Source of the Nile', in Ludwig Fischer and Christopher Helmut Mahling (eds), *Festschrift Walter Wiora zum 30 Dezember 1966*, Kassel: Barenreiter, pp. 583-92.

Wachsmann, Klaus P. (1971), 'Musical Instruments in the Kiganda Tradition and their Place in the East African Scene', in K. P. Wachsmann (ed.), *Essays on Music and History in Africa*, Evanston, IL: Northwestern University Press, pp. 93-134. This chapter first appeared in *World of Music* (1992), **34** (1).

9 Warrior Composers: Maasai Boys and Men

Malcolm Floyd

'Tinyakampa' ('it's in trouble!') is a song I know well, having heard it sung everywhere I have visited in Maasailand. After hearing it several times I started to join in with the chorus, and I was encouraged to develop my own patterns to fit in with everyone else's, and in recent years I have occasionally been brave, or foolhardy, enough to take over the solo part, which demands that I sing about the places where I have caused trouble.

This sums up Maasai musicianship. It is based on individual and communal experience, and requires individual creativity within a well established framework, and with a recognisable repertoire of appropriate motifs, to which the individual is expected to add.

The Maasai and Samburu

The Maasai, and the very directly related Samburu, live on the floor of the Rift Valley, from Lake Turkana in Kenya to the Serengeti in Tanzania. It may be useful to spend some considering their route there, and the implications for cultural practices. It appears that in the first millennium BCE the people who included those who would become the Maasai, cultivated sorghum, finger and bulrush millets, had some livestock, and also depended on hunting, gathering and fishing (Ochieng', 1985: 27). By the start of the Common Era Nilo-Saharans had travelled as far south as Lake Turkana and in this arid region were obliged to adopt a semi-pastoral economy and transhumant lifestyle. Here they met with Eastern Cushites, and took up some of their prohibitions against eating game and fowl. This was also the time of the start of the Bantu migration into East Africa (McEvedy, 1983: 33; Ochieng', 1985: 27; Ogot, 1974: 161-2). By 200 CE Nilo-Saharans had moved further down the Rift Valley, while the Bantu had moved across to the Indian Ocean, which would ensure their control of the lands to the south. Meanwhile, Cushitic groups were established in what is now north and north-east Kenya (McEvedy, 1983: 35).

The next event major movement was down the Rift Valley by the Kalenjin group of Nilotes; this happened around 1350 (McEvedy, 1983: 59). In 1600 another Nilotic group, the Luo, moved down the Rift Valley to settle around Lake Victoria (McEvedy, 1983: 79). By 1625 the Maasai move south had begun, and they started to impose their language on the Kalenjin, Sirikwa and Dorobo, although they also borrowed many words. It is also probable that they borrowed Bantu words as they went on, particularly for their agricultural vocabulary (Ogot, 1974). They broke through Kalenjin and Kikuyu settlements, and by the late seventeenth century the Maasai had moved into the central Rift Valley, according to oral, archaeological and linguistic evidence, from the Maasai themselves, and the Kalenjin and Kikuyu. As well as borrowing words, the Maasai took a range of cultural ideas, including working with cattle, the cyclical age-set system, circumcision and clitoridectomy, and some armaments, including the oval shield, from the Kalenjin and Sirikwa (Ochieng' 1985: 27-28; Ogot, 1974: 162-63). In about 1750 the Maasai moved south to the Tanzanian steppe, as the Nilotic Tutsi moved south-west in turn, to become rulers of the Bantu Hutu (McEvedy, 1983: 89). However, the expansion of the Maasai was halted in Tanzania by the Gogo and Hehe who were increasing their own domains. In northern Kenya the Maasai were held in check by the Galla and Somali so their expansion continued into the western highlands, in the middle of Kalenjin territory, between the Nandi and Kipsigis. At this time the Maasai controlled an area about 500 miles by 200 miles, governing the Rift Valley, and the movement and settlement of other peoples (Ochieng', 1985: 29). From about 1800 their expansion was contained, so their aggression was turned towards each other, over such issues as grazing rights, with much cattle raiding in a whole series of internal wars, especially between the pastoral il-Maasai and agricultural il-Oikop, and with a struggle by the Purko group to gain leadership. There was also rivalry between the il-Oibonok (ritual leaders), gravitating first to Supeet, then to Mbatiany who was unchallenged up to 1884, followed by Olanana,[1] who was opposed by his brother Senteu (Ogot, 1974: 241-2; Spear, 1981: 64, 106). In 1885 the Maasai lands were divided between British and German 'spheres of influence', which later became British and German East Africa. After the First World War the lands were in British-controlled Kenya and Tanganyika (McEvedy, 1983: 111; Spear, 1981: 106).

In recent years they have become more agricultural across their dispersal, particularly the women, who see more efficient ways of feeding their families than relying solely on cattle. They remain, however, a people strongly attached to traditional mores and cultural practices. This is made possible for them by the fact that so many of their young men find employment in the armed forces, where the maintenance of their warrior ethos can be positively encouraged. These warriors are the principal focus of Maasai and Samburu society, and this is also apparent in its music.

I have studied with the Samburu at Lemisigyo near Maralal between 1984 and 1993, and with the Maasai at Makurian near Dol Dol, and near Arusha. Figure 9.1 shows these locations.

Figure 9.1 Map of Kenya, showing research locations

Peter Lekampus, a young Samburu *ol-murrani* (warrior), introduced me to
the life and music of his community in 1984. In that year he wrote his own
version of their history and pattern of existence:

> The meaning of the word *Samburu* is a special basket which
> was made by women for carrying such things as meat, fruit and
> calabashes. The basket was called *Sambur*. Their original
> homeland might have been the Sudan. But some stories say that
> the Maasai came from the sky: Samburu are the northern branch
> of the Maasai and even the language they talk is the same, their
> traditional beliefs are also similar, so they must have come from
> the same place. But whatever happened, most people believe
> that the Maasai and Samburu originated in the Sudan. Their
> movement down into Kenya was due to droughts in the north.
> They moved to where they could find enough pasture and water
> for their animals ... The part of the country [the Samburu] are
> living in does not receive enough rain, and that gives people
> their main occupation, as the climate decides the occupation of
> the people. The main occupation is pastoralism; the people
> believe that from the beginning 'no other tribe had the right to

keep cattle' and even now that still continues. That proves that from the beginning they had been cattle keepers.

He goes on to give a introductory sketch of significant features of Samburu and Maasai lifestyles:

> There are several traditional beliefs e.g. a warrior is not allowed to eat anything at home alone. Women are responsible for house duties while boys look after animals e.g. cattle, goats and sheep. Morans are kept free for the emergency cases. But some of the beliefs are now disappearing automatically. There are also some ceremonial parties ... birthday, circumcision which usually takes place to boys who are above 16 years old and to girls at the time of marriage. When boys are circumcised, they remain drinking blood mixed with milk for half a month and eating meat for another half. The work of the people is evenly shared according to traditional ways of life e.g. men take care of animals while all the manual work at home is taken by women. (Lekampus, unpublished manuscript)

By situating Lekampus in Samburu society we can gain a picture of its overall structure. He belongs to the Lempirikany family. Figure 9.2 shows this diagrammatically:

Figure 9.2　Diagram of Lempirikany family in Samburu society

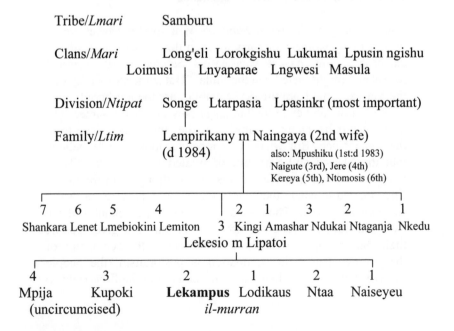

Music of the Maasai and Samburu

This chapter is based on the songs heard, recorded, and performed which are part of this lifestyle, and on discussions with performers. It deals principally with songs for males as I am male, and access to this male music was enthusiastically granted. While there was also access to the performed music of women, there was a reluctance to share more than this, in terms of functions, significance and references. However, I have considered as much as possible in constructing a paradigm of the place of music in Maasai and Samburu.

Figure 9.3 shows a model of the groups of performers, who can be identified as having a coherent performance practice in Maasai society, which appears to establish three principal repertoires; for infants, for warriors, and for women.

Figure 9.3   Model of Maasai repertoires

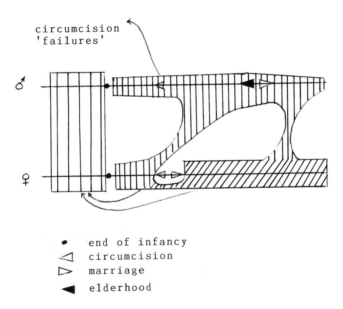

The music for infants is often led by older girls and young women, and there is no gender separation of children at this age. Songs are mostly call and response, with simple response parts, and may be interspersed with riddles to encourage mental and verbal dexterity. Mothers may move their sons in ways reminiscent of warriors' movements, as her worth will be judged eventually on how successful she has been in bringing up sons who are initiated without showing fear. Daughters are not, as a rule, played with in the same way. Figure 9.4 is an example of such a song:[2]

Figure 9.4 'Ntai ng'udi-ng'udi' infants' song

Infancy is considered to end, as in many cultures, around the age of five to seven, when second teeth are coming through, and it is considered that they are ready for an element of responsibility and training. However, the next repertoire is essentially that of warriors, *ilmurran*. There is almost no repertoire for children here; boys are learning the techniques they will need to perform warriors' songs when they are older, and the girls are joining in with the warriors themselves, picking up songs from the girls slightly older than them. This is a courting process, as marriage happens between a man of one age-set and a girl of the following age-set, and warriors will show their attachment to a girl by giving her bead decorations, although she may not yet be teenaged.

This period of training for boys, and courtship for girls, is completed by circumcision, which will lead to initiation into warriorhood for boys, and to marriage for girls. Lekampus describes the rituals of circumcision as ceremonies;

Figure 9.5 *Muratare* - circumcision

1st ceremony	*Arapu ilkilani*: wearing a skin ready for circumcision
2nd ceremony	*Nepuoi olbaa*: going to a very far place to get thin branches and gum from a certain tree
3rd ceremony	*Nebukokini ontolio kule*: elders come to bless the boy
4th ceremony	*Nepuoi enkare*: the boy goes to get water from the river with a calabash
5th ceremony	*Ndungoto enkaji*: a house is built where the initiated will stay
6th ceremony	*Nemiruni enkishu*: cattle are driven back to the manyatta (collection of houses) at about 2 p.m.
7th ceremony	*Nebukokini nkarer*: water is mixed with milk and an elder splashes it on the boy
8th ceremony	*Newon layeni*: the boy sits by the door and is circumcised

He goes on to describe the singing related to circumcision:

> Ceremonial [circumcision] songs are different, everybody [men and boys] sing. They are sung all night and during the ceremony. The songs are very bad and abuse you because you are not circumcised. All the morans sing them to make you brave. After the circumcision good songs are sung, about bravery.
>
> If you are not brave you have to be alone, and no songs are sung. You have to learn the abusive songs so that you can join in, and show you don't care about the knife.
>
> Boys start learning circumcision songs about two or three years before circumcision. Among the Samburu all boys are circumcised in the traditional manner. Some Maasai boys are circumcised in hospital, but many are not happy about it. It is not brave to be injected the morans say. (Interview, 16 September 1984)

At the end of their period as warriors, when they become junior elders and get married, men's singing is dramatically reduced. They may occasionally join in with the warriors, but only with the approval of the younger men, and they are mainly left with their memories.

Married women, on the other hand, are introduced to a whole new repertoire exclusive to them. It has two main aspects:

1. Prayers and praises for a range of things, particularly for children. These songs are called *Laomon*. This religious music is entirely reserved to married women.
2. Songs sung to praise warriors, particularly their physical attributes, and to mock their husbands. This 'ritual of rebellion' is perhaps not surprising when husbands may be considerably older than wives, and when the warriors, the glorious focus of Maasai society, are the same age as the younger wives. These songs are called *Kagisha*.

I want now to concentrate on the musical development of males, from the preparatory stage prior to initiation up to their social completion as *ilmurran*. A fundamental point to be made is that being able to take part fully in the music is important. Everyone needs to be able not only to join in, but to lead the music, at least for a short time, and inability is mocked. One version of 'Tinyakampa' says: 'if unable to praise you will come out with a yellow skin'. This gives considerable impetus to young boys to acquire techniques and abilities as fully as possible.

What specifically do they need to be able to do? There are three main aspects:

1. accompanimental motifs
2. solo melodic motifs
3. rhythmic hyperventilation, called *nkuluut*.

The nature of accompanimental motifs can be seen in 'Endike' (Figure 9.6).

Figure 9.6 'Endike'

It is possible to note the use of something akin to a triad as a structural parameter. Rhythm interlocks, and has an overarching two-beat structure, but within that may subdivide into, three, four or six.

Solo melodic motifs tend to start at a point relatively high in the performer's range, then move to a rather higher note, and from there descend. This pattern may be repeated, and the descent may be over more than an octave. This can be seen in 'Entemer' and 'Esesiai' (Figures 9.7 and 9.8);

Figure 9.7 'Entemer'

Figure 9.8 'Esesiai'

In *nkuluut*, or rhythmic hyperventilation, the breathing is heavy, and can lead to momentary fits, or a catatonic seizure, and is part of the warriors' philosophy of being so angry that control is barely possible. This cultural phenomenon is explored in Spencer (1988: 120-29)

What do the warriors sing about? There are two main topics, which often overlap: descriptions of personal bravery and ferocity, and sexual relations.

The Maasai have a saying: 'boasting and a man cannot be separated', and this is certainly apparent in the songs of the first type describing their exploits. There is also a desire to remind the whole of society of the fundamental nature and function of warriors. Examples from texts include:

> The tendency of *ilmurran* is temper ...
> We live at Lenchanguai while waiting for night to come, when we get angry ...
> Where the troop of warriors sleep is where they raid and kill the enemies ...

Songs about sexual relations occur in two forms. First, those sung by the whole group in front of everyone, in which warriors refer to their girls:

> The feather of my girl swings like the leaves of a tree ...
> I came across a good person, shining like electricity, tell her mother to talk with me ...
> I love the girl who doesn't talk much ...

The second form is the song sung by an individual, without an obvious audience, which is part warning to others and part seduction. The text can be very referential and at times obscure because of this:

'Lkirongoi'

Oiyie, kolo lmurani lapitin lengai oopishana, maibung'a nkaina ntonata neaku sororua nkapune.
Behold a warrior can go seven good months without 'talking to a woman' and the pubic hair becomes like a bush.

Oyie lmuran ootii singira lentito nanyokie empung'o ketipiwa lmurani lentito nanyekie.
O morans at the cube of the brown girl (my girlfriend) move away for the warrior of that girl has come to life.

Oiyie motonyi ldia nalo, oiyie metuonyi lebarta lootung'ana, tanarishe ninya loosipa poro lemomuai naa tanaalaroki nikinya.
You flying bird follow me, if I am killed then you eat fresh meat which is not diseased.

Oyie nkuruk ai eiborie namara long' opang'i eiborie keewo tanaibor kiyaa eiborita.
O my crow that whitens not at our place, but right from the white while white.

Oiyie nkusia lai mikijo lomelek, lmurani litibit ltenege llknua muratat esedi, lemeduakini mperoto.
O my mother don't call me beloved one, call me long penis, of these later ages, of whom nobody has witnessed the death.

Oiyie tejo ntitooino namelok nijo lmoruo lino lomelok, mikijo nanu lomelok, tejo lolitilit lterege lekuna towotin esedi lemoduakini mperoto.
O call your daughter and your husband beloved and not me; call me long penis man of these later ages, nobody has witnessed his death.
(sung by Olmusere, November 1984, Lemisigyo)

To approach an understanding of the music of these warriors, it may be useful to compare several versions of 'Tinyakampa', collected from various places at various times. These are given in summary form in Figure 9.9, except for song number two which is given in its complete form:

Figure 9.9 Versions of 'Tinyakampa'

1. Recording made by the national music and dance troupe at 'Bomas of Kenya' (ZAIT 511: nd, *c.* 1982)

Sample from text:

Iyie	*Iyie*
Tinyakampa hampe	It's in trouble
O Nanyekie, tinyakampa hampe	[Nanyuki]
O Nakuro ti ...	[Nakuru]
O Mombasa ti ...	
O Lomuruti ti ...	[Rumuruti]
O Naimarau ti ...	[Maralal]
O Nairobi ti ...	
O Nanyekie ti ...	[Nanyuki]
Mombasa ti ...	
Lomuruti ti ...	[Rumuruti]
Naimarau ti ...	[Maralal]
Mombasa ti ...	
Nanyekie ti ...	[Nanyuki]

2. Young teen-age boys at Lemisigyo near Maralal (August 1984)

Sample from text:

Hoi Naivasha, tinyakampa	O Naivasha, it's in trouble
Hoi Nairobi, ti ...	O Nairobi ...
Hoo Lomuruti ti ...	O Rumuruti ...
Hoo yioye ti ...	O yioye ...
Ho kituwoitie ti ...	We migrated ...
Ho marti elay ti ...	Plateau of lava ...
Ho lbarta ruma ti ...	Slopey Baragoi [town] ...
Ho Naisiolo ti ...	O Isiolo ...
Ho Lomuruti ti ...	O Rumuruti ...
Emu ngopipi kumo ti ...	Many are the countries ...
Hoi tarapuja ti ...	Jump now ...
Hoiyie leiyo ti ...	Hoiyie leiyo ...
Hoi Nanyekie ti ...	O Nanyuki ...
Hoi Nairobi ti ...	O Nairobi ...
Hoi Kisumu ti ...	O Kisumu ...
Katidira ti ...	I climbed ...
Lowa mara ti ...	Brown mountain ...
Naromaki kop ntoiyie ti ...	To see the girls ...

3. Boys and warriors at Makurian (November 1988)

Sample from text:

O tinyakampa hampe
Ntoiyie ilmurran, italian ilai longeresa, tinyakampa hampe
Tasieku ade, tinyakampa ...
Penya letuduenya lokalaile, penya letduenya, tinyakampa ...
Kipir lodua, tinyakampa ...

oyie leiyio hampe
Kimhung'a ntai tana iltuliun oyle,
Loimerilang' hampe,
Erukoki, tinyakampa ...

O it's in trouble,
Girls and warriors, Italian person, English person, it's in trouble
Come early another time, it's in ...
Sing, you others who don't sing, it's in ...
Oyie leiyio hampe, [vocables]
We have caught you like the Italian person,
Loimerilang' [name] hampe,
High voice, it's in ...

4. Warriors at Makurian (November 1988)

Sample from text:

Oyie tinyakampa hampe
Kamandora tinyakampa
Mowo laro kegededed ti ...
Oyie ti ...
Erangie erany ti ...
Oyie simpas entudumu ti ...
Ensha taa elo.

Oyie it's in trouble
Makandora [nr Makurian] its ...
The buffalo's horn is not catching
the owner properly it's ...
Oyie it's ...
Let us sing with the neck it's ...
Oyie there are greetings it's ...
Let it go.

5. Young warriors at Arusha (August 1993)

Sample of text:

Olaleiyo tinyakampa
Longirisa lelelontai ti ...
Makurian nai kerikito murani lang Ngenshe lai ti ...
Mowo laro lolewa eruko mara iltilo kanguyana ti ...
Lerikisho ti ...
Muran kumok ti ...

Olaleiyio it's in trouble
I can't forget the American it's ...
Ngenshe is a warrior it's ...
I climb the horn of a buffalo it's ...
Ole Rikisho [boy's name] it's ...
Many warriors were called it's ...

Is it possible to identify features in these songs which point to a fundamental structure for the 'Tinyakampa' song type, and which may point to a generic 'warrior song' style? It is certainly the case that some interesting points arise.

The texts usually include the naming of places, (song 3 is the only exception to this), and talk of particular events (except in song 1). Songs 3, 4 and 5 include references to people, often performers or visitors. The word 'tinyakampa' itself is most often included in the solo, although in song 1 it appears in the chorus part as well, and in song 2 only in the chorus part.

These are songs exclusive to males, both solo and chorus parts, except for song 1 in which there is a female chorus part. (This is not true of all warriors' songs, as there are many which require girls and young women to join them.)

The melodies of the solo parts descend in all songs in a gapped pattern of notes, over a range of a sixth (in songs 1, 2, 4 and 5) or an octave (in song

3). In addition, however, there is often a prominent chorus part (the exception is song 2). This goes in the opposite direction, ascending, and could be described as having a triadic pattern, over the range of a fifth, with the part in song 4 having an ancillary lower note. These main melodic parts alternate in all but song 4, where they are roughly contemporaneous, and in songs 1, 3 and 5 the alternating parts overlap briefly.

The *nkuluut* anticipates the main pulse structure of the solo in songs 1 and 4, and has its own pulse based pattern, while in songs 2, 3 and 5 it subdivides the pulse into threes. This information is tabulated in Figure 9.10.

Figure 9.10 Comparison of 'Tinyakampa' versions

		Song 1	2	3	4	5
text:	places	y	y	n	y	y
	people	n	n	y	y	y
	events	n	y	y	y	y
performers:	male solo	y	y	y	y	y
	male chorus	y	y	y	y	y
	female chorus	y	n	n	n	n
'Tinyakampa' in solo		y	n	y	y	y
in chorus		y	y	n	n	n
solo descends [range]		y[6th]	y[6th]	y[8v]	y[6th]	y[6th]
chorus part ascends [range]		y[5th]	n		y[5th]	y[5th]	y[5th]
oppositional movement of parts		y	n	y	y	y
alternation of melodies		y	y	y	n	y
syncopated *nkuluut*		y	n	n	y	n
triplet *nkuluut*		n	y	y	n	y

Songs 1 and 2 have factors which will affect their reliability in looking for a typical 'Tinyakampa'. Song 1 is performed by a national music and dance troupe, made up of performers from across Kenya, not only Maasai and Samburu. It performs what will be attractive to the mainly tourist audience who come to see them, although attention to authenticity is one of their principles. Their Maasai medley starts with a warriors' song, then a women's song, so that everyone is one stage and can be included in the 'Tinyakampa' finale. So the gender makeup and possibilities of performance are adjusted with this in mind. Song 2 is sung by relatively young boys, who had not been circumcised, but were practising for the day when they would become warriors. At this point they had not started including the chorus melody, and they avoid the potential difficulty of overlapping the solo and *nkuluut* parts by having a clear alternation.

Bearing this in mind, can we posit an archetypal 'Tinyakampa'? Figure 9.11 suggests a framework for the composition/performance of this song:

Figure 9.11   A framework for 'Tinyakampa'

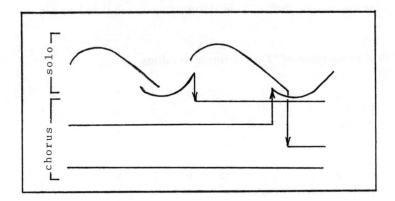

This shows the importance of the continuity of all parts, although the actual performer of any particular part not only could vary, but should vary during the course of the song. The essential patterns are the oppositional relationship of solo and principal chorus parts, over a background of the relatively stable pitch patterns of the *nkuluut*. The timbral quality of the parts is also indicated; the tonal patterning given by words used in the alternating prominent parts contrasts with the fundamentally word-less *nkuluut*, with its intentional breathiness. The sort of melodic patterns from which the *laranyani* create their solos are also indicated.

How do boys start the process of becoming able to take part in singing such songs? How do they approach the challenge? Obviously imitation is a large part of the process, but cannot be the only part, as so much depends on the individual's ability to improvise within certain parameters, about the things he has done. The learning is done at a distance, and is based mainly on snippets heard late at night from inside the family home. This exclusion is mixed with frequent verbal and physical 'abuse' to ensure that the boys are keen to be circumcised and will have the courage to go through it without flinching, at least officially.

Figure 9.12 shows songs sung by a group of boys aged about six to eight years old:

Figure 9.12   Songs of young boys

In the performance of these songs they have started to work on accompanimental motifs, although these are still relatively simple, and often shadow the melody, even singing in unison, rather than attempting the diversity that will be required of them later. There are some attempts at *nkuluut*, and they are working at the vocables 'hi-di', followed by an audible even-pitched note, which is used to encourage rapid deep breathing. They are not very adept at using solo motifs, finding it difficult to maintain pitch, and after a few standard phrases tend to break down. During the performance there was also a degree of discussion about what is right, and what should happen. The text is along the right lines, if rather tame, with some wishful thinking, for example; 'my girl is nice, where we kept the cows we raided'.

This phase of learning seems to me to be described very clearly by Boyce-Tillman in 'A Framework for Intercultural Dialogue in Music':

> All through their lives [children] have been surrounded by the sounds of their particular culture and now they are endeavouring to join it, by using expressive gestures taken from

it. That is why this phase is called the *vernacular*. (Boyce-
Tillman, 1996: 59)

By the age of 16 individual skills are more highly developed;
accompanimental motifs have been well rehearsed, and some more
complicated ones are being sung in unison; *nkuluut* is quite highly
developed, and solo motifs have been assimilated, and there is some skill at
maintaining the part. It is becoming more *idiomatic*, a phrase used by
Boyce-Tillman to describe this phase of musical development (ibid.). The
lack of maturity could be heard in the performance in problems of balance,
particularly in listening to the soloist and making sure he is heard, and in
coordinating the moves between sections.

Of course, by this stage boys will have had more experience of life on
which to draw to make their songs. They are also physically developed
enough to handle *nkuluut* effectively. They will have been with the
warriors looking after the cattle; will have heard them sing many times, and
may have joined in on the periphery. The younger boys do not have this
access to the warriors, and if they are sensible will not attempt to gain it.
One performance of boys practising 'Esesiai' includes the following words:

This song is sung by boys
Let us keep *ilmurran* away from us
We are not yet their age
Ilmurran are as fierce as the Air Force

(The Air Force were the principal movers behind the 'disturbances' or
attempted coup in Kenya in 1982.)

For Maasai men musicianship has to do with recognition and
assimilation of short accompanimental motifs and progression beyond that
to the creation of new motifs, which will need to be approved by the group
in performance, and which will then become part of the individual's
repertoire which can be drawn on as occasions demand.

Musicianship also requires mastery of the *nkuluut* technique, as another
type of accompanying figure created by the performer, and as an
expression of warrior philosophy.

The third part of male Maasai musicianship is the assimilation of
melodic motifs to be used as a basis for singing one's own song, to boast of
one's heroism and to encourage female admirers.

Each boy has to work at these aspects, balancing individual achievement
within communal performance. This may lead us to a model which
indicates the nature of musical composition in a way similar to Figure 9.13:

Figure 9.13   Model of composition

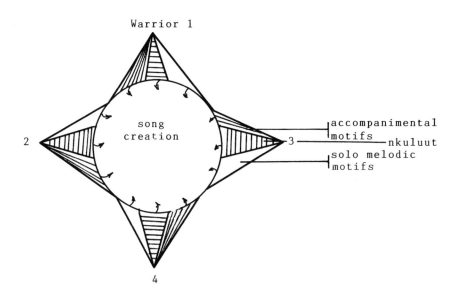

This shows minimal beginnings, expanding into individual motif banks, and with greater effect as the *nkuluut* is enhanced with physical growth, and fuller confidence in the use of solo melodies. All these individual skills come together to create group performances, and for each performance the individual selects what to contribute.

It is appropriate to bring in the warriors' own thoughts about their music at this point, and first I want to return to Lekampus and his friend Kanchory. They said that they started to sing when they were born, and could sing well at 8 years of age, (Kanchory) or 12 (Lekampus), and they learnt the songs of the older group, who did not object to this. After initiation when they joined in the songs of warriors their feelings depended upon their place in the song; for example they felt bad when the names of the brave, and those who had raided cattle from the Turkana were mentioned, if they were not among them, but very good if they were (they also made the legal point that it was bad to have raided cattle or killed a lion, which immediately placed them in a quandary: how can you feel 'good' if you are only mentioned in the songs when you have done something 'bad'?). They described the songs sung outside as being easy, while the songs sung inside homes were difficult. *Nkuluut* was also a difficult thing to do. They were only aware of a small range of songs:

What do girls sing?
They sing lullabies or not at all. [K, L]
What is sung at marriage ceremonies?
The men sing about raids. There is nothing concerned with those being married. [L] The women [among the Maasai] sing to welcome the girl. [K]
Are there singing games? *No* [K, L] Humorous songs? *No* [K, L] Love songs? *No* [K, L] Work songs? *No* [K, L] (Interview, 16 September 1984)

But singing was important:

It is good to know songs, and to be a good singer. You will be laughed at if you can't sing well, but nobody teaches singing; it is picked up from the older group. [L]

It is enjoyable to sing and to listen to others singing, particularly the *laranyani* [good singer]. [K]. (Ibid.)

They also had views about the music of other peoples; first about Kenyan groups:

Singing with instruments is bad, and it is bad-mannered to dance while singing. [L]

and secondly about the singing of 'Westerners':

It is controlled, and has a variety of levels [pitch and volume]. It is better than the singing of other tribes. [L]. (Ibid.)

Hussein Mohamed Hassan (17-year-old Samburu-Somali) wrote some of his thoughts in August 1992. He was particularly concerned to declare his view that music was the clearest expression of a culture he valued:

So to me Music is highly for keeping culture around us. Music sung in praise of old historical memory. Kenyans do memorize [what] occurred with traditional music... Traditional Music is our cultural memory, and to us ... losing or forgetting your culture is slavery. (Letter, 27 August 1982)

My most recent discussion on these issues has been with a group of Maasai/WaArusha secondary school students, who during the school holidays returned to their warrior lifestyle, in August 1995. Their comments are given below:

Silas Lararo: My music is so well I want to stay there. Our music is so beautiful that [it] can make you feel very happy and forget all your problems ... So I want to challenge all young men who belong to our tribe to like our tribe more than those foreign ones.

Silanga Sabore: [I like to sing traditional songs] because it makes me to refresh myself, also it makes me proud of myself for what I did.

William Sanare: [From our songs] I have learnt to be a strong man, to defend your society, to work hard, able to control your family ... they make you not to worry about things, it teaches us more about our culture, to become a real 'morani'.

There was also a very interesting comment from another of the students, which makes clear the impact of Christianity on expressions of traditional culture:

> Nothing I can write because I am no traditional music. Because ... I have been saved ... Christians in my religion are not allowed to sing traditional music because if you sing you will make sin to God ... Traditional songs glorified traditional values (things). That is why as a Christian I don't like to sing them. (Name withheld)

The influence of religion on music has varied among the communities I have worked with; from the extreme situation of rejecting everything that is not new and specifically part of the religion, to a very *laissez-faire* approach to things which are not actually offensive, with a range of modes of direction of people's lifestyles in between. It does not seem to be denominationally specific either, as Protestant denominations around Arusha have been engaged in employing traditional music as appropriate in Christian worship, while in Maralal Protestant missions have required that converts give up all traditional practices, including the wearing of beads, and singing of songs (two defining cultural features). This may, indeed, have had the effect of isolating these people (almost exclusively women) from those in the surrounding communities, but it would be possible to argue that the replacement of these by the (mainly non-Samburu) Christian community has not been as complete as it might have. What other influences are there on song construction and perception?

Figure 9.14 shows the geography of the family encampment (manyatta) of the Lempirikany family at Lemisigyo. It shows houses, fencing used to contain livestock, and the two churches (one Anglican, one Roman Catholic).

Figure 9.14 Lempirikany *manyatta*

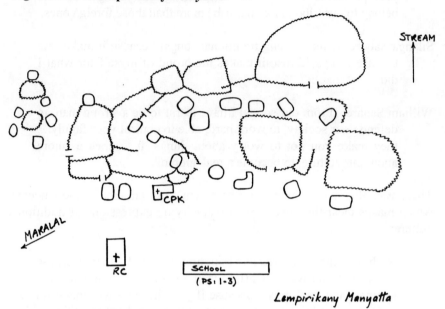

Figure 9.15 shows the progression of performance by warriors on one particular evening;

Figure 9.15 Warrior movements

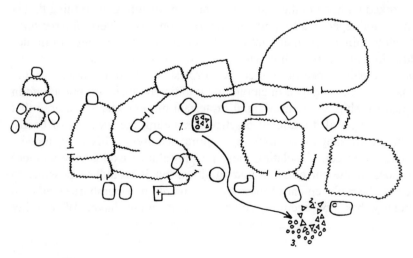

The group consists of 12 junior and senior warriors. They start at about 7.00 p m inside the home of the mother of Olmiuseie, a senior warrior respected for his musical expertise. Here they sing two versions of 'Esesiai', which is a boasting song involving improvising words to archetypal melodic patterns, with warriors taking turns to outdo each other. This arouses the spirits of the group and they then move to position 2, outside the home of Lempirikany's first wife, as the group included two of her sons. In the first home the group was rather squashed in, now they are outside they move into a typical circular shape, with the less experienced singers creating a second row where they stay close to an expert. In position 2 they sing two more competition songs, 'Eokore' and 'Emparo'. After this they start to call for the girls to come and join them, singing 'Entemer', before going on to yet another version of 'Esesiai'. As the peri-adolescent girls arrive they join the group as shown in position 3. As the night goes on the songs are specifically for moving and jumping with, although the Maasai decry the notion that this is anything so effete as dancing. The songs on this particular night are 'Eiyoler' and the extremely popular 'Entoremama'. The music concludes with another version of 'Emparo', and 'Lodo', a circumcision song. By this time it is 12.30 a.m.

The community of listeners, the audience, consists of the warriors themselves, especially when they are not the ones improvising the solos, but concentrating on providing the accompaniment. The girls join the immediate audience after they hear 'Entemer', and only join in singing for the version of 'Esesiai' that follows it. However, there are other groups in audience, even if not obviously. Young children can hear, and their mothers will often sing along surreptitiously, so that their infant sons start learning their eventual repertoire. Boys gather together in homes, and are partly fearful of the warriors' display of prowess, partly eager to join them, and partly involved in picking up aspects of the songs to include in their own practice versions. Old men will typically move away from the *manyatta*, and join friends for beer and conversation at another one. In larger *manyattas* they may just move to the furthest home from the warriors.

Some of the married women stay in their homes, to welcome the warriors in, to look after their children, or the uncircumcised boys. Others go off together and sing their own songs.

We have noticed that *ilmurran* are first inside a home, and then for the rest of the evening are outside, next to another home. The first home is fairly central in the *manyatta*, the second at the edge of it. Initially the songs are to do with mutual encouragement in the areas of bravery and relationships. When they move outside the songs change, so girls are called for, and obviously everyone in the *manyatta* can hear what is going on as girls from all parts of it come to join in.

Why do the *ilmurran* move to the edge of the *manyatta* for their singing, when it is obviously still audible? A clue may come in the way the songs develop. Intimacy between *ilmurran* and their girlfriends is expected and accepted. However, intercourse resulting in pregnancy is not, as it causes considerable complications in arranging payments for the girl at her marriage. 'Adultery' is fairly commonplace, but in such cases the warrior concerned is directly challenging the authority and respect due to an elder. The case is most serious where the husband is two age-sets or more older than the warrior, when he has the right and power to curse the warrior.

Performing venues are chosen because they allow a construct to be established that there is no audience beyond the performers themselves. Therefore, it is as if the songs are sung beyond the hearing of the elders. The elders play along with this during the performances of the *ilmurran* by moving away, by ceding ground to the younger men, and thus not being required to respond to this act of apparent public rebellion. *Ilmurran* feel this need to rebel partly because of their attraction towards the women, and partly because of the perceived avarice and self-centredness of elders, contrasted with the warrior's ideals of being subservient to the will of the collective, yet having a role in shaping it, and having property in common. This often includes girlfriends and, but much more rarely, cattle.

This is in line with Gluckman's argument that forces of opposition generated by absolute systems may be dissipated through ritual protest (Spencer, 1988: 99).

It is the choosing of the venue by the performers to create the desired audience, and the fact that song is the medium of expression and it is not channelled directly at the elders, that makes it possible for these rituals of rebellion to occur among the Maasai, and ultimately go beyond legitimising conflict to emphasising the fundamental underpinning concept of the entire community, which rises beyond any particular group.

To summarise, the Maasai and Samburu have been a migrating, transhumant people, developing a strong warrior ethos to maintain their progress, and their social cohesion while on the move, although they have been prepared to borrow widely, linguistically and culturally. This ethos has also led to a significant status being accorded to the warriors. Music has also enhanced this warrior status, as the warriors are at the centre of the Maasai musical world, (there is also a strength in the music of married women, but this tends to be reserved mainly for the women themselves). Musical skill is required from all the warriors, for performance within a socio-musical framework, and there are physiological implications in the use of hyperventilation in *nkuluut*. Texts also reinforce the importance of bravery, and shame any reluctance to be 'what a warrior should be'. All this is given further social consequence as the composition/performance happens where it will have the appropriate and most impact.

As for me, I have aged with my Maasai and Samburu friends and have passed the *ol murrani* stage. In future I will only be able to listen to the boys and young men singing 'Tinyakampa', while there are still places where they can cause trouble. And, of course, reminisce with my age-mates about the places, people and events who have been involved in the trouble we caused.

Notes

1. There are various ways of spelling these names, the main alternatives to the ones I have mentioned here are: Supet, Mbatian and Lenana.
2. The issue of notation is always complex, and certainly the transcriptions and resultant descriptions used in this chapter are based on Western models. This is, of course, inevitable to an extent, as it is difficult for me to discard my ways of thinking musically, and the questions that interest me are not always those that interest the Maasai and Samburu. All the transcriptions should be read as approximations, which, while not complete, attempt to give something of the essence and flavour of these songs. For those interested to hear the actual music the British Library National Sound Archive holds a range of recordings of Maasai and Samburu music, including those of the songs discussed here.

Bibliography

Alpers, E. A. (1974), 'The Nineteenth Century: Prelude to Colonialism', in B. A. Ogot (ed.), *Zamani. A Survey of East African History*, Nairobi: Longman and East African Publishing House, pp. 229-48.

Boyce-Tillman, June (1996) 'A Framework for Intercultural Dialogue in Music', in Malcolm Floyd, (ed.), *World Musics in Education*, Aldershot: Scolar Press.

Ehret, C. (1974), 'Cushites and the Highland and Plains Nilotes to AD 1800' in B. A. Ogot (ed.), *Zamani. A Survey of East African History*, Nairobi: Longman and East African Publishing House, pp. 150-69.

Floyd, Malcolm (ed.) (1996), *World Musics in Education*, Aldershot: Scolar Press.

Kipury, Naomi (1983), *Oral Literature of the Maasai*, Nairobi: Heinemann.

McEvedy, Colin (1983), *The Penguin Atlas of African History*, London: Penguin.

Mitzlaff, Ulrike von (1988), *Maasai Women. Life in a Patriarchal Society*, Munich: Trickster Verlag; Dar es Salaam: Tanzania Publishing House.

Ochieng', W. R. (1985), *A History of Kenya*, Nairobi: Macmillan.

Oddie, Catherine (1994), *Enkop Ai. My Life with the Maasai*, East Runswick, NSW: Simon and Schuster.

Ogot, B. A. (ed.) (1974), *Zamani. A Survey of East African History*, Nairobi: Longman and East African Publishing House.

Saibull, Solomon ole and Carr, Rachel (1981), *Herd and Spear. The Maasai of East Africa*, London: Collins and Harvill Press.

Saitoti, Tepilit ole (1986), *The Worlds of a Maasai Warrior*, New York: Random House.

Sankan, S. S. (1971), *The Maasai*, Nairobi: Kenya Literature Bureau.

Spear, Thomas (1981), *Kenya's Past: An Introduction to Historical Method in Africa*, London: Longman.

Spear, Thomas (1997), *Mountain Farmers*, Dar es Salaam: Mkuki na Nyota; Berkeley, CA: University of California Press; Oxford: James Currey.

Spear, Thomas and Waller, Richard (eds) (1993), *Being Maasai*, Dar es Salaam: Mkuki na Nyota; Nairobi: East African Educational Publishers; Athens, OH: Ohio University Press; London: James Currey.

Spencer, Paul (1988), *The Maasai of Matapato*, London: Manchester University Press for the International African Institute.

Tucker, A. N. and Mpaayei, J. Tompo ole (1955), *A Maasai Grammar with Vocabulary*, London: Longmans, Green and Co.

10 New Lyres in Northern Kenya: the *Enchamunge* of the Samburu and the *Kilumba* of the Turkana

Malcolm Floyd

I first came across the *enchamunge* late in 1989. It was being played by a Samburu watchman at Turi, near Nakuru in Kenya, (for all locations see map at Figure 10.1) where I then worked. It struck me as being interesting in several ways: it is a Maasai/Samburu string instrument where, according to my investigations, none had existed before; it showed the assimilation of techniques and concepts from at least two other cultures; and it reveals a process in action for the dissemination of musical instruments and practices. It also arouses questions to do with definitions of instruments: is it an absolute art, or does it depend on the intentions and perceptions of composer/performer and audiences? In this particular case should the instrument be regarded as a lyre with the body adapted to ideas of guitar patterns, which is what it looks like to the etic observer, or is it a guitar with the neck exchanged for the more usual type of lyre construction found in Kenya, as is the view of the emic participants?

I came across the instrument type again in 1993, while visiting Maralal towards the north of Kenya. On this visit I saw it being played by a teenage Samburu male initiate at a compound in Bahaua Location. It was also on this visit that I encountered the Turkana equivalent; the *kilumba*, being played at a house in Loikas village, on the outskirts of Maralal itself. The two Samburu instruments of 1989 and 1993 were very similar, the Turkana version was more like a traditional lyre in the construction of the soundbox, although used in a similar way to the *enchamunge*.

To begin to provide a context for this study it may be useful to spend some time exploring the general spread of traditional musical instruments across Kenya. Comparatively little has been written on the topic, and what there is has usually been in the form of small-scale works, or as information included in more general texts. Much of the detailed work that has been done has been on the music and instruments of a specific people or community.

There is a significant range of musical instruments to be found in Kenya, some for specialists, some available for all, some complex in construction, others made from household implements. The influences on Kenya's musical instruments seem to come from three principal directions; down the Nile, from inland areas to the west and south, and from Arabs at the coast. There is a specific issue concerned with pastoralism, which appears to limit instrument construction and use. It is also the case that pastoralists in Kenya

Figure 10.1   Map of Kenya showing locations

have developed comparatively complex harmonic systems and rhythmic vocal techniques. Spontaneous improvisation and extemporisation are other important features of their music. This may all mean that to add melodic or accompanying instruments would be perceived as being very problematic. It would seem that for instruments to be adopted into a culture there needs to be a predominantly agricultural or at least sedentary mode of existence, and a certain stability.

Figure 10.2 shows where various peoples are to be found in Kenya, and indicates rough, and rather imprecise, groupings common in discussions of East African anthropology, namely Bantu, Cushitic, and Nilotic.[1]

Figure 10.2   Social groupings in Kenya

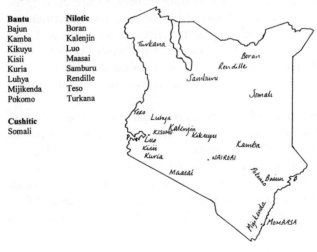

Bantu	**Nilotic**
Bajun	Boran
Kamba	Kalenjin
Kikuyu	Luo
Kisii	Maasai
Kuria	Samburu
Luhya	Rendille
Mijikenda	Teso
Pokomo	Turkana

Cushitic
Somali

Graham Hyslop's book (1975) was the first attempt to review instruments across the country, and in addition is summarised in *African Music* (1958, vol. 2, no. 1). However it was only able to contain significant information from the coastal and western areas of Kenya, because the musicians in those places were the only ones to complete the questionnaires sent out by Hyslop, on which his information was based.

There is a useful supply of information in the *Kenya Churches Handbook* (Barrett, 1973). It lists 177 instruments, and is unique in including relatively accurate, if very small, drawings of so many instruments. However, instruments are only included which are used in Christian worship in Kenya, most of which are found among the independent churches, and so this catalogue is intentionally selective. The next writer to assay a look at instruments throughout the country was Paul Kavyu (1980). He describes briefly the main types of instruments, and gives the names used by several peoples. He also provides maps showing the distribution of instruments. There is not, however, an exhaustive list of the instruments, and Kavyu does not comment further on them. In 1982 Gerhard Kubik's East Africa volume of VEB Deuthscher Verlag für Musik's *Musikgeschichte in Bildern* appeared, and this is one of the most fully illustrated and detailed texts on aspects of the topic. The Kenyan elements relate specifically to lyres, and their movements in the region, which are particularly relevant to this study, and the historical music of the Swahili coast. The most recent book (up to 1997) to include a significant discussion of the topic is by George Senoga-Zake, *Folk Music in Kenya* (1986). It gives names of instruments in several cultures, and very brief descriptions. This is another book which satisfies its aim of providing basic information, without attempting explanations beyond the comprehension of its intended audience in schools.

This is very much a feature of most recent writing. Since 1984 there has been a significant increase in music textbooks, as music became one of the examined subjects for the Kenya Certificate of Primary Education (KCPE). Most of these new books include basic information on the best known instruments, including instructions for making them. Naturally, none of these attempts to be exhaustive, although several instruments are mentioned only in these school texts. (All texts studied are listed in the Bibliography.)

Altogether, there are over 560 instrument names to be found in all these books. Figure 10.3 is an indication of where these instruments are to be found.

Figure 10.3   Map of the distribution of instruments in Kenya

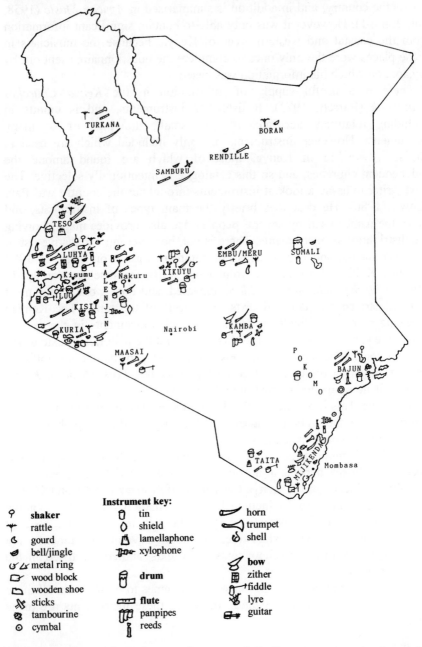

Often no orthography exists, so that several similar names may be found for the same instrument. There are also, however, occasions when two different names indicate the same instrument, and others where one name stands for two quite different instruments. Bearing these problems in mind, here follows a summary of which instruments can be found where. Figure 10.4 shows the spread of idiophones, using the simple classification employed by Nketia (1979) with additions and adaptations as required.

Figure 10.4 Idiophones found in Kenya

IDIOPHONES

shaken	shakers	
	rattles	
	gourds	
struck &	bells and jingles	plate
concussion	metal rings and triangles	tin
	wood block	shield
	wooden shoes	hoe
	sticks	cymbal
	tambourine	
tuned	'thumb piano' (lamellaphone)	
	xylophone	

There is also the bull-roarer, although this is not really used as a musical instrument, and is only found amongst the Kipsigis, who use its fierce animal sound in an attempt to frighten circumcision candidates.

Shakers are fairly wide-spread, with notable exceptions. The whole of the north and north-east are without shakers. This includes the Samburu - along with their southern cousins the Maasai, all the Cushitic peoples and the Turkana. The reason for this may be a lack of available suitable materials. There is, however, anecdotal evidence to suggest that there is a growing tendency to use dried seed pods where these occur.

Rattles are more widely spread. Only Samburu, Somali and other Cushitic groups appear to have no rattles. There are no rattles marked for the Taita, but performances at music festivals and so on suggest a thorough adoption of the Mijikenda reed rattle *Kayamba*. The Turkana, among others, use a string of bottle-tops between the two arms of a Y-shaped twig, reminiscent of the Ethiopian *sistrum*.

Gourds are principally used as containers for a variety of seeds and pebbles. As gourds are commonly part of household contents it is not surprising to find these from the Luhya in the west, to the Mijikenda at the coast, although it appears to be a predominantly Bantu phenomenon. There is nothing recorded for Nilotic and Cushitic groups.

Bells and jingles seem to be found almost everywhere an the variety of bells found is enormous; from large single metal pods strapped to the thigh, to a collection of many small jingles tied around the upper arm The only gap in this dispersal is among the Pokomo. Considering the evidence of other coastal Bantu musics, however, one may be inclined to think that the apparent lack of instruments for which there is evidence among the Pokomo is due to a lack of research, or because the Pokomo themselves have not yet moved much beyond traditional boundaries.

Metal rings and triangles are found in western Kenya, among the Kalenjin[2] group of peoples, the Kikuyu, and in the Mijikenda occupied part of the coast. Major groups which do not have rings or triangles are Cushitic, the Turkana, and the Maa speaking group. The reason might appear to be a lack of suitable metal, although metallic noises are often made by banging spear heads together. More surprising omissions are the Central Bantu groups such as the Embu and Meru, even though they are closely related to the Kikuyu, and the Kamba who occupy the land to the east of these groups. One reason put to the author in personal conversation is that it is felt that such instruments are not truly African, but come rather from European influence, hence their appearance in the areas with the longest and strongest European presence.

Wood blocks hit with sticks have a fairly restricted distribution, being quite common only in the densely populated western area around Lake Victoria and Mount Elgon. The only other place with any evidence for wood blocks is at the coast, among the Mijikenda.

Wooden shoes are used for musical accompaniment only in one small group in the west; the Kuria or Watende. The shoes add several inches to a dancer's height, and the style of dancing includes a strong percussive leg movement, which is enhanced by these wooden shoes. It seems possible that this has been adopted from a group outside Kenya, perhaps from Tanzania, as the Kuria straddle the border, but there is insufficient information to be sure.

Sticks are not very commonly used as musical instruments. Among the Samburu, however, they are required by every male singer, although in many cases they make do with striking their club (*rungu*) against the spear shaft. The other groups with a documented use of sticks as percussive instruments are the Luhya, Kikuyu and Kamba, all of which are Bantu.

Apparently the only place in Kenya where the tambourine is found is on the Lamu archipelago, on the north Kenya coast, where it is called *Twari*. It is probably an adopted instrument, from the mainly Arab countries which have traded extensively with Lamu.

Cymbals are also limited to the coast, and suggest another adoption. Similarly plates are referred to as being used only at the coast.

Tins are used as struck instruments only among the Somali, and are among a variety of instruments made from everyday objects, which also include the hoe.

Shields are used by warriors in a limited number of cases, and in some instances are decorated with jingles.

'Thumb pianos' are restricted to the Luhya and Teso on the extreme west of Kenya, and the Taita to the east of Mount Kilimanjaro. In both cases they have been adopted from near neighbours, but have stopped in their current situations without further dispersal. It does not seem to be an instrument highly regarded by Kenyans, and has found very few imitators. The examples made are often of relatively limited musical potential, sometimes being restricted to six tongues. This is, perhaps, surprising as there are considerably larger examples in other parts of Africa, indeed as close as Tanzania.

Although xylophones are common throughout many parts of Africa, in Kenya they are to be found mainly at the coast and in the west. There are a few examples among the Kalenjin, who may have learnt its construction from the Teso, who live close to several Kalenjin sub groups on Mount Elgon.

Membranophones are to be found in Kenya in large numbers. The only friction drums are the Kikuyu *ndarama* (also the name of a men's dance), and the Nandi *cheplanget*. There is a great range, however, of struck drums.

The only peoples apparently without drums are the nomadic and semi-nomadic pastoralists; the Turkana, Maasai, Samburu, Rendille and Boran. It may be that the growing level of education in schools could have the effect here of ensuring that drums do not become a part of the music of such groups, as the current situation is proclaimed and reinforced through public performances with a high regard for concepts of 'authenticity'. If so this might be an interesting feature of modern Kenyan education; that textbooks on traditional practices supplant the traditional processes of instrumental development and migration through settling down and interacting with other groups. On the other hand, the ubiquitous radio with its drum driven regularity may be more persuasive.

Figure 10.5   Aerophones found in Kenya

Flute	vertical
	transverse
Panpipes	
Reed	double reed only
Horn	
Trumpet	
Sea shell	

Flutes are widespread throughout Kenya. There is a general preference for transverse types. It is so common that it is a possibility that the few groups without evidence of flutes indeed have them, but information is not as yet as available. For example, if the Samburu have flutes, it is possible that their southern brothers the Maasai have them as well. However, it does seem that most of the Cushitic peoples, apart from the Bajuni, are not flute players.

Panpipes are to be found only among part of the Central Bantu group, namely the Kamba and Kikuyu. This is an interesting alternative to what was common for several of the idiophones which were found only at the coast and in the west. The materials for making panpipes are freely available in many parts of the country, yet they are not widely used, and references are scanty.

Of reed instruments only double reed instruments are to be found in Kenya, and they are without exception at the coast. They have not even penetrated as far inland as the Taita. They may have originated as imports from Arab traders, adventurers and settlers, who have influenced so much of the coast's culture for over 1,000 years.

The essential difference between horns and trumpets is their basic material. Horns are made out of animal horns, or carved out of ivory. Trumpets are made from vegetable material such as gourds, wood, millet stems and so on. The only groups apparently without horns or trumpets are the Somali, Pokomo and Boran. It must be acknowledged that not all tribes use these instruments in an exclusively 'musical' way. Many of the pastoralists (Nilotic and Cushitic) use theirs more frequently to summon warriors, announce danger, and for various other extra-musical purposes. For the rest, trumpets and horns are rarely used melodically; most typically they are used for almost percussive interpolation between song verses, and to indicate changes in the programme.

The only written reference for the use of sea shells (usually conches) as musical instruments is among the Somali. However, the author has also seen them used, as would be expected, along the Kenya coast. Among the Bajun of the Lamu archipelago they arre used in place of the trumpets and horns of inland Kenya. They have a remarkably full and loud tone.

Figure 10.6   Chordophones in Kenya

    Bow
    Zither
    Lutes   Fiddle
                Lyre
                Guitar

There are no lutes of the bow-lute, harp-lute or harp types in Kenya.

The musical bow can be found in an arc that stretches from the west, among the Kuria and Luhya, through the Kalenjin to the Mijikenda and Bajun at the coast. It may be that this indicates the route of its transmission.

Zithers are all of the reed zither type, and are only to be found in the west, among the Luo and Luhya. An origin further west is suggested by these people.

Fiddles are popular throughout Kenya, except among the pastoralists and at the coast. It is not certain why they are not found at the coast as there are certainly Arab instruments like it, and coast melodies are playable on it. It may be that they prefer all melodies to be played on reed instruments of the *nzumari* and *bung'o* types or on flutes such as the *chivoti*. The number of strings a fiddle has is either one or two. Where there are two, one is usually a drone string.

Lyres are very popular in most of Kenya, the exceptions being among the Central Bantu and the pastoralists. There is a great deal of variety in the shape and construction of these lyres. It is quite possible that they arrived in Kenya from two different directions; down the Nile, and from central and western parts of Africa.

Versions of guitars are now spreading rapidly, and in many cases are beginning to supplant the more traditional lyre forms.

Enchamunge and *Kilumba*

To put the *enchamunge* and *kilumba* into more detailed context Figure 10.7 draws together the material available on Turkana and Samburu/Maasai instruments:

Figure 10.7   Turkana and Maasai instruments

Turkana	bell/jingle	*echorot*
	drum	*ebure*
	transverse flute	*apili, ebunoo, elamaru*
	trumpet	*atoroth*
Samburu/	bell/jingle	*ntualan/oltuala*
Maasai	sticks	*sobwani*
	transverse flute	*ndule/ndurerut* (also Kalenjin)

There are a few additional items that are noted for the Maasai but not the Samburu:

'idiophone'	*enkalulunga*
shield	*ngo* (also Kalenjin)
horn	*emowuo*
fiddle	*pugandit*

It is difficult to comment further on the unspecified idiophone, although it is conceivable that it refers to the sticks (*sobwani*) that the Samburu also have. The fiddle (*pugandit*) referred to by Wahome (1986b: 215) is attributed to the Maasai around Mt Elgon in the west of Kenya, who are a settled group, and the name is very similar to names of instruments played by close Kalenjin groups, such as the fiddle *kipugantet* (Nandi), and the lyre *pakan/pagan/pugan/pukan* (Pokot), and the *bukandit* lyre attricuted to the Kalenjin generally. This similarity of names can be seen also in the *ngo*, and *ndurerut*.

To show the chordophone context for the *enchamunge* and *kilumba* Figure 10.8 shows the distribution of the 32 lyres and guitars to be found throughout Kenya.

Figure 10.8   Distribution of lyres in Kenya

Figure 10.9 lists lyres by group.

Figure 10.9 Lyres in Kenya

Group:	Lyre names:
Bantu	
Kisii (Gusii)	*Obokano*
Kuria	*Iritungu, Litungu*
Luhya (including Bukusu and	*Litungu, Bukhana*
Tachoni sub-groups)	
Tiriki (sub-group)	*Lukhuje*
Swahili	*Udi*
Nilotic	
Kalenjin	*Chepkong'o, Chemonge*
Keiyo-Marakwet (sub-group)	*Kibukandet*
Kipsigis (sub-group)	*Achemonge, Chepkesem, Chepkeser, Kibugader*
Nandi (sub-group)	*Achemonge, Ketuba, Kibgandent, Kibkandet, Kibucondet, Kipkesemit, Kitubet*
Pokot (sub-group)	*Pagan, Pakan, Pugan, Pukan*
Sabaot (sub-group)	*Bugandit, Kipkandit*
Tugen (sub-group)	*Kibukan*
Luo	*Kambanane, Nyatiti, Obukhana, Skika, Thum, Thum nyaluo*
Samburu	*Enchamunge*
Turkana	*Kilumba*

There are many differences between these, in terms of numbers of strings, details of construction, tuning (which often varies between individuals anyway), and precise performing techniques, but otherwise all of them are recognisably the same essential instrument; a lyre with bowl shaped soundbox, skin sound table and asymetrical arms. The *kilumba* is consistent with this description, which is a bowl lyre, and classified by Sachs and Hornbostel as 321.22, and by Dournon in her adaptation (1992) as 381.2. The *enchamunge* is rather different, having a box resonator with wooden soundboard, but it does have asymmetrical arms, classified as a box lyre (Sachs and Hornbostel 321.22, Dournon 382). This does raise issues which have been connected with the classification of instruments from its beginnings as a scientific study. And that is, perhaps, the first point of discussion. Organology has most frrquently been seen as as scientific tool for those studying instruments, such as curators of collections, ethnomusicologists and so on, aiming for an empirically based system which is universally applicable, rather than being a reification of instrinsic or functional concepts. There are examples of organological systems from various parts of the world, and Dournon (1992: 250-51) briefly discusses theoretical systems from China and India, and two 'ethnic systems', of the Bassari of Senegal and the 'Are'are of the Solomon Islands, based on the way sounds are produced, although the 'Are'are subdivide the classification depending upon whether the playing is 'individual or collective' (ibid.). The system of Hornbostel and Sachs also uses the ways in which sound is produced as a basis for classification, which are determined 'only on those features which can be identified from the visible form of the instrument avoiding subjective preferences' (ibid.). Schaeffner, however, while obviously influenced by the work of Hornbostel and Sachs, has as one of his major subdivisions of instruments the materials of which they are constructed, and in this is close to the Chinese model (ibid.: 253). Dournon then posits her own synthesis of some of these systems. Her intention is again to provide a particular type of user (curator, ethnomusicologist, student) with a tool suitable for 'practical and didactic purposes'. She does this principally through combining the systems of Hornbostel and Sachs and Schaeffner, so that:

> The distinction of instruments within each of the categories thus defined is based on the relation between the ways in which they are set in vibration and the structure of the instrument. (Ibid.: 254)

So in the Hornbostel and Sachs system, 321.21 means that the *enchamunge* is a composite chordophone (consisting of a combination of a string bearer and resonator), of the 'box lyre' type. The *kilumba*'s classification would be 321.21 as it is a bowl lyre (Hornbostel and Sachs, 1992: 457). For Dournon, the *kilumba* can be classified at 381: a lyre with strings stretched between soundbox and yoke, linked by two arms, plucked, with a bowl shaped soundbox with skin sound-table. However, the *enchamunge* is rather more problematic as it fits into her category 38, as a lyre, but she only establishes two types of soundboxes, bowl shaped or flat, whereas the resonator of the *enchamunge* is very definitely a box. However, she allows for extension in her discussion, and so perhaps it is appropriate to classify the instrument at 383.2; a lyre with strings, which are plucked, stretched between a box-shaped resonator and yoke, which are linked by two assymetrical arms (Dournon, 1992: 279).

That may go some way to satisfying a penchant for the neatness and sense of completion that manipulation of any classificatory system is supposed to bring, but it is still working with a tool that is perhaps only usable for those who have created the need for such a tool. It is an abstraction which aids the person studying, but does not necessarily provide anything useful for the person who 'uses' the instrument, as composer, performer, listener and so on. Of course, it does not have to, that is not the intention of such a system, but the problem is posed because the perception of the participants is at odds with our classification. For the Samburu and Turkana, these instruments are guitars plain and simple. That is because they are used in the place of guitars in the composition and performance of the sort of music that guitars play. Elements of construction differ, quite markedly, from guitars as usually made, but in this instance the over-riding parameter of classification is function. Wachsmann (1995: 237-45) briefly discussed two systems, which attempt to acknowledge the importance of culturally situated organography in establishing a taxonomic organology. Part of the point of the work of both Hood and Heyde is that organography is capable of local adaptation, and would include performance techniques, function, decoration, and a range of 'socio-cultural consideration' (ibid.). In Hood's organology the consideration of these aspects creates a 'symbolic taxonomy', leading to 'organograms' combining symbols and diagram. This replacing of language with scientific symbolism in diagrammatic form is also a feature of the work of Heyde. It will be interesting to see if the construction of such diagrams through the perceptions of the *enchamunge* and *kilumba* performers themselves will throw up any more pertinent classification.

It can be seen from Figure 10.9 that the Samburu name has most probably been adapted from the Nilotic Kalenjin names *achemonge* and *chemonge*. The Samburu adaptation of the name can be seen in the use of the feminine singular prefix *en-*. The probability of this route is based not only on this linguistic evidence, but also on the historical links and relationships between the two groups. There is indeed one group which appears to combine elements of both groups: the Ilchamus (Samburu name) or Njemps (Kalenjin name) of Lake Baringo.

We face another problem here, and that is the existence and name of the Turkana kilumba. The first assumption might be that the *enchamunge* has been adopted from the Samburu, as the instruments have been found very close to each other, but the relationship between the Turkana and Samburu has not been an amicable one, throughout the twentieth century at least. The Turkana have been considered as aggressive and bent on expansion from the time of their exodus from north-eastern Uganda over 200 years ago. This continues to the present day, as they move down the Rift Valley into Pokot and Samburu territory. The geography of the area has given them protection from the harrassment of other groups, but has also meant that it would be difficult for the Samburu to move out of their reach into new lands, which, in the direction they would have to travel, are already well populated and highly agriculturalised. The practices of the Turkana and Samburu are also different on significant matters; cows and milk do not have the mystical importance for the Turkana that the Samburu bestow upon them,[3] there is no age-set system among the Turkana, and most importantly the Turkana do not circumcise at initiation, and feel superior to those who do, but which evokes scorn from the Samburu (Fedders and Salvadori, 1977). Of course, the route of the lyre from the Kalenjin via the Samburu to the Turkana is still possible, as conquerors have always taken what they want from the vanquished. It has, however, proved impossible to date to find any linguistic evidence to support his, or indeed any other route.

An example of an *enchamunge* can be seen in Figure 10.10 which is a diagram showing all the measurements of the original instrument studied at Turi in 1989. The other instruments have varied quite a lot in size, but the basic proportions have remained the same.

Figure 10.10 *Enchamunge*

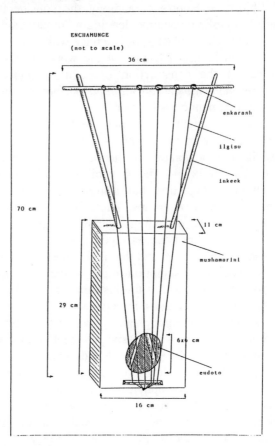

In this case, the resonator is a wooden box with a small hole cut in the middle of the front side, (another instrument owned by the same player,

Layan ole Liripin, was made from an old ammunition box, with the holes being much smaller and cut in the corners of the front facing side). The arms go from the base of the box, through holes in the top side (as the instrument stands) and into the yoke. The tuning rings are made from plant fibre, in this case strips from banana leaves. The strings have in all cases been wires, which join the tuning rings, and then pass through notches on the bridge to a nail which acts as a tail piece.

Similarities with the bukandit/chemonge/pukan of various Kalenjin groups can be seen clearly in this description of the Kalenjin instruments by Senoga-Zake:

> It has five or six wire strings, which are plucked ... The sound-box is [half] a log, about 17cm long, and 26 cm wide. This ... is hollowed [and is] 15 cm deep [and] covered with a cow hide. It has two sticks(arms) projecting from the sound-box and also a cross-bar at the widest part of the two sticks. (Senoga-Zake, 1986: 136)

Moving on to performance practice, the *enchamunge* is played in a sitting position, with the base on the left knee, and the yoke uppermost, with the hole in the resonator facing outwards. The left hand stops the strings from behind, at the harmonic nodes required. The desire to do this is the apparent reason for the rejection of the usual neck construction found on a guitar. The right hand picks the strings, usually in groups of three. This method of playing is common in Kenyan guitar music, as Low makes clear in his *History of Kenyan Guitar Music* (Low, 1982: 17-36). It is also used in some traditional lyres, namely the *litungu* and the *chemonge*. Senoga-Zake describes a particular *chemonge* technique:

> At times two strings are plucked simultaneously in fourths, and this, sounding like the western banjo, tempts the western educated to more attentive listening. (Ibid.)

If Senoga-Zake is right, perhaps this is what attracted me to the *enchamunge* and *kilumba* in the first place.

Other lyres use both hands for plucking the strings: on an eight-stringed lyre such as the *nyatiti* of the Luo each hand is responsible for for four strings, which has encouraged, or at least enabled, the use of rapid repetitions of the same note, between strings one and seven, or two and eight.

The tuning on this instrument can be seen in Figure 10.11:

Figure 10.11   *Enchamunge* **tuning**

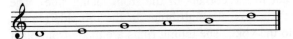

The arrangement of relative pitches is broadly similar in the two Samburu instruments and the Turkana instrument I have observed. Several other Kenyan lyres are tuned in two sets of pitches, where the middle two of eight strings are an octave apart, and several examples are given by Senoga-Zake in *Folk Music of Kenya* (1986), including the tuning of a *licheni* (played among the Marachi) seen in Figure 10.12

Figure 10.12   *Licheni* **tuning**

(*Source*: Senoga-Zake, 1986: 139)

This can also be seen in the tuning of the Luo *nyatiti*:

Figure 10.13   *Nyatiti* **tuning**

(*Source*: Omondi, 1984: 271)

It will be noticed here that the pitches of strings one and two are repeated for strings seven and eight, thus allowing rapid repetitions of these notes. There are also, however, instruments that are tuned similarly to the *enchamunge* and *kilumba*, namely the *litungu* of the Bukusu:

Figure 10.14   *Litungu* **tuning**

(*Source*: Senoga-Zake, 1986: 142)

and the *chemonge* of the Kalenjin, providing further evidence of a link with the Samburu instruments:

Figure 10.15   Tunings of the *chemonge* [All transposed to the same starting point to facilitate comparison]

(*Source*: Ibid.: 136)

It will be observed that all of the tunings cover the span of an octave. Some have the extremes of the octave between the middle strings, others, including the *enchamunge* and *kilumba*, spread the octave from first to last strings.

Layan ole Liripin, the performer who introduced me to this instrument, had been playing for two years at that time, and was originally taught by ole Lokamorian at Ong'ata Rongai. The Turkana player I observed was rather older than the Samburu players, at about 40 years of age. It was ole Liripin's assessment that all the Maasai and Samburu liked the *enchamunge*, although only young people play it. Ole Liripin was also quite certain that the idea for the instrument came from guitars, with the adjustment of neck and tuning designed for the greater convenience of the performer. It is interesting to note that the Samburu themselves say that traditional songs cannot be sung to an *enchamunge* accompaniment, and that singing has to be changed to fit the instrument. All *enchamunge* songs have been newly made up, and rely heavily on the sounds of the instrument for inspiration. For ole Liripin, the composition process consists of listening to oneself improvising rhythmic chordal patterns on the *enchamunge* and then adding a vocal line to them. The resulting compositions with all three performers consist of short repeated chord sequences on the instrument, with a sung tune above, which is rhythmically and melodically linked to the instrumental part, and is usually a descending figure.

The transcriptions that follow are derived from recordings, and discussion with the performers. They do not attempt to show all, or even much, of the musical detail, but give an indication of the basic material which the performers draw upon in performance. Figures 10.16 and 10.17 are by Layan ole Liripin, performed at Turi in 1989, Figures 10.18 and 10.19 are by the Turkana player at Loikas, and Figures 10.20 and 10.21 by the young Samburu initiate at Bahaua, both recorded in 1993.

Figure 10.16   Song text typical of warriors' songs, mentioning places the singer has been to, and the girls he has known

Figure 10.17   Song about girls' stomachs, highly appreciated by the Samburu and Maasai male

It may be noted that the rhythm of the *enchamunge* part is identical in both pieces, and that the vocal rhythm is not as closely tied to the accompaniment as might be expected.

Figure 10.18 A song about a girl called Monica, and the ways the singer has tried to win her love

Figure 10.19 Song enjoining all children to love their parents

The two performances in Figures 10.18 and 10.19 use very similar chord sequences.

Figure 10.20 A song thanking mothers for looking after the boys while young, and promising to be a source of pride in the future

The tune sung is the same as the top notes of the *enchamunge* part.

Figure 10.21 A version of a circumcision song, calling for bravery on the part of all the boys being circumcised

The Samburu initiate uses much smaller repeated units, and is limited in his choice of chords.

The structures of the six songs can be seen and compared in Figure 10.22:

Figure 10.22   Structures of *enchamunge* and *kilumba* songs

Piece Fig.:	10.16	10.17	10.18	10.19	10.20	10.21
Speed (♩ =)	140	142	104	112	108	108
Base pitch	D	D	A	A	C	C
Playings of patterns	45v	83v	2i	1i	15v	25v
i: instrument only;	4i	4i	9v	4v	2i	1i
v: with voice			2i	2i		4v
			6v	2v		
			3i	7i		
			3v	3v		
			1i	1i		
			6v			
			3i			
Ends with slow strum?	yes	yes	yes	yes	no	no

What else can we learn from these transcriptions (which are significantly less than the complete song, but perhaps provide us with a starting point)? If we consider the vocal part first it is noticeable that the range is quite varied, not only between performers, but between the two songs of the Samburu performers. The range is as follows:

Figure 10.23   Song ranges

Samburu (Turi)	Figure 10.16	10th
	Figure 10.17	5th
Turkana	Figure 10.18	7th
	Figure 10.19	8ve
Samburu (Bahaua)	Figure 10.20	2nd
	Figure 10.21	5th

The Turkana songs make most consistent use of a fair range, while the older Samburu performer has the widest range of all in one song, although he is much more restricted in the other. The Samburu initiate has a very limited range for both songs, with the first being almost all on one note.

The melodic shape is generally a descending arc, although with some variety within that; the second Turkana song has the most complex pattern, and the restricted compass of the initiate's songs make the arc less of a feature, although it is apparent in the second of his songs.

Figure 10.24 Melodic shape

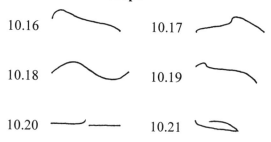

Turning to the guitar/lyre parts themselves, the number of different notes used varies from 4 in songs 20 and 21, through 5 and 6 in songs 16 and 17, to 7 and 8 for songs 18 and 19. This includes notes reappearing in different octaves, and the extra Turkana notes are mostly of this sort, with notes other than the open strings being created.

Single notes are very rare, only occurring in these examples as an opening 'anacrusis' to song in Figure 10.18. Two part chords are common to the Turkana songs (Figures 10.18 and 10.19), and to those of the Samburu initiate (Figures 10.20 and 10.21), while they do not appear at all in the songs of the older Samburu performer. Three part chords are used by all performers, although only in one of the initiate's songs. The Samburu players use noticeably fewer chords than the Turkana, however; songs in Figures 10.16, 10.17 and 10.21 use three chords, and song in Figure 10.20 uses four, while the Turkana songs use seven (Figure 10.18) and nine (Figure 10.19).

The length of the repeating instrumental pattern is mostly eight beats (Figures 10.16, 10.17, 10.19 and 10.20 as transcribed here), although the initiate's song in Figure 10.21 has only a fou-beat pattern, while the Turkana song in Figure 10.18 has a 16-beat pattern.

The ordering of combined vocal and instrumental notes into modal suggestions indicate a pentatonic element, which is particularly clear in Figures 10.16, 10.20 and 10.21, although this is altered or extended in the other three songs, to create a hemitonic hexatonic mode for the song in Figure 10.17, and an alternation of notes, and thus modes, in Figures 10.18 and 10.19, with the song in Figure 10.18 having increased semitonal possibilities (between B - C - C# - D):

Figure 10.25   Derived modes

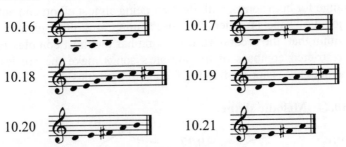

What are the differences between the traditional music of the Samburu adult male and this new enchamunge music? To act as a focus for comparison here are transcriptions of two traditional songs (Figures 10.26 and 10.27).

Figure 10.26   'Ntoremama'

This talks of migration, and particularly of how 'my girl's feather swings like leaves on a tree'.

Figure 10.27   'Tesho'

This is a friendship song, Tesho being the friend's name, 'sharing one stick ... club mother ... father ... etc'.

First, then, *enchamunge* songs are solo. There is no place at present for the polyphony of Ntoremama (Figure 10.26), which is very typical of Samburu male singing, and all observation and discussion points to the *enchamunge* being performed exclusively by males. These may be things that will alter with time as the *enchamunge* and its songs become better known, but they were not considered appropriate by my informants. Secondly, traditional songs are rhythmically much more varied than *enchamunge* songs, which are all performed (and transcribed) in a strictly controlled four beats in a bar, whereas 'Tesho' comes closest to:

$$(1)\ 7\ 4\ 7\ 4$$
$$(8)\ 8\ 4\ 8\ 4$$

Thirdly, the use of harmonies in chordal sequences is quite different from the single chord structures found in traditional songs.

Fourthly, in the previous chapter, a feature of 'Tinyakampa' was the directional opposition of soloist, and principal chorus part. This is not so clear in these songs, and indeed does not appear in the Turkana songs, or in one of the initiate's songs. However, there may be more of a link with the songs of the older Samburu performer.

There are, indeed, many facets of the new music that have been carried in from the traditional:

1. A strong tendency to employ descending melodic lines.

2. Vigorous maintenance of regular rhythms where these occur, using either the *enchamunge*, or the *nkuluut* technique of rhythmic hyper-ventilation as an accompanying part.

3. Extensive repetition of short phrases, with occasional altered notes or phrases.

4. A strong pentatonic element in both melody and accompaniment.

5. The vocal ranges are broadly similar, from a fifth to a tenth.

6. The 'contrary motion' of parts is particularly noticeable in the songs of Layan ole Liripin.

How far is the music created for the *enchamunge* and *kilumba* societally distinctive and how far is it common to lyre music throughout Kenya? There is not enough space here to discuss that in detail, but it may be worth considering briefly the music of the Luo *nyatiti* because of the significance accorded to it in all writings on Kenyan music, and because of its importance in underlying the popular *Benga* style which originated among Luo musicians, although it has now spread significantly further, and hence could be a feature one might expect to see in other music moving towards contemporary popular idioms. Figure 10.28 shows the principal formula of a nyatiti-accompanied song performed by Ochieng' Waganda. No title or other information is given on the cassette.

Figure 10.28   *Nyatiti* performance by Ochieng' Waganda

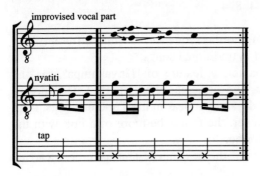

The piece can be compared with the *enchamunge* and *kilumba* pieces in Figure 10.29.

Figure 10.29   *Enchamunge, kilumba* and *nyatiti* patterns

Fig:	16	17	18	19	20	21	28
Speed (♩ =)	140	142	104	112	108	108	120
Base pitch	D	D	A	A	C	C	C
Playings of patterns	45v	83v	2i	1i	15v	25v	143v[1]
i: instrument only;	4i	4i	9v	4v	2i	1i	
v: with voice			2i	2i		4v	
			6v	2v			
			3i	7i			
			3v	3v			
			1i	1i			
			6v				
			3i				
Ends with slow strum?	yes	yes	yes	yes	no	no	no[2]

Notes

1, There are occasional phrases where the singer does not sing, never for more than one phrase at a time.
2. The piece begins and ends with a fast tremolo on the two 'C' strings.

What is immediately noticeable in this comparison is the considerable length of the Luo performance, far exceeding any of the others. The vocal range is a fifth, (about the average of the other songs), and five different notes are used (the others using from four to eight). Single notes are quite common in the *nyatiti* part, with use also of two-part chords. In this performance there are no three-part chords (in the other songs three-part chords were most common, followed by two-part chords, with almost no single notes). The length of the repeated pattern is at the shorter end of the range, being four beats long. There is no appparent contrary motion between instrumental and vocal parts, and although the melodic shape is often a descending arc, it also appears as a wave:

I stated earlier that the performer's intentions were significant in analysing what was happening in the use of this instrument. Although there is much that is clearly adapted from traditional musical processes - elements of the instrument's construction, tuning, melodic outlines and so on - the performers see themselves as being within the tributaries to the mainstream of popular music, as players of instruments as conveniently close to guitars as possible, incorporating the guitarists ways of developing structure through chord sequences. This is their expressed intention, and they are intentionally working towards an assimilation with which they can feel culturally comfortable.

It is intriguing also to see the development of composing as an individual creative activity, as an expansion of traditional methods of extemporisation upon known vocabularies of appropriate musical phrases. This is not a case of cultures in conflict, but of new growth from a meeting of musics which has engendered mutual respect.

Notes

1. For a fuller historical discussion of these terms it is worth reading Ogot (1974).
2. Recent newspaper reports in Kenya suggest a growing reluctance to accept this grouping, and a wish rather to be acknowledged as separate communities.

3. However, I have noticed that the Turkana sing songs about their prize animals, as do the Samburu, and they also make movements with their arms in representation of the animals' horns, while the Samburu do not.

Bibliography

Akuno, Emily (1994), *Music for Schools Standards 4 to 8*, Nairobi: East African Educational Publishers.

Amunga, Wahu (1991), *Music Course for Standard 4*, Nairobi: Muziki Wetu.

Barrett, A. (1988), *English Turkana Dictionary*, Nairobi: Macmillan.

Barrett, D. B. (ed.) (1973), *Kenya Churches Handbook*, Nairobi: Evangel.

Bomas of Kenya (n.d.), Performance programme.

Darkwa, A. (ed.) (1983), *African Musicology*, **1** (1).

Darkwa, Asante (1984), 'The Marakwets and Keiyo', in *The Black Perspective in Music*, Chicago: Chicago University Press.

Dournon, Genevieve (1992), 'Organology', in Helen Myers (ed.), *Ethnomusicology: an Introduction*, London: New Grove Handbooks in Musicology, pp. 245-300.

Fanshawe, David (1975), *African Sanctus*, London: Collins and Harvel.

Fedders, A. and Salvadori, C. (1977), *Turkana: Pastoral Craftsmen*, Nairobi: Transafrica.

Floyd, Malcolm (1985), *Music Makers 7 & 8*, Nairobi: Oxford University Press.

Floyd, Malcolm (1987), *Revision Music*, Nairobi: Oxford University Press.

Floyd, Malcolm (1989), *Music Makers 5 & 6*, Nairobi: Oxford University Press.

Gichimu, Chege (n.d.), *Music for Modern KCPE Pupils Standard 8*, Kijabe: Kijabe Press.

Gichimu, Chege (1992), *Music for Standard 3*, Nairobi: Savani's Book Centre.

Hollis, A. C. (1969), *The Nandi: Their Language and Folklore*, London: Oxford University Press.

Hornbostel, E. M. von and Sachs, Curt (1992), 'Classification of Musical Instruments', in Helen Myers (ed.), *Ethnomusicology: an Introduction*, London: New Grove Handbooks in Musicology, pp. 444-61 (reprinted from the English translation of 1961 of the original article of 1914).

Hyslop, Graham (1958), 'African Musical Instruments in Kenya', *African Music*, **2** (1), 31-6.

Hyslop, Graham (1975), *Musical Instruments of East Africa. Vol. 1: Kenya*, Nairobi: Nelson.

Institute of African Studies, University of Nairobi (papers given):

Omondi, W. A. (1971), 'An Introduction to the Music of the Luo', March.

Kavyu, P. N. (1972), 'Some Kamba Dance Songs', April.

Kavyu, P. N. (1973), 'Some Kamba Dance Songs II', February.

Mwaniki, H. S. K. (1973), 'Categories and Substance of Embu Traditional Folksongs', March.

Campbell, C. A. (1976), 'An Introduction to the Music of Swahili Women', October.

Boyd, R. (1977), 'The Zumari: a Musical Instrument of Lamu Area', February.

Chacha, C. N. (1979), 'Musical Instruments of the Abakuria (Unesco seminar, Kisumu)', April.

Isack, Hussein Adam (1986), *People of the North: Boran*, Nairobi: Evans.

Jones, A. M. (1974), 'Luo Music and its Rhythm', *African Music*, **5** (3), pp. 43-54.

Karanja, Njoroge (1990), *A Standard 6 Music Companion*, Limuru: Companion.

Karonji, R. M. and Akuno, E. (1992), *Revision Music for KCPE*, Nairobi: East African Educational Publishers.

Kavyu, P. N. (1977), *An Introduction to Kamba Music*, Nairobi: East African Literature Bureau.

Kavyu, P. N. (1980), *Traditional Musical Instruments of Kenya*, Nairobi: Kenya Literature Bureau.

Kenya Institute of Education (1977), *Music in Adult Education*, Nairobi.

Kenya Institute of Education (1980), *Notes on Traditional Music Instruments of Kenya*, Nairobi.

Kubik, Gerhard (1982), *Musikgeschichte in Bildern: Ostafrika*, Leipzig: VEB Deuscher Verlag für Musik.

Low, J. (1982), 'History of Kenyan Guitar Music', *African Music*, **6** (2), 17-36.

Mbugua, D. M. (n.d.), *Music Foundation*, Nairobi: Daista Books.

Muriuki, G. (1978), *People Round Mount Kenya, Kikuyu*, Nairobi: Evans.

Ndeti, K. (1972), *Elements of Akamba Life*, Nairobi: East African Publishing House.

Nketia, J. H. Kwabena (1979), *The Music of Africa*, London: Gollancz.

Nzioka, Sammy (1982), *Akamba*, Nairobi: Evans.

Nzioka, Sammy (1990), *Music Time*, Nairobi: East African Educational Publishers.

Ochieng', William (1985), *People Round the Lake: Luo*, Nairobi: Evans.

Ochieng', William (1986), *People of the South Western Highlands: Gusii*, Nairobi: Evans.

Ogot, B. A. (ed.) (1974), *Zamani: a Survey of East African History*, Nairobi: Longman and East African Publishing House.

Omondi, W. A. (1984), 'Tuning of the Thum, the Luo Lyre: a Systematic Analysis', in J. H. K. Nketia and J. C. DjeDje (eds), *Selected Reports in Ethnomusicology, vol. 5. Studies in African Music*, Los Angeles: University of California at Los Angeles, pp. 263-84.

Sassoon, Hamo (1975), *The Siwas of Lamu*, Lamu: The Lamu Society.

Senoga-Zake, G. (1986), *Folk Music of Kenya*, Nairobi: Uzima.

Senoga-Zake, G. and Eldon, K. (1981), *Making Music in Kenya*, Nairobi: Macmillan.

Varnum, John P. (1970), 'The Ibirongwe of the Kuria', *Ethnomusicology*, **14**, pp. 462-7.

Varnum, John P. (1971), 'The Obokano of the Gusii', *Ethnomusicology*, **15**, pp. 242-7.

Wachsmann, Klaus (1995), 'Instruments: Classification of', in *New Grove Dictionary of Music and Musicians*, London: Macmillan, vol. 9, pp. 237-45.

Waganda, Ochieng' et al. (n.d.), *Luo Traditional Nyatiti*, Kisumu: TMC 005 (cassette).

Wahome, J. K. (1984), *Learning Music*, Nairobi: Transafrica.

Wahome, J. K. (1986), *Music Exercises and Answers*, Nairobi: Jemisik.

Wahome, J. K. (1986), *Musical Instruments*, Nairobi: Jemisik.

Wahome, J. K. (1991), *Beginning Music*, Nairobi: Jemisik.

Wahome, J. K. (1993), *Learn Music Standard 7*, Nairobi: Jemisik.

Wanjala, H. N. (1990), *Gateway Primary Revision Music*, Nairobi: Longman.

(Wahome, H. N.?) (1987), *History of Traditional Music of Kenya*, Nairobi: Jemisik.

Part II

The Changing Faces of Music

11 Consumer-led Creation: *Taarab* Music Composition in Zanzibar

Janet Topp Fargion

> ... when we speak of popular music in Africa, we have to look at the conditions which allow for the creation of the music, whether the various systems of patronage or the technological and civil environment of the society or the presence of people who can dance to it. (Chernoff, in Bender, 1991: xvi)

Taarab is a style of music played for entertainment at weddings and other festive occasions all along the Swahili coast of East Africa. This vast area runs in roughly a 10-mile strip from northern Mozambique to southern Somalia, including the adjacent islands of Pemba, Zanzibar, Mafia and the archipelagos of Lamu and Comores. Since the late nineteenth century, Swahili culture has spread inland so that now even parts of eastern Zaire, where the Swahili dialect known as kiNgwana is spoken, could be seen as part of it. Swahili is one of Africa's fifty 'major languages' and depending on how the Swahili people are defined, it could be claimed that the language is in fact spoken by up to 70 million people (Shariff, 1973: 71), making it one of Africa's most widespread languages. Wherever Swahili is spoken, taarab forms an important part of the local musical scenario. At least two performing groups have emerged as far inland as Burundi and as many as five in Uganda, with three in Kampala alone.[1]

Taarab contains all the features of a typical Indian Ocean music, combining influences from Egypt, the Arabian peninsula, India and the West with local music practices. Although Zanzibar is geographically miniscule in the context of this vast Swahili region, its political and economic influence has been historically significant. Zanzibar's contribution in terms of the development of *taarab* has been enormous: the style was started there; it was popularised all over the East African coast by the legendary Zanzibari singer, Siti binti Saad; and today musicians from Zanzibar are continually in demand to play at weddings and as teachers in all corners of this Swahili-speaking area. This music plays such an important part in the lives of all Zanzibaris that it has come to form part of the characterisation of the island itself. Along with Zanzibar being described as 'the island of cloves' - for cloves have formed the backbone of the island's economy since the spice was brought there in the early nineteenth century by Arabs from Oman - it has also been described as 'the island of *taarab*' (Seif Salim Saleh, lecture at Holland Park, London, 18 July 1985).

Figure 11.1 Map of Zanzibar Town

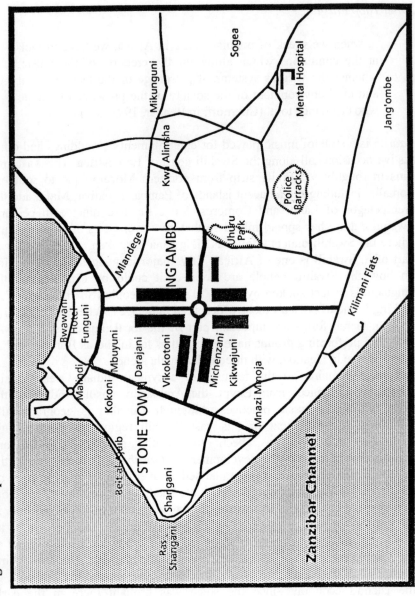

Three forms of *taarab* can be identified: a) a 'traditional' or 'ideal',[2] modelled on Egyptian forms of urban secular music, serving the more affluent, primarily Arab orientated sectors of the society inhabiting Stone Town or areas close to it; b) a counter-style known as *kidumbak* that has all the characteristics of indigenous musical forms (*ngoma za kienyeji*), developed by people of African descent in the further outlying Ng'ambo and rural districts as a popular response to the 'ideal' from which they were excluded primarily for economic reasons; c) *taarab ya wanawake* (women's *taarab*) modelled aesthetically on the 'ideal', but featuring performance practices normally associated with other specifically female *ngoma*. All three categories must be considered together to formulate a definition of *taarab*. They are closely inter-linked and interdependable, sharing much of the same repertoire. It is vital to point out that all three categories now have the same audience, that is, women.

This chapter will look at the significance of Chernoff's statement, quoted above, in relation to *taarab* music in Zanzibar. In order to see its place in society it will be necessary to go into some detail in describing the history and current manifestations of the style on Zanzibar island. I hope to show that it is principally through demands made on composers and performers by non-musical elements - in this case, by the audience/consumers - that this style has developed into a hugely popular and socially significant feature of this Swahili identity.

Historical background of the *taarab* environment

To understand entirely what *taarab* is, one must appreciate the fact that the East African coast has been largely under the control of peoples from the Middle East, except for the 200 years of Portuguese occupation from 1498, and the 30 to 35 years since independence. Furthermore, the impact of various Indian traders, who have also been in contact with the region since before the Christian era, should not be underestimated. Contact was well established between countries bordering on the Indian Ocean by the first century A. D. John Gray writes:

> ... in about A.D. 60 an unknown Greek compiled a treatise known as *The Periplus of the Erythrean Sea*. In this description of the East African coast the author tells us that: 'the Mapharitic Chief governs it under some ancient right, that subjects it to the sovereignty of the State that has become the frst in Arabia. The people of Muza (Mocha?) now hold it under his authority, and send thither many large ships, using Arab captains and agents, who are familiar with the natives and intermarry with

them and who know the whole coast and understand the
language. (1962: 11)

A great influx of immigrants from the Middle East (probably from Shiraz
in Persia) took place during the eleventh and twelfth centuries. This Shirazi
dynasty lasted until the Portuguese conquest of the entire region in the
early sixteenth century. The Portuguese held on to their rule in East Africa
for 200 years. They were finally ousted after a series of revolts aided by
Arabs from Oman. In 1828 the Omani sultan, Seyyid Said bin Sultan, came
to East Africa to assert his power in the face of threats to it from the local
leaders in Mombasa. Upon his first visit to Zanzibar he is said to have
immediately decided to take up residence there, thus making it the
headquarters of his Omani sultanate (Gray, 1962: 126). This he did
officially in 1832. The Omanis remained in power until 1890, when
European powers, particularly Britain, began to play a role in the
administration of the island and of other countries of the Arab East African
empire.

Evaluating the social significance of this group of Omani Arabs in
Zanzibar, Berg describes the period thus:

> It is difficult to weigh the importance of their presence in the
> early 18th century, but by the end of the century a process of re-
> Arabisation seems to have begun on the coast, in which Arab
> kinship, values and some elements of material culture. In the
> long run Swahili society was considerably modified by this
> process, a process that gained impetus after Omani authority
> was reasserted in the 1820s and 1830s. The Oman Arab period
> thus ranks with the era of Shirazi colonisation as one in which
> the impact of the Middle East upon the coast was highly
> significant. (1968: 132)

It is also clear from works such as *The Periplus* that Indians had been
actively involved in the commercial and financial aspects of East African
history. There was one major difference between the settlement patterns of
the Arabs and those of the Indians, however. At least until the beginning of
the nineteenth century, Indians do not appear to have been involved in
organised migration and settlement in East Africa like the Arabs were. It
was not until the large-scale recruitment of Indian labour by the British for
the construction of the Kenya-Uganda railway in 1895 that Indians began
immigrating systematically. Nevertheless, as Lofchi writes:

> Even after they had created a permanently settled community in
> Zanzibar they did not enter into a close cultural relationship

with the local African population. For this reason, the indigenous Africans of Zanzibar (and other East African countries) have adopted practically nothing of Asian culture for their own. (1965: 27)

Zanzibar obtained independence from the British in 1963, with the Arab-orientated Zanzibar Nationalist Party forming the first government. In January 1964 a revolution was mounted against it which put the predominantly African Afro-Shirazi Party in power under the leadership of Abeid Karume. This marked the beginning of a concentrated 'Africanisation', or de-Arabisation, process which saw the expulsion of between 12,000 and 15,000 Arabs from the island, the Arabic language dropped from the curriculum, education for women, and greatly increased integration of the sexes.

This very brief overview of Zanzibar's social and political history should provide a background for the arrival and development of *taarab* on Zanzibar.

Origins of the style

Taarab music is as old as the first visitors from eastern countries who arrived in their white-sailed dhows that were blown by the north-east and south-west monsoons to east Africa every year, [but] the organisation of modern orchestras and compositions of contemporary music ... is an evolution of nearly one century. (Seif Salim Saleh, lecture at Holland Park, London, 18 July 1985)

Although Zanzibaris acknowledge that Arab music must have had some kind of impact through the hundreds of years of contact, they are generally unable to pinpoint anything specific until at least 1870, the start of the reign of Sultan Barghash bin Said (1870-88). He was the third Omani sultan to take the throne since 1832 when Seyyid Said bin Sultan made Zanzibar the seat of the Omani Sultanate. Sultan Barghash is reputed to have been 'an energetic and enlightened prince who did much to improve the amenities of Zanzibar town' (Hollingsworth, 1953: 12). He 'was one of the ablest Arab administrators that ever governed Zanzibar. The impress of his masterful spirit is still found in the island' (Newman, 1898: 54). Remembered as being a man who greatly enjoyed luxury, he had five palaces built around the island, including the famous landmark, the Beit al-Ajaib (House of Wonders), which he used as his town residence. He also had a conduit built from the spring in the north of the island to the town to provide the citizens with running water. But in musical circles he is best remembered for introducing *taarab*.

Sultan Barghash sent a musician in his employ, Mohamed bin Ibrahim, to Egypt to study the music he had enjoyed so much on a recent stop-over there. Ibrahim either returned with Egyptian musicians or he taught Zanzibar palace musicians what he had learnt. In either case, around the turn of this century Egyptian music, sung in Arabic, was played in Zanzibar for the entertainment of the sultan and his upper-class Arab guests. At this time, the music of the *takht* (pl. *tukhut*; platform, dais) ensemble was what Racy has called 'the backbone of Cairo's secular music' (1988: 139). The musicians were specialised performers, playing for an audience in a situation not dissimilar from the Western concert. During the nineteenth century at least, male and female *takht* ensembles existed side by side, performing separate repertoires for audiences of their respective sexes only and with different instrumentation. Male ensembles featured a solo singer with four or five male singers in a chorus, a *qanun* (trapezoidal board zither), *'ud* (short-necked plucked lute), *nay* (oblique-blown flute), violin and a *riqq* (small round frame drum with metal jingles). Female groups were more percussively orientated, including beside the singers, at least one *darabukka*, more than one *tar* (large frame drum with metal jingles, closely associated with music of the harem), a *riqq* and a lone melody instrument, the *'ud*. The repertoire of the male groups was dominated by the *waslah*, a sequence of vocal and instrumental pieces in the same *maqam* (scale/mode) the performance of which lasted roughly an hour. Female *takht* ensembles primarily performed one form, the *taqtuqah*, a relatively short song with a strophic form and short refrain. These songs used colloquial Arabic texts and dealt with sentimental themes.

The more accessible *taqtuqah* came to dominate the Cairene musical scene due to its adaptability to the requirements of the recording industry which began to operate in Cairo in 1904. It lost its female associations as sexual segregation became less stringent after the First World War. Female singers often went on to become celebrities backed by male accompanists in a male *takht* ensemble. Non-traditional influences of the time gave rise to the increased incorporation of Western instruments. By the 1940s more violins, one or two celli, a double bass and later a piano accordion, electric guitar and electronic keyboards were added, the new enlarged orchestra being called *firqah*. Still playing compositions based on the *taqtuqah*; this music flooded the film and recording industry at least until the 1970s. This is the tradition that was brought to Zanzibar in the 1870s, and which has continued to provide the model for the development of 'ideal' *taarab* music.

The 'ideal'

The year 1905 saw the emergence of the first independent *taarab* group on Zanzibar. Starting as one of many male social clubs of the time, Akhwani Safaa formerly constituted itself in this year with the name Nadi Ibnaul Watan Li Jum-iyat Ikhwanissafaa [*sic*] (Club of the Citizens of the Group of Pure Brothers). The choice of the name is a reference to the Ikhwan as-Safa' (Brotherhood of Purity), an influential secret society of intellectuals founded around the year 951 in Iraq.[3] It is also indicative of the Arab orientation of the membership. Certainly one member was a musician who was closely affliated with palace musicians and had frequently performed with them. This musician, Shaib Abeid, is credited for inciting other members of his club to learn music and recruiting palace musicians, Mohamed Ibrahim among them, to teach them. By 1907 they had acquired a full set of the ideal instruments, that is, the instruments of the male *takht* ensemble as described above. They performed at festive occasions for family and friends and frequently at the palace. Rival groups soon emerged, but it was only Akhwani Safaa among them that has survived. Having the finances to do it, the club bought more of the instruments of their Egyptian model. The orchestra has eight violins, a *kanuni* (*qanun*), *udi* ('*ud*), *rika* (*riqq*), *nai* (*nay*), *dumbak* (*darabukka*), one or two bongos, cello, double bass, piano accordion, electronic organ, electric guitar and roughly thirty singers, approximately ten of whom are soloists. They continued to sing in Arabic until 1955.

An Akhwani Safaa event is a formal occasion which has the orchestra on a stage and the audience seated in rows. The audience is made up of adult women and the dress is extremely formal. There is applause at the end of each song, while during the song members of the audience can show their appreciation by going to give money to the singer (*kutunza*). Dancing is frowned upon, though some more daring women may dance momentarily at the front of the stage before they depart with their money and return hurriedly to their seats.

The democratisation of *taarab*

It was in 1911 that a woman, significantly of African descent, who was to become a *taarab* legend, arrived from her home village of Fumba in the south of Zanzibar island. This was Siti binti Saad. Her artistic contribution to *taarab* is undisputed: her remarkable voice and the fact that she could sing in Swahili, Arabic and Hindi is highly acclaimed. Siti binti Saad effectively brought *taarab* out of the palace and into the hearts of the majority who were ordinary Swahili-speaking Zanzibaris. In so doing she broke with Arab-orientated, traditional ideals and models, and earned herself the title 'mother of *taarab*': for many of these people this is where *taarab* began.

Siti binti Saad made numerous recordings for His Master's Voice and Columbia, the first to be made by any artist in the Swahili language. These circulated extensively in Zanzibar and throughout the Swahili coast. While only the wealthy could afford to buy the gramophones and the discs, the records nevertheless reached a much wider audience: they were played in coffee shops and eating houses, and people who played them inside their houses were frequently astonished to hear applause and encores from listeners gathered outside the windows (Suleiman, 1969: 88).

The impact of Siti's songs was largely due to the fact that they were sung in Swahili rather than in Arabic, and that instead of typical *taarab* themes of sentimental, romantic love, Siti sang of everyday life in Zanzibar. One classic example is found in the song 'Muhogo ya Jang'ombe' ('Cassava of Jang'ombe', Jang'ombe being a district in the outlying areas of Zanzibar town). Cassava, one of the staple foods of rural Zanzibar, is used here as a metaphor for 'ulevi' (drunkenness) suggesting the ubiquity of drunkenness during this most oppressive period of colonialism. The song was composed by Mwalimu Shaaban, one of the members of Siti's performing group, who transcribes and interprets it as follows:

Muhogo ya Jang'ombe	Cassava of Jang'ombe
sijauramba mwiko	I haven't yet licked the spoon
Msitukane wakunga	You shouldn't interrupt the midwives
na uzazi ungaliko	or girls' sexual instructresses when the baby is coming

I haven't had anything to drink in the shamba (rural area) since one will get caught by the authorities. Don't upset the women since it is they who have to bear us (Jahadhmy, in Whiteley, 1966: 60).

Two important responses to Siti's work emerged, resulting in forms of *taarab* that are in many ways more relevant, since they are more accessible, for the majority of the Zanzibari population. African musicians living primarily in outlying Ng'ambo areas of Zanzibar town formed small informal groups to play Siti's songs for their own recreation and for the entertainment of guests (mainly women) at wedding parties. Initially they accompanied themselves only on two home-made drums fashioned on the y-shaped *dumbak*, itself fashioned on the Arab *darabukka*. These drums were called *kidumbak* (pl. *vidumbak*, meaning small dumbak) and this became the name of the music style that resulted. As the larger 'ideal' *taarab* groups began to expand their ensembles along the lines of the Cairene *firqah* orchestras, *kidumbak* musicians drew on them further and their ensembles became standardised to include beside the two *vidumbak*, a *sanduku* (lit., box: a single-string tea-chest bass instrument modelled on the double bass), a violin, a pair of *cherewa* (coconut shell maracas; used in many local *ngoma*) and a pair of *mkwasa* (sticks either beaten together or on a table; probably imported from styles performed on the mainland). In stark contrast to 'ideal' *taarab* events, these informal performances have the musicians sitting outdoors in a group with the audience gathered in a tight circle around them. Closely aligned to the *kidumbak* groups and also as a result of Siti binti Saad's inspiration, a large network of women's *taarab* groups emerged during the late 1930s and into the 1940s. The musical activities of these groups constitutes the third category of *taarab*, namely *taarab ya wanawake*. The first of these groups already existed as *lelemama* associations, the female version of early *beni* clubs.[4] *Lelemama* groups were primarily self-help associations for women but they also provided a forum for the public performance of song and dance characterised by a favourite Swahili activity - 'disputation and the expression of competition through song and dance' (Ranger, 1975: 18). Margaret Strobel's account of *lelemama* performance in Mombasa highlights this.

> Dancing sedately, they sang old favorites or newly composed songs that revealed the misdeeds of people in the community, publicly shamed individuals, or challenged rival *lelemama* associations by ridiculing their dancing abilities. Associations usually formed competing pairs, following a pattern common to coastal societies ... Occasionally the rivalry became vicious ... (Strobel, 1976: 187)

The clubs in Mombasa subsequently turned into more political entities concerned with the social position of women. In Zanzibar, under the influence of Siti, they began to perform *taarab*. They brought to *taarab* the traditional Swahili tradition of rivalry expressed in sung poetry. Not playing instruments, the women hired *kidumbak* musicians to accompany them at weddings and other women's celebrations. A number of clubs emerged during this time, five of which are still active today. These are: Nuru el-Uyun, Royal Air Force, Royal Navy, Banati al-Khairiyah and Sahib al-Ari. *Taarab* thus moved further into the public domain and began to be influenced more by local practices than by developments in Egypt.

Women's *taarab* is much more informal and quite different from the 'ideal' taarab of the larger, male-dominated clubs. The difference lies not so much in the music, for often the women's groups merely play cover versions of popular songs of the larger groups. Instead, the main distinction is in their approach to the music and in the atmosphere at events at which they perform. Because it can be expensive to hire a full orchestra, instruments at these performances tend to include a basic core of melody and percussion, usually a piano accordion and/or small electric keyboard, one or two violins, two bongos and *rika*. Zanzibari women are a fun-loving and highly excitable part of the community, and at these performances where few men are present, many members of the audience lose their inhibitions. When they leave their seats to reward (*kutunza*) a singer, instead of walking calmly to the stage and returning directly, many dance openly and without restraint, remaining at the stage to sing and clap in an expression of joy and acknowledgement of the effectiveness of the lyrics. In 1965, the new African revolutionary government brought together musicians from outlying areas of the town to form a new club. They were principally of African descent and players in *kidumbak* and women's *taarab* circles. The group was called Culture Musical Club and was constituted under the Culture Department, which fitted it out with all the instruments of an 'ideal' *taarab* orchestra of the time. It came to be Akhwani Safaa's only rival. Culture Musical Club events are very much like those of Akhwani Safaa in that the orchestra is positioned on a stage in front of an audience seated on chairs in rows. The atmosphere is somewhat less formal, however, though this is due to the nature of the songs and the audience response (as will be discussed later) rather than any situational or contextual differences.

Popular art?

Writing of popular arts in Africa, Karin Barber writes:

> They loudly proclaim their own importance in the lives of large numbers of African people. They are everywhere. They flourish without encouragement or recognition from official bodies, and sometimes in defiance of them. People too poor to contemplate spending money on luxuries do spend it on popular arts, sustaining them and constantly infusing them with new life ... they are expressive acts. Their most important attribute is their power to communicate ... (Barber, 1987: 1-2)

Since the time of Siti binti Saad, in the late 1920s and early 1930s, *taarab* has developed from an exclusive and elite form into an all-pervasive living tradition. It is both produced and consumed by the people. No celebration is complete without a performance of one type or another and money must be found, often in the face of great poverty, to ensure that it happens.

Who are the primary consumers?

Chernoff, in the quote at the beginning of this chapter, recognises the importance of the audience for the creation and thus for the suivival of popular musics. We have been introduced to the main forums for production of *taarab*, that is, 'ideal' *taarab* orchestras (Akhwani Safaa and Culture Musical Club), *kidumbak* groups and women's *taarab* clubs. This section looks at who the audiences of *taarab* are and how they behave in the different *taarab* contexts.

Performances of all types of *taarab* are primarily held at parties celebrating stages in the life cycle such as circumcision or, most frequently, marriage. But *taarab* music plays no part in the ceremonies themselves other than to provide entertainment for the guests. The onus is on the host and organiser of the event - for a marriage, usually the mother of the bride - to provide suitable entertainment for the guests she has invited. In organising this a woman has various alternatives. If she is a member of a women's club, she will arrange for it to play. An added benefit here is that as women, the club members know all the songs connected with the various parts of the marriage ceremony and can participate in making these successful too. Although her own club would not charge a fee, the event would still be quite expensive: she would have to pay for the hiring of chairs and for the provision of electricity for the event. If this proves beyond her means, she may be forced to make other arrangements such as organising for a *kidumbak* group to play. This option is the only one available to a woman who is not a member of any club and is not wealthy. If she is not a member of any club but can afford it, she may hire Culture Musical Club or Akhwani Safaa. To some degree her choice as to which of the two she decides to hire is dependent on where she lives and on her personal preference: if she is in or close to Stone Town she is more likely to have connections with Akhwani Safaa than if she is a resident of the outlying Ng'ambo districts. As 'employers' of musicians these women can be responsible for the rise or fall in popularity of any of the *taarab* performance types.

The majority of the guests invited to all three categories of *taarab* performance on Zanzibar are married women, including widows and divorcees. Even at concerts of 'ideal' *taarab* organised independently of any specific celebration, married women form the main part of the audiences, though in these contexts a minority of men do attend, often to accompany their wives to these public events. Women of all economic brackets or ethnicities attend all performance types. It is their position as the primary consumers of the style which draws the categories together and causes changes in one to affect another.

Audiences behave differently at performances of the different types of *taarab*, making atmosphere, or the degree of freedom, the main difference between them. In 'ideal' *taarab* contexts the audience is very smartly dressed, the women being heavily involved in a so-called 'dress culture'. A great deal of money is handed to the singers and musicians as a reward by members of the audience, but dancing is discouraged and patrons are expected to remain in their chairs to listen to the music. According to Dr Farouk Topan (pers. comm., 12 May 1989)

> I would sit and listen in a *taarab* and expect to be entertained in a very soothing way. I am making a distinction between a *taarab* and a *ngoma*. *Ngoma* would be where there is a throbbing, violent participation, whereas in *taarab* it is soothing ... In other words it is melodious in the sense that would keep it apart from, let us say, a drum-based dance. It's quite different.

Musicians and singers do not improvise. Rather they must sing the songs as they have been composed and rehearsed.

Audiences at *kidumbak* performances on the other hand, are there primarily to dance, and they are at liberty to express themselves as explicitly as they wish. As these events are held outdoors, smart dresses would be spoiled; the women tend to wear plain outfits and are usually bare-footed. The only 'dress culture' in operation here is in the need to bring a *khanga* (cloth worn as skirt and veil) to be worn around the hips, accentuating their movement while dancing. The musicians are free to play whatever they think will excite the guests. *Kidumbak* musicians judge the success of the performance by the extent to which the audience participates through dancing. They perform popular 'ideal' *taarab* songs (though usually played at a faster tempo), tagging faster sections with improvised lyrics (*michapuzo*) on to the end, during which they make or break the performance. The string bass (*sanduku*) plays a large role in this through virtuosic rhythmic improvisation he creates a great deal of excitement (*msisimko*). '*Wale wachezaji sisi ndio wanaotutia mori wa kufanza kila kitu kiwe kizuri*' ['It is those dancers who give us the inspiration (*mori*, lit., 'great bravery, anger, or ferocity, such as of male animals when fighting for the females ... '); Johnson, 1939: 295 to make everything good'] (Rashid Makame Shani, pers. comm., 4 October 1989).

The atmosphere at *taarab ya wanawake* events lies somewhere between 'ideal' *taarab* and *kidumbak*. Seating is arranged at *taarab ya wanawake* events but the atmosphere is much less formal than in 'ideal' *taarab* contexts. The performance area frequently becomes full of women dancing, singing and clapping and musicians, particularly bongos players, improvise to add *msisimko*.

Some Zanzibaris would argue that this desire to dance is in part caused by world trends in which they believe popular music has tended to get faster and, beginning with rock 'n roll in the 1950s, arguably more danceable. However, we must look at Zanzibari *taarab* itself to understand recent developments in the style, particularly within the 'ideal'. Until the mid-1960s, that is after the revolution, the *kidumbak* and women's *taarab* circuits were in many ways cut off from the 'ideal'. The sedate 'ideal' *taarab* performance, until that time with a predominantly male audience, was quite separate from the *ngoma*-like, participative *kidumbak* and the overtly responsive *taarab ya wanawake* contexts both performed for women. But the gap has narrowed. In the first instance, women have gained influence in the 'ideal', facilitated by the general de-Arabisation programme of the African revolutionary government. As part of this programme the government forced Akhwani Safaa to admit, for the first time, women as members. Moreover, women were free to join Culture Musical Club from its inception in 1965. Linked to this, the inauguration of Culture Musical Club made up largely of musicians from the smaller *kidumbak* and women's groups provided a channel for both musical and performance practices common in these areas to make their way into the 'ideal'.

What is the audience looking for?

We have seen that *taarab* is first and foremost an entertainment music. Sultan Barghash brought it to Zanzibar as a commodity to be consumed in the comfort of his palace, and the style has been used ever since to amuse guests at festive gatherings. But much, or even most, of the entertainment value comes from meaningful lyrics. These form a part of the very definition of *taarab* and play a major part in consumers' appreciation of it.

These aspects are made clear if we look at the meaning and derivation of the term. The word *taarab* comes from the Arabic abstract noun *tarab* meaning 'joy, pleasure, delight, rapture, amusement, entertainment, music' (Wehr, 1974: 555). *Tarab* in turn derives from the verb *tariba*, which means 'to be moved (with joy or grief; to be delighted, overjoyed; to be transported with joy' (Wehr, 1974: 555). *Tariba* also signifies 'to delight, fill with delight; to enrapture, please, gratify' and hence 'to sing; to make music' (ibid.). *Mutrib* and *mutriba*, the active participles of tarab, meaning literally 'he' and 'she who moves people' (Rouget, 1985: 282), are the words for male and female musicians respectively. The terms are applied primarily to singers rather than to instrumentalists. Hence another aspect of the emotional state defined as *tarab* is revealed, namely that it is brought about primarily through 'the combined action of the beauty of the voice and the emotional power of the words' (ibid.: 283). It is indeed poetry that has brought about changes in *taarab*: poetry brought to *taarab* by women.

The 'ideal' poetic formula

Ideally, taarab songs adhere more or less strictly to one poetic formula. *Shairi* (lit., poem, pl. *mashairi*) could be loosely used to refer to all Swahili poetry. The term encompasses a number of poetic forms categorised according to the number of lines (*mshororo*) in a stanza (*ubeti*), how lines are divided into segments (*vipande*, sing. *kipande*), the number of syllables (*harufi*) in a line, and the rhyme scheme. *Taarab* poetry fits into a category known as *wimbo* (lit., song pl. *nyimbo*) employing any one of three metres as listed in the table below. *Nyimbo* is also the basis of *ngoma* songs. The most common *wimbo* metre is one in which each of three or four lines has 16 syllables with a caesura after the eighth. Within a verse all line-final syllables usually rhyme with each other, and the syllables before the caesura also rhyme.

No. of lines in verse	No. of syllables in line	Caesura	Rhyme
3 or 4	12	6+6	ab ab ab
	12	4+8 *	or
	16	8+8	ab ab ab ab

* The first segment is often repeated, making this 8+8.

The poems normally have three or four verses each alternating with a chorus (*kiitikio*) of two lines. This poem called 'Tushikane' ('We should hold each other'), written by Salim Bimany of Akhwani Safaa and performed at the Idd el-Hadj concert in July 1989, is a good example. (A translation by Ally Saleh follows the Swahili. The caesura are marked with slashes.)

Pendo letu limefana/na jua linochomoza
Na watu watafutana/huku kamba tukikaza
Nasi vyema tushikane/mahaba kuyaongeza
Njema huba tuivune/kwa mbegu tulopandiza

Msijitie vitani/kutaka liangamiza
Msidhani ni utani/kwamba mwaweza tucheza
Letu imara si duni/pendo linajieleza
Njama zetu kweupeni/vizizi mtamaliza

Tunu yangu ya miaka/kwangu imejisogeza

Anga ikipambazuka/kheri ikajijaliza
Kufika ikanitaka/ili moyo kuupozu
Hapo ikakubalika/kushika namba ya kwanza

Akinena hebu shika/tushikane tukikuza
Kwa kwangu ondoa shaka/hilo akasisitiza
Nafasi nilokuweka/pekee mekupendeza
Tua kisha burudika/ndugu zangu kwako laza

Kiitikio:
Nilo nae anitosha/bure mnahangaika
Hamuwezi muondosha/kwangu amehifadhika

Our love has risen like the rising sun
May it make people search themselves while we tighten the rope
While we hold each other earnestly, more affectionate we become
While we reap the best of love from the seeds we have sown

Be warned of waging war to destroy it
Do not take it as a joke and fool around with us
Ours [our love] is strong and not weak, and the love expresses
itself
Exposed are your devious activities, you will finish yours
[your love]

My long-time wish has approached me
There is sunshine when dawn came; I have been blessed with happiness
On arrival it wants me so that it can comfort my heart
There it was agreed to hold the number one position

He then said: 'Hold onto me, we should hold one another as we
cultivate our love
Cast no doubt on me', this he insisted
'The place I have seated you suits no other
Sit tight with all the ease, your efforts will not be in vain'

Chorus:
He/She is enough to me, you are merely troubling yourselves
You can not take him/her away, he/she is protected here.

Thus even these Egyptian-style groups are using 'traditional' Swahili poetic forms. But they are still singing Egyptian-style lyrics. It is the content rather than the form that is significant. We have seen that content played a large role in the early democratisation of *taarab*: Siti sang words with local relevance for the African majority, in their language, and this helped to popularise the style.

'Ideal' music

Music is not notated. Poems are written down in the club's book and often the first note of the melody is also given. For the rest, the musicians must rely on memory. For the most part, 'ideal' *taarab* songs are strophic. Every song opens with an instrumental introduction, and verses are usually separated by an instrumental interlude. These instrumental sections are called *bashraf* (the Arabic name used for purely instrumental compositions, normally played to open each half of a concert). They may be shorter or longer as the composer desires though Akhwani Safaa songs are frequently characterised by their use of very long *bashraf* and usually allow for each leading melody - violin, *udi, nai, kanuni*, accordion and electric keyboard - instrumentalist to perform a *taqsim* (improvised solo usually in free rhythm). The orchestra almost always heralds the start of a verse by repeating a short phrase twice or three times. This usually comprises the final few notes of the instrumental section just played, but it may also be a longer phrase.

   Both Western diatonic scales and Arabic *maqamat* (Ar. modes/scales) are used in composition.

> ... *njia zitumikazo hadi hiyi* [*sic*] *sasa katika kuliza nyimbo za taarab ni zile zile zitumiwazo na Waarabu ambazo ni maarufu kwa majina kama Hijazi, Sika, Banyati* [*sic*], *Rasti, Nahawandi, Shuni* [*sic*], *Saba, Ginka na kadhalika.*
> [... keys (scales, modes) which are used even today in the production of *taarab* songs are those same ones used by Arabs which are known by names like *Hijazi, Sika, Bayati, Rasti, Nahawandi, Shuri, Saba, Ginka*, etc.] (ibid.) (*Njia* literally means 'ways or roads'. This word was used to refer both *maqamat* and Western diatonic scales.) [Seif Salim Saleh, pers. comm., 1989]

It is clear that these are indeed the most well-known and well-used *maqamat* in Zanzibar. In a short music handbook which Idi Farhan (one of my main consultants) prepared for teaching, he includes a page listing 'nine Arabic keys of the *kanuni*'. He lists *bayati, hijazi, saba, shuri, rast, sika, hussein, nahawandi, hijaz kar* [*sic*]. In contemporary practice *maqamat* have more or less been replaced with Western diatonic scales which musicians refer to using tonic-solfa terminology, using the fixed 'do' system (do = c, re = d, mi = e, and so on).

While percussion parts are considered indispensable as time keepers, they are meant to remain subdued in the 'ideal' orchestra. The instruments (*dumbak*, *bongos* and *rika*) are all small drums and are much quieter than the larger drums used in most *ngoma*. Seif Salim Saleh writes of them: '*zina sauti hafifu, laini na nyororo*' (1980: 43) ['they have insignificant, thin and soft sounds']. At Akhwani Safaa rehearsals, the percussionists were frequently told to play softer. These instruments take on far more significance in the *kidumbak* and *taarab ya wanawake* ensembles as the music and context becomes more like *ngoma*.

One of the most commonly used rhythms in contemporary 'ideal' *taarab* songs is called *wahed unus*, meaning one-and-a-half (Idi Farhan, pers. comm., 29 May 1989). In my analysis this is possibly derived from a rhythm often used in Egyptian popular songs, called *wahdah sayirah*. *Wahdah sayirah* is in turn derived from the wahdah (meaning unit) rhythmic pattern frequently used in the *taqtuqah* form.

Figure 11.2 *Wahdah*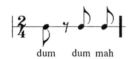

dum   dum mah

Neither the *wahdah* nor the *wahdah sariyah* are clearly defined rhythmic patterns. Instead, the names denote metres of either 4/8 or 2/4, that is, they encompass an overall duration of a minim. According to D'Erlanger, everything after the first 'dum' is only included to fill in what would otherwise be a long silence, and to make it easier to play the metre more accurately. He asserts though, that due to ignorance or laziness, many musicians do play these metres as rhythmic patterns when they wish to simplify a composition (D'Erlanger, 1956: 32). The Zanzibari *wahed unus* has perhaps been derived in the same way. This rhythm comprises one 'unit' with the characteristic 'dum' at the start. The rest of the unit could be fill-ins. The half unit in *wahed unus* while it has the same duration as a whole unit, is less ornamented and the 'dum' stroke is less pronounced. This is possibly why the second half of the pattern is thought of as a half unit.

Figure 11.3 *Wahed unus*

1 unit   1/2 unit

Players normally ornament the pattern after playing it once or twice in this simplified way. The above diagram is only an outline.

The *wahed unus* is readily interchangeable with what Zanzibaris call a rumba rhythm. The former rhythm is often employed by composers in

Akhwani Safaa as a slight variation of the rumba, the latter generally being preferred.

Figure 11.4   Rumba

Other commonly used rhythms include waltz, fox-trots and marches and *sharaha*, a frequently-used rhythm originating in the Hadramawt.

Poems are always written first. In some cases poets also compose the music though more often a poet gives his or her work to a musician to set. The composer needs to set it to suitable music: the nature of the lyrics or the content of the poem thus dictates parametres such as tempo and rhythm. The 'ideal' poem quoted above was set to a slow rumba, for example. We shall see what changes in the nature of the poetry have meant for musical settings.

Post-revolutionary poetry and music

During the six years immediately following the revolution *taarab* was employed by the new government to educate people as to their policies and to the new union with the mainland. The radio was the primary means of dissemination. The government ensured that all *taarab* songs broadcast were political in content. During this time, only songs with titles such as 'Usawa na Ushirika' (Equality and Cooperation), 'Uhuru' (Freedom), or simply 'Tanzania' were broadcast. One example is a song written by Khatib in 1964, called 'Muungano' (The Union) (translated by Ally Saleh). It clearly demonstrates the didactic nature of many of these political poems. (See Khatib, 1984: 52-65 for other examples.)

Muungano umetimu/	The union is complete
Unguja na Tanganyika	Zanzibar and Tanganyika
Tumeishika hatamu/	Onto the lead we hold
wananchi kwa shirika	together, all the citizens
Tunaujenga kwa hamu/	With zeal we build it
kwa umoja twatumika	in unison we serve
Muungano wa halali/	This is a legal union
wenyewe tumeridhika	we are all content
Msingi wake wa kweli/	Truthfulness is its base
imara umejengeka	it was erected with strength

Sote tumeukubali/	We have all accepted it
katu hautovunjika	it will never be broken
Raisi wetu wa dhati/	Our beloved president
Nyerere tumemweka	Nyerere we exalted him
Mwenye sifa tofauti/	Possesses various qualities
njema zilokamilika	good and perfect ones
Na kauli madhubuti/	With firm words
ambazo hazina shaka	that cannot be doubted
Nchi yetu Tanzania/	Our country Tanzania
Mungu aipe baraka	God should bless it
Dua tunaiombea/	We ask that it
ipate nyingi fanaka	should have plenty of success
Tuzidi kuendelea/	We move further ahead
tupate tunaotaka	so that we should get our wishes

While the poetic structure of the songs was not altered, these new lyrics caused the music to change. For the first time *taarab* musicians were moving away from the 'traditional' slow rumbas to include rhythms of a more military nature. (These rhythms were often more typical of African and Latin American military bands, featuring the characteristic pattern: x . x . x . . x . x . .)

This post-revolutionary period is never quoted as a high point in the history and development of this 'ideal' *taarab* style. Many poets in Akhwani Safaa, such as Idi Farhan and Seif Salim Saleh, claim to have stopped writing songs altogether during this period. But *kidumbak* and women's *taarab*, which did not form part of the official function of *taarab*, was less affected by these developments. It did not take long for the authorities to realise that *taarab* was only popular if it gave the consumers what they wanted. Soon the tide changed and love songs once again became the order of the day.

The *mpasho* phenomenon: women's poetry

For centuries women in Zanzibar have been actively involved in the creation of poetry. Many of their poems relate to activities attached to their roles in society. Members in women's associations sang among themselves while carrying out their various domestic chores. These lyrics are concerned with everyday life and the general social condition, in striking contrast to the aloofness desired of the poetry of 'ideal' *taarab*. The merging of these two types of lyrics not only marked the beginning of *kidumbak* and women's *taarab* but was also the start of the Africanisation of 'ideal' *taarab*. By the time of the revolution *taarab* poetry was no longer contained within the élite circle - Siti binti Saad had not been forgotten.

We have seen that with the influence of Siti, women's *lelemama* associations changed to make the performance of *taarab* their main focus. The intense rivalry and the tradition of expressing this in sung poetry was carried through.

This kind of poetry is known in Zanzibar as *mpasho* (pl. *mipasho*). The word derives from the verb *kupasha* [the causative of *kupata*, the broad meaning of which is 'to get'] which means 'to cause to get, or to cause to have' (Johnson, 1939: 369). It is used in the sense that the poet causes the person who is the subject of the poem, or to whom the poem is directed, to 'get the message': the message is clear and direct so there can be no misunderstanding about what is meant and who it is directed at.

Lyrics are also composed following the *taarab* 'formula' to be sung accompanied by the women's version of the *taarab* ensemble. While almost all *taarab* poetry uses proverbs, riddles and hidden meanings, *mipasho* songs are different in that they are directed at a specific rival group, be it a single member or the group as a whole. The sole intention of the songs is to insult and attack. *Mipasho* songs use very strong and abusive language (*maneno makali; maneno matusi*) with the intention of hurting and degrading the subject in the eyes of the public. They use sarcastic, cutting, ironical language (*vijembe*) to be direct and hard-hitting. They have been described as 'out of line *kabisa*' or 'hot *kabisa*' (Khamis Shehe, pers. comm., 17 September 1980). [*Kabisa* means 'utterly, altogether' (Johnson, 1939: 164). In this context it was said with emphasis on each syllable.]

Mpasho is the main factor contributing to the distinctiveness of women's *taarab*. Many Zanzibaris, both men and women, agree that women's *taarab* is much 'hotter'. Ummie Alley elaborates:

> I can say that the women themselves are much more active and livelier on the stage on the wedding day than the men. I believe that the celebrations of marriages in our culture are solely female programmes. Suppose you call the Malindi (Akhwani Safaa)[5] group [to play for your celebration], their music is sentimental and classical. But with our female groups we enjoy this type with interchanges of words of rivalry and jealousy. So I feel if I sing this song, it's so active that somebody will get it that I'm telling her. Then the fans who come and pay a token [to the singer] as a gesture of appreciation make it much more lively. (pers. comm., 29 June 1989)

It is not only between the two protagonists of an argument that a *mpasho* song is effective: the 'use' of *mipusho* songs extends to the audience as well as to the poets who wrote them. If, for example, two women are arguing, they may hear something pertinent to their argument in a *mpasho* song. One might go up to *kutunza* (reward the singer), making sure that her rival sees her, and then say: 'There! That is for you!' (Idi Farhan, pers. comm., 25 May 1989).

Even in Siti binti Saad's time this practice of *kusengenyana* (lit., mutual back-biting) was in operation. Attacks were made against her by competing singers, especially from Mombasa; it is perhaps natural to expect that somebody so much in the public eye, and a woman at that, should attract comment in this society. Furthermore, Royal Air Force and Royal Navy were in opposition from their earliest days at least until the beginning of the *wakati wa siasa* (period of electoral politics) in roughly 1958. Some of the most severe exchanges, however, occurred between Royal Air Force and Nuru el-Uyun between 1978 and 1984. It happened that a member of Nuru el-Uyun handed a copy of the Koran to the 'pilot' of Royal Air Force. (Both protagonists are of Comorian descent.) This act was intended as a personal attack, insinuating that it was thought that the 'pilot' was 'too old' to still be involved in *taarab* and that she 'should settle down and read her Koran' (Saada Jaffer, pers. comm., 19 August 1989). The 'pilot' composed a song in answer to this provocation, and consequently further insults and accusations passed between the groups. Many women said that it was advisable to remain at home when one or other of these groups were performing, since the events frequently degenerated into physical brawls in which stones were thrown and people were hurt. Nevertheless, they were events not to be missed!

This *taarab* poem by a member of Nuru el-Uyun demonstrates clearly their competition with Royal Air Force. It also suggests that location was a factor in the struggles (translated by Ally Saleh; *Fosi* refers to Royal Air Force):

Ndege lawaka	The plane is ablaze
Nasema siyanyamazi/	I can no longer keep quiet
Leo nitayaeleza	Today I shall spill it
Kuna baraza fulani/	There is a certain meeting place
Nikipita huapizwa	I am always cursed when I pass it
Nimewakoseni nini	What wrong have I done to you? -
Wenzangu nawauliza	if I may ask you
Ati wanajitia kunena/	They pretend to talk about it
Na mambo wanayajua	While they surely know the facts
Hayo wanayo yasemal	Indeed what they are saying

Si kweli ninayakana	I dare refute
Nuru mbele Fosi nyuma/	It's Nuru ahead and Royal behind
Na dalili mwaziona	And you can see the signs

Nitakapo nitapata/	I shall get where I want
Na wala sitojikhini	And will not shrink from my endeavours

Anajikuna kwa kwata/	She scratches herself with hooves
Amejigeuza jini	Turning herself into a spirit
Kikwajuni sitoacha/	I shall never leave Kikwajuni
Japo majabalini	Though it is said to be the rocky area
Sitoijali Royal/	I shall never care about Royal
Iliyo ikwao Funguni	Which has its headquarters in Funguni

By about 1984, the dispute had become so serious that not only did the Zanzibari government intervene, but a group of Comorian diplomats came to Zanzibar to investigate (Saada Jaffer, pers. comm., 19 September 1989). The government forced all the groups to register with the Ministry of Information, Culture and Tourism under the Department of Culture. The department set up a Censorship Board and all were obliged to submit each poem for scrutiny. According to Idi Farhan, the Censorship Board looks for poems which 'might put the Zanzibari government in a bad light', and they also censor 'strong *mipasho* songs to try to prevent fighting' (pers. comm., 4 May 90). In addition the women's groups were encouraged to form a union which would facilitate cooperation. This had a degree of success.

The following extracts from two poems (translated by Ally Saleh) demonstrate well the level of the insults which were thrown backwards and forwards between these two groups. Nuru el-Uyun wrote a poem directed at the leader (the 'pilot') of Royal Air Force:

Piloti wakumbuka/	You still remember it, Pilot
Usiseme huelewi	Don't say you don't understand or have forgotten
Kakayo kaolewa Chwaka/	Your brother was married in Chwaka
Kwa ngoma na hoihoi	With all the festivities
Mambo yalipochafuka/	When the scandal broke loose
Kenda uzia Dubai	He has gone to be a prostitute in Dubai

(It was said that the brother was homosexual and that he left his wife in Chwaka - a village on the east coast of Zanzibar island - to become a prostitute in Dubai.)

One of Royal Air Force's responses was this poem attacking Nuru el Uyun for their alleged involvement in lesbianism:

Kumezuka papa kuu	There is a threatening shark
Si jike wala si dume	Neither female or male
Lina miguu mitatu/	It has three legs
Na mikono yake minne	And four hands
Wafunikeni watoto/	Protect your children
Papa lisiwatafune	So they will not be eaten by it

(The 'threatening shark' is Nuru el-Uyun, the alleged lesbians. '*Papa*' is also a crude word for female genitalia.)

The fact that the rivalry had to be stopped by the authorities demonstrates how serious the situation had become. Shariff writes of Swahili poetry:

> The reasons for the heavy use of metaphor in Swahili poetry and Swahili speech are complex. In a nutshell, it has to do with the fact that the societies' very survival depended on the cooperation of its members ... Among the things that are highly valued by the societies are pride and honor. Shame is frowned upon and every effort is made to avoid it, most especially because when one family member is shamed, the rest suffer the consequences and ultimately the community itself pays a price ... Serious inter-family quarrels have been avoided because people were not shamed in public and there was no question of honor to be defended as a result of using metaphoric language. (1981: 7)

Mipasho poetry violates all of these cultural norms, as the two poems above demonstrate. Poets probe the private lives of their opponents to involve them in scandals. The offended party inquires equally as deeply into the lives of opponents in order to retaliate. The aim is to destroy people's reputations, and the effectiveness of *mipasho* songs is based on the fact that reputation is a public matter by definition (Dubisch, 1986: 20). In this way people are shamed publicly, pride and honour of families have to be defended, cooperation dwindles and the society's 'very survival' is threatened.

The seriousness of the *mpasho* interaction between Royal Air Force and Nuru el-Uyun and the government action it provoked effectively put women's *taarab* into a state of decline. Since the government's intervention and the formation of the union of women's groups in 1984, relative peace has prevailed. The *mpasho*-type poem, however, is by no means dead: it is merely less explicit. Often the target of a poem is not clear except to the chief protagonists of an argument. For example, the song 'Na mnikome', sung by Sahib al-Ari, has the following chorus (translated with the help of Sheikh Yayha Ali Omar):

Na mnikome waja na	You (pl.) should leave me alone, you
mnikome (x3)	nosy people
Mimi yenu siyataki	I do not mind your business
Yangu mwayatakiyani	What do you want with mine?

If *mipasho* lyrics have become milder within the women's *taarab* network, in *kidumbak* they have been taken to their limits. The informal *kidumbak* groups are not answerable to the Censorship Board. *Kidumbak* thus has a freedom which no other area of *taarab* has, which is certainly one reason for its soaring popularity. It should be noted that lyrics sung in the improvised sections in *kidumbak* are often composed spontaneously in performance. They are thus probably never repeated exactly, and they do not always follow the formulaic rules of rhyme and scansion usually expected in *taarab* poetry. One example publicly reveals an illicit love affair, even mentioning the woman's name (transcribed from my own recording and translated by Ally Saleh):

Kipenzi changu Mwajuma	My dear Mwajuma
Naomba dua ifane	I pray for fulfilment of my prayers
Bila ya kutimu mwezi	Before the end of the month
Naomba mume akwache	I ask that your husband divorces you
Likome jambo la wizi	So we can stop this theft

The song speaks to a specific person of an adulterous affair. Another song talks of a brothel, again identifying a particular person:

Chorus:

Wamo wamo wamejaa tele	They are there in full presence
Banda la uani msela lala	The sailor occupies the rear
mwenyewe	room
Kwanza nataka kusema	I would first like to speak
Lakini naona haya	But I feel shy
Chupi ya dada Mwatima	Sister Mwatima's panties
Imetoboka pabaya	Have a hole in a bad place

Since women have been permitted to participate in 'ideal' *taarab*, they have come to vastly out-number men as fans even in this previously male-dominated sphere. Accordingly, women have exerted pressure on these groups to provide the type of excitement which the women had become accustomed to within their own *taarab* network. This became particularly acute after 1984, once the intense *mipasho* interchanges had been quelled. It has caused even the traditionalists of Akhwani Safaa to produce *mipasho* songs. As Idi Farhan explained: 'It is good business to play *mipasho* songs' (pers. comm., 17 April 1990). The group has gained financially - through the sale of concert tickets - from a string of songs composed by Abdalla Issa (who actually now lives in Dubai but remains very closely connected with the club by making annual visits for the Idd el-Fitr celebrations). It is commonly known that he had a very bitter romantic experience which he used as the basis for all the songs he produced in 1989 and 1990. One of these, called 'I am sorry', raised him to 'pop-star' status; one person even dubbed him the 'Elvis ya Unguja' ('Elvis of Zanzibar'). The chorus (translated by Ally Saleh) states:

Tafuta wakuchezeya!	Look for another to deceive
Watu wote sio sare	All people are not alike
Mimi kwako kurejeya!	As for me ever returning to you,
Nasema 'I am sorry'	All I can say 'I am sorry'
	(that is, forget it!)

Another of his songs is one of the strongest *mpasho* songs to emerge from within 'ideal' *taarab*. It concerns an hypothetical person called Adisadi who is a well-known 'Don Juan':

Adisadi/	Adisadi
Maringo mkwaju	Airs and graces like a tamarind tree
Adisadi/	Adisadi
Ufae nini	What should you do
Huna moja ufaacho (x2)	You have no function at all

Although no names are mentioned, the whole community knows the history behind Issa's songs, which therefore have their intended effect of social criticism.

Men are therefore now also involved in *mpasho*. Such competition is not alien to them. With reference to *beni* associations in Kenya, for example, Ranger writes:

> Dance societies of this kind had long been important in the Swahili cities because they were competitive, and because they expressed their competition through elaborate dance and through song. For if two things characterised urban Swahili civilization more than anything else, and distinguished it from the 'tribal' cultures of the interior, they were precisely locational

factionalism and an elaborate verbal and musical culture based
on literacy. (1975: 18)

Thus competition was rife within traditions of both the male and the female
sectors of Swahili towns. Although there are points in the history of
Akhwani Safaa which suggest some degree of competition did exist
competition does not seem to have been a feature affecting the music of
male-dominated 'ideal' *taarab*. It was more likely through women that this
eastern African phenomenon of competition and rivalry expressed through
dance and song was brought to *taarab*. Beginning with Siti binti Saad's
involvement in back-biting through song; reinforced as the women's
lelemama associations transformed into *taarab* clubs; and solidified as
women became the primary consumers of the style, *taarab* became the
main forum for this characteristically Swahili competition. *Taarab* thus
began to be Africanised.

Mpasho music

With these *mipasho* lyrics, the accompanying music was bound to change.
The slow rumbas, waltzes and *wahed unus* used in *taarab* hitherto were
well suited to the sentimental poetry of 'ideal' *taarab*, but in the face of the
bluntness and crudeness of *mipasho* lyrics, they were totally unsatisfactory.
Not being composers, women normally set their poems to existing 'ideal'
taarab songs or invited male musicians to compose the music for them.
Both these solutions were unsatisfactory as they relied on men who were
often too conservative. Women thus found that they had to look further
afield for music that would be more suitable. According to Khadija
Baramia, leader of the women's club Nuru el-Uyun, her group was the
leader of this new trend. Members began to set their poetry to songs from
Mombasa which did use more lively rhythms. Male instrumentalists hired
to play for the women were asked to imitate this music from cassette
recordings, and the women would replace the words with their own
(Khadija Baramia, pers. comm., 1 May 1990). Thus women were
innovators not only as poets but also as musicians, for although they did
not play instruments or compose music, they demanded musical changes to
suit their needs as poets.

In the same way, and for the same purpose, women also introduced the
concept of using rhythms from other styles of music local to Zanzibar to
accompany their *mipasho* lyrics. It is thus no coincidence that the most
popularly used of these local rhythms ('local beats') is the one that is most
meaningful to women, namely *unyago*. This *ngoma* is concerned with the
instruction of girls during their puberty rites. One of its primary purposes is

to teach the girls how to sexually satisfy their prospective husbands. The accompanying hip gyrating dance, called *kiuno* (pl. *viuno*, lit. 'loin, flank, waist, the part just above the hips and groin'; Johnson, 1939: 212), is used demonstratively to this end. *Unyago* is also performed by married women for entertainment at wedding celebrations. In this context the *kiuno* is danced more competitively: two women dance together to demonstrate their sexual prowess. Men are forbidden to attend.

These changes were relatively well contained within women's *taarab* until the activities of this network were restricted by the authorities in about 1984. Following this, women turned to the other forms of *taarab* demanding the same sort of excitement that they had become accustomed to in the context of women-only performances. The informality and *ngoma*-like context of *kidumbak* was more conducive to the accommodation of these demands than 'ideal' *taarab* and the popularity of this form began to soar.

Musicians in Culture Musical Club provide a link between women's and *kidumbak* on the one hand, and 'ideal' *taarab* on the other. Many members play both in *kidumbak* ensembles and for women's clubs. They have first hand experience of the atmosphere at both sorts of events and are thus more attuned to their audience. One of the ways in which this is manifested in the music is that Culture Musical Club composers write much shorter instrumental pieces (*bashrafs*) and instrumental interludes within songs than Akhwani Safaa composers, and use more 'local beats'. *Bashrafs* are generally only appreciated by the better trained musicians, that is, male instrumentalists. At 'ideal' *taarab* events, members of the audience tend to chat among themselves during a *bashraf*, and seem not to pay much heed to the performance; their attention is caught once the verses begin. Consider the remarks of Seif Salim Saleh, himself a violinist, singer, poet and composer in Akhwani Safaa. He declared that 'some people like to listen to *taqasim* [free-rhythm instrumental solos] more than to songs'. When asked to explain who he thought those people are, he opined that it was 'those people who love to play an instrument. Any musician who likes to play an instrument would enjoy *taqsim*' (pers. comm., 5 July 1989). The women of the *taarab* audiences invariably have no specific musical training other than in singing. I suggest that it is through these women's interest in the lyrics of taarab songs rather than in purely musical parameters that their influence is felt.

It is largely because of these connections that the musicians have had something other than Egyptian forms to model their music on, namely local African styles. One of the earliest *taarab* songs to use a 'local beat' was Pakacha, written by Saidi Mwinyi Chande of Culture Musical Club in 1967. It used the rhythm from a style originally from Pemba, called *msewe*. It is perhaps not surprising that this particular rhythm should have been used. *Msewe* is one of the styles promoted by the government and normally forms part of any official exhibition of local culture. This early example of the use of 'local beats' in *taarab* stands in isolation, however. Only towards the mid- 1980s - that is, at the height of the '*mpasho* era' – did Culture Musical Club begin to use 'local beats' frequently. Today a programme may be dominated by compositions using these sorts of rhythms.

Currently the most commonly used 'local beats' in the composition of *taarab* songs are *unyago* and *kumbwaya*. *Kumbwaya* is an *ngoma* associated with spirit beliefs and is mainly played on Pemba and in the very north of Zanzibar island. Another rhythm also classified as a 'local beat' (though it in fact originates in Zaire) is called *tukulanga*. This rhythm has been used in only a few songs.

Of these three rhythms, *unyago* is by far the most common. In its original context, the performance of *unyago* requires three large drums. One plays a regular beat, a second subdivides this beat into three while accenting the second stroke of each group, and the third acts as a 'master drummer', improvising over the triplet base (Abeid Muhsin, pers. comm., 23 August 1989). Songs are usually led by the master drummer, with the dancing participants providing the chorus and hand-clapping.[6]

Figure 11.5 *Unyago* rhythm

This rhythm is used in the song 'Na mnikome' ('You should leave me alone') sung by Sahib al-Ari, quoted above. The hand-clapping establishes the regular beat in place of the first drum. The *rika* subdivides the beat into three together with one pair of bongos, while the second bongos player acts as master drummer. The use of 'hot' percussion - as Zanzibaris refer to it - is reminiscent of the use of the *sanduku* (string bass) in *kidumbak*: it provides *msisimko*.

The Akhwani Safaa song 'Adisadi' (quoted above) is a typical example of the way that the *unyago* rhythm is used in 'ideal' *taarab* songs. The *dumbak* begins the piece by establishing a regular beat and the bongos divide this into three. Improvisation is kept to a minimum and is very subtle. The *rika* sets up a different rhythmic pattern, which contrasts with the duple division by the *dumbak* in a relationship of two against three. Adisadi was amongst the club's most popular songs when it came out in 1990. It is proposed here that this popularity is due to the *mipasho* lyrics and 'local beat'.

Finally, the *kiuno* dance of *unyago* is performed often very explicitly at *kidumbak*, somewhat more sedately at women's *taarab* events, but is virtually forbidden in 'ideal' *taarab* contexts.

A further development, more characteristic of Culture Musical Club than of Akhwani Safaa, is a move away from the 'ideal' strophic structuring of songs. Frequently the traditional *taarab* rhythms are replaced by 'hotter' ones for the final two verses and this is accompanied by an increase in melodic and rhythmic density. Probably in imitation of *kidumbak*, the purpose is to provide variety. An extreme example of this is the song Mwambieni, a Culture Musical Club song composed by Abbas Machano and first performed in 1988. It features two such changes. The first verse is set to the Arabic rhythm *wahed unus*, the second and third verses to a rhythm known as *bonero* (possibly from Zaire), and the rhythm used in the fourth verse is described as *unyago*. *Mwambieni* was an instant success and besides being adopted by Sahib al-Ari, it is also frequently played by *kidumbak* musicians.

Although Idi Farhan explained that 'we [Akhwani Safaa] must keep up with the time' (pers. comm., 21 March 1990), his group did not begin to use 'local beats' until about 1987. Perhaps the change has come too late: many people say that they are tired of the 'slow' music played by Akhwani Safaa and have shifted their interest to Culture Musical Club. What 'ideal' *taarab* musicians have to 'keep up with' is precisely the new desire for more exciting lyrics and for dance music. It is argued here that the fact that 'Zanzibaris want to dance' (Maryam Hamdani, pers. comm., 21 August 1989) is essentially a product of the force of women as the primary consumers. Particularly in the years since women's *taarab* activity has been quelled, that is, since the mid-1980s, women are forcing men in *kidumbak* and, more importantly, in 'ideal' *taarab* to produce the kind of music that they want.

In Zanzibar, women are the primary consumers of *taarab* as audiences and as organisers of the events at which the music occurs. It is they who influence decisions concerning the kinds of musical events that take place. Not only do they decide which forms of music should be played, but in *taarab* they determine how the music should be played. It is thus the consumers, in their manipulation of this music to suit their own aesthetics, have dictated the character of *taarab*.

Notes

1. Thanks to Dr Peter Cooke for the information regarding the groups in Uganda (pers. comm., 23 October 1990). He reported that he had heard of three *taarab* groups in Kampala and two in Jinja. The typical instrumentation is: two electric keyboards, *tabla*, bongos, drum kit, guitar, jingle frame drum, male or female solo singer and a male chorus.
2. The word 'ideal' was used by one consultant in reference to the five instruments that make up the Egyptian *takht* ensemble on which *taarab* is based (see below). These instruments now form the core of the orchestras that superseded as the *takht* and now also exist in Zanzibar. While acknowledging that ideals are constantly changing, I have extended this use of the word to refer to the category of music played by these larger orchestras in Zanzibar. This music is least removed from the Egyptian form, and provides a model in its turn, for the other categories of *taarab* (see below).
3. It published a treatise which incorporated numerous works in philosophy, theology, metaphysics, cosmology, the natural sciences and music. The 'Abbasid al-Mustayid, who succeeded to the Khalifate in 1160, destroyed their works, but their extensive influence continued. (See Glasse, 1989.)
4. See Ranger (1975) and Strobel (1976 and 1979) for in-depth discussions of *beni* and Lelemama
5. As part of the revolutionary government's 'Africanisation' programme all clubs were required to take African names. Akhwani Safaa became Ndugu Wanaopendana (Brothers/Comrades Who Love One Another) though this name never took on. Instead they became widely known as Malindi, the name of the town district whose jurisdiction they came under.
6. The second drum part is written with upward stems to represent its higher pitch relative to the others. The symbols + and - represent longer and shorter durations respectively. The hand-clapping part is placed in parentheses because it only occurs intermittently.

Consultants

Ummie Alley: leader, composer and singer in Banati al-Khairiyah
Idi Farhan: udi player with Akhwani Safaa and one of the oldest and most respected *taarab* musicians in Zanzibar. He has the reputation of being an 'encyclopedia' of *taarab*. He is employed in the Department of Culture and Arts where his duties are to keep records of all musicians and clubs.

Maryam Hamdani: wife of the leader of Twinkling Stars for which she writes poems. She is one of the few women who composes music. She is the director of Sauti ya Tanzania, Zanzibar (the Zanzibar radio station).

Saada Jaffer: ex-leader of the women's *taarab* group, Royal Air Force.

Abeid Muhsin: bongos player with Akhwani Safaa and occasionally plays with Royal Air Force.

Sheikh Yahya Ali Omar: assistant in Swahili conversation at the School of Oriental and African Studies, London University. He is from Mombasa and returns there at least once a year.

Ally Saleh: *taarab* poet and member of Akhwani Safaa (not a musician). He is also a law student at the University of Dar es Salaam.

Seif Salim Saleh: director of the Department of Culture and Arts in the Ministry of Information, Culture and Tourism. He is a prolific composer of *taarab* poems and songs, a lead violinist and singer with Akhwani Safaa.

Rashidi Makame Shani: prolific *taarab* poet, composer, violinist (until January 1990, with Culture Musical Club, but now with the Bwawani Hotel group) and sanduku player. He is also very active as a violinist and composer in Sahib al-Ari. He is self-employed, making a living from music and selling soap in the informal sector.

Khamisi Shehe: director of music and lead violinist and composer in Culture Musical Club. He often plays and composes for Sahib al-Ari.

Dr Farouk Topan: lecturer at the Institute of Ismaili Studies. He was born and brought up in Zanzibar.

Bibliography

Barber, Karin (1987), 'Popular Arts in Africa', *African Studies Review*, **30** (3).

Bender, W. (1991), *SWEET MOTHER: Modern African Music*, Chicago: Chicago University Press, foreword by John Miller Chernoff.

Berg, F. J. (1968), 'The Coast from the Portuguese Invasion to the Rise of the Zanzibar Sultanate', in B. A. Ogot and J. A. Kiernan (eds), *Zamani: a Survey of East African History*, London: Longmans Green.

D'Erlanger, Baron Rudolphe (1959), *La musique arabe*, vol. 6. Paris: Librairie Orientaliste Paul Geuthner.

Dubisch, Jill (ed.) (1986), *Gender and Power in Rural Greece*, Princeton, NJ: Princeton University Press.

Glass, Cyril (ed.) (1989), *Concise Encyclopedia of Islam*, London: Stacey International.

Gray, John (1962), *History of Zanzibar from the Middle Ages to 1856*, London: Oxford University Press.

Hollingsworth, L. W. (1953), *Zanzibar under the Foreign Office: 1890-1913*, London: Macmillan.

Johnson, F. (1939), *A Standard Swahili-English Dictionary*, Nairobi: Oxford University Press.

Khatib, Mohammed Seif (1984), *Taarab Zanzibar*, Dar es Salaam: Tanzania Publishing House.

Lofchie, Michael F. (1965), *Zanzibar: Background to Revolution*, Princeton, NJ: Princeton University Press.

Newman, Henry Stanley (1898), *Banani: the Transition from Slavery to Freedom in Zanzibar and Pemba*, Leominster: The Orphan's Printing Press.

Racy, Jihad (1988), 'Sound and Society: the Takht Music of Early-Twentieth-Century Cairo', *Selected Reports in Ethnomusicology, Vol. 7: Issues of Conceptualisation of Music*, Los Angeles: University of California.

Ranger, T. O. (1975), *Dance and Society in Eastern Africa 1890-1970: the Beni Ngoma*, London: Heinemann Educational Books.

Rouget, G. (1985), *Music and Trance: a Theory of the Relations Between Music and Possession*, trans. by Brunhilde Biebuyck in collaboration with the author, Chicago: University of Chicago Press.

Shariff, I. N. (1973), 'Waswahili and their Language: Some Misconceptions', *Kiswahili*, **43** (2).

Shariff, I. N.(1981), '"Knappert Tells More Tales". Horn of Africa', Summit, NJ, *Horn of Africa Journal*, **4** (3).

Suleiman, A. A. (1969), 'The Swahili Singing Star Siti binti Saad and the Tarab Tradition in Zanzibar', *Swahili*, **39**, pp. 87-90.

Strobel, M. (1976), 'From Lelemama to Lobbying: Women's Associations in Mombasa, Kenya', in Nancy J. Hafkin and Edna G. Bay (eds), *Women in Africa: Studies in Social and Economic Change*, Stanford, CA: Stanford University Press.

Strobel, M. (1979), *Muslim Women in Mombasa, 1890-1975*, New Haven, CT: Yale University Press.

Wehr, H. (1974), *Dictionary of Modern Written Arabic*, London and Beirut.

Whiteley, W. H. (1966), *Waimbaji wa Juzi*, Dar es Salaam: Chuo cha uchunguzi wa Lugha ya Kiswahili.

12 *Kwela*: the Structure and Sound of Pennywhistle Music

Lara Allen

Kwela is an urban South African popular music style which developed in Johannesburg's black townships during the 1950s. Originally played on pennywhistles by small boys, adolescents and young adults, *kwela* was later also performed on saxophones. An eclectic mix of 'traditional' South African music and American popular music styles of the day, it was the first township style to cross the colour bar and attract a substantial white following.

Although it is possible to draw certain conclusions about the internal musical characteristics and compositional principles inherent in 'typical' *kwela* numbers, in practice the term *kwela* is used to refer to a wide range of musical styles. Compositions called *kwela* range from pennywhistle blues and boogie-woogie to numbers which could equally be classed as African Jazz or *mbaqanga*.[1] The perceptions presented in this chapter derive from a detailed analysis of over 250 compositions classified as *kwela* by musicians, on record labels, in advertisements and record reviews.

The fusion of traditional South African and African-American musical elements is a process of constant negotiation within *kwela*. Although beyond the scope of this chapter, this process both reflects and expresses the stresses and constant flux experienced by township dwellers in their search for, and definition of, black urban identity. African-Americans were perceived as having achieved success and social status under similar conditions of racial intolerance and discrimination. Appreciation and emulation of American music and culture therefore appeared to be one of the manifestations of, if not pathways to, prestige and prosperity. American dress, behaviour and language codes gleaned from films almost attained cult status. This was particularly true in the more cosmopolitan 'melting pot' areas such as Sophiatown, where the intellectual élite were inspired by the cultural and social achievements of black America, and the principal gang (called The Americans) modelled themselves on Hollywood's Chicago gangsters.

Interestingly, however, highly Americanized pennywhistle numbers generally did not sell as well as those compositions more strongly influenced by South African musical elements. Evidently the buying public preferred music which referenced America but was also firmly rooted in South Africa. Although Willard Cele's 'Pennywhistle Blues' and 'Pennywhistle Boogie' were released in 1951, the '*kwela* boom' did not occur until late in 1954 when Spokes Mashiyane made his first recordings.

The latter sold exceptionally well, their immediate and overwhelming success generally being attributed to Mashiyane's use of local musical elements. Albert Ralulimi, a friend and pennywhistle colleague explained the appeal of his music in this way:

> Spokes became more popular because he took tunes from the community, something that he felt. He went about *stokvels*[2] and watching people singing their old songs ... So Spokes improvised the pattern of the type of music that was sung by anybody - or small boys playing on the street ... [3]

The fusion and interplay between American and South African elements forms a recurrent theme in the following discussion of the construction and production of kwela music. For instance, 'traditional' African principles of musical organisation such as cyclicity and 'call-and-response' are merged with the imperatives of western functional harmony. In *kwela* jazz-style development of musical material and improvisation is often indiscernible from procedures of ornamentation and variation intrinsic to much 'traditional' African music.

The following investigation into the compositional principles of *kwela* music starts with a brief examination of the style's harmonic, melodic and rhythmic characteristics, and its common formal structures.[4] This is followed by a discussion of the definitive aspect of *kwela*: instrumentation. After an examination of the contribution of the backing instruments to the formation and development of this style, the chapter concludes with a detailed exploration of the pennywhistle's role in the composition of *kwela*.

Structure, melody, harmony and rhythm in *kwela* music

Structurally *kwela* music consists of the repetition of a short harmonic cycle over which a series of short melodies or motifs, usually the length of the cycle, are repeated and varied. The internal structure of a *kwela* number is delineated by melodic variation rather than by harmonic movement and there are two fundamental methods of organising melodic material over the harmonic cycle: either a series of motifs are repeated and alternated with improvisatory passages; or a solo is improvised over an ostinato backing riff. Other variants of structural organisation include: combinations of the above, versions of the blues form and, occasionally, longer progressions of primary chords which are repeated like verses of a song.

The cyclical repetition of a short harmonic progression of primary chords fuses the fundamental organising principles of African and Western music: cyclicity and functional harmony respectively. Another primary structural element which locates *kwela* within the African and African-American musical traditions is the style's utilisation of the call-and-response principle. In compositions constructed from motifs and solo sections, the solos represent the 'call' and the motivic sections the 'response'. In compositions of the solo-over-ostinato variety, the ostinato backing riff can be interpreted as fulfilling the response function. Call-and-response also frequently occurs between a solo instrument and its backing chorus.

Harmonic structure is one of the areas of continuity between *kwela* and other urban South African musical styles such as *marabi* and *mbaqanga*.[5] There is no specific *kwela* chord progression although two progressions, I I IV V and I IV V I, are particularly prevalent. *Kwela* compositions are constructed almost exclusively of the primary chords, generally in their triadic form. Seventh or substitution chords occur only in compositions strongly influenced by jazz.

The short repetitive melodic motifs, often closely modelled on the chord tones of the harmonic progression, are the most important and memorable components of any *kwela* number. Each composition is defined by these motifs and their creator is recognised as the composer. Although large parts of the rest of a *kwela* number, for instance the solos and backing, are added by other members of the band, they do not lay claim to partial composition. The melodic structure of much *kwela*, within both motifs and solos, tends to be dominated by arpeggiated figures and scalar passages.

Kwela rhythm is defined primarily by the guitar rather than the drum-set and can be described as a 'lilting shuffle'. The most important rhythmic difference between *kwela* and *marabi* or *mbaqanga*, is that the former is 'swung', whilst the beat in the latter two styles is usually 'straight'.

Kwela instrumentation

Although the structural, harmonic, melodic and rhythmic criteria discussed above are important, the definitive component of *kwela* music is instrumentation. A composition may contain all the most typical elements indicated above, but without the sound of a pennywhistle, or a solo saxophone, such a composition would generally not be recognised as *kwela* by musicians or by the general public.

Various combinations of instruments constitute the front line in a *kwela* ensemble. The earliest line-up was simply a solo pennywhistle accompanied by a guitar. Later the solo pennywhistle was accompanied by the typical *kwela* rhythm section: a guitar, a string-bass and a drum set. Although the use of one solo pennywhistle was characteristic of the early days of *kwela*, it remained popular as the style developed and all the major stars made solo recordings without the normal chorus of backing pennywhistles. The most stereotypical *kwela* line-up is, however, a solo pennywhistle backed by a pennywhistle chorus and a basic rhythm section. 'Tom Hark' which rose high on the British Hit Parade in 1956 and catalysed the '*kwela* boom' in South Africa, is one of the most famous examples of such instrumentation.

The hierarchy in pennywhistle bands was very much one of a virtuoso leader backed by a supporting band. Peter Macontela's description of a *kwela* performance cogently illustrates this power relationship:

> The three, or four, or six guys stand around me in an arc form, then they just play in parts. They are not actually playing a song, they are backing in harmony. Then I start building a repetition of what I do. Then I must be above them and do all that, they just go ba ba ba. I'm going to let them know that I am stopping abruptly then they all 'bvoir' [demonstration of the final note] they stop, and it's another song again.[6]

Such issues of hierarchy and leadership were so important that a *kwela* band formed by two pennywhistling brothers, Elias and Jake Lerole, recorded under different names according to who was leading. The same band performed variously as The Shamber Boys, Elias and his Zig-Zag-Jive Flutes and The Black Mambazos.

The occurrence of a *kwela* recording in which two pennywhistles are, musically speaking, equally important is so contrary to the normal hierarchy of *kwela* bands that it occurred only as a result of external pressures. The most famous *kwela* 'duets' were recorded by Lemmy 'Special' Mabaso and Spokes Mashiyane just after Mashiyane joined Gallo (the record company which already had Mabaso under contract). As it made commercial sense for Gallo to publicise the fact that they now 'owned' both of the most famous pennywhistlers, it is possible that the two stars were requested to perform together. This provided opportunities for such statements as the following introduction to 'Manyatela' played by Spokes Mashiyane and Lemmy Special:

> Ladies and Gentlemen, for the first time in the history of South Africa we have the two *kwela* kings: On my right hand I have King of Kings, Lemmy Special [Signature tune and dubbed cheers.] On my left hand I have King of Kwela, Spokes Mashiyane (Signature tune and more dubbed cheers.][7]

In 1958, Spokes made his first saxophone recordings, 'D.O.C.C.' and 'Sweet Sax'. From this point forward, the line-up of musicians in *kwela* recordings included saxophonists as soloists and members of backing choruses. Many of the solo saxophone and rhythm section *kwela* recordings were made by

Spokes Mashiyane, and he constructs these numbers exactly as he would have on the pennywhistle. they mostly consist of two varied motifs alternated with solo sections.

One consequence of the introduction of the saxophone into the *kwela* line-up was that, in compositions for saxophones and pennywhistles, the latter had to be amplified. The pennywhistle *kwela* compositions discussed so far are essentially the same as those performed on the streets. The addition of the saxophone, however, meant that this music could not be successfully performed on the streets or in the townships if studio-type equipment, such as amplifiers and mixers, was not available. Musicians who did not have the financial means to provide this equipment therefore became dependent on record companies for the organisation of live shows as well as recordings. With the introduction of the saxophone, *kwela* still sounded like *kwela*, but the relationship between musicians, the record industry and the market started to change. The foundation for 1960s *mbaqanga* was being established.

The *kwela* rhythm section

The move from the streets into the studios had a significant impact on the instrumentation of *kwela* rhythm sections. Willard Cele, the first pennywhistler to achieve widespread fame, started off playing completely alone on the streets of Alexandra Township. The guitar, bass and drum-set evident in his recordings 'Penny Whistle Blues' and 'Penny Whistle Boogie' were added in the recording studio.[8] The *marabi*-based pennywhistle street music which proliferated in the early 1950s was, however, commonly played on pennywhistle(s) and guitar(s). Spokes Mashiyane, for instance, consolidated his style playing with a guitarist, Frans Pilane, long before his first recording in 1954.

There are a few recordings which document how early *kwela*, as it was played on the streets, may have sounded. 'Ngiyabonga' and 'Kupela' by Jerrypenny Flute, for example, are recorded on pennywhistle and guitar without other backing. These recordings were produced by Charles Berman of BB Records and it is to his credit that Jerrypenny Flute's compositions were not tampered with, or 'improved' with additional backing, as happened in virtually all other studios. Dan Hill, musical director of Gallo in the 1950s, admits that pennywhistles and guitars are the only instruments needed to play *kwela*. He explains, however, that it was generally felt that recordings required the 'fullness of sound' provided by the addition of bass and drums. Pennywhistle and guitar 'sounds thin on a recording. You have to have a bass because it gives it body, and you have to have drums for the beat really'.[9]

A fluid relationship existed between *kwela* recordings and street *kwela* during the mid-1950s. As the style's popularity swept the country, a plethora of bands took to the streets. These groups imitated *kwela* compositions as they existed on hit records, that is, with a bass and drum-set. In this way a modification instigated by the record companies was absorbed into, and accepted as an integral part of, kwela as a 'grassroots' musical style. Even some musicians who had busked for years with pennywhistles and guitars, and who were already successful recording artists, introduced the tea-box bass into their street performances. The Lerole brothers were a case in point: Elias Lerole remembers playing in the streets with two guitars and four pennywhistles.[10] Later, Jake Lerole reports, their street band consisted of two or three guitars, four to seven pennywhistlers and a tea-box bass.[11] Other groups did not wish to go to so much trouble as Barney Rachabane explains: 'No we just used guitar and flutes that's all. It was a problem to have that box you know - how you going to get into the bus?'[12]

By the late 1950s, a rhythm section consisting of at least two guitars, a bass and drum set had become the norm in live *kwela* performances as well as in recordings. Jake Lerole's memories of this line-up in *stokvel* performances is corroborated by a newspaper report of a dance party in 1959: 'Swaying couples were dancing to hot pennywhistle music given out by Aaron 'Jake' Lerole and his Black Mambazo band ... Several guitarists and a double bass player thumped out the beat.'[13]

The bass players and drummers provided by recording studios to back black groups were often white. This occurred in most studios but at Gallo, under the musical directorship of Dan Hill, it was particularly common. Hill himself played saxophone or clarinet on the recordings of many black artists, as he explains: 'in those days we just used to fill in whatever we could'.[14] Hill's justification for using white musicians was ostensibly a commercial one: 'we often used white drummers because they were actually better at the time ... We used them because it was more efficient, a black guy didn't have the experience usually to play neatly and that'. He was also of the opinion that as the bass and drums were not part of street *kwela*, it was of little importance who played them in the studio: as 'street music it was often just pennywhistles and guitar ... the bass and drums were added but you didn't really need it ... the *kwela* rhythm itself was mainly the guitars doing this shuffle type of beat and the drummer just played you know'.[15]

Despite such attitudes, white backing musicians were not the norm in *kwela* recordings. There were many black session musicians available, and groups often had their own drum and bass players. Backing musicians (of any race) were rarely acknowledged on record labels in the 1950s and, apart from the memories of living musicians, few clues remain as to who played in which recordings.[16]

Elias Lerole reports that his street band included a drummer playing on a side drum.[17] This, however, does not appear to have been the norm in other *kwela* groups. When Peter Macontela played *kwela* at *stokvels*, his band consisted of three pennywhistles and a guitar. The rhythm was provided by any one of the *stokvel*'s clientele who could play the spoons. 'The drums they used to take the dessert spoons and put them upside down, I don't know how, and put a finger in between there and then he just [makes clicks]: Two spoons back to back'.[18]

Elias Lerole maintains that drummers who had learnt on homemade instruments had little difficulty in adapting to the commercially produced instruments available in the studios.[19] This is corroborated by Dan Hill who adds that black musicians rarely used the whole drum-set: 'most of the time they just used the side drum, the snare drum with brushes and the cymbal going and that was it'.[20] On occasion only one drum was used. Barney Rachabane describes the modification of a snare drum to produce the right sound for a *kwela* recording: 'You put a cardboard [from a cardboard box] on top of the snare drum and you use brushes ... there is a certain sound that's wanted. You get a very different sound, a *kwela* or *mbaqanga* sound which you couldn't really imitate'.[21]

The Lerole brothers' *kwela* band was reportedly the first to use a tea-box bass regularly in street performances. The Alexandra Bright Boys, led by Lemmy Special, and several other groups soon included the tea-box bass in their line-up, but the instrument was never adopted by Spokes Mashiyane.[22] The inclusion of a tea-box bass made busking a less mobile, and therefore a more risky, operation. Peter Macontela explains: 'the problem is if the flying squad comes you must run'.[23] Furthermore, bus drivers were singularly unsympathetic to the needs of young *kwela* bands, as Duze Magwaza reports: 'We used to go and hide that thing because it was a very big thing to keep it in the bus and the drivers used to shout at us. We had to hide it somewhere. Each time we have to play, we come to find it. Sometimes we don't find it'.[24] If the bass was lost, stolen or broken by police another one was constructed.

The technique of playing a one-stringed tea-box bass is quite unlike that required to play a double bass. It is likely, therefore, that the bass lines of *kwela* numbers played on the streets would have been different to those in *kwela* recordings. Owing to the lack in availability of street recordings, the following comments on *kwela* bass lines refer purely to recorded *kwela*, in which a string bass was employed.

Jazz bass player Monde Futshane explains that the function of the bass in *kwela* music is to provide a fundamental harmonic outline of the chord progression and to hold the composition together rhythmically by continuously playing on the beat.[25] Although bass movement on the crotchet is the norm, the bass line also occasionally moves in minims or swung quavers. This 'walking bass', so common in *kwela* recordings, is another aspect of the American big-band legacy inherited by *kwela* musicians from local big-bands. Albert Ralulimi asserts that walking bass was also a feature of street *kwela*: 'when our fellows started using tea chests as basses you can feel that they are also following the footsteps of the walking bass style'.[26] Although *kwela* walking bass lines are intrinsically similar to their American prototypes, however, the cyclical repetition of a short harmonic progression demands a slightly different pattern from, for example, the blues progression. Another distinctive trait of a *kwela* bass line is the fast upbeat to the basic crotchet at significant moments in the music. Futshane recounts: 'Bra Jake said you play on the crotchet except for those moments when you kind of kick start it to give it a boost'.[27] This technique is also used by *kwela* drummers and guitarists to provide the forward propulsion intrinsic to music created primarily for dancing.

The guitar is the only instrument of the *kwela* rhythm section which belonged to the original *kwela* bands of the pre-recording era. It therefore plays a far more significant role than do either the bass or drum-set. In fact, the rhythm produced by the way in which the guitarist strums is frequently quoted as one of the definitive aspects of *kwela*. Dan Hill explains that '*kwela* evolved in the townships. It evolved from having a cheap guitar and strumming it a certain way. That became the norm, the rhythm that caught on'.[28]

The four-crotchets-per-bar, on-the-beat strumming is typical of many early *kwela* recordings. Stylistically, it is a hallmark of Frans Pilane, Spokes Mashiyane's first guitarist. The timbre of Pilane's guitar is quite 'tinny', and he uses the most basic strumming technique consisting of downward strokes only. This strumming method develops naturally into the definitive *kwela* shuffle-type rhythm: a shorter, softer upward stroke precedes each downward strum which occurs on the beat. It is a spontaneous result of the wrist movement required to produce a downward stroke. This strumming technique produces the 'swing feel' that distinguishes *kwela* from 1960s *mbaqanga*.

Figure 12.1   The shuffle-type *kwela* rhythm[29]

Figure 12.2 illustrates some variations on the basic shuffle beat commonly played by rhythm guitarists in *kwela*. Such rhythms generally exist in pennywhistle compositions which are influenced by jazz.

Figure 12.2a   Variation on the swing beat in 'See You Later' and 'Little Lemmy' by Dan Hill

Figure 12.2b   Variation on the swing beat in 'Year 1962 Blues' by Allen Kwela

As *kwela* developed, guitar parts became more sophisticated and the instrument played an increasingly prominent role. It gradually became the norm for a *kwela* band to include both a rhythm and a lead guitar. The rhythm guitar was occasionally replaced by a banjo. As the lead guitar increased in importance it took on a contrapuntal rather than a backing harmonic role. This was especially the case after electric guitars became popular and is one of the primary indications of the metamorphosis of *kwela* into *mbaqanga*. Occasionally lead guitars provided introductions and increasingly took solos. The latter varied in length from four to 24 bars.

The tendency of the guitar line to become more important is taken to extremes in two compositions, 'Fish & Chips Kwela' and 'City Kwela' by Jerry Mhlanga (one of the most important *kwela* guitarists). Both recordings are typical of *kwela* in every way except that the instrumentation is bass, drum set, rhythm guitar, and lead guitar. It includes neither a pennywhistle nor a saxophone. The structure of 'Fish & Chips Kwela' is three motifs with solo sections, the basic harmonic progression is I IV V V, and the drums play the shuffle rhythm whilst the bass and rhythm guitar play on the crotchet. The part customarily played on the pennywhistle, that of the motifs and solos, is played by the lead guitar. Although these compositions are typical in many other ways, as a result of the absence of a pennywhistle they are unlikely to be widely recognised as *kwela*.

The solo sections of 'Fish & Chips Kwela' illustrate one of the most characteristic element of *kwela* guitar lines, a supertonic ostinato. As is generally the case, the rhythm of the ostinato figure is swung quavers, and it lasts for at least one cycle, often more. During his solo Jerry Mhlanga demonstrates a second particularly characteristic element of the *kwela* sound by playing open fifths and fourths (see Figure 12.3). This is a particularly African element of *kwela*: Voice leading and spacing which results in open fifths and fourths is common in much black Southern African 'traditional' and neo-traditional music.

Figure 12.3   Open fifths and fourths on the lead guitar in 'Fish & Chips Kwela' by Jerry Mhlanga

A further device commonly incorporated into *kwela* guitar solos is that of the cross-rhythm. The electric guitar in 'Woza Woza' by Spokes Mashiyane, for instance, plays a series of triplet crotchets on the dominant producing the most typical cross-rhythm in *kwela,* two-against-three. On occasion the lead guitar plays a short motif at the end of each cycle. The function of this motif is the same as the typical drum-set 'kick', that is to mark the end of one cycle and introduce a new one.

The introduction of a lead guitar into *kwela* and the advent of electrification happened almost simultaneously, although the electrification of guitars occurred in two stages. To begin with *kwela* guitarists attached a 'pick-up' microphone to their acoustic instruments. This amplified the sound, making guitar solos possible, but did not change it and the character of pennywhistle *kwela* was not essentially altered. In the late 1950s, however, the introduction of the electric guitar heralded the coming of *mbaqanga*. Peter Macontela suggests that although rock musicians had little impact on black South African music 'they brought the instruments into usage'.[30] The use of glissandi, a technique associated with electric guitars, became quite common in guitar lines after 1958. Glissandi are clearly evident in 'Hit and Beat' by The Sewer Rats. In this recording the guitarist slides from the tonic down a semitone and back again over the time span of a minim.

Figure 12.4   Glissandi in 'Hit and Beat' by The Sewer Rats

According to guitarist Zami Duze, the main difference between *kwela* and *mbaqanga* guitar technique is that *mbaqanga* is faster, requiring the guitarist to be 'more technically proficient'. Furthermore, a *mbaqanga* lead guitarist plays an independent melody line throughout containing 'fast singing lines' and 'special kind of fill-ins', and typically plays 'lots of parallel thirds'.[31]

In spite of their fundamental importance, *kwela* guitarists have tended to be as unacknowledged as bass players and drummers. However, because guitarists were generally permanent members of bands rather than itinerant session musicians, they are remembered by pennywhistle players more clearly than other members of the rhythm section. Jake Lerole recalls recording at Troubadour with guitarist Rex Shongwe in 1952, although Peter Khumalo was the main guitarist with the various Lerole family bands during the height of *kwela*'s popularity.[32] Ben Nkosi was a guitarist and bass player, and when he was not recording his own pennywhistle numbers, he played as a session musician on other artists' recordings.

The changing role of the guitar in *kwela* music is exemplified by the series of guitarists who played with Spokes Mashiyane: Frans Pilane was Mashiyane's first guitarist, they played together before entering the studios and for Mashiyane's first recordings for Trutone. Pilane, with his basic rhythm guitar style, was ousted by Jerry Mhlanga when acoustic guitars became amplified. Albert Ralulimi recalls:

> Then when guitars started to be electrified he [Pilane] lost touch, so surely we couldn't use him. He didn't have that zeal, because we needed push really ... Jerry had a pick up on his guitar. Whereby, when Spokes recorded 'Kwela Claude' Frans couldn't cope up with the arrangement which had that western touch in it, so they had to bring in Jerry Mhlanga.[33]

Jerry Mhlanga recorded with Spokes Mashiyane until Mashiyane left Trutone for Gallo in 1958. Mashiyane and Mhlanga continued to perform together in live shows for years afterwards even though they recorded at different studios. Jerry Mhlanga was the most acknowledged *kwela* guitarist. Ralulimi points out, for instance, that at one stage Mashiyane and Mhlanga were given equal publicity: 'he became even on the King Kwela album. There is Spokes Mashiyane's and Jerry Mhlanga's photos on that'.[34] At Gallo Spokes recorded most often with guitarist Allen Kwela, who went on to become a jazz musician, and Reggie Msomi, a Zulu guitarist who later became an *mbaqanga* saxophonist.[35]

The importance of the rhythm guitar in *kwela* had already been severely eroded through the increasing role played by the lead guitar, when the introduction of the banjo threatened to make rhythm guitars completely redundant. The appeal of the banjo lay in the continuous strumming technique which increased the volume of the backing section and filled in the gaps. Albert Ralulimi explains: 'let's say the guy [rhythm guitarist] is playing 4/4 type of strumming, it leaves open gaps. But now the banjo fills in'.[36]

In 1957 Saul Malahela, a banjo player from the Eastern Transvaal, joined the Gallo stable. Originally a guitarist, Malahela was given a banjo by his employer (a farmer and keen *Boeremusiek* musician)[37] which he soon adopted as his primary instrument. Malahela met Billy Zambi, a saxophonist from Zimbabwe (then Southern Rhodesia), and together they travelled to Johannesburg. At Gallo Billy Zambi, Saul Malahela, Allen Kwela and Spokes Mashiyane formed a 'brotherhood' and made many recordings together. Banjo thus quickly became integrated into *kwela* and Malahela was frequently 'borrowed' by other studios. Other banjo players who recorded *kwela* were Saul Nkosi and Marks Mankwane, who later became the top exponent of *mbaqanga* guitar.[38]

The influence of Afrikaans *Boeremusiek* is evident in the banjo style of several kwela recordings. Figure 12.5 illustrates the banjo rhythms of three kwela recordings by Spokes Mashiyane which exhibit strong *Boeremusiek* characteristics. All three recordings are extremely fast.

Figure 12.5   Banjo rhythms which suggest the influence of *Boeremusik*

a) 'Caledon River' by Spokes Mashiyane and his Big Five

b) 'Lona Na Lona' by Spokes Mashiyane and his Big Five.

c) 'Phesheya' by Spokes Mashiyane and his All Star Flutes.

In many *kwela* recordings the banjo replaces the rhythm guitar only to play exactly what the latter would have played, namely the shuffle rhythm illustrated in Figure 12.l. Although the banjo occasionally plays this rhythm alone it more often occurs in unison with the drum-set. The close relationship between the banjo and rhythm guitar lines is further exemplified by two Mashiyane compositions ('Don't be Mad' and 'Girls, What about Jerry?') in which the rhythm guitar plays the most characteristic banjo rhythm, triplet quavers. In 'Deep Heat', by Lemmy Special and the Alexandra Bright Boys, the banjo plays triplet quavers continuously from the second motif to the end. This figure does 'fill up the gaps', providing the 'zest' described by Albert Ralulimi in his explanation of the importance of the banjo in *kwela*. Using 'Double Qwela' by Lemmy Special as an example, Figure 12.6 illustrates one of the most typical rhythmic relationships between the banjo and the rest of the rhythm section.

Figure 12.6   A typical set of rhythmic relationships between the instruments of a *kwela* rhythm section

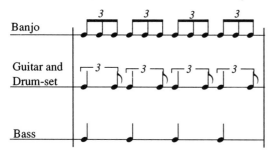

Triplet quavers and the shuffle rhythm are readily compatible. This accounts for the ease with which the banjo player in 'Maseru Special', by Spokes Mashiyane and his New Sound Band, alternates triplet quavers with sections of the shuffle rhythm. Figure 12.7 illustrates two banjo backing riffs which result from the amalgamation of these rhythmic figures.

Figure 12.7   An amalgamation of the shuffle rhythm and triplet quavers in backing riffs

'Woza Woza' by Spokes Mashiyane   'Mama Ndiyeke' by Lemmy Special
and his All Star Flutes   and the Alexandra Bright Boys

Kwela compositions may be divided into two fundamental rhythmic groups: those which are swung and those based on a straight beat. The basic crotchet beat of the former is subdivided into three and the latter into two or four. The swing beat is a legacy of the *kwela*'s jazz roots whilst the straight beat stems from Southern African 'traditional' music. *Kwela* compositions belonging to the second group exemplify the general trend away from jazz towards a neo-traditional African style which culminated in *mbaqanga*. Figure 12.8 illustrates some of the straight-beat banjo figures used in *kwela* compositions.

Figure 12.8   Straight-beat banjo figures

'London Special' by Lemmy Special   'Dingo' by Lemmy Special

'Godini' by Lemmy Special   'Jazz Kwela' by Lemmy Special

The occurrence of other instruments in *kwela*

Some *kwela* recordings include instruments other than the typical line-up discussed above. These often resulted from collaborations between *kwela* musicians and white South African musicians, or visiting jazz musicians from America.

One of the most heralded American visitors in the 1950s was clarinetist Tony Scott, who made several recordings with pennywhistlers. Tony Scott recorded an LP album titled 'Tony Scott in Africa' with the Alexandra Dead End Kids. The reconciliation of jazz clarinet with pennywhistle kwela on this album is accomplished more effectively on some tracks than on others. A more successful synthesis of these instruments and styles is 'Something New from Africa' by Peter Macontela.[39] White South African clarinetist Dan Hill and pennywhistler Ben Nkosi play jazz solos supported with backing riffs provided by a pennywhistle chorus. This composition demonstrates the expertise with which the pennywhistlers were able to imitate big-band swing. The best integration of the clarinet into the *kwela* idiom, however, was accomplished by Kippie Moeketsi in 'Clarinet Kwela' and 'Goli Kwela'.[40] Besides the substitution of the solo pennywhistle or saxophone with a clarinet, both recordings are good examples of the *kwela* style.

The only other instrument occasionally included in the front line of a *kwela* band, is the violin. Spokes Mashiyane made several recordings with violinist Robert Cele. Two of these, 'Manotcha' and 'Simple Simon', consist of typical motifs on the part of the pennywhistle supported by a violin riff which relies heavily on the dominant. In Albert Ralulimi's 'G-String Kwela', however, the violinist (probably also Robert Cele) plays a more prominent role taking two solos and providing the introduction.

Two recordings which brought widespread fame to Spokes Mashiyane, 'Kwela Claudet' and 'Sheshisa!', were made with visiting American jazz pianist Claude Williamson.[41] Both compositions are fundamentally *kwela*, although the former includes a piano solo strongly grounded in the jazz idiom. Subsequent to the success of these recordings, the piano became an acceptable supplement to the *kwela* line-up. Nor were the pianists always visiting whites: a newspaper report of a kwela performance by The Black Mambazos, for instance, reveals that their backing included black South

African jazz pianist and composer Gideon Nxumalo.[42] The role of the piano in *kwela* compositions is that which is normally fulfilled by a guitar: that is, to provide the harmonic framework and occasionally take a solo. Sometimes, as in the case of 'Mambo Spokes' by Mashiyane, the piano completely replaces the guitar.

Another common alteration of the regular *kwela* rhythm section is the augmentation, or replacement, of the bass with a trombone. The trombone is used more frequently with saxophones than with pennywhistles, and its inclusion is indicative of the tendency exhibited by some *kwela* players towards African jazz.[43]

The pennywhistle was recorded with vocal music throughout the entire period of the instrument's popularity. During the height of the '*kwela* boom' many pennywhistle and vocal recordings were made, particularly with female close harmony groups. Of these, Spokes Mashiyane's recordings with Miriam Makeba and the Skylarks were the most highly publicised.[44] Like most instrumentalists who recorded township music in the 1950s singers who took part in *kwela* recordings were virtually never credited. Neither were pennywhistlers who accompanied vocal numbers. The relationship between the vocal and pennywhistle parts in *kwela* numbers ranges from dialogue sounding within a typical *kwela* composition, to compositions which are essentially songs with an added pennywhistle improvisation,[45] although compositions belonging to the latter group are the most common.

The role of the pennywhistle in *kwela* music

The pennywhistle is the most important instrument in *kwela* music. It was popular with *kwela* players, most of whom came from financially impoverished backgrounds, because it was relatively inexpensive. As children some *kwela* musicians could not even afford metal pennywhistles. Peter Macontela describes the plastic instruments he played on as a child:

> The first plastic flute that came in was shaped like a trumpet. It was this small [10 cm] and it had three holes. Then I started with that [in] 1949, 1950 ... [it was] shaped like a trumpet, made of plastic, but it's so little. But you play something, you can build up a song. You used to buy it for a tickey. Then from there '50, '51, '52 came a fish flute. It's broad - made just exactly like a fish. It had a hole underneath like a recorder now. That was a difficult one, broader here at the mouth ... After that came this straight pennywhistle, with six holes on top with the mouthpiece

you could dismantle like a sax. It used to be white and mouthpiece yellow or red or green, it was colourful ... nobody recorded with that ... you can get it from any shop in Soweto ... I got hold of my first flute in 1955 I think, the metal one. ... You sort of graduate from plastic to that.[46]

Other young aspirant musicians made their own instruments. In rural areas reeds provided the basic material whilst a bicycle pump, or any other available metal tubing, was used in the towns. Albert Ralulimi describes his early attempts at instrument building: 'I remember pinching my uncle's bicycle pump. It was made from steel. I looked for stronger nails to punch holes in it and I was even given a hiding for that. But after they listened how I made use of it, they became excited'.[47]

The pennywhistles available in South Africa in the 1930s, 1940s and early 1950s were made of brass.[48] In 1958, however, the Hohner Company in Trossingen, Germany, started mass-producing nickel-plated pennywhistles for the South African market apparently using a 'home-made flute acquired from a South African youngster in Johannesburg' as a prototype.[49] British nickel-plated pennywhistles were also sold in South Africa under the trade name 'Generation'. Musicians who were accustomed to brass pennywhistles found the nickel instruments inferior: Peter Macontela declares 'the Hohner was too tinny, too light. I have never recorded with that'. Describing his preference in pennywhistles Macontela says: 'I have my brass, copper you know when it fades, the genuine ones ... it's silver coated. But as it wears off you could see there's brass coming. But you can hit it and it dents. Those were our pennywhistles'. All the Solven Whistlers, including Ben Nkosi, played on these 'genuine' instruments because, as Macontela explains, 'you have to have the correct sound, you must be uniform. All play same make otherwise they don't tune the same way'.[50]

In the early 1950s it was fairly diffcult to obtain metal pennywhistles. By 1955, however, Indian shopkeepers in central Johannesburg were stocking the instruments. Peter Macontela reports: 'Indian shops where you could cut suits and things, that's where we would get our pennywhistles from'.[51] In other areas the most likely place to sell pennywhistles was the local bicycle shop. Macontela remembers that the price of a pennywhistle in downtown Johannesburg was 5s. 6d. This was substantially less expensive than music shops in the city centre where, in 1956, B flat and C pennywhistles were advertised for 8s. 6d. and 7s. 6d. respectively.[52]

The limitations and possibilities inherent in the pennywhistle as an instrument had a significant effect on *kwela* composition. In the 1950s, the pennywhistle was made of a cylindrical metal tube moulded at one end into a fipple mouthpiece. Pennywhistles have six reasonably evenly spaced finger holes, the top hole placed approximately in the centre of the instrument. The diameter of each finger hole is slightly different, which controls the tuning of the instrument; the larger the hole, the sharper the note. As a pennywhistle does not have a thumb hole it may only be conveniently played in one major key. The most commonly available pennywhistles were those in B flat and G with the result that most *kwela* compositions were recorded in these keys. The key of a pennywhistle is taken to be that note which is sounded when all the finger holes are covered so that the air stream vibrates along the entire length of the tube. The range of the pennywhistle is two octaves, the second octave being obtained by over blowing. Figure 12.9 illustrates the fingerings required to produce a scale of B flat major on a B flat pennywhistle.

Figure 12.9   The fingering of B flat major on a B flat pennywhistle

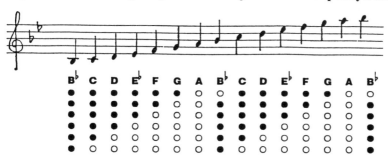

Notes foreign to the particular major scale a pennywhistle is designed to produce may be obtained either through the use of cross-fingering, or by partially covering the tone holes. The absence of a thumb hole at the back of the instrument limits the scope of cross-fingering: only the minor seventh is successfully sounded using this method. Figure 12.10 illustrates fingerings which may be used to play the minor seventh which, on a B flat instrument, would be A flat. The first fingering in Figure 12.10 is easier and more in tune than the other two options. Utilisation of this cross-fingering results in the ability to play in the subdominant major key with relative ease, that is for instance, the key of E flat major on a B flat pennywhistle.

Figure 12.10   Cross-fingerings which produce the minor seventh

Commentators frequently express amazement at how pennywhistlers play chromatic notes on their 'limited' instruments. Although some fundamental errors are made in the following newspaper report of the show 'Township Jazz', the journalist colourfully expresses the sense of awe instilled by complicated pennywhistle fingering techniques. 'The tin whistle has only eight notes, but these boys, out of their own ingenuity can produce 13 [*sic*] ... They played sharps and flats and sixths and sevenths and all those things found in a musical dictionary ... all out of the simple eight-holed [*sic*] whistle'.[53]

Most *kwela* compositions are, in fact, strongly based in the major mode and the occurrence of notes foreign to the key of the instrument is quite rare. Chromatic notes customarily occur in compositions influenced by jazz or other forms of American popular music such as rock 'n' roll. There are two reasons why, in these instances, the method of playing chromatic notes is generally one of partially closing the tone holes rather than through the use of cross-fingering. First, there are few successful cross-fingerings available on a six-holed instrument. Secondly, the method of partially covering holes allows far greater scope as to the actual pitch of a non-scalar note. Providing that other variables, such as breath speed, remain constant the pitch of a cross-fingered tone is specific; whereas a partially covered tone hole will produce a pitch anywhere between the note of that hole and the note of the hole above. This allows the performer flexibility and a greater expressive range, which is particularly important in jazz-influenced *kwela* compositions since the flattened third and seventh of the blues scale are not sung (or played) according to the well-tempered scale.

Using the chromatic finger technique of partially covering the tone holes glissando and 'bent' notes may also be achieved. Ben Nkosi, who was technically and musically one of the most creative pennywhistlers, uses both methods of ornamentation frequently. Some of his expertise may be heard in the pennywhistle solos of 'Something New in Africa'.[54] Lemmy Special also makes extensive use of chromatic notes, bent notes, and glissandi (see, for example, Figure 12.11).

Figure 12.11   Extract from 'Tsamaea' by Lemmy Special

None of the above ornamental effects can be successfully achieved if the fingers are rounded with the fingertips covering the holes. For ease and flexibility the fingers must be placed flat on the pennywhistle with the crease under the first knuckle, or the pad between the first and second knuckles, over the tone holes. The fingers are bent backwards to achieve a rising glissando or higher chromatic note and vice versa to play lower. The emotive range such techniques make available is very important to *kwela* musicians. For Jake Lerole the ease with which notes may be bent is one of the main attractions of the pennywhistle:

> When I was playing this piano I didn't like it because it didn't give me the sound exactly what I wanted, because you can't twist a piano note and do it exactly what you want it to do, like a wind instrument ... It can be in between, it can be semitone but sometime you find it's not a semitone in fact it's a tone of its own.[55]

The other set of techniques which give South African pennywhistle music its distinctive quality are those related to the manipulation of the air stream through the fipple mouthpiece. Factory-manufactured pennywhistles always needed to be altered slightly before they could produce the volume and timbre sought by *kwela* musicians. Ralulimi describes this operation: 'So a pennywhistle has to be tuned as well. It needs something like a pocket knife just to open the mouth piece for it to give you the correct volume'.[56] The pocket knife is used to enlarge the air passage in the mouthpiece and to press down the centre of the lip so that it is 'V' shaped.

Figure 12.12   The alteration made to a pennywhistle mouthpiece

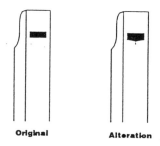

Original   Alteration

It is impossible to play *kwela* on the pennywhistles available commercially today because they have plastic mouthpieces, and plastic cannot be bent or altered in the manner described above. More importantly, it is not possible to play with the typical *kwela* embouchure because the mouthpiece is a different shape. The distance between the fipple opening and the end of the mouthpiece is almost a centimetre longer on the plastic pennywhistles, which makes it extremely uncomfortable to place the mouthpiece in the mouth far enough for the lips to partially cover the fipple opening. Even if one's mouth is big enough to do this without choking, the shape of the fipple opening is such that a rather feeble sound is emitted when the opening is partially covered. In a demonstration of the different sounds obtainable from the old and new pennywhistles, Frederick Maphisa states: 'Plastic one I don't like at all - it gives you this tone [plays a very straight, soft, thin note with no vibrato]. It doesn't give you this [plays louder and fuller with vibrato and a buzzy timbre]'.[57]

The typical *kwela* embouchure was devised by pennywhistlers to command a louder, richer sound from the instrument. Rachabane explains: 'a pennywhistle sounds very rich when you put it that way [at an angle], then you get a better tone. If you do it that way [straight] you get a very small sound - thin'.[58] By partially covering the fipple opening with the lips it is possible to direct more air through the instrument without over-blowing and mistakenly play a higher octave.

To achieve this effect, the mouthpiece is placed in the mouth cushioned on the tongue, the tip of which is directly under the fipple opening. The tongue protrudes beyond the bottom teeth and extends the bottom lip forward. The pennywhistle is rotated 45 degrees to the player's right so that the left edge of the mouthpiece may be gently held between the front top teeth. The top lip is then extended forward in order to partially cover the fipple opening. If the head is tilted slightly to the left the shape of the lips covering the opening is altered, resulting in improvement in tone quality. The pitch of the instrument is flattened in proportion to the degree to which the fipple opening is covered. This differs between individual musicians, but on average the pitch is lowered by a semitone. A composition played on a B flat pennywhistle will therefore usually sound in A major. Occasionally a glissando effect is produced by moving the lips forwards and backwards over the fipple opening. This is the only way of producing a glissando on the tonic as the fingering requires that all the holes be covered.

A contemporary newspaper report described how pennywhistlers looked whilst playing: 'lips mouthing the mouthpiece in a big round O fashion, eyes drooping and the Adam's apple working up and down like an old-fashioned petrol pump'.[59] Since the *kwela* embouchure renders the tongue unavailable for purposes of articulation, the only functional method of separating notes is to contract and release the vocal chords as one would in order to say 'koo'. This accounts for the extraordinary movement of the Adam's apple noted in the newspaper report.

Ben Nkosi frequently used a flutter-tonguing effect in his compositions. As a result of the embouchure described above, this flutter-tonguing would technically require a throat growl rather than a tongue roll. Although flutter-tonguing was a technique which distinguished Ben Nkosi's style, it was occasionally used by other pennywhistlers. A fast throat vibrato is also periodically used as a method of ornamentation in *kwela*, more often by Spokes Mashiyane than anyone else.

Another method of sound manipulation available to pennywhistlers or saxophonists is control of the air stream by the diaphragm. A sudden contraction of the diaphragm muscle dispels a greater quantity of breath faster, which results in an accent. A modified version of this technique is used by Spokes Mashiyane and his New Sound Band in 'Maseru Special': a diaphragm contraction on the part of the saxophonists results in a 'doo-up' effect stylistically reminiscent of American big-bands. In 'Ben's Special' Ben Nkosi uses a slower contraction of the diaphragm to simulate on the pennywhistle the crescendos typical of big-band horn and brass lines.

Another category of ornamentation used by pennywhistlers comprises various types of trills. Trills in *kwela* typically occur on the tonic and dominant, although there are exceptions (for instance 'Davytown Special' by the Dube Satellites, which contains trills on the mediant). The most common method of trilling is a fast fluctuation between a note and the note above or below. On occasion, *kwela* musicians experiment beyond this basic trill, for instance the minor third trills in 'Steak & Porridge' by Themba Madondo. A further example is a figure based on the trill principle (generally occurring between the tonic and the leading-note) which is measured rather than being played as fast as possible. In 'Tamatie Sauce Swing' by the African Dizzy Fingers for instance, this trill-type figure occurs in the rhythm of swung quavers.

The single most striking attribute of pennywhistle or saxophone solos in *kwela* music is the occurrence of dominant and tonic ostinato patterns or pedal notes. These are always at least the length of one harmonic cycle, often longer, and mostly occur in a high range where they are most audible. Pedal notes and ostinato figures occur more often on the dominant than on the tonic, although the latter is very common. In some compositions (for example Lemmy Special's 'Phansi', (see Figure 12.14) both appear. Figures on the dominant also occur in guitar solos, (for instance 'Phansi' by Lemmy Special (see Figure 12.14e) although ostinatos on the super-tonic are far more prevalent on this instrument. Occasionally *kwela* solos are comprised solely of pedal notes or ostinato figures: for example, in 'Zoo Lake Jive', Spokes Mashiyane's saxophone solo is merely a held note on the dominant and there is no other significant improvisation. Generally, however, pedal notes occur as part of an improvisation, for example the tonic pedal in 'Phansi', by Lemmy Special (see Figure 12.14c), and the dominant pedals in 'Midnight Party Jive', 'Spokes Jump' and 'Bennies 2nd Avenue Special' by Spokes Mashiyane. *Kwela* musicians utilised various techniques to vary the pedal notes in solos. The trill, one of the most basic methods of variation, is used for this purpose on the tonic in 'Mashashane' by Aron, Pieter and David, and on the dominant in Mashiyane's 'Vela Bahleke'. Oscillation between octaves, another method of imbuing a pedal note with interest, is used on the dominant by Kippie Moeketsi in 'Goli Kwela'.[60] Mashiyane's solos in 'Sheshisa!' illustrate both the exploration of octaves rhythmically and measured trilling (see Figure 12.13).[61]

Figure 12.13 Octave oscillation and measured trilling in 'Sheshisa!' by Spokes Mashiyane

Rhythmic patterns on a single note embody an intermediary phase between pedal notes and ostinato figures. The two most common rhythmic patterns are both utilised by Lemmy Special in 'Phansi': The shuffle rhythm is played on the dominant during the first pennywhistle solo (see Figure 12.14b); while the second pennywhistle solo contains crotchet triplets (see Figure 12.14f). 'Phansi' further illustrates the use of the note below the tonic or dominant in ostinato patterns The first pennywhistle solo contains glissandi up to crotchets on the tonic (see Figure 12.14a) and later, the tonic and leading-note alternate in the shuffle rhythm (see Figure 12.14d.) The latter also occurs during the guitar solo between the dominant and subdominant (see Figure 12.14e).

Figure 12.14 Variations of pedal notes in 'Phansi' by Lemmy Mabaso

In 'Girls, What about Jerry?', Mashiyane demonstrates three additional ways of varying a pedal note: fast grace-notes leading from the subdominant on to crotchet triplets on the dominant (see Figure 12.15a), triplet quavers (see Figure 12.15b), and flutter-tonguing on a pedal note (see Figure 12.15c).

Figure 12.15 **Variations of pedal notes in 'Girls, What about Jerry?' by Spokes Mashiyane**

In 'Phehello' and 'Emily Ngoma', Mashiyane plays figures which combine the two-against-three cross-rhythm with a tonic ostinato in the former, and a dominant ostinato in the latter.

Figure 12.16 **Tonic ostinato combined with two-against-three cross-rhythm**

'Phehello'
- Arr. Mashiyane

'Emily Ngoma'
- Mashiyane

Not suprisingly it is within the solo passages that the individuality of each musician is expressed. Certain features are characteristic of particular soloists and tend to distinguish their personal styles. Variations on a dominant or tonic pedal, for example, are universal in *kwela* solos and particularly prevalent in performances by Spokes Mashiyane. Mashiyane's solos tend to be quite motivic, rarely straying from the primary chords of the harmonic progression. In contrast, Lemmy Special's solo style is particularly flamboyant, containing many quick notes and fast scalar passages. He also plays many more chromatic notes than Mashiyane. 'Tsamaea' (see Figure 12.11) illustrates Mabaso's extensive use of the flattened thirds and sevenths characteristic of the blues scale.

Ben Nkosi's style is easily identifiable through his utilisation of jazz scales, chromaticism and various ornamental techniques such as glissando and flutter-tonguing. A remarkable innovation contributed by Ben Nkosi to pennywhistle technique is the method of playing two pennywhistles simultaneously. He was not the only pennywhistler to master this technique, but he was the first to make recordings using it. A newspaper article eulogising Ben Nkosi's prowess at the new technique observes that 'not only does he play the two but he produces two different tones, like a duet'.[62] This effect is achieved by using pennywhistles in different keys: B flat and G. The instruments are placed in the mouth so that there is approximately a 45 degree angle between them. The mouthpieces are only inserted a short way as it is not possible to use the *kwela* embouchure whilst playing two pennywhistles. Each hand controls the first three holes of each instrument which makes the chromatic scale from the subdominant to the leading-note on each instrument available.

**Figure 12.17   The range of notes available when B flat and G
pennywhistles are played simultaneously**

The parts played on each instrument move simultaneously, and generally the fingering is identical. This results in chordal movement at intervals of a minor third or major sixth depending on octave displacement. Most double-flute compositions played on B flat and G instruments are based in C major although there is always a great deal of chromaticism. The following extract from Ben Nkosi's 'Two-One Special' illustrates the intervalic relationship between the two pennywhistles which provides the haunting chromaticism characteristic of this technique.

**Figure 12.18   The pennywhistle intervalic relationship between the
pennywhistles in 'Two-One Special' by Ben Nkosi**

Exceptions to the practice of identical fingering on each instrument occur only when harmonically necessary. Non-identical fingering occurs most often in relation to the third hole of the B flat pennywhistle which, when fully covered, produces E flat. It is frequently necessary to cover half of this third hole in order to produce an E natural, the major third in C major.

Figure 12.19   Alteration in identical fingering necessitated by the harmony in 'Ben's Hawk' by Ben Nkosi

G pennywhistle   B flat pennywhistle

Figure 12.20 llustrates this altered fingering in context. The chords marked (x) are played with a half-hole fingering on the B flat pennywhistle to produce the major-third in C major. The chord marked (y) illustrates a situation in which E flat is acceptable because it forms the seventh of IV7 in C major.

Figure 12.20   'Ben's Hawk' by Ben Nkosi

The soloist in a *kwela* band customarily contributes the distinctive qualities of each composition whilst aspects of the pennywhistle or saxophone chorus parts, such as the backing riffs and the ways in which compositions begin and end, provide a sense of continuity and homogeneity.

One of the most basic backing riffs played by pennywhistle or saxophone choruses consists merely of the harmonic progression in which the start of each chord is anticipated. This type of backing riff is played by a saxophone chorus in 'Zulu Khayalami' by the Mashiyane and Msomi Double Five, and by a pennywhistle chorus in 'Tsaba Tsaba' by Jake Lerole.

Figure 12.21   The pennywhistle backing of 'Tsaba Tsaba' by Jake Lerole[63]

Chordal harmonic outline played by the backing chorus is often varied through rhythmic manipulation. The most routine of these is the shuffle rhythm (see Figure 12.1). A more complex series of rhythms is played by the pennywhistle chorus in 'Deep Heat' by Lemmy Special.

Figure 12.22   Variations of the shuffle rhythm in the pennywhistle backing riff of 'Deep Heat' by Lemmy Special

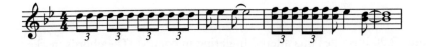

The parts of most backing riffs are not usually restricted to one pitch per chord, but move between chord tones generating short melodies. Each line of the chorus parts in 'Tom Hark', for example, is able to stand on its own as a melody (see Figure 12.23). Backing riffs are often varied slightly as occurs in 'One Way' by Jake Lerole (see Figure 12.24)

Figure 12.23   The chorus parts of 'Tom Hark' by Elias and the Zig Zag Jive Flutes

Figure 12.24   The pennywhistle backing riff of 'One Way' by Jake Lerole

The backing parts of compositions for double-flutes are played on both B flat and G pennywhistles, and chromatic fingerings are used in order to produce the desired harmonies. Figure 12.25 illustrates the ways in which the backing parts of Jake Lerole's 'Thata Slow' are voiced and altered, resulting in a composition in C major.

Figure 12.25   The pennywhistle backing of Jake Lerole's 'Thata Slow' for double flutes

Kwela compositions often begin with one cycle of the first motif played by the solo pennywhistle or saxophone alone, followed by repetitions of the first motif played by the whole *kwela* band. 'Laughing Kwela' by Jake Lerole (see Figure 12.26) illustrates this type of introduction. The hierarchical structure of *kwela* bands explains why it is normally the solo pennywhistler or saxophonist who sets the tempo and character of a composition. Only very occasionally is the first motif played by other members of the band.

Figure 12.26   The beginning of 'Laughing Kwela' by Jake Lerole

The problem of how to end a cyclical composition is solved in many *kwela* recordings by a 'fade out' executed at the discretion of the recording engineer or producer. This type of ending exemplifies of one of the effects of the recording process on *kwela*: the 78-rpm shellac discs lasted just under three minutes, and recordings were simply faded out at the end of that time.

Kwela compositions which finish before the point of 'fade out', however, generally use one of three categories of endings. The first category consists of an extended tonic chord whilst the second comprises compositions which end with a descending major arpeggio on the tonic. The third and largest category of endings contains various forms of the major scale from the dominant up to the tonic. Common variants of the dominant to tonic scalar ending are illustrated in Figure 12.27.

Figure 12.27   Variants of the dominant to tonic scalar ending

e.g. 'Mashashane' by Aron, Pieter, David e.g. 'Ulthomile' by Spokes
                                                  Mashiyane
'Mama Ndiyeke' by Lemmy Mabaso   'Six Down' by Lemmy Mabaso

e.g. 'Hae Phokeng' by Spokes Mashiyane   e.g. 'Moreletsane' by Spokes
                                                Mashiyane
    'Phansi' by Lemmy Mabaso   'Blues Ngaphanzi' by Jake Lerole

e.g. 'Xmas Jump' by Mashiyane
'Tobetsa' by African Dizzy Fingers

Spokes Mashiyane used this type of ending more often than any other *kwela* musician and further variants found in his compositions are illustrated in Figure 12.28.

Figure 12.28   Dominant to tonic scalar endings in compositions by Spokes Mashiyane

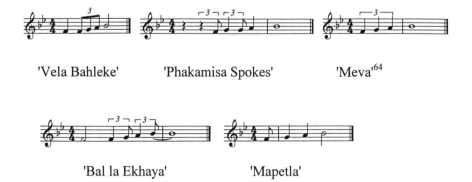

'Vela Bahleke'   'Phakamisa Spokes'   'Meva'[64]

'Bal la Ekhaya'   'Mapetla'

A feature which imparts a poignant touch to this dominantly exuberant musical style, is the addition of the submediant to the final tonic chord. Figure 12.29 illustrates several such endings.

Figure 12.29   Inclusion of the submediant in the final tonic chord

e.g. 'Copper Avenue' by Spokes Mashiyane and Lemmy Special
'Maseru Special' by Spokes Mashiyane

e.g. 'Phansi' by Lemmy Special   e.g. 'Mfana Ka Nkosi' by Peter Makana

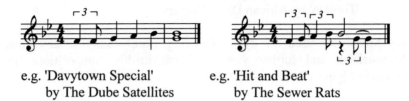

e.g. 'Davytown Special'   e.g. 'Hit and Beat'
   by The Dube Satellites   by The Sewer Rats

Drawing on his study of Malawian *kwela*, Gerhard Kubik maintains that
the relationship between dominant, subdominant and tonic chords is not
that of functional harmony as utilised in the west.[65] However, all the above
endings emphasise the tonic as a place of rest, and the scale from the
dominant to the tonic has particularly strong harmonic implications. I
therefore suggest that the ways in which South African *kwela* compositions
end (when they are not faded out), indicate that the basic tenets of
functional harmony have impacted upon this style.

**Hierarchy and the interplay between local and foreign musical
elements**

The above explanation of the internal musical characteristics and
compositional principles of *kwela* is necessarily fairly generalised since the
style was not a pre-fixed static entity but a constantly changing creative
process. It is possible, however, to isolate some broad chronological trends
in the development of *kwela* and its subsequent mutation into *mbaqanga*.

As regards the fusion and interplay between South African and American
musical elements, the overarching movement is away from American big-

band swing towards South African *mbaqanga*. Structurally and harmonically there were no major changes, although the blues form tended to be utilised more in the early years. Melodic structure is one of the areas of continuity between *kwela* and *mbaqanga*. Typical pennywhistle scalar and arpeggiated passages as well as many of the characteristics of *kwela* solos, such as ostinato patterns and pedal notes on the tonic and dominant, are clearly evident in the *mbaqanga* saxophone style of the 1960s and 1970s.[66] The rhythmic transition from a lilting shuffle to a heavy straight beat is one of the prime indications of *kwela*'s metamorphosis into *mbaqanga*.

Ultimately the definitive parameter is instrumentation and the chronological trend tends away from the dominance of the pennywhistle. To begin with *kwela* was played on just two instruments, pennywhistle and guitar. More instruments were added until a fairly large band became the norm and the pennywhistle was eventually replaced by the saxophone. The shift from acoustic backing instruments to electric guitars and basses coincided with the move from the streets into the studios as primary venues.

Finally the hierarchy between musicians changed. In *kwela* the solo pennywhistler was the leader and star, both musically and in terms of billing and publicity. The lead pennywhistle played the melodies and improvisations whilst the other instruments provided harmonic and rhythmic support. Gradually the lead guitar and bass became more prominent until each instrument boasted an independent melodic line resulting in the contrapuntal texture of *mbaqanga*. *Kwela* was regularly advertized as being played by an individual backed by a band: Lemmy Special and the Alexandra Bright Boys, for instance. In contrast, the leading instrumental exponents of *mbaqanga,* the Makhona Tsohle Band, were billed as a group with no individual gaining special credit. The shift to *mbaqanga* was a process of 'indigenisation' and, intentionally or not, the musical and hierarchical equalization within bands defied western notions of individualism and individual glorification. *Mbaqanga* embodied a triumph of local musical elements over the influence of American popular culture and indigenous musical elements came to dominate urban South African popular music, for a while at least.

Notes

1. Mbaganga is a style of township music which became popular in the early 1960s. It is played on electrified or amplified instruments and is characterized by a heavy straight beat and strong contrapuntal lines. Internationally, the most famous *mbaqanga* exponents are Mahlathini and the Mahotella Queens.

2. A *stokvel* is a fund-raising party; a method of raising money for individuals, often to save for sudden big expenses like funerals. Members of a particular a *stokvel* association each host a party in rotation. The other members of the association agree to attend the party and encourage the attendance of non-*stokvel* members. The host keeps the profits accumulated from the sale of alcohol (and sometimes food) and an entrance fee.
3. Albert Ralulimi. Author's interview, 12 February 1990.
4. In my analysis I use terms which might be considered Eurocentric because they are borrowed from Western calssical music and jazz. I do so because *kwela* musicians commonly employ terminology drawn from both these traditions when they discuss and describe their music.
5. Marabi was 'the name given to the "hot" highly rhythmic repetitive single-themed dance tunes' of the period from the 1910s to the early 1930s. It was primarily a keyboard, banjo or guitar style based on a cyclical harmonic pattern. It originated in Johannesburg's slumyards and was associated with the consumption of alcohol and wild 'low-life'. (See Ballantine, 1993: 25-7.)
6. Peter Macontela. Author's interview, 13 July 1990.
7. Spoken introduction to 'Manyatela' composed by Spokes Mashiyane, Gallo GALP 1049.
8. Ntemi Piliso. Author's interview, 4 September 1990; and Albert Ralulimi. Author's interview, 15 July 1990.
9. Dan Hill. Author's interview, 5 September 1990.
10. Elias Lerole. Author's interview, 16 February 1990.
11. Jake Lerole. Author's interview, 19 May 1991.
12. Barney Rachabane. Author's interview, 16 September 1989.
13. *World*, 29 August 1959.
14. For example: 'See You Later' and 'Little Lemmy' composed by Hill and played by Little Lemmy and Big Joc.
15. Dan Hill. Author's interview, 5 September 1990.
16. Rob Allingham does provide complete discographical information on some recent CD reissues, e.g. *From Marabi to Disco: 42 Years of Township Music*, Gallo Music Publishers, CDZAC 61.
17. Elias Lerole. Author's interview, 16 February 1990.
18. Peter Macontela. Author's interview, 13 July 1990.
19. Elias Lerole. Author's interview, 16 February 1990.
20. Dan Hill. Author's interview, 5 September 1990.
21. Barney Rachabane. Author's interview, 16 September 1989.
22. Albert Ralulimi. Author's interview, 15 July 1990.
23. Peter Macontela. Author's interview, 13 July 1990.
24. Duzi Magwaza. Author's interview, 11 March 1990.

25. Monde Futshane. Author's interview, 10 June 1992. Most of Futshane's knowledge about bass playing in *kwela* was learnt from Jake Lerole during rehearsals for a *kwela* revival concert held at the University of Natal on 17 May 1991.
26. Albert Ralulimi. Author's interview, 15 July 1990.
27. Monde Futshane. Author's inteiview, 10 June 1992.
28. Dan Hill. Author's interview, 5 September 1990.
29. Although I am aware of the accusations of Eurocentricism levelled when 'staff' notation is used in the analysis of African music I have nevertheless decided to use this set of tools. Staff notation is a useful descriptive and didactic device because I, and probably most readers of this book, are familiar with its conventions. It may also be more acceptably utilised in the representation and analysis of *kwela* than in 'traditional' African music because *kwela* is so influenced by jazz. I use staff notation in much the same loose way as it is employcd in jazz; as a generalised 'map' of the proceedings. This mode of representation provides only a general impression and I makc no attempt or claim to notate nuances of rhythm, pitch, timbre or any of the other finer details which endow *kwela* with its particular sound identity.
30. Peter Macontela. Author's interview, 13 July 1990.
31. Zami Duze worked with me on aspects of this research as part of the Natal University Internship Program. He was also the guitarist in the *kwela* revival concert held at thc University of Natal on 17 May 1991.
32. Jake Lerole. Interviewed by Christopher Ballantine, 15 January 1986.
33. Albert Ralulimi. Author's interview, 15 July 1990.
34. Unfortunately the original cover is not used on the CD reissue of this album.
35. Albert Ralulimi. Author's interview, 15 July 1990.
36. Ibid.
37. A *Boereorkes* is a band which plays a style of Afrikaans folk music known as *Boeremusiek*.
38. Albert Ralulimi. Author's interview, 15 July 1990.
39. See *From Marabi to Disco: 42 Years of Township Music,* track 10.
40. Ibid., track 11.
41. See *King Kwela,* tracks 5 and 9.
42. *World,* 1 March 1958.
43. Examples of African Jazz are available on the following compact discs: *From Marabi to Disco: 42 Years of Township Music. Township Swing Jazz Volume I.*
44. See *Miriam Makeba and the Skylarks: Volume 1,* tracks 1 and 12; *Miriam Makeba and the Skylarks: Volume 2,* tracks 1, 4 and 10; and *From Marabi to Disco: 42 Years of Township Music,* CDZAC 61, track 12.

45. See, for example, 'Inkomo Zodwa', *Miriam Makeba and the Skylarks: Volume I,* track 1; and 'Vula Amasango', *Miriam Makeba and the Skylarks: Volume 2,* track 4.
46. Peter Macontela. Author's interview, 13 July 1990.
47. Albert Ralulimi. Author's interview, 12 February 1990.
48. Fredrick Maphisa. Author's interview, 11 July 1990.
49. Kubik (1987), p. 19.
50. Peter Macontela. Author's interview, 13 July 1990.
51. Ibid.
52. *World,* 25 August 1956.
53. *Drum,* August 1956.
54. See *From Marabi to Disco: 42 Years of Township Music,* track 10.
55. Jake Lerole. Author's interview, 13 July 1990.
56. Albert Ralulimi. Author's interview, 15 July 1990.
57. Fredrick Maphisa. Author's interview, 11 July 1990.
58. Barney Rachabane. Author's interview, 16 September 1989.
59. *World,* 11 October 1958.
60. See *From Marabi to Disco: 42 Years of Township Music,* track 11.
61. See *King Kwela,* track 9.
62. *World,* 19 November 1960.
63. The following backing riffs from compositions by Jake Lerole were taught to the author by Lerole in preparation for a *kwela* revival concert held at the University of Natal, South Africa, on 17 May 1991.
64. *King Kwela,* track 1.
65. Kubik (1969), p. 94.
66. See, for example, *Sixteen Original Jive Hits: West Nkosi.*

Bibliography

Ballantine, Christopher (1993), *Marabi Nights: Early South African Jazz and Vaudeville,* Johannesburg: Ravan Press.

Kubik, Gerhard (1969), 'Afrikanische Elemente im Jazz: Jazzelemente in der popularen Musik Afrikas', *Jazzforschung,* 1, 84-98.

Kubik, Gerhard (1987), *Malawian Music: a Framework for Analysis,* Zomba: The Centre for Social Research and The Department of Fine and Performing Arts, University of Malawi.

Discography

78 rpm records

Bal La Ekhay (arr. Stamford), Spokes Mashiyane, Gallo New Sound GB 3399.

Bennies 2nd Avenue Special (Spokes Mashiyane), Spokes Mashiyane, Rave RGM 1192.

Ben's Hawk (Ben Nkosi), Ben Nkosi and his Double Flutes, HMV JP 622.

Ben's Special (-), Ben Nkosi, LP Rave RMG 1047.

Big Joe Special (Spokes Mashiyane), Spokes Mashiyane, Rave RMG 1 I92.

Blues Ngaphanzi (J. Lerole), Jake Lerole and his Rhythm, Quality TJ 210.

Caledon River (A. Rametsi), Spokes Mashiyane and His Big Five, New Sound GB3149.

City Kwela (J. Mhlanga), Jerry Mhlanga, TJ 854.

Clarinet Kwela (Moeketsi), Kippie Moeketsi with The Marabi Kings, USA Records African Records USA 60.

Copper Avenue (J. Monaheng), Spokes Mashiyane and Lemmy Special, New Sound GB 3045.

Davytown Special (Lipondo), The Dube Satellites, USA 8.

Deep Heat (L. Mabaso), Lemmy Special and the Alexandra Bright Boys, Gallo New Sound GB 3479.

Don't be Mad (Spokes Mashiyane), Spokes Mashiyane, Rave RMG 1192.

Double Qwela (Mabaso), Lemmy, New Sound GB 3391.

Emily Ngoma (Spokes Mashiyane), Spokes Mashiyane, Rave RMG 1192.

Fish & Chips Kwela (J. Mhlanga), Jerry Mhlanga, TJ 854.

Girls, What about Jerry? (Spokes Mashiyane), Spokes Mashiyane, Rave RMG 1192.

Goli Kwela (Trad.), Kippie Moeketsi with the Marabi Kings, USA Records African Records USA 60; also GMP CDZA 61.

G-String Kwela (Strike), The Blackjack Hitters, Decca LK 4292.

Hae Phokeng (Spokes Mashiyane), Spokes Mashiyane, 3.Gallo GALP 1049.

Hit and Beat (Kid Monacho), The Sewer Rats, USA Records African Records USA 129.

Kupela (Jerry Ndhlovu), Jerrypenny Flute, JP 2017.

Kwela Claude (Spokes Mashiyane), Claude Williamson Trio with Spokes Mashiyane, Quality (Special), TJ 222; also GMF CDZAC 50.

Laughing Kwela (J. Lerole), Jake Lerole and his Rhythm, Quality TJ 210.

Little Lemmy (Hill), Little Lemmy and Big Joe, Gallotone GALP 1246.

Lona Na Lona (T. Remadi), Spokes Mashiyane and his Big Five, New Sound GB 3189.

Mama Ndiyeke (L. Mabaso), Lemmy Special and the Alexandra Bright Boys, Gallo New Sound GB 3479.

Mambo Spokes (Spokes Mashiyane), Spokes Mashiyane, Gallo SGALP 1049.

Manotcha (Jill Desmond), Spokes Mashiyane and Robert Cele, TJ 213.

Manyatela (Spokes Mashiyane, L. Mabaso), Spokes Mashiyane, Gallo GALP 1049.

Mapetla (R. Msomi), Spokes Mashiyane, New Sound GB 3002.

Maseru Special (Spokes Mashiyane), Spokes Mashiyane and his New Sound Band, Gallotone New Sound GB 2967.

Mashashane (D. Ramosa), Aron, Pieter and David, HMV JP 514.

Meva (-), Spokes Mashiyane and his Rhythm, Quality TJ 21; also GMP CDZAC 50.

Mfana Ka Nkosi (P. Makana), Peter 'Blues' Mkakana, Envee NV 3069.

Midnight Party Jive (Spokes Mashiyane), Spokes Mashiyane and his Magic Sax, Quality (Special) TJ 505.

Moreletsane (Spokes Mashiyane), Spokes Mashiyane and his Golden Sax, New Sound GB 3249.

Ngiyabonga (Jerry Ndhlovu), Jerrypenny Flute, JP 2017.

Pennywhistle Blues (Willard Cele), Willard Cele, Gallotone GE 1123.

Pennywhistle Boogie (Willard Cele), Willard Cele, Gallotone GE 1123.

Phakamisa Spokes (J. Monaheng), Spokes Mashiyane and his Golden Saxophone, New Sound GB 3128.

Phansi (M. Mabaso), Lemmy Special, New Sound GB 3124.

Phehello (Arr. Mashiyane), Spokes Mashiyane, Gallo New Sound GB 3402.

Phesheya (H. Tau), Spokes Mashiyane and his All Star Flutes, New Sound GB 3001.

See You Later (Hill), Little Lemmy Special and Big Joe, Gallotone Jive GB 2774

Sheshisa! (Be Alive!) (Mashiyane), Claude Williamson Trio with Spokes Mashiyane, Quality (Special) TJ 222; also GMP CDZAC 50.

Simple Simon (Jill Desmond), Spokes Mashiyane and Robert Cele, TJ 213.

Six Down (L. Mabaso), Alexandra Junior Bright Boys with Lemmy Special, Decca LK 4292; also Gallotone GALP 1246.

Something New from Africa (Mokonotela), Solven Whistlers, Decca LK 4292; also GMP CDZAC 61.

Spokes Jump (Spokes Mashiyane), Spokes Mashiyane and his Big Five, New Sound GB 3270.

Steak & Porridge (Madondo), Themba Madondo, Goli RA 158.

Tamatie Sauce Swing (Arr. Daniel Rankofi), African Dizzy Fingers, Envee NV 3010.

Tobetsa (Daniel Rankofi), African Dizzy Fingers, Envee NV 3010.

Tom Hark (R. Bopape), Elias and his Zig-Zag Jive Flutes, Columbia YE 164.

Two-One Special (Ben Nkosi), Ben Nkosi and his Double Flutes, HMV JP 6??

Uthomile (Spokes Mashiyane), Spokes Mashiyane and his Golden Sax, New Sound G3249.

Vela Bahleke (Spokes Mashiyane), Spokes Mashiyane, Gallo GALP 1049.

Woza Woza (H. Tau), Spokes Mashiyane and his All Star Flutes, New Sound GB 3001.

Xmas Jump (-), Spokes Mashiyane, LP Rave RMG 1047.

Year 1962 Blues (A. Kwela), Allen Kwela, Winner OK 072.

Zoo Lake Jive (Spokes Mashiyane), Spokes Mashiyane and his Magic Sax, Quality TJ 204.

Zulu Khayalami (arr. R. Msomi, H. Mathaba), Mashiyane and Msomi Double Five, New Sound GB 3247.

Long-playing records

Kwela with Lemmy and other Pennywhistlers, Gallotone GALP 1246.

Something New from Africa, Decca LK 4292.

Spokes of Africa, Gallo GALP 1049.

Tony Scott in South Africa: Tony Scott with the Tony Scott South African Quartet and the Alexandra Dead End Kids, RCA Popular Record 31104.

Compact discs

King Kwela. Gallo Music Publishers, CDZAC 50, 1990.

Marabi to Disco: 41 Years of Township Music. Gallo Music Publishers, CDZAC 61, 1994.

Miriam Makeba and the Skylarks: Volume 1. Teal Records. TELDC 2303, 1991.

Miriam Makeba and the Skylarks: Volume 2. Teal Records, TELDC 2315, 1991.

Township Swing Jazz: Volume 1. Gallo Music Publishers, CDZAC 53, 1991.

Township Swing Jazz: Volume 2. Gallo Music Publishers, CDZAC 54, 1991.

West Nkosi: Sixteen Original Sax Jive Hits. Gallo Music Publishers. CDZAC 57, 1991.

13 Keeping our Ears to the Ground: Cross-Culturalism and the Composer in South Africa, 'Old' and 'New'

Hans Roosenschoon

> The art constituting the essence of a nation is born of the needs of that nation, and is of the very substance of all who experience the collective crisis. (Dietrich Fischer-Dieskau: *Wagner and Nietzsche*)

Prolegomenon

Since 2 February 1990, the eyes and ears of the world have turned towards South Africa, and creative artists in many lands must surely have been curious, with all the new concepts and structures to be assimilated by our country, what the situation of our composers has hitherto been and could become.

That the discords of an old South Africa had finally begun to die away became a concordant fact of life on 17 March 1992, when its dominant minority voted overwhelmingly - to continue the musical metaphor - in favour of resolution to the tonic for the full gamut of society in our culturally chromatic country.

During several decades prior to that, however, South African creative artists, many of them composers, voiced their conceptual rejection of apartheid not only verbally, but also, and perhaps more deeply, via the elemental voice of their art. Structurally, too, a number of bodies supporting musically creative endeavours either started their operations with a non-discriminatory policy or began moving in that direction some time before the rest of the establishment came to realise that a divisive way of life was, in the end, an existential *cul de sac*.

The contributions by South African composers and their support bodies to change (especially, through music, at the important level of the subconscious) are worthy, therefore, of recognition.

Cross-culturalism and musical cross-fertilization

No overview of musical life in a society as varied and pluralistic as that found at the southern end of the African continent can start without some examination of the problems posed by cultural diversity, whether real or ideologically imagined.

In a paper entitled 'The Composer in Africa', which was presented at the Fifth Annual Symposium on Ethno-Musicology held at the University of Cape Town in 1984, a leading figure in South African composition, Professor Peter Klatzow, discussed the use of indigenous material by Western-trained musical creators. His conclusion was that any such composer wishing to include African elements in his or her work had, *in fine*, only two options - 'nationalism' or 'exoticism':

> My impression is that at this stage of our musical development, we are in a crucial stage of transition both politically, culturally and in terms of our awareness of the country that we live in and its traditions, and there may well be an anology between our situation and situation that Bartok and Kodaly found them-selves in.[1]

Whereas 'nationalist' music, in Klatzow's sense, wholly absorbs the traditional music of a country, using it self-containedly as the basic material of composition, 'exotic' music selects only certain elements from it, developing them in the context of an individual and personal music style. Bartok's *Mikrokosmos* and Stravinsky's *Petrushka* are good examples of the two genres respectively.

An 'exotic' composer, Klatzow goes on to explain,

> reaches outside (his or her) particular area for new materials and methods. This, to a certain extent, also indicates a restlessness amongst creative people and the need to stretch their imaginations towards entirely new challenges.[2]

Where, then, in the face of this dichotomy, do the 'roots' of the South African composer lie? For many, Europe - the centre of 'the great musical tradition' - is where one naturally turns for compositional study and new ideas. But what of one's African origins, and how exactly does one assimilate them?

An expert on South African 'serious' music, Michael Levy, put forward another perspective on the issue in the *South African Journal of Musicology* (*SAMUS*):

> even those composers who take note of ['nationalist']) precedents clearly desire to approach the problem in an original and individual way.[3]

Should those composers who wish to absorb African elements then become ethnomusicologists, making field trips or diligently studying tape recordings? But in what way does one study such material - in terms of its anthropological background and the function of the music in the societal structures from which it emanates, or through the analysis of elements that indicate inter-traditional congruity, leading to comparison of one system with another and extrapolation of parallels with, or differences from, the more familiar Western musical matrix? And if one rationalises such discoveries, what of their innermost evocations, those atavistic echoes that sound beyond the rational process but none the less make a subtle impact on one's own creative impulses?

In the indigenous music of our country, as in folk music from other parts of the world, the musical component is not independent of the socio-cultural context within which it occurs: its ritualistic function is intrinsic, with language, music and mimetics forming an integrated whole. The gap between it and Western music is particularly wide, and in my opinion, therefore, it is impossible for a composer of Western art-music, when taking material from African sources, to be anything else except an 'exoticist'. Musical purism is for scholars, not for composers, who must be free to paraphrase, to juxtapose different styles and instrumental forces, or to do whatever else their creative consciences dictate.

Questions are sometimes raised as to whether the incorporated indigenous material should be 'recognisable'. The issue here, as I see it, is one of degree, and also of aesthetic viewpoint, that is, whether one hears with 'African' or with 'Western' ears. It seems possible that, through an upsurge in cross-cultural endeavour currently taking place in South Africa, a new aesthetic of ethnically integrated music may be evolved. The young composer, David Hoenigsberg, however, pinpoints some of the problems which are fundamental to any attempt at synthesis:

> the assimilation is difficult - if not impossible - when basic musical elements such as tonality/pitch, rhythm/metre and timbre/instrumentation are concerned. A type of cargo-cultism is reached, rather than the emergence of a new formalism.[4]

Personally, I have always maintained that there are three choices open to the composer in Africa. First, one may wish to remain faithful to one's European heritage and distil one's inspiration from contemporary Western trends. In this regard I should mention, *inter alia*, the South Africans Arnold van Wyk, Blanche Gerstman, Hubert du Plessis, Stefans Grove, Graham Newcater and Peter Klatzow, who, though their musical speech is inevitably tinged with a certain South African accent, have remained essentially in the European mainstream, and were recognised internationally a good while before the Cultural Boycott. Secondly, one may decide on a purist approach to one's African roots, and go with ethnomusicology. Thirdly, there is the option of cross-culturalism, to a greater or lesser degree, though whether one can ultimately do equal justice to both worlds remains, aesthetically and musically, a rather moot point.

Amongst South African composers in the black community, only one that I am aware of, Michael Moerane, has attempted to approach Western art-music 'from the other side', in his orchestral tone-poem 'Fatse la Heso' ('My Country') (1941), which uses African folk music in a late Romantic context *a la* Smetana's 'Ma Vlast', and was played by the BBC Symphony Orchestra and also in New York and Paris under the black American conductor, Dean Dixon.[5]

From the middle generation of South African composers currently making an impact on cross-cultural composition I must single out Carl van Wyk, Jeanne Zaidel-Rudolph and Johan Cloete, while the 69 year-old Grove, since his return to this country in 1972 after many years as Professor of Composition at the Peabody Institute in Baltimore, has latterly also turned towards such forms.

At bottom, I believe, musical composition is, and must ever remain, an entirely subjective statement about one's approach to art and life. Factual objectivity cannot enter into the case, and legitimacy must automatically be accorded to any 'work of the spirit' which comes into being through an original impulse, whatever the trigger may be. From the purely practical point of view, however, as Carl van Wyk has observed:

> even the most drastically different styles can be mated if the know-how exists. For clues, re-examine the Berg Violin Concerto.[6]

Finally, I believe, it must be stated quite openly that having a conscience about the South African situation in the socio-political sense is a personal crux, while addressing such topics in one's music is a matter of choice - as in the case of John Simon's 'Threnody for Steve Biko'.

But to place the fact that one is or is not doing so above quintessential issues like the artistic integrity of one's work is, to me at least, utter nonsense.

Cross-culturalism as a concept and socio-political relevance as a contextual reference are secondary issues to the establishing of a musical framework or hierarchy before the productive process begins. Whether one's choice fall on a tone-row, a chord-structure or on typological elements taken from African music, the essential pre-compositional task is to discover and plot the potentials of one's material as a prelude to the creative act.

Cross-culturalism and the ANC Cultural Desk

The cultural dichotomy of the South African situation is well illustrated, on the one hand, by a book-review that appeared in *SAMUS* and, on the other, by an address given by Ms Barbara Masekela, Head of the ANC's Cultural Desk in 1990, at the National Festival of the Arts in Grahamstown that year.

Veit Erlmann of the University of Natal, in a *SAMUS* review of the *South African Music Encyclopedia*, made a valid criticism:

> (the volumes) contain articles on (black) African composers, music in African schools, but the general bias of the encyclopedia is unmistakably towards Western music, thereby reflecting the dominant 'white' culture and the way in which it wishes to present itself. It is in the logic of this bias, for instance, that one Hubert du Plessis, pianist and composer, is entitled to an entry of six pages, while R(euben) Caluza, one of the most influential and innovatory composers in South Africa, only qualifies for sixty-seven lines.[7]

With reference to the 'Products of Apartheid' and the role and responsibility of the 'Mass Democratic Movement' in what the ANC calls 'The Reconstruction' Ms Masekela stated that:

> we need to rethink our definitions, particularly the line that apartheid has drawn between art and craft ... for us, culture is not a separate category of life from politics.[8]

In developing the voice of challenge and resistance in its Cultural Workers, and in its understandable effort to find a substitute for the current hegemonic system in South African society, the ANC seems to be opting for a neo-totalitarianism in which all art-forms are simply jumbled together under the blanker concept of 'People's Culture'.

This stance becomes clearer in its persistent labelling of white art-forms as Eurocentric.

In such a context, a review in *SAMUS*, by Dr Jonathon Drury of the University of South Africa (UNISA), of David B. Coplan's In Township Tonight, a socio-musicological study of *mbaqanga* or township jazz, is enlightening:

> despite some references to the plural nature of South African society and to the general problems of urbanisation in Africa as a whole, Coplan seems to view the development of black townships as wholly aimed at the suppression of Africans and the promotion of black disunity ... While many blacks might

accept this point of view, it reeks of ideology instead of
scholarship, which would at least present other points of view
and complicating circumstances, not all of which are nefarious.[9]

It is a fact that the overwhelming majority of black South African
composers are interested almost exclusively in 'light' or 'contemporary
popular' music, and are quite substantially - if not predominantly - subject
to the influence of Western and, especially, American trends. Although a
sense of their African heritage does come through in 'township jazz',
ethnomusicologists fear that, owing to commercial influences, its
indigenous flavour could quickly fade.

In this sense, black South African 'popular' or 'people's' music might
equally be considered 'Eurocentric'.

Cross-culturalism and music education

Until comparatively recently, would-be composers from the black
community did not study at 'white' universities. This was because of
discriminatory legislation, or because of their unfortunate failure, through
an inferior high school system, to meet the required standards of entry, or
else because of their own personal convictions or attitudes dictated by their
peer groups. The standard of music at black universities, too, has been
limited, so that not enough students have been exposed to it in ways which
are conductive to ignition of the creative spark that flames in an
accomplished composer.

From the cross-cultural point of view, two courses of action have been
posited for solving the problem: to introduce high-level 'mixed' musical
curricula into the education programme of all sectors of South African
society, or else significantly to raise the standard of Western music
education amongst blacks.

Professor Elizabeth Oehrle, in her opening address at the First National
Music Educators' Conference held at the University of Natal in 1985, said,
in referring to Unesco's International Society for Music Education (ISME),
that

> music educators throughout the world are moving towards a
> global philosophy of music education. On the one hand, to deny
> a place for the musical metaphors, forms and behaviours of
> other cultures is to deny students access to sources integral with
> human life and experience. On the other hand, the learning of

music as the knowledge of a single set of cultural 'objects', as opposed to an array of innate human behaviours, would direct the practice of music education towards the end of having musical understanding at the expense of being musical.[10]

Another perspective, though from a different point of view, is given by Professor Khabi Mngoma, a venerable black South African music educator who was also, in his time, an accomplished performer of the Western art-music repertoire:

> I want to emphasise that the teaching of Western music to the exclusion of African music at all levels in the South African setting is both narrow and bigoted. It stultifies the black student because it dispenses with the performance practices obtaining in his own culture; it 'de-musicates' him; it reduces his capacity to enjoy music and to be musically creative.[11]

But in attempting to upgrade musical skills amongst young South Africans, it is a fact that there as yet exists no state-subsidised tuition at an expert level for the disadvantaged student. Concerned music educators thus become involved in privately sponsored supplementary programmes as part of their cathexis with the black community and its musical future.

Several such programmes exist throughout the country on a somewhat informal basis, but at tertiary level the most notable is the 'Music Enrichment Workshops' (MEWS), patterned on Berkeley's 'Young Musicians Programme' and begun in 1987 by the University of the Witwatersrand, Johannesburg, with sponsorship from the Southern African Music Rights Organisation (SAMRO).[12]

Each year, 30 talented students are chosen from amongst many applicants, on the basis of accredited music aptitude tests, for free tuition enabling them to qualify for admission to degree or diploma courses in music at the university. MEWS also helps combat the threat to music education posed by more trying financial times and ever-escalating study fees - economic and cultural boycotts, whatever ethical or politico-logistical pleas are advanced for or against them, are interactive in their effect.

South Africa, however, is not the only country where introduction of a mixed music curriculum has posed difficulties, as Professor Oehrie further observes in discussing ISME principles:

> despite the fact that the principle of multicultural music education has been accepted in the USA since the late sixties,

there continue to be problems encountered in the implementation of this principle.[13]

But in the view of Andrew Tracey, Director of the International Library of African Music (ILAM) at Rhodes University in Grahamstown and one of our best known authorities on indigenous music, a cross-cultural hope for igniting the creative musical spark in coming generations may well be intrinsic to our situation. With reference to the context of a Western cultural oligarchy, he describes

> the inherent duality of co-operation/conflict, or, if you like, dependence/independence, at the roof of African music. Much of the enjoyment is found directly in this basic duality.[14]

Cross-culturalism and the Southern African Music Rights Organisation (SAMRO)

The Southern African Music Rights Organisation Limited, is our national society of composers and authors, and is a member of the Confederation Internationale des Societes d'Auteurs et Compositeurs (CISAC), with a seat on its Administrative Council. SAMRO's task is to protect, administer and promote the musical works not only of its own composer/author-members but also the works of members of its sister societies in more than seventy countries throughout the world, for almost the whole of Southern Africa, including Botswana, Swaziland and Lesotho.

Prior to the setting up of SAMRO in 1962, copyright in Southern Africa was administered by the Performing Right Society in London. Owing to the distance involved, this was not a very practical state of affairs. At SAMRO's founding, however, it faced a rather difficult problem in that, under apartheid legislation, non-racial membership was permitted to no statutory body whatsoever, not even to academic or scientific societies. But SAMRO simply went ahead along non-discriminatory lines; music, after all, knows no colour bar, although at that time a certain discretion was necessary.

Today SAMRO's enrolment has grown from some 60 members at its inception, only one of whom was a black South African, to some 2,300, with membership now about equally distributed among all population groups.[15]

Its function as a promoter of the South African composer and his or her original works has been of considerable importance.

In 1962, the preponderant bulk of the repertoire heard in SAMRO's territory was of foreign origin. Today, a significant proportion of the music publicly performed in our country is by South Africans, reflecting also the growth of the local music industry over that period. In terms of royalty moneys collected for distribution both to local composers and foreign affiliates, the three decades of SAMRO's operations have seen a two-hundredfold increase in its gross annual turnover. Its most significant growth-year yet was 1991, with a total income approaching $20 000 000.[16]

Another aspect of SAMRO's work is its 'Encouragement of the National Arts', funded through a minimal deduction on royalties permitted by CISAC to its affiliated societies so as to expand the opportunities for creative musical activity in each individual member country.

Under this dispensation, SAMRO's Board of Directors instituted, during the first year of its existence, South Africa's most important Overseas Scholarship for Composers, and in 1968 extended this award to include performers. In 1980 it also established a generous number of Undergraduate Bursaries for Music Study in South Africa, while from 1989, the number of all these awards was doubled to accommodate both 'serious' and 'contemporary popular' genres, thereby making SAMRO's scholarships and bursaries the largest and most comprehensive group of music study awards on the subcontinent.

These are given purely on the basis of musical merit, with allocation being made by non-racial selection panels. A steadily increasing number of talented young black musicians are qualifying for such assistance with their studies, and this year almost half the applications for SAMRO's Undergraduate Bursaries in both genres have been from black students, who currently make up just over 40 per cent of qualifying candidates in the 'contemporary popular' category and some 15 per cent in the 'serious' music category.[17]

SAMRO also stimulates music in a host of other ways by funding master classes, concerts and musicological research, publishing academic theses, conference proceedings and other books and/or music of educational value (including SAMUS), as well as by substantially sponsoring several contemporary music groups. But even more significant for the composer is the fact that SAMRO regularly gives out commissions for new works.

In 1992, the thirtieth anniversary year of its operation, it awarded some 30 major commissions for music ranging from large symphonic compositions performed to mark special occasions, jazz concertos and other popular music, to chamber and solo pieces, some for use as the prescribed South African repertoire in UNISA's ever-growing biennial International Music Competitions, for which SAMRO, in addition, sponsors one of the top prizes.

1992 also saw through acquisition of the latest music-typesetting technology, the inaugural edition of 'SAMRO Scores', a publication project aimed at both the local and international promotion of new musical works commissioned by the organisation. The first volume in this series, 'Two South African Dialogues for Guitar', contains a complementary coupling of cross-cultural/cross-genre compositions - a 'serious' work by Jeanne Azidel-Rudolph including elements of 'township jazz' and a jazz suite by Darius Brubeck based not only on Zulu musical material but also on its traditional manner of performance.

As part of the documentation of South African music necessary for copyright protection and royalty payment purposes, SAMRO has over the years amassed a Music Library of Scores and related material which is of major importance. SAMRO's *Catalogue of Serious Music ... by Southern African Composers and Arrangers*, compiled by its Organiser: Serious Music, Michael Levy, has just been issued in a revised and enlarged thirtieth-anniversary edition. This is a most compendious work of reference for both librarians and scholars as well as for performers and concert presenters, containing not only the customary listings of the works of each individual South African 'serious' music composer, but also details in respect of instrumentation, performing times, text authors/translators, commissioning bodies, and the dates of composition and first performance.[18]

Composers of 'serious' music make up approximately 5 per cent of SAMRO's total membership, and of these, 3 per cent are black South Africans. With enhancement of opportunities for South African creative musicians abroad, an expected upsurge of interest in cross-cultural and indigenous music, and a steady increase in the number of disadvantaged students in our country who qualify both academically and economically to enter tertiary institutes of music education - many of them through SAMRO sponsorship - these figures seem to have the prospect of some improvement in the future.

Commenting in their Annual Report for the year 1991 on the new South Africa, SAMRO's Board of Directors observed that

> for our Organisations this did not require any change of policy, for since its inception, SAMRO has never practised any distinction of membership on any basis whatsoever - neither race, nor colour, nor creed, nor sex.[19]

Cross-culturalism and the Foundation for the Creative Arts

Since the early 1960s, state-subsidised Performing Arts Councils, each serving one of South Africa's four provinces (a fifth, now defunct, was in Namibia), have played an important part in fostering the arts in this country. In some cases - such as the pioneering commission for the cross-cultural ballet 'Raka' by the Performing Arts Council of the Transvaal (PACT) they have actively supported South African creative work, but a regrettable public tendency to avoid new music has meant that the box-office (Stravinsky's *box populi* ...), particularly in view of increasing economic pressure from both outside and inside the country, has militated against such involvement.

By the early 1980s it had become clear that a special initiative was called for, and the authorities accordingly appointed a Commission of Enquiry into the Promotion of the Creative Arts. Under the able Chairmanship of Dr Jan Schutte, and with enlightened members like the late Professor Anton Hartman (whose services to composers are mentioned below), the commission's brief was to enquire into and report on the stimulation and promotion, among all South Africa's population groups, of creative activity in music, literature and the plastic arts. Economic issues were of paramount importance, and the commission's brief was well defined. It had to examine:

1.   The fostering of an appreciation of art in the community by means of formal and informal education.

2.   The introduction of creative artists and their works to the public, and the role to be played therein by museums, libraries, Performing Arts Councils, radio and television, the printed media, and so on.

3.   Existing bodies for the promotion of the creative arts, or bodies to be established for that purpose, and the question of financial aid to such bodies.

4.   The role of art-criticism.

5.   The training of creative artists and training facilities for them.

6.   Commissions to creative artists, together with awards, prizes and similar incentives.

7.   The desirability of measures guaranteeing a minimum livelihood to deserving creative artists, having due regard to the restricted market for the literary arts in Afrikaans and other indigenous languages.

8.   The manner in which such deserving artists might be identified.

9.   The desirability of statutory measures for promoting the creative arts and for ensuring financial aid to creative artists.

10.   Any other issues pertaining to the above.[20]

Individuals and organisations over a broad social and cultural spectrum were asked for opinions, but some were sceptical and refused to become involved. The commission's report was submitted to Parliament in 1984, and, in 1986, almost all its recommendations were accepted. A controversial issue was the suggestion that the State itself should set up, administer and finance a body specifically to foster the creative arts. In mid-1988, therefore, a 'Deliberation on the Arts' was held in Stellenbosch, and the then Minister of National Education, Mr F. W. de Klerk, expressed his opinion that state involvement in such a body was undesirable in order to ensure its political independence. Mr De Klerk's view was that a private company would be the most satisfactory answer.

The Foundation for the Creative Arts was accordingly established in 1989 as a non-profitmaking body, its principal objective being to promote the creative arts by mobilising funds from both the public and private sectors. Its stated aims are to foster knowledge and appreciation of the creative arts in South Africa, and to make them accessible to all sections of the population throughout the country, providing as far as possible for the needs of every cultural and language group.

In the field of music, the foundation has, during its short span of existence, taken some notable initiatives, commissioning over thirty works from more than twenty composers, and being instrumental in organising a fact-finding visit to South Africa by Professor Lupwishi Mbuyamba of Zaire at that time President of Unesco's International Music Council.

Amongst the cross-cultural works commissioned by the foundation to date have been Lourens Faul's 'Multiracial Choral Cycle', with texts in English, Afrikaans and Zulu, Stefans Grove's suite of 'Songs and Dances from Africa' for piano, Paul Loeb van Zuilenberg's 'Twelve Marches on Indigenous Themes' for brass ensemble, and Henk Temmingh's Zulu Requiem, 'Imisa Labafileyo'.

It has been said by some that the foundation's initiatives so far have tended towards the conservative, but, given its reliance on private sector sponsorship, this may, in the light of the following case, seem not entirely incomprehensible.

One of South Africa's biggest commercial concerns in the basic food industry, which depends on a sizeable unskilled workforce, had for a number of years sponsored one of our major orchestras, albeit to a fairly modest degree given the company's global economic parameters. Owing to pressure from its Social Responsibility Committee, however, and under an implicit threat of strike, these funds had to be diverted to what the Committee called 'grassroots' causes.[21]

Although it is undeniable that many millions will have to be poured into social upliftment and the narrowing of the poverty gap in South Africa, it is also a truism that nations which neglect their own inner nourishment through the arts will remain forever poverty-stricken from the spiritual point of view.

While the mists of political newspeak still hang heavily in the air, it is difficult, apropos of long-term national cultural goals, to discern the wood from the trees, and in order to provide commercial sponsors with a purely practical incentive to greater clarity of vision, perhaps the expected new multi-racial South African government might consider putting at least a proportion of its money where a predecessor's mouth has been by making private and corporate funding of the arts tax deductible, as has so successfully been done in the United States.

One of our society's problems is that its cultural diversity can become an excuse for ideological divisiveness with regard to the attainment of ultimate ends.

In the interests of a financially viable future for the arts in South Africa, some kind of cross-cultural economic *rapprochement* seems a necessity.

Cross-culturalism and the South African Broadcasting Corporation (SABC)

The South African Broadcasting Corporation, founded some 55 years ago as a statutory body based on the model of the British Broadcasting Corporation, today has 22 internal radio services broadcasting in eleven different languages, together with two principal television channels (television having been introduced to South Africa only in 1976). The first of these alternates English and Afrikaans, while the second, formerly an ethnic language channel, was recently converted to a community service with a variety of entertainment, actuality and educational programmes in a multi-lingual/multi-cultural format.

The greater part of the Corporation's income (72 per cent) derives from sponsorship through commercial advertising, which makes for a somewhat delicate situation, as pointed out above, where its transmission of cultural material is concerned.[22] The current economic recession in South Africa has further exacerbated the position of cultural programmes, especially since involvement with advertising has led the SABC to implement strictly cost-effective principles.

Even drama productions (usually the last art-form to be jettisoned in financially straitened times), whether of a 'high art' nature or of the 'soap opera' variety, have suffered rather drastic cuts during the past two years, so that SAMRO's subsidiary, the Dramatic, Artistic and Literary Rights Organisation (DALRO), was obliged to report that, for 1991,

> applications for television rights in respect of existing prose works, whether for single programmes or for serials, virtually ceased.[23]

The continued depression of our currency makes even ready-made imports difficult to afford, while the British Actors' Equity ban has meant that what is amongst the best dramatic and musico-dramatic radio and television material available today has in any case been impossible to obtain, thus denying South African audiences a window on world culture and leading to a drop in standards not only amongst our viewers but also in local performance criteria and, to a lesser extent, creative endeavour. Lifting of the British Musicians' Union ban on 30 March 1991, however, is bound to have a bearing on the re-opening of doors.

As in other countries, it is the SABC's radio services which give the greatest prominence to music programmes *per se*.

Radio South Africa, the national service in English, with an estimated average listenership of some 400,000, had a musical content in 1990 of around 30 per cent, of which about half was 'serious' music. Radio Suid-Afrika, the national service in Afrikaans, with an estimated average listenership of some 900,000, had a musical content during the same period of about 20 per cent, with a similar proportion of 'serious' music. These figures, musically speaking, are quite encouraging.

The total daily radio audience throughout the country is about 12 million, with Radio Zulu having the largest share, namely some 3 million listeners.

The smallest audience was that of Radio Allegro, the national 'serious' music station, which broadcast in both English and Afrikaans and had an average audience of around 30,000. Whereas Radio Zulu broadcasts for an average of 18 hours per day, Radio Allegro was kept to only four fairly unsociable hours each day, from 9 p.m. to 1 a.m. Started in 1984, its low listenership led, for economic reasons, to its demise during the latter part of 1991.

Despite this regrettable and retrogressive step, the SABC continues to maintain a commitment to art-music, supporting a full-time symphony orchestra of some 75 players, the National Symphony Orchestra of the SABC, founded during the late 1950s and now infused with a number of outstanding principal players from Eastern Europe and the former Soviet Union; a semi-professional chamber choir of some 20 voices; and a much larger choral group of able amateurs constituted along British lines, the SABC Choir, of about 150 singers.

The membership of these bodies is mainly, though not entirely, drawn from amongst the white South African community. Recent massed performances of standard repertoire works, however, have seen them combined with one of the best among the may black choirs which abound in the Johannesburg area and throughout the whole of South Africa, serving a valuable community music function despite some rather varying standards.

At its headquarters in Johannesburg, the SABC has five large music production studios, including an orchestral studio-cum-concert hall containing a versatile pipe-organ. Two record libraries, one for 'serious' music and one for 'light' music, are stocked with many thousands of records, tapes and compact discs.

The Radio Archives also aim at preserving recordings of South African works, together with special interviews and documentary/magazine programmes which feature indigenous composers, while an extensive Music Library contains the most comprehensive collection of 'serious' South African scores in the country.

The corporation's support of South African musical creators, especially when its Music Department was under Anton Hartman (a pupil of Albert Coates and Igor Markevich) during the 1960s and 1970s, has been substantial, with visits during that period by Igor Stravinsky, Pierre Boulez, Henk Badings and Karl-Heinz Stockhausen to present or discuss their own and other works, thus exposing both public and composers on home ground to great musical minds.

More latterly, under Hartman's successor, Bennie Bierman, economic cuts and the 'Cultural Boycott' have made such visits by internationally acknowledged creative musicians a comparative rarity, though the late Morton Feldman came to conduct some of his works and give lectures and composition masterclasses at an SABC Contemporary Music Festival held in 1983.

A significant serious of commissions was given by the SABC Music Department in 1986, the centenary year of Johannesburg as well as the fiftieth anniversary of the Corporation's founding, bringing the total number of SABC-commissions at the end of 1987 to *circa* 120. For the 1986 celebrations, it was decided to ask for music which depicted all the other major cities of South Africa in addition to Johannesburg, and amongst the cross-cultural works to emerge from these commissions were the following, from the composers' notes on which I quote:

Jeanne Zaidel-Rudolph - 'Fanfare Festival Overture'

the music has a strong indigenous flavour ... the percussion section features prominently, using authentic African instruments, among them the Chopi 'piano' (a marimba-type), cow-bells and cabassa.

Hans Roosenschoon - 'Architectura!'

The Cape Town theme is hardly a new one, since Blanche Gerstman wrote a 'Table Mountain Overture' and Richard Cherry a 'Van Riebeeck Festival Overture' to name but two ... as in my other works, reaching out to the indigenous was inevitable, and I decided on the (Cape Malay) folk-song 'Daar Kom die Alibama'.

Henk Temmingh - 'Baai Baai' - A P(ort) E(lizabeth) Piece

like our society, and (the city of) Port Elizabeth, this work is characterised by contrasts ... my aim was to incorporate a Western as well as an African theme.

Stefans Grove - 'Dance Rhapsody: An African City'

I accepted the invitation to pay musical homage to the city of Pretoria with enthusiasm, for this metropolis fascinatingly blends First-World cosmopolitanism with the vibrancy of Africa ... only a few blocks away from the glittering, high-tech skyscrapers, pulse the sights and sounds of the Third World ... it is an articulation of my profound hope for a future in which all the peoples of Pretoria may share equally and harmoniously of her bounty.[24]

Unfortunately, the SABC, in tightening its belt during the current economic crisis so as to maintain at least the *status quo* for its Music Department, Orchestra and related facilities, has virtually ceased commissioning new works independently, joining forces for this purpose in an informal association with the Foundation for the Creative Arts and SAMRO.

To predicate the destiny of the Corporation and its role in a 'new' South Africa, particularly with regard to the creative arts and music, is at this moment difficult, especially given the uncertainty surrounding policy statements by those who appear likely to have a ruling voice in future government. The ANC's main concerns for the SABC at present are equity in news reporting and the gaining for itself of a political platform in the electronic media. While wishing to see the SABC freed of what it deems undue bias towards the interests of the white minority, whether in general programming or in the fostering of so-called 'Eurocentric' art-forms, it has, as yet, no explicitly stated policy regarding the support of artistic creativity in a liberal and free-spirited manner.[25]

Essentially, the end-issues for an independent-minded musician in the current politico-economic impasse are those I have alluded to earlier, that is, individualism versus submersion: in compositional terms, 'exoticism' versus 'nationalism'; in terms of financial viability for creative work: privatisation versus nationalisation - with the hope of cross-culturalism as a connecting principle.

Cross-culturalism and the creative arts in South Africa: some conclusions on its function as a connecting principle

While some have seen in privatisation an answer to the economic problems that have gathered momentum following international devaluation of our currency since President Botha's disastrous 'Rubicon' speech of 1985, the political Left has naturally inclined to socialist principles, holding differing views on the issue of nationalisation as it wavers between pure Marxist theory on the one hand and concessions to a mixed economy on the other.

The situation of bodies like the Foundation for the Creative Arts and the SABC mirrors this dichotomy and its inherent dangers. To survive in his or her chosen *métier*, the creative musician in South Africa is caught between the Scylla and Charybdis of depending either on a private sector subject to pressure from its workforce and with few sponsorship incentives, or on a state-funding system which might well get caught up in the toils of an ideological posturing that is ultimately destructive to freedom of expression in art. In the past year, neither the visiting Sinfonieorchester Baden-Baden under Maestro Michael Gielen nor the pop singer Paul Simon, performing with the indigenous group Ladysmith Black Mambazo, have been spared the *agitprop* sloganism of the Far Left.

Special initiatives in the field of musical creativity by the individual Maecenas seem also, with some notable exceptions, to be on the decline at present. Various individual and corporate sponsors and, in some cases, state-funded bodies, have in the past supported music festivals concentrating on the South African composer. They include the pharmaceutical company, Adcock Ingram, which sponsored a National Music Conference and Composers' Festival held at the University of the Witwatersrand in 1981. The SABC's Contemporary Music Festival of 1983, mentioned above, featured a similar Composer's Conference.

Michael Levy reported in SAMUS on the conference's panel discussion about 'The Future Direction of Music in South Africa', where composers were:

united in the opinion that not enough was being done by government or private enterprise to support or foster serious contemporary music ... whether by commissions for new works, recordings of indigenous works, performances of contemporary music, publishing of new music or by the award of grants which would allow representatives to attend international music congress ... The founding of a composers' union was proposed and agreed upon; such a union would be in a better position to present the composers' case for sponsorship, both to government and commerce.[26]

Much water has run under the bridge in the decade since these statements were made, and only some of the problems have been solved, not many of them - it must be conceded - by concerted efforts on the part of composers themselves. The setting up of the Foundation for the Creative Arts and its generous number of commissions over the past two years has been a positive step forward, but is countered somewhat by the economic difficulties of the SABC and its resultant inability to grant a satisfactory number of independent commissions. The work of SAMRO in this direction, however, is growing, and a Committee on Commissions was recently appointed to make recommendations to its Board of Directors. Apart from considering requests for commissions initiated by composers themselves, the committee also has a brief to identify areas of the repertoire in which it feels new works should be written, and to motivate the offering of commissions for them, including cross-cultural works.

The SABC continues to make transcription recordings of works by South African composers, and, through the dedication and tenacity of a small private company in Cape Town, a number of tapes and compact discs of important works by South African composers, many of them in the cross-cultural genre, have been issued over the past few years.

Visits to music festivals overseas are increasingly more difficult to afford, and the Department of National Education, which can dispose of an increasingly limited amount of funds for such purposes, is, owing to the need for marshalling its resources, unfortunately not able to make them available without certain rather academically oriented provisos.

SAMRO has hitherto been fairly generous with help in this regard, but it too, though copyright societies are to a certain extent protected from recessionary tendencies, needs at present to exercise some prudence. Fortunately, an advance on royalties can usually be offered, although, for the average 'serious' music composer in South Africa, the amount involved will not be very great.

But the position in this connection may gradually improve through an influx of foreign royalty revenue for 'serious' music, especially with changing attitudes abroad, a greater interest internationally in South African musical products, especially of the cross-cultural variety, and with the growth of dissemination projects like 'Musications', a publication company begun over a decade ago by Peter Klatzow, the more recent 'Amanuensis Editions', and 'SAMRO Scores'.

A step in the direction of a composers' union was taken with the formation of The Composers Guild some three years ago, but this as yet fairly fledgling body is aimed primarily at raising the commercial status of the 'light' music composer, and the proportion of 'serious' music creators remains low within its still not fully representative ranks: culturally divisive elements in South African society, its historical partition into discrete provinces and some 40 years of statutory apartheid have led to a certain provincialism of attitude and the building of inward-looking walls amongst all its peoples, the creative artist not excepted.

Some private sector initiatives, however, do hold out more hope for the future. The oil company Total (South Africa), through the interest of a senior executive and an enlightened corporate policy, has not only built up a fine visual arts collection which is on display to the public, but also established, in 1986, the Total Music Collection, holding an annual Composers' Competition at which specially commissioned pieces are performed in addition to the winning works. The list of new compositions which have so far entered the collection, many of them containing cross-cultural elements, is not unimpressive:

1986	Carl van Wyk	Concerto for Piano and Percussion
	Pieter de Villiers	Johannesburg: Song-Cycle
	Stefans Grove	Quintet for flute, clarinet, viola, cello and harp
	Jeanne Zaidel-Rudolph	Tempus Fugit
	David Kosviner	Botosani
1987	Peter Klatzow	States of Light
	Arthur Wegelin	Perel van Suid-Afrika
	David Hoenigsberg	Sonata for Double String Orchestra
	Pieter Smit	Scenario
1988	Hans Roosenschoon	Mantis
	Livio Ventura	De Rerum Musicalis
	Roelof Temmingh	Autumn
1989	Christopher James	Midnight of the Soul
	Lourens Faul	Sonata for Chamber Orchestra
	Michael Rosenzweig	Sinfonietta

1990 Thomas Rajna   Harp Concerto
          Peter Louis van Dijk   San Chronicle
          Johan Cloete   En Reponse au Soleil

1991 Warren Katz   Reflections
          Barry Jordan   Elise Meiring se Disa
          Graham Newcater   Songs of the Inner Voices[27]

The National Festival of the Arts, held annually in Grahamstown with funding from The Standard Bank of South Africa, was mentioned *en passant* earlier on. It is perhaps the most encouraging of all those thermometers indicating that a cross-cultural reconciliation of South Africans through the arts may well present a paradigm for the eventual solution of our current problems.

Every year the number of South Africans, both black and white, who join each other there in the celebration of art increases, while the festival's presentation of new plays, sculptures, paintings and musical compositions that reflect a bringing together and blending of diverse cultural roots is growing very rapidly. My own composition, 'Timbila' (see Chapter 14) commissioned by the Oude Meester Foundation and premiered at the festival in 1985, was the first in a fast-expanding series of works which venture to combine such apparently irreconcilable elements as the *materia musicae* and traditional performance practices of marimba players from the Chopi people of Mozambique and a Western symphony orchestra.[28]

Now, with the liberation of South African life that has taken place through the lifting of political censorship, the festival has taken a lead in airing works by artists whose creative products were previously under prohibition. This year, a song-cycle by Peter Klatzow on texts by Dennis Brutus (who was in prison with Nelson Mandela), will be presented during the festival in Grahamstown. Commissioned by the Foundation for the Creative Arts, its performance will be sponsored by SAMRO.

The de-politicization of art which is the *sine qua non* for a free creative climate has thus begun to make its essential statement in South African society, holding out hope for a future in which the artistic integrity of 'works of the spirit' will ultimately be the sole criterion for their creation and public presentation.

It can be argued that the creative artist encompasses within himself or herself, and in his or her artistic strivings, an image of reconciliation that is emblematic of unity in human endeavour. Composition, after all, is 'a bringing together'. The melding of opposites which Carl van Wyk mentioned in his reference to the Berg Violin Concerto involves a continuing exchange of concepts and the learning of combinatory techniques, whether in politics, social readjustment or in musical composition. For composers, the solution lies, surely, in listening, by 'keeping our ears to the ground', for that elemental voice which prompts us toward action that is creative in every sense.

Plinius coined the aphorism *ex Africa semper aliquid novi* and Richard Wagner counselled his disciples: *Kinder, schaff' Neues*!

The leitmotif of renewal that is sounding in South Africa will, if we keep on listening inwardly to the *Zukunftsmusik* in our hearts, continue to be heard. Already it has meant that the international musical community is once more lending its ears to us. I have a strong conviction that, despite some transitional difficulties, all the many cross-cultural strains in our country will at last be transformed symphonically into a truly new South Africa, and that all our composers will join with one another in 'keeping their ears to the ground'.

Appendix: select list of cross-cultural works by Southern African composers

BRUBECK, Darius
The Maskanda

CALUZA, Reuben
Reminiscences of Africa
Rondo for Orchestra
UTokoloshe

CLOETE, Johan
Celebration
Festival
Sangoma
Township I
Township II
The Voyager

GROVE, Stefans
Concertato Overture: Five Salutations on Two Zulu Themes
Dance Rhapsody: A Cosmopolitan City
Sewe Boesman-Verse
Sonata on African Motives
Songs and Dances from Africa

HOENIGSBERG, David
Fantasy on African Themes
Three African Excursions
Toccata Africaine

JAMES, Christopher
An African Safari for Keyboard Instruments
Grahamstown Buzz!
Images from Africa

KHUMALO, James
Ingoma Kantsikana
Iph' Indlov' Edl' Umntanami
Izulu Elisha
Preamble Ladum' Izulu and Isibongo Zikashaka
Ushaka Kasenzangakhona

KHOSA, Joseph
Afrika Lontshwa (New Africa)

KINSEY, Avril
Bushmen (Spirit of the Wilderness)
Domba Dance
Four Sacred Songs
Modjadji (Rain Queen)
Mokoro (Song of Water)
Sangoma

KIRBY, Percival
Three African Idylls
Salane Vamakweru

KLATZOW, Peter
Overture: Citiscape
Ovamboland (film score)
Raka: Symphonic Poem

KLEIN, Herbert
African Metamorphosis
Die Gevalle Zoeloe-Indoena
Introduction and African Dance

KOSVINER, David

Ciascun apra ben gli orecchi
Hamba Kahle
Worksong

LaPIERRE, Gerald

Picture Songs of Natal

MASKE, Hans

Sechuana Dances

MOERANE, Michael

Fatse La Heso

NEWCATER, Graham

Mosaics
Raka
The Rain Queen

N'TZOMA, Sam

Orchestral Fantasia
Dachu Bayo
Diem D'ja Tanda Wena
Thula Umntwana
Wuka Zamile

MXUMALO, Gideon

Fantasia
Wedding Day in Zululand

O'REILLY, Stephen

Dingaka (film score)
Overture: Umkhosi

ROOSENSCHOON, Hans

Architectura I
Circle of Light
Firebowl
Ghomma
Helios
Horison, Naghemel en Landskap
Makietie

Mantis
Die Sonnevanger
Timbila

TEMMINGH, Henk
Baai Baai - A P(ort) E(lizabeth) Piece
Imisa Labafileyo (Zulu Requiem)

TEMMINGH, Roelof
Lobola
Natal Festival Overture
Three Sonnets for String Orchestra
White Integration

Van DIJK, Peter Louis
The Prodigal Son
San Chronicles
San Gloria
Songs of Celebration

Van WYK, Carl
Concerto for Piano and Orchestra
Little Dance for the Picaninny
Overture for a Birthday City

Van ZUILENBERG, Paul Loeb
African Echoes
Twelve Marches for Symphonic Wind Band

VOLANS, Kevin
African Paraphrases
Cover Him With Grass
Journal
Kneeling Song
Leaping Dance
Lesotho Mountain Village
Mbira
She Who Sleeps With A Small Blanket
White Man Sleeps

ZAIDEL-RUDOLPH, Jeanne
Abantubomlambo (The River People)
An African Dream (film score)

Fanfare Festival Overture
Five African Sketches
Peace
Tempus Fugit

Notes

1. Klatzow, P. (1984), 'The Composer in Africa', in transcript of talk given at the Fifth Annual Symposium on Ethno-Musicology, University of Cape Town.
2. Ibid.
3. Levy, M. (1986), 'African and Western Music: Shall The Twain Ever Meet?', *The South African Journal of Musicology* (hereafter *SAMUS*), 111-15.
4. Quoted in ibid., 115.
5. Vide Huskisson, Y. (1969), 'The Bantu Composers of Southern Africa', s.v.; recorded on CD GSE 1513: 'TIMBILA - Orchestral Works Inspired by Elements in African Music' (hereafter, TIMBILA CD), Claremont Records, Cape Town (1991).
6. Quoted in Levy, M. (1986), *SAMUS*, 115.
7. Erlmann, V. (1984), review of Malan, J. P. (ed.), 'South African Music Encyclopedia', *SAMUS*, **4**, 73-5, 73.
8. Masakela, B. (1990?), 'Culture in the New South Africa', in African National Congress, Department of Art and Culture, address presented at the Standard Bank National Arts Festival, Grahamstown s.d., 2 ff.
9. Drury, J. (1986), review of Coplan, D. B., 'In Township Tonight!', *SAMUS*, 4, 93-4, 94.
10. Oehrle, E. (1986), 'The First South African National Music Educators' Conference in the Context of World Music Education', *Proceedings of the First National Music Educators' Conference* (hereafter 'SANMEC Procs'), Durban: University of Natal, 7-18, 17.
11. Mngoma, K. (1990), 'The Teaching of Music in South Africa', *SAMUS*, 10, 121-6, 126.
12. See Shepherd-Smith, A. (1992), 'Encouraging Musical Talent Amongst the Underprivileged', in J. Eichbaum, (ed.) *Scenaria* (international edition: 'The Performing Arts in South Africa - 1992'), 54-5.
13. Oehrle, E. (1986), *SANMEC Procs* 10.
14. Tracey, A. (1986), 'Keywords in African Music', *SANMEC Procs*, **1**, 29-45, 37.
15. SAMRO: Thirtieth Annual Report, 1991 (hereafter 'SAMRO Annual Report'), p. 3.
16. Ibid., p. 4.

17. SAMRO: General Report (G.295), 124th Meeting of the Board of Directors, p. 38.
18. Levy, M. (1992), *Catalogue of Serious Music, Original Works, Arrangements and Orchestrations, Published and in Manuscript, by Southern African Composers and Arrangers*, 2nd edition, 3 vols.
19. SAMRO (1991), Annual Report, p. 3.
20. Paraphrased ex-*South African Government Gazette*, xix/7583, 15 May 1981, 1-2.
21. See also Ludman, B. (1992), 'No More Corporate Cash for the Arts?', *The Weekly Mail*, Johannesburg, 10-15 April, 30.
22. For all broadcasting statistics see *SABC: Annual Report*, 1991, 16 ff. and *This is the SABC*, Johannesburg, 1992, *passim*.
23. SAMRO (1991), Annual Report, p. 8.
24. Ex-SABC music archive material.
25. See anon. (1992), 'ANC Moots Interim Authority for Media', *The Star*, Johannesburg, 23 March, 6.
26. Levy, M. (1984), 'Tenth Musicological Congress', *SAMUS*, 4, 84-6, 85.
27. Programme details ex-SAMRO Serious Music Department archives.
28. Recorded on TIMBILA CD, q.v. supra.

14 Timbila[1]

Hans Roosenschoon

After hearing the work by Ali Rahbari, 'Half Moon', it occurred to me that it would be quite a change to write a work which combined a Western symphony orchestra with an African instrumental group as opposed to choir.

In September 1984 I was commissioned by the Oude Meester Foundation for the Performing Arts to write such a work with Amampondo in mind. But when they were approached on the matter, they showed no interest.[2] It was then that Andrew Tracey suggested that I should try out a group of Chopi players with whom he had contact.

In January 1985 I first went to Grahamstown to have discussions with Andrew, and from there, I went to the Wildebeestfontein in North Mine near Rustenberg to meet the leader of the Chopi xylophone (*timbila*) orchestra, Venancio Mbande.

Originally, the Chopi hail from southern Mozambique and they are well known for their music and for the very fine and powerful instruments they make.

The daunting task was to find common ground. The first problem was the tuning of their instruments. As they divide the octave into seven equal parts, there was no point in trying to adapt the Western instruments accordingly, and because I had in mind to use indefinite pitches such as very high or extremely low notes, or complex structures such as clusters, I soon realised that discrepancy in tuning would actually enhance the music.

Secondly, because the Chopi do not read music, I was obliged to use one of their pieces of music with which they were familiar, and I had to devise a form scheme in which they could play this music *together* with a symphony orchestra. But the biggest headache was to find the 'right' piece of music. The music that I decided to use in the end is a 'Mtsitso' which acts as an introduction to the 'Mgodo'. It was Andrew Tracey who suggested a 'Mtsitso' because of its clear structure and in fact he told me of a 'Mtsitso' that was played for the chief at Kenga in Chopiland in 1973, where it was recorded for a film on the Chopi. At the time that I met Venancio, he could only play me short fragments that he remembered, while his group did not know it at all. Only after obtaining a cassette copy of the 1973 recordings from the Traditional Music Documentation Project in Washington, was I able to hear this 'Mtsitso Kenge' of Venancio played by a full ensemble, and start on the composition.

By this time I had read a lot about the Chopi and their musical traditions in Hugh Tracey's book, *Chopi Musicians*.[3] In the meantime, Venancio agreed to teach his group this particular song and it was only at their first rehearsal that we saw each other again.

Something about the Chopi *timbila*: the word *mbila* refers to a single key on the xylophone, likewise *timbila* is the plural. Indirectly *timbila* refers to the sound being made. The instruments that they play are made in three different sizes:

Sanje	tenor/baritone	*c.* 19 keys
Dibhinda	baritone/bass	*c.* 11 keys
Chinzumana	double bass	*c.* 3 to 4 keys
Njele	rattle	

Orchestras can comprise be comprised of 15 to 30, or even more instruments.

The 'Mgodo' is akin to other organised social dancing in Africa and consists of seven different movements (of which the Mtsitso is the first) and lasts for over an hour. Very often the songs address critical issues. For instance, the people do not criticise their chief directly, they do it through the music!

Apart from the fact that Venancio's 'Mtsitso Kenge' contains a very simple 'do-re-mi-do' motif, it has an ABC form. The A section consists of a number of 'short starts' which the leader opens and which is answered by the rest of the group in unison/octaves. In the B section everyone is playing a cyclical pattern together, and in the C section the 'do-re-mi-do' motif becomes a prominent feature of the whole group, marking as it does in this song, the end of every cycle. It is only the leader who now makes all sorts of excursions in an improvisatory manner. It is also interesting to note that this motif has a significant function as a kind of signal device in the music of the Chopi.

The structure of the music offered by the Western orchestra takes its cue from the Chopi music and one finds passages in strict metre interchanging with *senza misura* passages all the time. This procedure makes it possible for the orchestra to play *colla parte* with the Chopi and because of the very strong rhythmic impact of the latter, the *senza misura* is often not perceived as such by the listener. While the Chopi are busy with their B section, the symphony orchestra tries to 'impose' the 'do-re-mi-do' motif, and eventually they succeed in convincing the Chopi to follow suit. This is when the C section starts. The orchestra now has floating material, the texture of which gradually becomes louder and more dense.

What actually happens is a double canon in the orchestra based on notes that one can pick out after a repeated listening to the Chopi song. The 'do-re-mi-do' motif leads, as far as I am concerned, towards its logical conclusion in the rendering of 'Frere Jacques' by the horns playing it *campana in aria* whilst standing up. After this 'anthem' effect, references to the opening of the work bring it to a gentle close.

'Timbila', completed on 25 May 1985, was first performed at the Standard Bank National Arts Festival by the National Symphony Orchestra of the SABC, conducted by the American conductor, Christian Tiermeyer, and the Chopi xylophone orchestra from the Wildebeestfontein North Mine, leader Venancio Mbande, on 12 and 13 July 1985. The CD recording was made a week prior to these dates.

A final thought: maybe I learnt from the Chopi not to criticise my 'chief' directly, but rather, through the music?

Notes

1. This short item is a brief description of the author's working processes in his composition 'Timbila', which can be heard on the Timbila CD, Claremont Records, GSE 1513, Cape Town (1991).
2. However, the foundation supported the recording of the eventual composition.
3. Tracey, H. (1948), *Chopi Musicians*, London: Oxford University Press.

15 Black - White - Rainbow: a Personal View on what African Music means to the Contemporary Western Composer

Geoffrey Poole

When two cultures intermarry, their issue is not merely the sum of their attributes, it is a multiplication, a vast spectrum of possibilities. Yet looked at another way, one might say the defining factor is the subtraction of attributes, the calling into question of that which had been assumed within each culture.

One might have thought that contemporary Western concert music had precious few assumptions left to question. But suppose I write this:

Example 15.1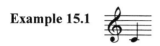

Nothing complicated: from Grade 1 Recorder to Wagner and Birtwistle, we all know what a crotchet middle-C is. But when you listen to the Japanese *shakuhachi* you realise that notes need not have been focused like this, that there is a universe of windy unfocused notes, and others whose overtones vie with the fundamental to shift your perception away from earthy certainty towards the diffusion of sky. The crotchet (quarter-note) itself implies strict arithmetical counting, but much of the world's folk song moves (as does plainsong) in a flowing manner that defies the notion of a regular beat. Meanwhile the grid of pitches indicated by the stave, and claimed by Westerners from Pythagoras to Paul Hindemith as a natural (indeed God-given) endowment to mankind, is merely one tuning system amongst many, to take its place alongside the Javanese *pélog* and *sléndro*, the Hindu modes, the pentatonic and equiheptatonic scales and so forth. When we encounter West African drumming ensembles we are likely to find ourselves totally unable to describe what we hear: the pitch and timbre meld together and this meld is further transformed by the strength and positioning of the impact on the drumskins. Finally the downbeats (if such they be) are largely non-intersecting, and the dense, almost repetitive but not exactly, packets of rhythmic energy pass by at such a speed that we cannot rationally assimilate anything. Yet we are totally drawn into listening. The fact that this is achieved entirely by oral tradition is chastening.

It is well known that African song pays little regard to absolute pitch; nobody in a village is about to conjure an A440 tuning fork from his trouser pocket or run to the concert grand to sound the first chord. Music may bubble up at any time, perhaps beginning as 'singing to oneself' but also immediately solidifying into a social tie. The singer is answered by another, a friend, who may vie to cut in with a new song. Every new song is an affirmation: I'm here, this is me. And probably because of the wall-less social setting of the outdoor village, it is the tone of voice, the primal call that matters above other considerations. The ethnomusicologist John Blacking was fond of telling how an African singer, asked to sing 'la', would sing several degrees too high, and given further tests would do so repeatedly. Not because he was tone deaf, but on the contrary because he was timbrally alert (in a way that we are not) to the lie of the voice and the 'feel of the cry'. Timbre and corporeal resonance were the parameters that most mattered to him when reproducing what he had heard.

All a far cry - interesting that this English turn of phrase is reserved for alienation - from the inhibited intonations of Anglican Evensong! And the significance goes far beyond the anecdote. It reaffirms one's suspicion that 'our' music may have paid too dear a price for its sophistication. There is a capacity for music within us that has been cramped by even the most primary of the processes of notation, squeezed out of the design of our instruments, suppressed in the interpretative training of practitioners and - it has to be said - forever disadvantaged by the over-structures, safely engineered 'objective worth' criteria of the submitted score required in order to meet with the approval of reading panels and teachers and examiners and conductors. Yet if a contemporary composer recognises the need to respond to the quality of the primal cry, just how much can be conveyed by means of the score? A *forte* with descending pentatonic phrases? A performing instruction such as 'rough, ecstatic, like the holloa of a Yoruba lament'? Clearly something essential gets lost in the translation, for sadly such indications in a score leave a hollow impression of striving after a borrowed effect, and melodic material of - on paper - perhaps no great distinction. Only the singer-composer, for whom the barrier of notation is obliterated, can hope to access the spirit of the cry directly. Which is probably the reason why the byways of rock and folk have generally got closer to Africa than we have in the concert tradition.

What we may realistically strive to do within the contemporary classical field is not, therefore, to present reliable copies of transcriptions of what already exist in another place (even assuming one had no scruples about the blatant theft of artistic property) but to assimilate the spirit, or rather to allow African music to stimulate the dormant quarters of our own musicality, and use that as the basis to create something new. Fortunately the limitations of one's home culture are also potential strengths: defining, enabling constructs. Consider Debussy, and the fact that he never, even in 'Pagodes', stooped to merely copying the Javanese gamelan, but perceived how the principles of heterophony, non-functional harmony, and fluidity of tempo could serve his needs as an innovative artist. Mallarmé and Poe,

Monet and Manet, Liszt and Wagner, Chabrier, Hokusai, the Golden Section - all were necessary ingredients, alongside the gamelan, in the composition of 'La Mer'.[1]

But how different is Britten's interpretation of gamelan (indebted to his experience of performing four-hand arrangements and compositions by Colin McPhee) in the sparkling morning curtain riser to Act 2 of 'Peter Grimes'. How different again the American individualist Harry Partch, who redesigned the whole armoury of instruments, their tuning, and abolished the composer-performer rift by singing in his own raucous but highly effective voice. Or John Cage, inventing the prepared piano as a one-man gamelan fit for anything from dance improvisation to such sophisticated compositions as 'Sonatas and Interludes'. Different offspring from different mixed marriages.

Thus when we discuss the impact of African music in our own creative environment, we should not expect any uniformity in the result. There is no 'school'. What African music has to offer - and heavens, it is bad enough that one should lump this whole complex continent of subtle traditions into one! - is very largely a question of the hopes invested from this side, every love affair being more a miracle of imaginative projection than a rational match.

The imaginary Africa

Quite apart from the real Africa, the European has a potent cultural sense of Africa as symbol. It is a complex symbol, in which Jean-Jacques Rousseau's well-intentioned notion of the uncorrupted noble savage is interwoven with an exotic expectation of sensuousness and magic, further overlaid with both pride and guilt at the memory of colonialism. Pride in the establishment of roads rails and trade routes, civil service, education and medicine (and for some, the Christian message), and guilt at the awful conditions of the old slave trade, the rape of natural resources, and the assumption of white superiority, continuing into today's iniquitous and artificial manipulations of 'international debt'. For my generation, for whom the obstinacy of white South Africa was an abomination, the symbol of black Africa is primarily one of power returned where it belongs, to the people; the creation of a post-industrial future along egalitarian, co-operative lines; sincerity; the reassertion of a deep reservoir of human energies that we suspect ourselves to have traded perhaps unwisely for a Faustian programme of material benefit.

This at least is the sort of symbol I had in mind when I first made reference to things African in my own work, in the context of a BBC commission. It was 1979, late enough for philosophically inclined/Greenish

Westerners to have assimilated the Oil War message that future power and assets may not be unlimited, but just before the political decision was made to ignore the problems and shoot the messengers. Like many others at that time I was drawn to ancient and esoteric interpretations of the larger rhythms of political and personal energy, such as 'I Ching' and astrology, and I had not long been acquainted with the theory of 'gyres' and complimentary tinctures set out in the fascinating book *A Vision* by W. B. Yeats and encapsulated in his famous poem 'The Second Coming'. This poem became the model for the one-movement form of my 'Chamber Concerto'.

> Turning and turning
> (*the inexorable vortex of fate*)
> In the widening gyre
> The falcon cannot hear the falconer;
> (*we approach the millennial stage of disintegration and rebirth*)
> Things fall apart, the centre cannot hold;
> Mere anarchy is loosed upon the world ...

The form of the poem called for three main sections plus a fourth that must be different. The three main sections were related to 1) the widening of the gyres (birdcalls, stretching into great orbits), 2) the rising of evil energies, as

> The ceremony of innocence is drowned;
> The best lack all conviction, while the worst
> Are full of passionate intensity.

Then the thrilling realisation 3)

> Surely some revelation is at hand;
> Surely the Second Coming is at hand,

all done in my best contemporary European (more or less Ligeti-disciple) style, though admittedly with a blatancy that would horrify that master. Now I was faced with 4), the deeply disturbing first glimpse of the New Age when

> somewhere in the sands of the desert
> A shape with lion body and he head of a man,
> A gaze blank and pitiless as the sun,
> Is moving its slow thighs

- a truly disturbing vision of the impending leo-aquarius era, ending with rhetorical dismay

> What rough beast, its hour come round at last
> Slouches towards Bethlehem to be born?

Clearly, what I needed for 4) was a type of music that would *sound* radically different, and would employ audibly different means, while conveying the poetic implication of a viable civilisation after the cataclysm. The solution that presented itself was that the ten instrumentalists should exchange their normal instruments to become a polyrhythmic percussion ensemble (the conductor forsaking the dominating baton to join *primus inter pares* on claves), a musical solution that would also invoke Africa - long regarded as a 'rough beast' by the outgoing Christian/piscean era, Yeats included - as the saviour of the aquarian epoch to follow. All this fell together by association of ideas just as naturally as, in the poem, things fall apart. The decision to turn the corner and create an extremely open form (A - B - A' crisis - Z), a 'hook' form, does indeed make it fall apart. But in compensation, the sharp attack of the neo-African percussion ensemble was projected back into the choice of a harshly non-blending instrumentation (no horns, violas, or low flutes: plenty of trumpet, clarinet, drums) and the technique of polyrhythmic layering had been planted in the A section in various ways, in order to underline the inevitability of the transformation and to make one feel that Z is, after all, the proper course of the future.

Had I been aware of contemporary African literature at that time, I might have been more cautious about my symbols. *Things Fall Apart* is of course the title of Chinua Achebe's classic novel (1958) which tells of the destruction of traditional Nigerian power structures (embodied in the personality of Okonkwo) under the intolerable invasion of white colonialism. Later, during my two-year residence at Nairobi, I would come to recognise something of the gulf that separates the Western myth from the reality of Africa. For the time being, though, a door had been opened. It was necessary to develop the purely technical implications of the stylistic corner I had turned at the end of the 'Chamber Concerto', and work duly began on a percussion sextet. However, the sextet seemed to require a uniform sonority such as pitched drums throughout, and in the course of playing possibilities at the piano, I found the piano itself could do even more than the six percussionists. I was fortunate enough to have met an outstanding interpreter of contemporary piano music based near me in Manchester, and thus wrote 'Ten' for Peter Lawson.[2]

In order to 'think African' on to the quintessentially European pianoforte, and in an abstract work analogous to a sonata, a composer must confront some difficult decisions. The tone of the piano carries very little of the 'feel of the cry' of African song. In fact it carries precious little *tessitura* at all. To get some approximation to that feel it would be necessary either to enrich a monody by thickening it (compare Messiaen's monophonic chorales), or to magnify the voice's octave range by a factor of 6 or 7, say, which would fill the piano's range proportionately but at some considerable risk to its communicative power as vocalise. One might do both. What one cannot do, in the context of such a powerful instrument with such a breadth of sophisticated repertoire, is to use African music the way the proverbial ostrich uses the sand, and write *simplistico* pentatonic quaver melodies - or at least, I don't find that either genuine or interesting. But to flail around on some general pretext of enriching and widening a melody is itself to court instant banality unless the composer supplies some sonorous and/or formal ambitions.

Sonority and form are the key factors in 'Ten'. The audible imperative is the clash of not-quite-simultaneous stresses, analogous to the military drummer's flam and the West African drum ensemble's polyrhythmic counter-rhythm. In order to stimulate such clashes (or to control their relaxation), it was necessary to superimpose two, three or four independent rhythmic strands rather on the model of A. M. Jones's transcriptions of Ghanaian music,[3] but actually according to rules which I shall explain shortly. This gave an ur-rhythmic structure such as the following:

Example 15.2 (a)

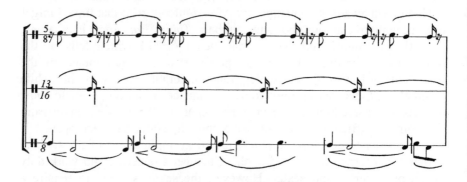

The next stage was to flesh out the basic rhythmic structure in such a way as to articulate the clashes. Thus there was no harmonic principle as such, and virtually no melody as such: the pitched elements were extrapolated out of the rhythm. (The famous 'Danse Sacrale' from Stravinsky's 'Rite of Spring' is an early example of this approach, insofar as its chords are not 'functional', they are chosen as a suitable articulation and colouring of the all-important rhythmic pattern.) In 'Ten', each drumstroke might be rendered as a single note, a dyad or triad or 'handful', an evenly spaced chord, a top-heavy or bottom-heavy chord, a concave or a convex chord. Thus the given example becomes:

Example 15.2 (b)

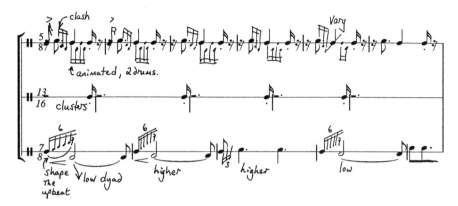

Complementing the 'sonorous imperative' outlined above, 'Ten' is entirely subjugated to a severe rhythmic discipline - so severe the constraints may sound positively unmusical. The reason for this is not unrelated to the political stresses in the summer of 1981, amid street riots, the destruction of 25 per cent of British industry, the ceaseless anti-Soviet warmongering and nuclear build-up, and so forth. The tenor is also indicated by the short poem of Osip Mandelstam, implicitly addressed to Stalin, which prefaces the score:

> You took away all the oceans and all the room.
> You gave me my shoe-size in earth with bars around it.
> Where did it get you? Nowhere.
> You left me my lips, and they shape words, even in silence.

Thus the extra-musical resonances of asserting freedom despite oppression are such as to forge a secret link with the Africa symbol of the 'Chamber Concerto'. The unbending rule imposed on each of the ten movements was that it must be exactly 365 units long, comprising up to four polyrhythmic strata, each one comprising arithmetic squares. The squares are possible because of the remarkable fact that 10 tens plus 11 elevens plus 12 twelves add up to 365. Thus the work as a whole depicts a decade, if you like, during which impossible shackles are imposed but human values and energy must fight back.

Figure 15.1 'Ten' (first movement)

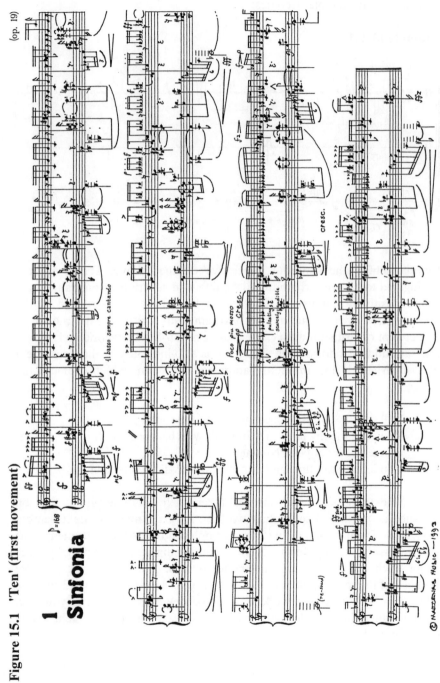

(op. 19)

1
Sinfonia

The articulated drumming of the upper voice is constructed on the basis of squares of 10, 11 and 12. The cantando bass uses squares of 14 then 13. The punctuating middle voices use squares of 13 then 14. The harmony and melody arise purely out of the colouring of polyrhythmic interaction.

Of course, what I have said about the composition of 'Ten' still leaves much out of account, for example the essential business of maintaining the continuity and surprise required of a tense abstract drama, and writing in such a way as to maximise the technical resources of the pianist. Yet perhaps most important factor was to ensure that every element was allocated sufficient 'acoustic' space. I subsequently happened to meet a very fine American composer living in Singapore, John Sharpley, who is of the conviction that Nature herself is a magnificent orchestrator of musical space. In the tropical forests of Java and Bali, he says, you may hear every creature clearly in its own registral and timbral niche, the whole ensemble vertically spaced just like the gamelan music of the people who live there. His own music is certainly 'heard' in that way, and it is a quality I have tried increasingly to emulate, something essential about good sound environments and all good music, yet something that will always elude those who think too much in terms of structure and analysis. To observe that the Javanese gamelan replicates its surroundings is not the same as the (deeply suspect) argument that art imitates nature: but it is indicative of the underlying principle that we are shaped by evolution and adapted to certain psycho-acoustic competencies and not to randomness - an awareness that was not without significance in the climate of re-evaluation and recovery from certain excesses of modernism and the *avant garde*.

During the early 1980s I found considerable creative stimulation in the collision of other cultures with our own. India, especially the Sarangi playing of Ram Narayan[4] was melded with a novel system of micro-tuning in my first string quartet, while the (imaginary) Cretan *aulos* and the (real) Chinese *ch'in* served to define the soundworld of pieces for winds and guitar duo respectively. In 1984, however, my interest in things African took a decisive turn when Beth Wiseman and I attended a week-long residential course at Holland Park, where the yucca lawn resounded with the dance of Zimbabwean warriors, the hypnotic court songs of The Gambia, contemporary folk from the Cameroon singer and writer Francis Bebey[5] and much else. It was there that we met the ethnomusicologist Professor John Blacking, who told us of two-year lectureships available at Kenyatta College, Nairobi, to whom we duly applied. And heard nothing for 12 months: only to be summoned immediately and on almost impossible conditions - the first of many experiences that were to combine exhilaration with setbacks that many, gifted with a stronger sense of self-preservation, might have ruled out as disastrous!

Kenya, 1985-87

'Spirit of place' is a difficult thing to capture in words, and I'm no Lawrence
Durrell. But even on the 'wrong' side of Africa (for tropical West Africa has
retained far more of its customs and wildlife) there was something
overwhelming. The gigantic sky, the radiant colours of the biannual
growing seasons, the implacable resistance of the dry ground and the
deluges: I felt as though I had never seen colours or heard sounds before in
my life. One also knew that, as a *msungu*, one didn't really belong here.
One of our most gifted students (now a lecturer) used to joke about history:
'Oh no, we don't know about that, we hadn't been discovered!' The
impertinence of the white settlers, to imagine they could 'own' this land!
Not even the Kenyans own the land, they have a saying 'It belongs to our
descendants, we are keeping it safe for them'. Now it became clear: Africa
had since the dawn of time been a self-contained (non-invading) social and
ecological unit in which every person had a recognised role; natural
iniquities were counterbalanced by belief structures that enabled people to
cope, it could have continued for ever, humanly (experientially) vibrant and
meaningful. There was violence and savagery and I do not pretend it was
Eden, but there was a solution to what is now a worldwide problem, and by
what right had unstable and avaricious aliens destroyed what was?

But it is one thing to feel a degree of remorse, and another thing to know
how to conduct oneself properly, as I soon learned from experience. For
example, I was appointed as an Adjudicator in the 1986 Kenya National
Music Festival - a superb annual display of choirs and folk performers from
the length and breadth of the land. Preparatory to the regional heats, I was
invited to give a day-long presentation to regional judges on the subject of
piano music, the set pieces being typically the Grade 3 Associated Board
repertoire. Unfortunately the organisers had not thought to provide a piano.
So there, in a large room, sat about 25 officials from all over the country, in
ties and dark business suits, while one white pianist in a casual white suit
fumbles his way through the impossible task of describing piano music
piece by piece without a piano. 'This next item is by Edgar Moy, no
relation,' I quip, 'it should be played quite fast, two beats in a bar, ta ta-ta ta
... ' I become aware of an unbearable heaviness in the air. Oh God! I am
facing two dozen Kenyan officials any one of whom would be ruined by
the first sign of deviation from the one-party KANU line, and I have just
alluded *casually* to His Excellency the President Daniel T. Arap Moi.
Suddenly I can see what they see, an arrogant and insensitive Englishman -
insult my leader and you insult me! - barely distinguishable from those who
'quelled' the Mau-Mau by bullet in the 1950s. The session was not
noticeably relieved by the nice man who jokingly observed that *con moto*
really meant something other than its Swahili translation 'on fire'.

Hearty laughter. But it was news to many, and I had begun to realise rather too late that many of the delegates were inexperienced in distinguishing a treble clef from a sustaining pedal. I was finally rewarded - or was it drummed out? - with a handclap of ominous slowness and persistence. No invitation arrived for the 1987 festival.

What this episode brought home to me was the fundamental difference of national attitude with regard to *respect*. It has often been said of hippy trailers who sit at the feet of gurus in India that they are the least equipped people in the world to do so, for they lack the fundamental requirement - unquestioning obedience to authority. If they had it, they would have stayed at home and listened to their parents. Coming from a culture where the government-led attitude to teachers was if anybody had got the brains and drive to open a Tie Rack stall or sell dodgy Spanish timeshares but still persisted in teaching then they deserved whatever derision they got, I was tremendously gratified to land in a place where *mwalimu* (teacher) is a term of respect and affection, and I was already addressed as *Mzee* (learned/older man) and there was some point in being one. But whereas I was accustomed to sounding off about Mrs Thatcher as I saw fit, my Kenyatta University counterparts would be 'picked up' in the night or even eliminated entirely for speaking against the president. It was dangerous even to sport a beard, since His Excellency does not like beards. 'Imagination' and 'originality' and 'independent intellectual judgement', yardsticks of value amongst my own people, were regarded as subversive. Thus when teaching composition in Kenya, I found no tradition of abstraction upon which to build: we would work concretely, from a known song towards its arrangement and elaboration. When I one day presented a little diatonic note-row to play with, my class laughed goodnaturedly: 'How can you make a song if you don't know the words?'

Well, there are ways of course, and I could show them, as I do in the UK. But *should* I? Jomo Kenyatta, in his scholarly study of the traditions of his own people who form the largest tribe of Kenya, wrote of the close integration of what we divide as art, religion, and social necessity as follows:

> The Gikuyu does not use printed books; instead, his social education is imparted to him by image and ritual, the rhythm of the dance and the words of the ceremonial song. For every stage of life there is an appropriate course of instruction through these means, and it is made as unforgettably dramatic as possible.[6]

This was quite a large part of why one wanted to go to Africa in any case. Now, under the guise of teaching neutral techniques, I could introduce my students to a handful of technical manipulations, 'how to develop the material'. And so the Africans would provide the raw material, while the Europeans manipulate it and repackage it? - there's a word for that: colonialism.

No. Rather than imposing predetermined methods, I decided to re-examine my own culture in terms of the distinction between primary material and process. English music tends to be impoverished in terms of primary experience, raw material. It is a problem that goes back far into our folk traditions. Why does English folksong and dance lack the verve and brinkmanship of so many other traditions? - Hungarian, Russian, Spanish, African? Surely the bus had left long before Cecil Sharp got there, but nobody seems to know when - Cromwell? the Enclosure Acts? Certainly whenever one attends the spectacle of Home Counties accountants revelling of a Saturday to a traditional Morris Dance, the music meted out cautious crotchet by crotchet, four-bars answering four-bars, the non-climaxing tunes (a - a' - b squarely refusing to do anything - a') with their fairly apportioned alternating dominant-tonic cadences ('I'll pay you, now you pay me'), one is acutely reminded of Napoleon's assessment of the English as a nation of shopkeepers, of a cast of mind whereby substance is entirely subservient to transaction.

Teaching composition in Kenya, one could no longer treat as merely theoretical John Blacking's aphorism that 'no musical style has its own terms: its terms are the terms of its society and culture, and the bodies of the human beings who listen to it, and create and perform it'.[7] To pretend that the manipulations that composers have applied to their material - inversion, imitation, augmentation, adding counterpoint or harmony, generating continuations and contrasts, serialism and so forth - are culturally neutral is a lazy assumption if not a lie perpetuated by our institutions of learning. All too often such techniques are simply an excuse for a lamentable shortage of primary ideas. In any case, one must have the deepest reservations about the concept of 'material' as a set of noteheads, as I remarked at the beginning of this essay. African music insists that one puts substance above transaction; real melody, colour, rhythmic movement and vitality above protocol.

And collective above individual, which is a bitter realisation for a creative artist as it would point logically to his own demise. The three years following my arrival in Kenya (two there, one back in the UK) marked the death of certain attitudes and skills that had taken 15 years to build up, and saw only one new work. It was written with maximum simplicity and directness, for that most African of mediums, unaccompanied collective voices. The words are from a black Madagascan poet who was literally destroyed by the pull of two cultures, his native Imerina and French Symbolism:

There, in the North, stand two stones, and they are somewhat alike:

One is black and one is white.
If I pick up the white one, the black one shames me.
If I pick up the black one, the white one shames me.
If I pick them both up, one is love, the other consolation.
               translated from Jean-Joseph Rabearivelo (1901-37)

Figure 15.2 'Imerina' first chorus, 'Two Stones'

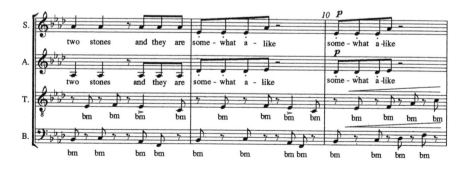

Thus the effect of the real Africa seems to have been humbling. 'Imerina' makes a strangely modest companion to the messianic 'Chamber Concerto'! But it does hand back creativity back to the performers and listeners: it achieves a comfortable sonority, movement and pacing: there are no clever refuges for faltering imagination. The harmony is neither of the tit-for-tat shopkeeping brand of tonality nor a contemporary concoction, but something close to the classic African taste for oscillating triads separated by a whole tone: the A-flat/G-flat juxtapositions give an air of neutral acceptance of two states, without the Western compulsion to debate and draw further conclusions. The required vocal performance style is hard edged and detached, and the preference for this rather than rounded or contiguous components of melody was to remain with me.

Integration

On the Equator anybody who finds it more interesting to sit at a desk writing symphonic scores than watching hippos and crested cranes, snorkelling in the Indian Ocean reefs, conversing with African and international friends and undertaking musical field-trips wants his or her head examined. Straining to extract all the available pleasure from the flight of gulls across Hull docks in January 1989 I found the situation reversed; composing was once again my passion, my *raison d'être*. Could I still do it, after a gap of three years? Why had I not managed to make something of the copious Nairobi sketches for an eight-movement spatial orchestral work of Mahlerian proportions (or perhaps I should say pretensions) called 'Karibu' (Welcome)? Or the five-act opera set in traditional Kikuyuland. Partly, it is true, because quitting the UK seemed to have wiped me off the map as far as performances and commissions were concerned. But more fundamentally because black music had shamed me into no longer wanting to write as I had before, while the things that appealed about African music were not, of themselves, transferable to the Western concert hall. For example, the astonishing singing in harmonics, practised by the ancestral nomadic Maasai and Samburu, must be accompanied by its curious high dancing of proud young warriors or it is nothing. The grimaces of a Luo *mzee*, singing while bent over his *nyatiti* (a lyre that has to be clasped by foot to the ground while plucked with both hands) are integral to the performance. Out of context, such phenomena seen almost ridiculous, like the stuffed head of an elk in a museum.

How have other composers coped with bringing Kenyan music home to England? From the 1960s we have David Fanshawe's 'African Sanctus', a hugely evocative and impressive work even if the literal incorporation of pioneering East African recordings into a slightly unfocused Western style leaves something of a travelogue impression, bonhomie speaking louder than the music. A few years later, the less well known but astonishingly inventive composer Frank Denyer made a prolonged study, living amongst the Samburu people. In 1991 I traced him to Dartington where we compared Kenyas: Denyer recalled how astonishing it was to live in the Samburu desert where the simplest invention - a nail was the example he gave - can be appreciated as a fantastic achievement, and life is managed without any such help. It is not surprising that somebody of such individuality in life is absolutely uncompromising in his selection of unusual sound-sources, even if this means that the majority of his music (like that of the American Harry Partch) can generally be performed only in special situations with the composer involved.

I found that the abiding lesson for me - perhaps this is related to travelling in the 1980s to a more urbanised Kenya and returning to a post-modernist, experiment-weary Europe that desperately needs to rebuilt its own moral and cultural centre - was the need to integrate whatever warmth and vigour one might have acquired within the collective, socially meaningful, forms and mediums of one's own tradition. So long as the African input is perceived as 'other', then one is in a sense relying on exoticism (like French *Chinoiserie* or the Mozartian flirtation with things Turkish), and to that extent failing to draw the fullest conclusions from one's model. Only when the elements have been absorbed and wholly integrated into a composer's sensibility - as I remarked *vis-à-vis* Debussy earlier - is the process complete to my way of thinking. It is true that assimilation taken to such lengths may pass unnoticed: I recall an occasion when I was obliged to deliver a presentation of my compositional ideas before an audience that included the pianist/professor Malcolm Troup, who protested 'You have done all these things in Africa, and come home to continue writing *stubbornly* as before!' I was dumbfounded, probably because of the unflattering 'stubbornly' as much as anything else. But do we castigate Bach for merely absorbing the Italian style into his Lutheran heritage when he could have copied Vivaldi pure and simple, or condemn Brahms for not becoming wholly Gypsy, or Stravinsky for retaining his Russianness? What do we actually think of the sort of person who changes completely with his surroundings? Nothing I have written in the 1990s has failed to be touched by my experience of African music, and I see no reason to write for noseflute and *mbira* in order to prove it.

The point is really that, by observing a foreign culture in which tradition is all-important but under threat, I came to appreciate the strengths, and indeed the fragility, of our own ways, and the constant need to renew the lifeblood of our own culture. The task of integration began with my 'String Quartet No. 2' (1990) - a medium associated with the very centre of the European concert tradition - and the stylistic shift may be seen in the balance between what is simple and what is complicated. Pitch relationships have become more obvious (often incorporating pentatonicism), while rhythm tends to be stretched out, as in the bodily-conceived 10/4 bars of the 'Song of the Gambia' movement (the inspiration for this rhythm was a beguilingly un-notatable Gambian Court song heard in Holland Park in 1984):

Figure 15.3   String Quartet No. 2, third movement

Cue B is an example of the longer, bodily-conceived type of rhythm. I tend to think of a physical dance that goes.

TREAD - 2 - 3 -
FINGERS OUTSTRETCHED - 5 - RELAX - 7 -
ROTATE TORSO - 9 - AND
TREAD - 2 - 3 - etc.

Also visible, in the introduction to the 'Song of the Gambia' in this extract is the 'squared' type of *fp*, borrowed from African singing as in 'Imerina', to be rendered by bow pressure and speed ⌑⊢ and not ▷.

The viola at B provides a gentle percussive effect, influenced by the sound of a large earthenware pot rhythmically cupped by hand. At cue C the chattering/murmuring is distantly related to one of John Blacking's recordings of Venda children engaged in rapid rhyme games: the concept of counterpoint throughout the quartet is one of participation rather than of notes working for their living. This is perhaps a tangible example of what I said at the beginning about the subtraction of assumptions: harmonic and contrapuntal devices have been marginalised in favour of a social perspective and a different attitude to rhythm and spaciousness, but the task was not complete (in my view) until everything was fully integrated into the medium of contemporary Western string performance.

A commission from the Broad African Representative Council in 1991 brought me into contact with the Ghanaian drummer Kwasi Asare, and we struck up a highly productive relationship based both on the oddball factor and tremendous mutual admiration. It is somewhat ironic to have travelled all the way to Nairobi in search of something when all the time it was alive and well on the eleventh floor of a block of flats in Salford. On the other hand, I would not have understood what use to make of this opportunity if I had not lived in Africa, learned something of how to think and talk appropriately, thought long and hard about the issue and studied drumming with a master drummer myself. Kwasi had come to Britain in 1956 as a mechanic, but his drumming had taken him to the USA working with Sun Ra, Duke Ellington and others, and he now ran a group called Kantamanto ('my word is my bond') doing gigs and educational workshops aided by North West Arts, whose then Music Officer, Gail Dudson, incidentally deserves the highest praise for her imaginative commitment both to Kwasi and to funding or collaboration. Kwasi has regularly returned home to his village in Ghana and was scathing of performers who had lost contact with their roots. His drumming tradition is of the standard Western African type in that he, as master drummer, will embellish at the foreground level while three or four other players provide a more or less consistent but polyrhythmically interlocking texture, but it is an entirely sacred tradition, inducing trance and serving the matrilinear priestesses who run in his family.

What I first wanted to do was create a multi-media event on the theme of 'Earth and Sky', with Dance, Lighting, and music in the round, mixing African and contemporary Western players. This was too expensive. But the composition that finally emerged, 'Two-Way Talking', retained significant elements of interplay between cultures and of intrusion into the audience, not least because of the spatial layout of five concertante groups around the soloist, as had been planned for the orchestral 'Karibu':

MASTER
DRUMMER

AFRO-GROUP   WAZEE (OLD MEN)
harp, percussion   horn, bassoon, trombone

MAIDENS
flute, viola

WARRIORS   HUNGARIAN BAND
violin, oboe, trumpet   cello, clarinet, double bass

Conductor

Hungarian Band? An essential component of the piece is the concept of a fundamental unity across two continents, not because 'Music is a universal language', which it is not, but because the love of music is a universal trait and the exchange of musical languages is exciting. The sonorous heart of Africa may be identified with the Talking Drums, but the sonorous heart of Europe? - I always think of the Danube, and the sort of band (if not precisely Hungarian) that plays its heart out, inside Haydn, Schubert and Mahler.

Besides going to several Kantamanto concerts, I eventually obtained a tape of one in order to make transcriptions of what Kwasi and his group actually play. Kwasi was most unwilling to let me have a tape: 'This is my music, you're going to steal my music, man.' We had to come to a (substantial) financial arrangement about the tape, and not until the first performance did Kwasi understand what I had been trying to explain, that I was not writing what he himself creates but I had to write *everything* else that other players would play.

It was by no means immediately clear how this should be done. Fortunately, a precedent had been provided in a most unlikely way, by the Machaut sexcentenary in 1977. At that time the musicologist David Fallows and I were newly appointed lecturers at Manchester University, and our specialisms were joined in regular New/Old concerts. David Fallows had shown me the wonderful repertoire of lays by Machaut, explaining the problem that 20-minute monophonic songs are difficult to take unaccompanied, however finely composed and sung, but nobody knew if and how they were originally accompanied: would I be interested in composing an ensemble around the original? So I wove canons and added mischievous scribblings - in retrospect Maxwell Davies' 'Missa Super L'Homme Arme' and Berio's 'Chemins IV' were probably models - and we performed 'Machaut Layers'. (The fact that Machaut and Africa were connected in my mind is also interesting. When I was not yet sacked as a Kenya Festival Adjudicator in 1986, a 12-year-old Luo boy from Nyanza by Lake Victoria sang a long impassioned unaccompanied piece which in style, structure and rambling *plainte* resembled nothing so much as a Machaut Lay. This set me thinking: the Luos are a Nilotic people, and 600 years ago they lived around the Nile delta, while medieval European music is thought to have been influenced by trading with North Africa. Perhaps this boy was performing his *plainte* in authentic Machaut style! Unfortunately, neither the Luo ethnomusicologists nor the medieval historians of my acquaintance appear to know of this genre in Nyanza. There is still a great deal of potential for research.)

Of six pieces Kwasi supplied on tape, three seemed to be of particular interest and these were transcribed into a cross between film cue sheet and notation, to form a cantus firmus which I would elaborate. The treatment of the five ensembles takes place on two levels, 1) the orchestrating out of rhythmic strands corresponding to the (now eliminated) accompanying drumming ensemble - a process which of course superimposes a more focused pitched component and therefore mediates towards the Western ensemble - and 2) free composition, responding to the material expected of the soloist, but also provoking the soloist into further responses, and adding fantastical interplay between the five groups themselves, or soloistic or other interjections. Freedom for cadenza extensions is provided by the use of specific extendible passages with repeating accompanimental texture, until released by he conductor's two-handed downbeat. In the example given from 'Tigare', the violin and viola have played pizzicato - glissandos which have provoked the master drummer into 'talking' on the *odundo* (small hour-glass string tension drum). At 414, the marimba and harp maintain the drum-ensemble accompaniment, taking over from the cello and bass whose pattern is disintegrating into further replies to the *odundo* at the bass register. A two-handed downbeat signals 415 at which the loudest instruments come to a climactic unison, then subsiding into the Round Dance.

Figure 15.4   'Two-Way Talking': from 'Tigare'

gently continue pizzicato conversation with drum

'Two-Way Talking' lasts over 30 minutes, and its panoramic intentions are provided by blocking opposing gestural types around the structural pillars of Ghanaian-based movements at the beginning, the centre, and the end of a seven-movement design:

1.   AKOM (traditional master drummer plus ensembles).

2.   TWO-WAY TALKING (organised improvised interaction of drums and groups).

3.   MANY TONGUES ONE GOD (without drummer)
       a) rueful East European heterophony
       b) far-away strains of melody.

       Master drummer traditional song, ensemble responses.

4.   TIGARE (traditional master drummer plus ensembles).

5.   ROUND DANCE
       a) effect of Central African pentatonic horn ensembles processing in circle, with master drummer and double bass conversing.
       b) Kora effect from harp and xylophone, African falling melodies

       collapses into held chord for:

6.   INVOCATION (traditional calling of the Chief of All Music).

7.   FONTOFROM (traditional master drummer plus grotesque ensembles).

Kwasi is accustomed to employing a variety of traditional drums in his performances, including a male and female *Tumpan* (which somewhat resemble congas), three *Miramabi* (agile drums like tomtoms), two monstrous male *From*, the rattling shoulder-hung *Brekete*, and string drums such as the *Ndundo* (or *Odundo*). One had to listen very carefully to the timbre of each, gradually extracting analogous densities for the pitched contemporary ensemble - though obviously, this is partly prefigured in the approach taken to composing 'Ten', where the piano textures were determined by the spaciousness required of imaginary drumming. (In both works there seems to be a preponderance of perfect fifths and fourths plus 'colouring', and an avoidance of harmonic system). I also became increasingly aware of the 'melodic' quality of drumming in the hands of a master such as Kwasi, and while it is just as impossible to notate this feature as it is the pedalling of a Chopin 'Ballade', for example, the awareness undoubtedly exerted its influence upon the instrumental traits of the composition.

'Tigare' traditionally passes at a velocity and complexity of cross-rhythm that defies apprehension in any detail, but the concerto concept of 'Two-Way Talking' meant that the drumming would need to be coordinated with a conducted ensemble, to the millisecond. While three main patterns could be identified when the music was relatively stable, these were separated by periods of clashing intersection and the confusion was a matter of delight to its exponent. 'Aha - Where is the downbeat! That is the question for *aaalll* music in Africa, where is the downbeat!' exclaimed Kwasi gleefully. For as I knew from Kenyan musicians, African music doesn't have 'downbeats' and no sooner has one musician apparently provided them by virtue of a regular pulse, than another will join in such a way as to make that pulse sound like the anacrusis, and then a third will wrongfoot them both and a dancer will gyrate to all three rhythms at once, one governing the feet, another the hips, another the shoulders. Nevertheless, Kwasi was able to help me find the background grid which could serve for notation, and this works perfectly well so long as the conductor thinks not in downbeats but in enabling constructs that permit a variety of rhythmic stress patterns.

Now as a general observation, the perception of a rhythmic stress is brought about by any one of three possible stimuli:

1.   Grouping (e.g. the long notes rather than the short in a French overture)
        or
2.   Accent (louder, or reinforced texture, or phonetic or verbal priority)
        or
3.   Pitch (an irregular pitch, usually very high or low).

The shifting of emphasis between these three possible stimuli offers enormous potential to engage the ear, and this is perhaps one of the greatest lessons one can learn from African drumming, because it is applicable to any other medium. Certainly I can see, in retrospect, that this is one of the chief animating features of 'Two-way Talking'. (At the level of language, that is: at the level of symbol and interrelation to the body politic, the concerto forms a sequel to the 'Chamber Concerto', animated by the breathtaking liberation of Nelson Mandela and the unstoppable promise of a black Africa, just when the East European spirit had simultaneously conquered its Soviet oppressors.) Thus, at the level of language, the principle may be illustrated by turning back to 'Tigare' at cue 414, where the harp and marimba imply a stress on semiquavers 1 and 7 according to

a) Grouping; yet their stress falls on semiquavers 3 and 9 in terms of b) Accent, while semiquavers 4 and 10 seem to protrude by virtue of c) Pitch. At 411 the wind and percussion take an opposite point of view from the strings, the two patterns co-existing. The fortissimo after 412 emphatically puts the accent on semiquavers 3 and 9, only to find the situation reinterpreted at 413. Listening to the music, I hope the effect is that of 'living in the moment', as patterns are re-orchestrated, re-accented, or otherwise transformed.

One of the more depressing results of African influence on the West is seen in the kind of a-rhythmic, mechanical repetitiveness practised by many of today's aspiring composers under the name of 'minimalism'. In my view, the early Steve Reich expunges quite enough of the underlying terror, error, and sonorous subtlety of West African drumming to make it acceptable to the comfortable first world, and he is to be praised for seeing the potential. But after him there are some who make a fetish of inertia and tedium, whereas nothing could be further from traditional African music at its best. Minimalism has lapsed into replacing the ungraspable sonorous catch with easily knowable notatable rhythms, on all-too-familiar instruments. It has even forgotten the most basic rule of interesting rhythm, which is to begin (or otherwise create a stress) at the 'wrong' moment of the repetitive cycle, thus setting up a counter-perception that enriches and compels the listening experience. (Having said that, my most recent score, a piano duo called 'The Impersonal Touch' (1995), began life as an attempt at minimalism. But I appear to be temperamentally incapable of the 'coolth' required to let the system run on automatic: Piano II wanted to but Piano I did not agree, thus a far more complex and ambiguous world had to be created.)

As I have mentioned, all other recent works of mine have been touched in some way by the breath of Africa. In 'Sailing With Archangels' for large Wind Band (1990), the influence is merely picturesque, the whole work tracing Vasco da Gama's epic voyage around the Cape of Good Hope to the little port of Malindi in Kenya, of which I was very fond, and across the Indian Ocean to Goa, and home. In 'The Magnification of the Virgin' (1992) (a Magnificat setting which pictures the Annunciation to an unusually sexy Madonna), drumming makes a special cameo appearance to represent Mary's vision of generation upon generation of mankind transformed by the wondrous child in her womb. In the largest and perhaps most focal work of mine, the secular requiem 'Blackbird' (1991-93), the effect of Africa is important not so much in the musical language, or the presence of texts by Rabearivelo and a Nigerian poet, as in the fact that if I had had no better model in mind than The oratorio I should not have felt the urge to write at all. However, two close friends had died, both mothers of young children, and I had become acutely aware of our contemporary inability to deal with Life's big issues - love, existence, demise, grief. That, surely, is what music should be doing, as it used to in the West, and as it still does in many other cultures. In this case, then, African culture had the very specific role of reassuring me as to the fundamental value of music as a healing presence and an intermediary to eternity. But it seemed essential that the music should involve the broader community and not simply a once-only professional visit. Therefore, although the BBC had begun to discuss the possibility of writing for the magnificent BBC Singers, I resolved that a large, amateur, choir should be addressed in this particular work. Maybe this reflects nothing more than the dying embers of the anti-establishment zeal that had informed my earlier works like 'Ten', but I suspect there is more to it than that - I refer to the suspicion that contemporary music has mortgaged itself increasingly to the narrow *success d'estime* on the plane of professionalism and egotism and the requirements of (dare one say it?) the human spirit, in all its richness and confusion. In the event it was heartening that the Sheffield Philharmonic Chorus not only agreed to commission the work, persuading Yorkshire Arts and the Arts Council to join in, but also enticed the BBC Philharmonic Orchestra to give the premiere. And in an interesting inversion of the New Music Ghetto situation, word spread and ticket sales for 'Blackbird' far exceeded those for earlier, more conventional concerts in the series. Whether one could still find the necessary sense of social cohesion in the South of England, or elsewhere, is not yet clear as it hasn't been tried. But for me, 'Blackbird' is a prime example of African-inspired revitalisation, and would still be one even if the African texts and the drums and steel pans were nowhere to be seen.

Towards a future

When writing 'Imerina', why was it necessary to choose a Madagascan poet from the 1920s, why not a contemporary Kenya? Because the Kenyan writers were, from Ngugi wa Thiong'o down, almost entirely preoccupied with the colonial inheritance, the urban poverty and violence, the corruption of the officials, the degrading terms of the international economy and tourism and so forth. There was a strong feeling (concentrated amongst the artists, intellectuals and religious leaders which is why they were perceived as dangerous) that white colonialism had merely given way to 'malteserism', with the *Wabenzi* (the Mercedes-Benz tribe) exploiting and betraying the aspirations of the ordinary people just as the white settlers had done. I got the impression that insofar as an author may have wished to question the wisdom of the present regime, he or she could do so only in disguise, by attacking the old white colonialists - for who in the government could disagree with that! Thus, with the exception of scholarly books on oral narrative, I could find only one novel that lived entirely within the era *before* Kenyans were 'discovered'. It took hold of me completely, and my attempts to trace the author led me through a series of false trails (defunct publishers, her old secondary school up country, previous offices, new name), before I eventually found her working for the Ministry of Education in Nairobi, married with four children, and very willing to take Beth and myself to her village at the foothills of Mount Kenya to meet relatives and see where the stories had taken place. Is it reprehensible to remain fascinated by ancient traditions rather than the present-day? I think not: for one thing, I am no less fascinated by my own ancestry and their social conditions in eighteenth- and nineteenth-century England. For another, the oral histories of Kenyan people go back at least 400 years while the period of white domination, counting from the heinous imposition of a one-penny poll tax that forced every citizen into the white employment market up to Independence, lasted only 40. I do not have such confidence in the sustainability of the present capitalist hegemony to imagine that, a hundred years from now, the colonial/malteser experiment will form much more than one episode of tribulation amongst the many famines and scourges in the long Kenyan memory. Look at the Polish, the Russians, the Scots, the Basques, the Haitians - governments come and go, but the underlying value systems remain. So paradoxically, my obsession may be the most real of the many Africas known to us.

Lydiah Nguya's novel, *The First Seed*, had come about in a curious way. It was largely the creation of her father, which Lydiah had assembled and written at the age of 16 around 1970. Her father was already in his eighties, Lydiah being a daughter by his fifth wife: his ideas were therefore already set, in many ways, by the turn of this century, before colonial government had made much of an impact in the hinterlands. His storytelling centred on a character called Kigaruri whose initiation group had been born around 1835 by our reckoning. So Nguya *père* would have picked up these stories rather as our children pick up reminiscences of the Second World War, from grandparents. Now I don't know exactly how real a character Kigaruri was: I dare say we are dealing with a collation, and probably an embroidered one. But in so far as Kigaruri loses his father in a Maasai cattle raid and the body was consumed by ants, Lydiah was able to take us to the place it happened, showing where huts had stood, exactly where the Maasai crossed the river, and so forth. She walked us around the home village Gathuini (or salt-lick), where the cattle were watered (and still are). And his hut, though whether she referred to her father, his father, or Kigaruri appeared negotiable. In *The First Seed* Kigaruri goes on to breach various taboos unavoidably; as a warrior he leads a vengeful raid back to he Maasai to capture cattle and, surprisingly, his first wife; then there are weird divination scenes and rituals, a comic sequence when he tries to attract a much younger and unwilling second wife, problems with drunks and so forth. All fantastic material for an opera! Yet all the time gnawing away beneath all this, the fatal flaw: God gives him daughters but no sons, and his authority is thereby somewhat compromised. He begins to question the traditions of the people, for example taking home the meat sacrificed beneath the sacred fig tree because he had come to realise that the hyenas ate it, not God (- we visited the said fig tree and, curiously, an ox femur was lying beneath it). Finally Kigaruri tries to rewrite the customs so as to pass his inheritance to his ablest daughter in lieu of a son. At this the people turn against him and - actually I have rewritten the ending, with Lydiah's approval, to make the story more dramatic.

Besides the story, I could see in Kigaruri the opportunity to develop a Kikuyu-based style of singing, rhythmical rather than bel-canto, forceful but interestingly falling from initial outbursts and settling on a rapidly repeated cadential pitch. The conversational duos would pick up something from the exciting cross-play of traditional call-response song. The instrumental writing would (as in 'Two-Way Talking') run close to repetitive minimalism but retain the rhythmic edge and uncertainty that makes it interesting. And the whole dramatic concept can be brought out in a novel way, extending the Brechtian dialogue of real-life involvement and distanciation. So a good question to pose at this point might be: why has the opera not been written, despite three drafts of libretto, considerable background research, and countless compositional sketches?

First, because in its original conception the scenes teem with life - pregnant women gathering wood and water, numerous children breaking into songs and rhymes, goats, cooking pots. But how can this succeed in the comfortable indoors bourgeois theatre? And whatever would it cost? Realistically, it would never be performed. In the ensuing attempt to make the drama fit within physical and budgetary requirements I found myself stripping down the scenarios and rewriting the libretto, three times. By the end of this process it had become merely the neat story of one man and five other characters accompanied by a chamber orchestra - so far from the original concept as to be a pointless enterprise (though actually, a separate and viable chamber opera project has grown out of it).

Secondly, I found an unduly large amount of performance time seemed to be needed to be expended establishing the social norms against which a specific event or action was to be understood. Here, to make the point, are two stories, Story A: a very fat man and his very fat sister capture a very thin old woman and make her work as their slave, starved and beaten. Story B: two drunks who are neighbours agree to reprimand their wives for not cooking properly and hatch up the plan that neither will stop beating before the other, but one is hoaxing and merely beating a carpet, simply in order to goad the other into beating is wife until she is dead. Two pretty nasty stories, and the question is, do you believe either could be true? In our surroundings? In primitive Africa? As it happens Story B is fictional, in *The First Seed*. Story A is true, it came to court in England in 1995. But whereas anybody who watched an opera set in England would supply their own cultural context in order to interpret what they saw as a revolting and absolutely atypical occurrence, a totally unfamiliar society leaves us perplexed as to an appropriate interpretation. Scenes might therefore be misconstrued in terms of drama, not to say construed as insulting in terms of race relations! In point of fact a Kikuyu man was expected to take many wives, by purchase, and it was not unknown for beatings to take place. The audience has somehow got to be persuaded that this is 'normal' - and not germaine to the drama - while on the other hand recognising that if a shepherd omits to pour goat blood over a newly mended fence, or if an uncircumcised youth buries the unattended corpse of a neighbour, such failings might result in plague and famine.

As an opera composer one can get away with almost anything by creating a theatrical fantasy-world with such fervour that the audience is carried by its own crazy logic ('The Magic Flute'), but simultaneously to present an unfamiliar real life without appearing patronising, and still have time to develop individual characters at odds with that - this is a tall order indeed. What might have been considered a major obstacle, the colour of the singers' skins, is not an issue, since I am principally attracted to the universal implications of the drama, and would wish for the personnel, like the staging, to extend beyond the particularities of Kikuyuland. But - this must be 'Thirdly' - there are further difficulties at the level of musical performance, considering that one would require unusual instrumental resources far removed from the standard orchestra, and cannot necessarily find anybody to play them. Or to look at it another way, African traditional musicians would (like Kwasi Asare) be able to contribute repertoire from their tradition, but not using notation, conducting, or the unfamiliar music I might come up with. Again, trained opera singers are required for their stage and ensemble skills yet they must be willing to project using the raw *anti-bel canto* manner of vocal production that has been mentioned. Regarding children, even the simplest call-response songs that African children sing are extremely difficult for English children to copy, since the basic skills of rapid interaction have not been built up. And as for the goats ... But, finally, it is open to doubt whether a composer chooses his/her subject matter. Perhaps it is the other way round. Despite nine years of setbacks (at some inevitable cost to other projects) 'Kigaruri' remains on my mind, and I wake up in the morning with fresh glimpses of it. It has returned to where it belongs, in the realm of the open air, like a folk festival or mummers play, with dance and including a large, enthusiastic amateur cast.

I have perhaps said enough to indicate some of the complexities inherent in bringing together African music and contemporary Western composition. As Rabearivelo observed in 'The Two Stones', the marriage of black and white is not easy: whichever stone you pick up, each fails in terms of the value systems of the other. The success of the graft depends crucially on what features are of value to the host culture. For example, Steve Reich and Philip Glass may be said to appeal to the American audience (and the Americanised audience) because they have polished he African input until it sparkles with instant non-threatening cleverness. Gyorgy Ligeti has made use of Simha Arom's researches into Central African music to enrich the rhythmic dimension of his recent 'Etudes' for piano, while retaining the European concert culture. Middle generation composers as diverse as James Wood and Rolf Gelhaar, Giles Swayne and Frank Denyer have, like Stockhausen and Xenakis, either rethought the language of music or else mixed ethic instruments with electronics to extend the resources of the European avant-garde; and it is scarcely necessary to mention how far popular music has benefited from waves of African-derived style from the origins of Dixieland jazz down to reggae and Paul Simon's fusion in 'Gracelands'.

But it is also interesting to consider grafts that did not 'take'. The young Pierre Boulez was captivated by African music and it shows in 'Le Marteau Sans Maitre', yet in the larger view of his *oeuvre* it is clear that this was a passing exoticism, irreconcilable with the abstraction and intellectual detachment that characterises the man. There is a sense in which the fundamental contribution of African music is the *mana* or sheer perceptual impact of the sound, and that its compositional techniques are such as to extend this highly energised *mana* (of the drum or voice or whatever) into permanence. In fact the most far-reaching effect of being dislocated from Europe and reviewing its history from the vantagepoint of Kenya was in my case a quite unexpected one, stimulated by the concern of ethno-musicologists such as Nketia to establish a universal field of music: it was to conduct extended research and ultimately to write a book on the psychological typologies of music.[8] To borrow a useful concept from Carl Jung, I would now say that the abstractions of Boulez (and Bach, Beethoven and Webern for example) are indicative of the intuitive psyche, whereas the sense-data impact of the primal cry belongs to the opposite end of the 'irrational spectrum'; no less powerful, not necessarily less sophisticated either, but fundamentally and categorically at odds. Similarly the thinking attitude shown in the need to externalise and objectify, as in Stravinsky or Mozart or Brechtian theatre, is directly antipodal to the Feeling values of most folk music and communality. I do not mean to give the impression that feeling and sensation are not well represented amongst Western composers; they are, but their strongest fields are song, opera, atmospheric music and so forth, rather than abstract form. If my theory amounts to anything it is to say the cultural assimilation issue is not merely one of techniques, but is governed by the individual need of each psyche to develop one superior function at the expense of its opposite: we have already seen how Gunther Schuller and numerous other composers failed to truly draw together the symphony and jazz, and I believe a similar absolute block is encountered, for psychological reasons, when African music tries to co-exist, unmodified, with absolute music. Indeed it only now occurs to me but in 'Ten' and the Second Quartet the African character had to be transmuted to meet the demands of an abstract work, whereas those works that use identifiably (perceptually) African music are both concertos, in which an oppositional context throws Europe and Africa into relief. Perhaps there is some sort of conclusion to be drawn from that.

However, a final conclusion would be quite out of place in what must, or certainly should, remain an open-ended quest. There is no doubt that African music has enormous treasures to offer materially - in its polyrhythmic techniques, its hocketing textures, its attitude to the perception of repetition, vocal sonorities, call-response activities, and unfamiliar instrumental resources. Unfortunately these treasures are seldom transferable directly, for all sorts of reasons. Thus the challenge is to understand how such music relates in its own terms (not as an 'exotic' extra) to African sensibilities and feeling, to custom, and to fundamental spiritual needs - and then to try to see how the warmth of that relationship might be transferred to the benefit our own post-everything situation. It is a difficult question, one that implies abstracting the sources of rhythmic and social energy and finding a new outlet for them, but one that probably has as many solutions as seekers.[9]

Notes

1. The still contentious theory of Debussy's use of the Golden Section is presented in Roy Howat (1983), *Debussy In Proportion*, Cambridge: Cambridge University Press.
2. See Andrew Burn, 'Geoffrey Poole - an Introduction to his music', *Tempo*, no. 145, Spring 1983. Also record sleevenote by the composer on Peter Lawson Plays, ECR 001.
3. This refers to the transcriptions of polyrhythmic music of the Ewe people as documented by A. M. Jones (1959), *Studies in African Music*, London and New York: Oxford University Press. Doubts have been expressed by Simha Arom (1991), *African Polyphony and Polyrhythm*, Cambridge: Cambridge University Press, in terms of the misleading impression of Jones's barring system.

4. Neil Sorrell and Ram Narayan (1980), *Indian Music in Performance*, Manchester: Manchester University Press, was particularly valuable here.
5. See Francis Bebey (1975), *African Music, a People's Art*, London: Harrap.
6. Jomo Kenyatta (1978), *Facing Mount Kenya*, Nairobi: Heinemann, p. 314.
7. John Blacking (1976), *How Musical is Man?*, London: Faber, p. 25.
8. This book was originally written in 1987-88, and revised in 1995 as *The Musical Psyche*, currently available only in manuscript.
9. It is encouraging to note the emergence of truly African 'Western contemporary concert' composers such as Timothy Njoora (Kenya) and Cosmas Mereku (Ghana). The difficulty of finding a nucleus of suitable performers and suitable performance outlets in their home countries is considerable at the present time, but the foundation of small pioneering groups is not out of the question.

Works by the author mentioned in the text

'Machaut-Layers' (1977) (in MS), first professional performance on Radio 3 in 1986, with Martin Best and Lontano conducted by Odaline de la Martinez.
'Chamber Concerto' (1979) (in MS), BBC commission, first broadcast by London Sinfonietta/Elgar Howarth.
'Ten' (1981) (Maecenas), for Peter Lawson. On disc ECR 001.
'Slow-Music' (1982) (Maecenas), quintet commissioned by Chester Festival, first London performance by Gemini, ICA, 31 October 1994.
'String Quartet No. 1' (1983) (Maecenas), Lindsay Quartet commission, first London performance Purcell Room 1985.
'Wild Goose/Weeping Widow' (1984) (Maecenas), Aquado Guitar Duo commission for world tour.
'Imerina' (1986) (Maecenas).
'Karibu' (1986-) abandoned symphonic suite for spatial orchestra.
'Sailing With Archangels' (1990) (Maecenas), RNCM Wind Orchestra commission, first London performance under Clark Rundell at Barbican, October 1993, CD (1996) SERCD 2400.
'String Quartet No. 2' (1990) (Maecenas), Lindsay Quartet commission, first London performance Wigmore Hall, September 1993.
'Two-Way Talking' (1991) (Maecenas), Broad African Representative Council commission, first London performance by Kwasi Asare and Gemini conducted by the composer, ICA, 31 October 1993, broadcast 23 July 1994.

'The Magnification of the Virgin' (1992) (Maecenas), Inaugural Sound Investments Commission for female voices of he Taverner Consort and Birmingham Contemporary Music Group, first performed Adrian Boult Hall with Andrew Parrott conducting, 9 February 1992 and broadcast 12 July 1994.

'Blackbird' (1991-93) (in MS), secular requiem for large chorus and orchestra, commissioned by Sheffield Philharmonic Chorus, who gave first performance with BBC Philharmonic Orchestra plus soloists 23 April 1994 and broadcast 25 July 1994.

'The Impersonal Touch' (1995) (Maecenas), Piano Duo.

'Kigaruri', opera based on *The First Seed* by Lydiah Nguyu (in progress).

Bibliography

Achebe, Chinua (1958), *Things Fall Apart*, London, Heinemann.

Nguya, Lydia (1975), *The First Seed*, Kampala, East African Literature Bureau.

Yeats, W. B. (1962), *A Vision*, London, Macmillan.

16 Egyptian Composition in the Twentieth Century

Adel Kamel

Introduction

The first formal Egyptian acquaintance with Western music goes back to the last years of the eighteenth century, and was connected with the founding of a school for military music by Mohamed Aly, governor of Egypt, as part of his plan to build a modernised Egyptian army. In this school, enlisted peasants started their musical studies in reading notation and playing Western brass instruments, instructed by Italian and French tutors.

Years later Aly's grandson, Khedevi Ismail, built the first opera house in the area to celebrate the opening of the Suez Canel in 1869 - following the European style. He requested the Italian composer, Verdi, to compose an opera for which he chose an Egyptian pharaonic subject. The resulting opera was 'Aida'. Thus, in the midst of Cairo grew a building indicating a meeting between two cultures, Egyptian and the European.

This meeting with European civilization resulted in the birth of new arts, which were not part of the country's inherited cultural life. This included a large theatre movement in which theatre groups, such as Kabani, Okasha sons and George Abyad, became famous. Musical plays were performed, which allowed more liberal singing than that performed by traditional music groups in closed singing parties. Then came Sayed Darwish (1892-1923), the 'knight' of Egyptian music in this period of transition. Though his life was short he left his mark on Egypt's culture and music. He developed the art of operetta, wrote music and national songs which were very popular. His songs were mostly for workers, glorifying the simple Egyptian man, picturing in words and music aspects of colonisation and abuse. These themes came from his reactions to, and sympathy with, the social and national events surrounding him.

Sayed Darwish helped the Egyptian listener to enjoy the singing and appreciate it, rather than listening to music with meaningless words that just affected his feelings subconsciously. Freedom movements, which reached their peak in the revolution of 1919,[1] moved Egyptian society deeply, and planted the seed of nationalism in the souls of Egyptian thinkers and artists. Under the call of 'Egypt for the Egyptians and complete evacuation' the way was clear for national Egyptian arts.

On the other hand, this meeting with European culture and its educational achievements affected Egyptian themselves deeply. Through the radio, gramophones and the movies, the Egyptians had a greater chance of being affected by Western culture and its arts. This meeting took a deeper form when formal education in arts and literature started with the opening of the

School of Fine Arts and the Egyptian University. However, when the feelings of nationalism broke, young Egyptian artists started to prove themselves and their 'Egyptianism' in new arts and new ways with deeper meanings and deeper feelings than they were used to under Ottoman rule.

When Mokhtar[2] finished his statue 'The awakening of Egypt', and when Youssef Greiss[3] wrote his symphony 'Egypt', each of them had to find a new method for his art, that was able to express the new meanings struggling in the souls of Egyptians.

For pioneer Egyptian composers such as Greiss, Khairat, and Rashid, being a composer in the 1940s was very difficult, for there was no academic framework in which musical composition was taught. This started to change at the end of the 1960s. All those Egyptians who studied music prior to this date either did it privately in Egypt or in European academies. This included the second generation of copmposers such as Aziz El Shawan, Refaat Garana, Halim El Dabh and Gamal Abd El Rehim.

The composers

Youssef Greiss (1899-1961)

He was born in the city of Cairo, to a rich Coptic[4] family from Upper Egypt. His talent for music was recognised at an early age, so he studied it side by side with his school subjects. In the year 1915 he started to study violin with the Sami El-Shawa and Mansour Awad, two of the most prominent professors of the time. Later he studied with Menasha and Samdy Ros Dol, harmony with Jeno Takacs, and composition with Joseph Wittel. Then he joined the law faculty, graduating in 1926, just to satisfy his family, then became completely devoted to music composition. In 1930 he was admitted as a member of the Association of Publishers and Composers in Paris after successfully passing its examinations. His house was a place where musicians and art lovers could meet. He welcomed to his house some of the composers who visited Egypt when the World Conference for Arabic music took place in 1932, including Bartok, Hindemith and the musicologist Curt Sachs. In 1942, together with other lovers of music, he founded the Egyptian Association for Talented Musicians aimed to spread music appreciation among Egyptians.

Youssef Greiss is considered to be the pioneer of Egyptian composers, perhaps even the pioneer of music composition in all Africa. He wrote his symphony 'Egypt' in 1932 expressing his love for Egypt and for what took place in the 1919 revolution. In his compositions Youssef Greiss tried to express the environment surrounding him, as well as the old times, and his style consists of the *Takaciem*[5] well known in Egyptian music. The pieces carry Egyptian and pharaonic names. He died on 7 April 1961, in the city of Venice in Italy on his was back from a trip for a medical examination.

Compositions for solo piano

> The Sudanese, op. 14 (1932)
> Asian in the Nile, op. 14, May (1932)
> Egyptian Prelude (Honesty), op. 27 (1932)
> Egyptian Prelude (Happiness), op. 28 (1932)
> Under the Palms (1944)
> Dance of the Boat on the Nile (1948)
> The Papyrus Flower (1949)
> The Egyptian Valley (1949)

For solo violin

> The Bedouin (1931)
> Son of the Valley (1943)
> Sphinx and the Violin (1947)
> Daughter of the Pyramids (1961) (his last composition)

For piano and violin

> The Potholder, op. 8 (1931)
> In the Desert, op. 4 (1932)
> The Camels, op. 32 (1932)
> Peasant Dance, op. 30 (1932)
> The Nile Singing (1950)

For piano and cello

> The Peasant Women, op. 15 (1931)

Orchestral compositions

> Symphonic Poem 'Misr'[6] (1932)
> 'The Pot Holder' for Violin and Orchestra (1932)
> Symphonic Poem 'Towards a Monastery in the Desert' (1934)
> Orchestral pictures: 'Prelude', 'the Peasant', 'the Bedouin'
> First Symphony 'Misr' (1935)
> Symphonic Poem 'The Nile and the Rose' (1943)
> Symphonic Poem 'Pyramids of the Pharaohs' (1960)
> The Third Symphony (1960)

Hassan Rasheed (1896-1969)

On 10 July 1896 Hassan Rasheed was born in the city of Cairo. He excelled in Arabic singing and in playing the lute. His excessive love for music caused him to neglect his studies, which made his family send him to England when he was 14, to be away from the music that attracted him all the time. After finishing school he went to university and in 1917 he received his degree in agriculture from Armstrong College at Durham University. While at the university he also studied music, and gained a diploma from the Royal College of Music in London. He was particularly involved in opera composition, for he was blessed with a beautiful operatic baritone voice.

In 1918 he returned to Egypt and set about opening a special broadcasting station in his house, which broadcast for three hours daily, starting on Friday 13 December 1929. It broadcast music and lectures, and continued till 1934 when Egyptian state broadcasting started.

Hassan Rasheed is considered to be the first composer able to set beautiful expressive melodies to Arabic poetry. He was the first to try to write an Egyptian opera, when he wrote 'The death of Antonio' in three scenes. It was based on the poem of Ahmed Shawky, 'The Death of Cleopatra'. Rasheed started composing it in 1945 and finished in 1947. He started to compose a ballet and an operetta after a story called 'Antar the Thief' but died in 1969 before finishing it.

Compositions

> An opera in three scenes, 'Death of Antonio' (1947)
> Youth songs
> 'The Time' for Soprano or Tenor
> 'Entreat' for Tenor
> 'Remember Me' for Tenor
> *'Ash el Watan'* 'Long Live the Nation'
> *'Ya Shabab el Wadi'* 'Youth of the Valley'
> 'Cleopatra's Prayer' for Mezzo Soprano
> 'Baladi' for mixed choir (not published)
> 'The Birds' (not published)
> 'Good Night' for Soprano and Tenor (not published)
> 'She Promised Me' for Tenor (not published)
> 'Pull the Sword', Prelude
> 'Everlasting Egypt'

He also wrote for children:
> 'Rabbit of the Valley' (not published)

Abou Baker Khairat (1910-63)

He is one of most outstanding members of the age of the pioneers, the national composers of Egypt, and the most important in its musical life.

He was born to an educated, well-cultured family whose house was a place for artists to meet. His mother was very fond of music, so his family encouraged him to learn the violin when he was a child, with Ahmed Dada, the Turkish musician. He studied the piano with European professors in Cairo, then joined Cairo University to study architecture, left for Paris, where he joined the Ecole des Beaux Arts and was interested in constructing buildings for the expressive arts. He also studied piano, harmony and composition with teachers from the conservatoire. On his return to Egypt he worked successfully as an architect and his work incorporated Egyptian designs. He started composing music in a romantic style, and his first composition, and some of his later ones, did not show any nationalist trend. This is true of the concerto (opus 1) for which he played the piano solo when it was played by the Cairo Symphony Orchestra.

Khairat was moved by the events taking place around him, and had an architectural and musical role in them. The Ministry of Culture asked him to design the Arts Institutes in the Pyramid Zone, which later became the Academy of Arts, including the Conservatoire, ballet, cinema, theatre and a concert hall. He was involved also in establishing the Conservatoire and organising the players, composers and singers following the European system. Thus he became the first Dean of this Institute, a post he kept until his death.

In the midst of all these things Khairat felt the psychological need to strengthen the connection between his compositions and Egyptian cultural music, which he was not much influenced by during his childhood.

Along with the society surrounding him, he started to feel the value of traditional culture, so from the 1950s his music headed towards nationalism. His work 'Suites on Folk Themes', first for the piano then for Orchestra, depends on tunes of *kanoun* (or *qanun* - a zither) songs like '*Atshan ya sabaya*' which he gave a military feeling, where brass instruments are obvious, as well as the tune of '*Weganentini y a bent ya beda*', or folklore songs common in the city like '*Yamama Helwa*' and '*Bafta Heendi*'.

In his second symphony called 'La Folklorique' there is a mixture of the national theme of Ṣayed Darwish, along with folkloric Alexandrian dances, its joyful rhythms, and with an African 'pentatonic influence'. This symphony was written in a way that shows his nationalist inclinations very clearly.

Compositions for piano

Five studies
Concert Studies, op. 13
Two Sonatas
Folkloric Studies, op. 25

Chamber music

Sextet for flute and five string instruments
Sonata for violin and string orchestra
'A Smile' for clarinet and piano
Sonata for flute and piano

Compositions for orchestra

Symphony no. 1, '*El-Sawra*' in F minor, op. 20 (1954)
Symphony no. 2, '*El-Shabeia*' in G minor, op. 21 (1955)
Folkloric Suite (1958)
Folkloric Overture in F major, op. 16 (1960) (a gift to the late President, Gamal Abdel Nasser)
Piano concerto No. 1 in C minor, op. 100 (1944)
Piano concerto No. 2 in F minor, op. 33 (1942)

Choral works

A new form of '*Lama bada Yatathanna*' for chorus and orchestra, op. 34, performed for the first time in April 1962
A new arrangement for Sayad Darwish's song '*Ain el Ebara*' for choir and orchestra
'Entreat' for choir and orchestra
'*Nesmet El Sabah*' for choir and orchestra in D minor, op. 31
'*Nazratun Wahedatun Tusedoni*' for Alto and piano in D minor, op. 28

Aziz El-Shawan (1916-93)

Born in Cairo, he got a Commercial Diploma at the French 'Freres' School, and studied the violin under Joseph Uberon. He studied composition with professors Minato and Orlovsky in Cairo, and later with Aram Khatchaturian in Moscow, at the Tchaikovsky Conservatory. He won the first prize in composition in 1965 from the Egyptian Ministry of Culture, the Medal of Science and Art of the First Degree from the Egyptian Government in 1967, presented to him by the late President Gamal Abdel

Nasser, and a medal from Oman given by Sultan Kabous in 1984 He worked as a Professor of Composition and Orchestration at the Arabic Conservatory.

El-Shawan aimed at creating an Egyptian national style of music and developed a distinct musical style which is characterised by the primacy of melodies, a tonal harmonic language characterised by an Egyptian modal flavour, characteristic orchestral colour and a new vocal style in which he expressively explores the phonetic features of the Arabic language.

His melodies are highly lyrical, and occupy a central place in his compositions. Some are inspired by, or quote, traditional Egyptian and African melodies. In his vocal music melodies are partly shaped by the words and their meaning. The African influences are clear in many of his melodic shapes as in 'Abu Simbel'.

He developed a distinct harmonic language within a tonal framework, with which he weaves elements from traditional Egyptian modes with chromatic harmony.

His orchestral palette employs all the potential of the full symphony orchestra to which he occasionally adds traditional percussion instruments. In his large orchestral and vocal works, he often used the wind section for building dramatic drive.

Compositions
First phase (approximately 1945-55)

> *'Atshanya Sabaa'*, Symphonic Poem (1947), a folklorique theme taken from Sayad Darwish
> Opera *'Antara'*, 3 Acts Poem by Ahmed Shawki (1948)
> Symphony No. 1 in Minor (1950-51)
> 'Arabesque' Nos 1 and 2 for Piano (1950)
> 'Fantasy' for Orchestra (1945)
> 'Arabesque' Nos 3 and 4 for Piano (1954)
> 10 Romantic and National songs for mixed choir
> 'Meditation' for Violin and Piano (1952)
> Symphony No. 2 (1952-53)

Second Phase (approximately 1955-65)

> 'The Call' for Piano (recorded)
> 3 Valses and Preludes Nos I, II, III and IV
> Ballet 'Isis and Osiris'
> Qunitet for string quartet and Oboe
> *'Anas Al-Wogoud'* Dances
> 'Abu Simbel', Symphonic Pictures for Orchestra and Chorus (1961)

In this last work El-Shawan presents episodes of Egyptian ancient history, exploiting his abilities in orchestral and choral writing, using a modern harmonic language and creating effective orchestral portraits. The Abu Simbel area contains two tombs carved in stone from the reign of Ramsis (1290-1223 BCE) This area is 280 kilometres away from Aswan. It was submerged after the construction of the High Dam, but later it was raised 60 metres with the help of Unesco. These two tombs were relocated to another safe place not far from the original place of the two tombs. This operation started in June 1964 and was completed successfully in the year 1968.

> Piano Concerto No. 1 (1958-59)
> Dancing Suite for Orchestra (1957)
> Rondo for Cello and Piano (1958)
> *'Biladi Biladi'*, Cantata for 4 Soloists (1960)
> 'The Oath' (*Al-Kassam*) for Orchestra and Chorus with Soprano and Tenor soloist and Chorale (1963)
> 'Africa ... Raise your Head'
> Cantanta for Tenor and Chorale (1960)
> Symphony No. 3, 'The Expulsion of Hyksos' (1964/65)

Third Phase (1966-93)

> 'Arabesques' Nos 5 and 6 for Piano (1966)
> Ballet 'Isis and Osiris' (completion), 2 Acts (1968-69)
> Opera *'Anas El Wogoud'* (1970-80)
> String Quartet (1982)
> Quintet for Strings and Harp (1982)

Kamel El Remali (b. 1922)

He was born on the first of October 1922 and loved and studied music from an early age. In 1948 Kamel El-Remali won the first prize in composition, and in 1950 he received his BA in Archaeology from the University of Alexandria. After graduation he continued his musical studies both in Rome and London, and in 1959 he received a certificate in the science of music composition from the Santa Cecilia Institute in Italy. In the same year he received a scholarship from Unesco to study composition, so he left Italy to go to Germany and Austria. In 1973 Kamel El-Remali gained the diploma of Licentiate of the Royal Schools of Music in theory. He still works as a composer, and many of his students have an active part in Egypt's musical life.

Compositions

> Opera 'Hassan El-Basry' - the second scene was performed in 1954
> Overture 'Suez Canal' (1957)
> 'Recital' for Orchestra (Folkloric pictures) consisting of five pieces which the composer based on some Egyptian folklore themes (1948).
> 'Fantasy' for Oboe and Orchestra
> Symphony in G major
> Suites for Orchestra, '*El-Robaiat*'
> Symphony, 'The Legendos Bird'
> Compositions for piano solo
> Variations on an oriental theme - 'Sonatina'
> String Quartet
> Songs accompanied by piano

Refaat Garana (b. 1924)

He was born in Cairo, and started to study composition with the Italian professor Minato, and used to play the trumpet.

In 1944 he joined the Institute of Music and graduated in 1948 with the grade of 'Excellent' in performance, then worked as a trumpet player in different orchestras. He continued his studies in composition for ten years where he gained a wide experience in writing music for different instruments.

He composed several pieces for orchestra, and a range of instruments, and received a prize in composition. Most of his compositions incline towards nationalism, deriving their subjects from Islam, like his work for choir and orchestra '*Intisar El-Islam*', or the Concerto for Lute, one of the movements of which contains the prayers of two Islamic feasts. Other compositions derive their subjects from social and national events.

Garana realises Egyptian atmosphere easily in his national compositions. This is achieved by using musical elements clearly from Arabic and traditional folklore music. The new elements overcame the traditional when using the *qanun* in his new concerto. He demands that the player uses two feathers in both hands instead of the traditional way of using one feather in each hand. In this way he imposed on the *qanun* (an Arabic instrument in origin) polyphony and arpeggio directions which were new for this instrument. In this concerto he realises a balance and a sweet dialogue between it and the orchestra, through the new orchestration, giving the *qanun* a chance to be shown and be clear without being overcome by the orchestra.

Compositions

Large orchestral pieces:

> 'Symphony 23 July' (1960)
> 'Arabia Symphony' (1962)
> 'Port Said' (1966) - In it he pictured the war that took place in Egypt in 1956 and used some of the national hymns that were present at that time. He also used 'La Marseillaise'.
> 'A trip to Chekoslovakia' (1968)
> '*Intisar el Islam*' (1971) in it he pictures the rise of Islam
> '*El-Nile*' in which he pictures the journey of the River Nile (1971)
> '*El Haye*' (1973)
> 'October 6' in this he pictures the war of the 6th of October 1973, and the crossing of Egyptian soldiers to the Suez Canal and their victory, which gave the Egyptians and the Arabs back their prestige (1974).
> 'Fugue Romantic Shabia' for flute and orchestra

Other compositions

> Suites from folklore 'Baladi' (1970) (not published)
> 'Impressions from Nubia' (1974)
> '*Motatabeat el Soar*' based on an exhibition of paintings

In addition to these there are several compositions for solo instruments and small groups:

> 4 pieces for piano: 'Marsh', '*Men Wahi el Khayal*', *Atshan ya Sabaya*' '*Mousika Shabia*'
> 'Fantasy' for violin and piano
> 'An Eastern Movement' for cello and piano
> Fugue on folklore theme '*A ya Zein*' for flute and strings
> Quintet for woodwind instruments

Halim El Dabh (b. 1921)

He belongs to a Coptic family from upper Egypt, and studied Western music in Cairo, as well as agriculture at the university. A Fulbright scholarship helped him to leave for the USA in 1950, where he studied music at New Mexico University, and the New England Conservatory in Boston. One of the strong influences in his development was studying composition at Tanglewood with Irving Fine and Aaron Copland.

He started composing music profusely in the early 1950s, and from the beginning he made sure he emphasised the African-Egyptian aspect in every respect. The tragedy 'Clytemnestra' marked a turning point in his musical life. For it happened that Martha Graham, the celebrated American ballet dancer and choreographer, heard this music in 1958, and was attracted by the scent of ancient history and the mystery that overwhelmed his music, a thing she was looking for in her dancing, and she presented it with her ballet troupe in 1958.

Martha Graham and El-Dabh started working together on dance dramas like 'Agamemnon' and 'Nazra Lelbarq' in 1962. In 1959 he got a Guggenheim scholarship; his music became widely known and he started to try new things, and became the first Egyptian-African to compose electronic music. In 1963 he composed 'Electronic Fanfare' and several other pieces in this new musical field, which was a feature of American music after the 1950s, including an electronic drama called 'Magnon Laila'.

Halim El Dabh taught at Harvard University, then the University of Kent State, Ohio, and is still teaching ethnomusicology programmes of African dancing and music. He maintains his relations with Egypt and the rest of Africa, where he has studied particularly the music of Ethiopia.

Western style composition

There is a whole section of his compositions which are far from his Egyptian roots, especially chamber music, and also in his work 'Sonics', a composition for instruments and singing where he introduces percussion. One of his great adventures was what he called the 'Orchestra of Sonic Vibrations', where he discovered many strange and new electronic sounds of new colours and shades.

Among his great works of this type are his three early symphonies, an opera, 'The Flies', which was based on students' violent demonstrations in his university at Kent in 1969. He also wrote a ballet 'Impressions from the art of Gaugin, Degas and Dali'.

Compositions from his Egyptian inheritance

The African background of Halim El Dabh, as well as his preoccupation with the value of the music from his Egyptian culture, is clear in his music, rhythms, instruments and the names of his works. The clearest example of this is his symphony 'Ramsis II no 9'. Actually, it is not the ninth but he meant by this number its symbolism, which indicates the nine strengths of the Pharaohs. It was composed for the opening of Ramsis II exhibition in Memphis in 1978, where it had its first performance. He has also written much simpler works, and has arranged Egyptian folk songs like '*Salma ya Salaa*' (1979) which he wrote for chorus.

Both Egyptian and African folk instruments have a prominent role in a number of his works. Either in solo works like his many works for *darabukka*[7] or those for groups. These include '*Tahmeel*' (1954), a concerto for string orchestra. He rewrote it in 1960, (it is also played with timpani instead of *darabukka*). It is worth noting that his wide experience in playing several folk instruments made him invent a special way for writing music for the drums.

Gamal Abd El-Rehim (1924-88)

He was born in Cairo in 1924 to a musical family. Unlike his father, who played several Egyptian instruments, his early contact was with Western music and he studied the piano. The family, however, did not encourage their son to take up a musical career. Nevertheless at Cairo University, while studying history, his musical talent was developed, and after graduation he decided to devote himself to music. A scholarship enabled him to fulfil his hopes of acquiring a professional training and he studied composition in Germany from 1950 to 1957.

After returning home he began a long search for an individual modern Egyptian idiom. His early background played an important role in paving the way for him. He deliberately avoids the alien major-minor system, and prefers the modality of his national, traditional and folk music. The typical oriental intervals of the augmented second (of the *Hijaz* genre), and the diminished fourth (of the *Saba* genre) are prevalent in his music although charged with new expressive potentialities. The same intervals largely condition his polyphonic writing and his harmonic progressions, hence the modern somewhat dissonant flavour. Rhythmically, one feels the immediate influence of the rich irregular rhythms (groups of 5, 7 and so on) of classical Arabic music. The rhythmic vitality is due to this element, as well as to the use of variable meters.

The nationalism in his style is the outcome of the recreation of folk and classical elements. He does not usually refer to direct quotations of folk themes, except in variation form. His style represents Eastern spirit and Western modern technique.

Gamal Abdel-Rahim has composed orchestral and choral works, piano and chamber music, as well as incidental music. His music ranges from the deeply meditative, to the warmly lyrical, and the vigorously energetic. He established the composition department at the Conservatoire and remained as head of it till he retired in 1984.

Works for Orchestra

Suite for Orchestra
Introduction and Rondo 'Baladi' for Orchestra.
Symphonic Variations on an Egyptian Theme.
'Isis', Symphonic Poem
'Lotus Pond' for Flute (or Oboe) and Orchestra.
'March of Amosis'
'Osiris' Suite for Percussion, Harp and Chamber Ensemble
Fantasy on an Egyptian Folktune, for Violin and Orchestra
Heroic dance for Flute and String Orchestra
Rhapsody for Cello and Orchestra
'*Samai*' for Orchestra
Concerto for Flute and Orchestra
'*Mowashah*' (Arabic form for singing) arranged for string Orchestra
with Flute and Violin

Works for choir and orchestra

'Awakening', Cantata for Baritone, mixed Choir and large Orchestra
'Sinai Epic', Cantata for mixed Choir, Children's Choir and Orchestra
'Egyptian Aspects' Vocal Suite for Choir and Orchestra (on four
Egyptian Folktunes)
'*Kadni'l hawa*' Cantata for mixed Choir and Orchestra (on a *Dawr* by
M. Osman)

Vocal and choral works

Seven Folk Songs in new polyphonic settings for mixed Choir
Nine children's songs in new polyphonic setting for children's Choir
'*Ibtihal*', religious chant for Tenor, men's Chorus and *Nay* (Flute)
Two songs from Aeschylos' 'Choephoroes', for Contralto (or mezzo)
and orchestra, 1. 'Weep Eye'; 2. 'O, God!'
'Fire and Words', Song for soprano (or tenor) and Orchestra (also
piano)
'The Happy Prince', Song for soprano, Contralto and Orchestra (also
piano)
'Money', Rhumba

Ballet music

'Osiris'
'Isis' Pas de deux

Chamber music

> Five little pieces for piano
> Six Free Variations on an Egyptian Folk tune for piano (published by Doblinger, Vienna)
> 'Heroic Dance' for flute and harp
> Sonata for Violin and Piano
> 'To Arab Martyrs' for piano: 'Lament-Conflict'
> 'The Lotus Pond' for flute (or Oboe) and piano
> 'Prayer' for an Egyptian Folktune for Violin and piano
> 'To Work!' Scherzino for Wind Nonet
> 'Elegy' for Cello and piano
> 'Little Trio on a Folkson' for children

Awards and decorations

> State Prize for Composition
> Order of Arts and Sciences 1967
> Award of Merit of the Academy of Arts 1977

Youssef Aziz (b. 1946)

Aziz graduated as an architect from the College of Fine Arts, then headed for the study of music at the age of 23, so joined the Conservatoire at Cairo in 1969, in the branch of theory and music composition. He studied composition with Gamal Abd El-Rehim and graduated with honours in composition in 1977. Then he emigrated to the United States to continue his studies where he also settled. His early compositions include a church cantata and some children's songs. He also wrote compositions for piano and a 'Romance' for horn and Orchestra.

Rageh Daoud (b. 1954)

He was born in Cairo. His father encouraged his musical inclinations, so he joined the Conservatoire in 1963 where he studied piano with Professor Polizi. In 1972 he joined the branch of music composition and theory where he studied with Gamal Abd El-Rehim. He graduated with an 'Excellent' grade in 1977 and works now as a teacher in the same section, after a scholarship to study in Vienna, where he received the degrees in composition.

He has written for piano and for choirs, and also wrote music for films, for which he received several prizes.

Mona Ghoneim (b. 1955)

Born in Cairo, she joined the conservatoire in 1972 where she studied piano with Professor Polizi, then she studied composition with Gamal Abd El-Rahim. In 1977 she graduated with 'Excellent' as a composer and works now as a teacher in the same section. In 1978 she received her BA in piano from the Conservatoire. She is known for her delicate style in her first compositions which were for the piano. She has also written some songs, and also music for films. Later, she studied at the Academy in Vienna, Austria where she received a higher degree in composition.

Adel Afifi (b. 1945)

Born in Cairo, he loved music from his boyhood, and played the piano and accordion. He joined the Police Academy and became the head of the music troop. In 1977 he graduated, and in addition to his job studied piano with Rachel Salib at the Cairo Conservatoire. In 1973 he became acquainted with the Russian composer, Sergei Balassanian, head of the composition department in Moscow, who encouraged him towards national music.

   He also studied composition by correspondence with the Royal Academy of Music in London for eight years, and in 1975 he received a diploma from the Royal Academy of Music, London. He works now as a Major-General in Cairo.

Compositions

> 'Romance' for string orchestra
> 12 songs for children accompanied by choir
> Music for three documentary films about mosques in Egypt
> Five pieces for the piano in polyphonic style
> Symphony of two movements in G minor
> Piano accompaniment for 4 pieces of Bach, from the book of Anna Magdalena - to be played by two players

Alaa El-Din Moustafa (b. 1947)

Born in Cairo, he was admitted to the Composition Department of the Cairo Conservatoire where he studied composition with Gamal Abd El-Rahim and counterpoint with Dr Awatef Abd El Karim until he graduated in 1985. He also studied with the German composer, Bertheld Hummel, Dean of the Freiburg Academy. He gained an MA and is preparing for his PhD. He has written numerous compositions for orchestra and chamber ensembles, and one of his two symphonies has been performed by the Cairo Symphony Orchestra.

Compositions

> 'The Egyptian Symphony'
> Symphonic Poem
> 'Egypt's Civilisation'
> 'Egyptian Fantasia' for violin and piano
> 'Oriental Memories' for cello and piano
> 'Egyptian Fantasia' for cello and piano
> 'Oriental Quartet' for strings
> 'Egyptian Fantasia' for two pianos

Adel Kamel (b. 1942)

Born to a Coptic family, he graduated from the Faculty of Music Training, where he studied with Awatef, harmony with Gamal Abd El-Rahim, then Abdel Karim at the Conservatoire. With Yousseff El-Sisi he studied counterpoint and composition.

In the years 1977 to 1978 he studied the Kodaly system and methods at the Kodaly Institute in Hungary. In 1992 he graduated from the Institute of Coptic Studies where he studied Coptic music.

During the 1960s he wrote his first compositions based on the themes of some Coptic hymns in harmonic style. In the last few years he has come to believe that polyphonic structures best fit this kind of old religious tune. He is the only Egyptian composer who creates modern compositions built on Coptic themes.

Compositions

> 'Fantasy' for Choir and piano based on the Coptic theme 'Aguios' (in Phrygian mode)
> Fugue on the Coptic theme 'Aripa Mevi' in F major

Notes

1. The first revolution by Egyptians asking for independency from the British occupation, its leader was named Saad Zaghloul.
2. The pioneer national sculptor.
3. The pioneer national composer.

4. Copts are the descendants of Ancient Egypt, who remained as Christians, after the Arab occupation in the seventh century CE.
5. A kind of improvisation in Egyptian traditional music.
6. Egypt.
7. A traditional drum.

Sources

Interviews with the composers: Refaat Garana, Kamel El-Remaly, Rageh Dawoud, Adel Afifi, Widow of Aziz El-Shawan, Alla El-Din Mustafa.

Bibliography

Abdel-Karim, Awatef (1993), 'The Vertical concept of Harmony in Gamal Abdel-Rahim's Compositions', in *Festschrift For Gamal Abdel-Rahim*, The Binational Fulbright Commission in Egypt.

Dawoud S. Gihad (1993), 'Traditionalism and Contemporaneity in Rhythm and Tempo in the Music of Gamal Abdel Rahim', in *Festschrift For Gamal Abdel-Rahim*, The Binational Fulbright Commission in Egypt.

El-Kholy-Samha (1992), *Nationalism in Music of the Twentieth Century*, Alamel-Maarefa: Al-Kowait.

El-Kholy-Samha (1993), 'Biographical Notes and List of Works', in *Festschrift For Gamal Abdel-Rahim*, The Binational Fulbright Commission in Egypt.

Kamel, Adel, articles about national symphonic music in Egypt in magazines: *Al-Fonoun* (1981), *Watani* (1982), Egypt.

Nassar Zein (1990), *The Egyptian Developed Music El-Maktaba*, El Sakafeia: National Book Organisation.

El-Sisi, Youssef (1981), *Invitation to Music*, Alam El-Marefa: Al-Kowait.

Index

KING ALFRED'S COLLEGE
LIBRARY

KING ALFRED'S COLLEGE
LIBRARY